Social History of Africa

COTTON IS THE MOTHER OF POVERTY

Social History of Africa
Series Editors: Allen Isaacman and Jean Hay

COTTON IS THE MOTHER OF POVERTY

PEASANTS, WORK, AND RURAL STRUGGLE IN COLONIAL MOZAMBIQUE, 1938–1961

Allen Isaacman

HEINEMANN
Portsmouth, NH

DAVID PHILIP
Cape Town

JAMES CURREY
London

Heinemann
A division of Reed Elsevier Inc.
361 Hanover Street
Portsmouth, NH 03801-3912

James Currey Ltd.
54b Thornhill Square
Islington
London N1 1BE

David Philip Publishers (Pty) Ltd
PO Box 23408
Claremont 7735
Cape Town, South Africa

Offices and agents throughout the world

ISBN 0-435-08976-5 (Heinemann cloth)
ISBN 0-435-08978-1 (Heinemann paper)
ISBN 0-85255-671-3 (James Currey cloth)
ISBN 0-85255-621-7 (James Currey paper)

Library of Congress Cataloging-in-Publication Data
Isaacman, Allen F.
    Cotton is the mother of poverty: peasants, work, and rural
struggle in colonial Mozambique, 1938–1961 / Allen Isaacman
        p. cm. — (Social history of Africa)
    Includes bibliographical references and index.
    ISBN 0-435-08976-5 (cloth). — ISBN 0-435-08978-1 (pbk.)
    1. Cotton growing—Mozambique—History—20th century.
    2. Peasants—Mozambique—History—20th century. 3. Mozambique—
Rural conditions.   I. Title. II. Series.
HD9087.M62I8   1996
338.1'7351'09679—dc20   96-14471
                                                               CIP

British Library Cataloging-in-Publication Data
Isaacman, Allen
    Cotton is the Mother of Poverty
    Peasants, Work and Rural Struggle in Colonial
    Mozambique, 1938–1961. —
    (Social History of Africa Series)
    I. Title II. Series
    338.1735109679

Cover design: Jenny Jensen Greenleaf
Cover photo: Mozambican women picking cotton. Courtesy of Arquivo Histórico de Moçambique. Rebelo Júnior, photographer.

Printed in the United States of America on acid-free paper
99 98 97 96 95 DA 1 2 3 4 5 6 7 8 9

To Barbara, Geoffrey, and Erik
who have given me so much

CONTENTS

LIST OF MAPS, TABLES, AND GRAPHS

ACKNOWLEDGMENTS

I owe a profound debt of gratitude to many friends and colleagues who provided moral and intellectual support during the fifteen years that I was working on this book. To Michael and June Stephen and Iain and Francise Christie, who were there from the start, my profound thanks. This study benefited from the energy and insights of Michael Stephen, Yussuf Adam, Eugenio Macamo, Augustinho Pililão, and Alpheus Manghezi, who worked with me as part of a research team from the Centro Estudos Africanos of the Universidade Eduardo Mondlane. Together we gathered oral data on peasant resistance to forced cotton cultivation during the colonial period. We were guided by the wisdom of the late Aquino de Bragança, director of the Centro Estudos Africanos, who appreciated the capacity of peasants to make their own history. I also learned a great deal from Paulo Zucula of the Ministry of Agriculture about Mozambique's complex and varied agro-environment. Of course, my best teachers were the women and men of the Mozambican countryside who generously shared their past with me.

The staff at the Arquivo Histórico de Moçambique provided valuable assistance. The director, Maria Ines Nogueira da Costa, deserves credit for preserving the archives' rich collections under very difficult conditions. António Sopa and Manuel Jorge Correia de Lemos shared their knowledge of the cotton material housed in the Archives. I am also grateful to Ms. J. Vautier Harries who collected important data on southern Mozambique housed in the Swiss Mission Archives in Geneva.

A number of scholars read this manuscript critically at various points in its formulation. The final product is much changed and far better, thanks to the detailed comments of Ron Aminzade, Tom Bassett, Sara Berry, Jane Guyer, James Johnson, Barbara Laslett, Elias Mandala, M. J. Maynes, Jeanne Penvenne, Anne Pitcher, Terence Ranger, Richard Roberts, Elizabeth Schmidt, and Jan Vansina. A special thanks to Steve Feierman and James Scott whose thoughtful critiques forced me to sharpen my arguments; their own writings on peasants have had a profound effect on my thinking. Those of us working on Mozambique have lost a real friend and committed colleague with the untimely passing of Otto Roesch. I learned a great deal about the country and its people from him. Finally, I want to thank Jean Hay, co-editor of the Heinemann Social History Series, for her thoughtful and supportive comments. It was a joy to work with her and with John Watson, president of Heinemann. My dear friend George Roberts taught me about the joys of writing.

The critical reading of a number of graduate students at the University of Minnesota made this a better book. Thanks to Thaddeus Sunseri, Osumaka Likaka,

Pier Larson, and Helena Pohlandt-McCormick. In addition to helpful comments from these four, Arlindo Chilundo and Heidi Gengenbach, who are both doing important research on Mozambique, read the entire manuscript highlighting areas that needed elaboration or refinement, or were just plain wrong. I also had the pleasure of doing fieldwork with Arlindo Chilundo in the summer of 1991.

I wish to thank the Social Science Research Council, the American Council of Learned Societies, and the National Endowment for the Humanities for their generous support. The Graduate School of the University of Minnesota and the College of Liberal Arts also provided financial assistance at critical junctures in this project. This book is graced with maps and graphs produced by the Cartography Laboratory of the University of Minnesota.

My greatest debt of gratitude, as usual, is to my wife Barbara, who allowed me to inflict my obsession with cotton on her night or day. She offered thoughtful and incisive responses, even to the most trivial questions I posed. To Barbara and to our sons Geoffrey and Erik I dedicate this book.

Allen Isaacman
Minneapolis, May 14, 1995

1

Introduction: The Labor Process and the Partial Autonomy of Mozambican Peasants

To this day, peasants throughout Mozambique insist that "cotton is the mother of poverty." Their antipathy toward cotton is hardly surprising, since the Portuguese colonial regime forced hundreds of thousands of peasants to cultivate the staple between 1938 and 1961, an obligation that for some actually began a decade earlier. By the 1940s more than three-quarters of a million Mozambicans were legally required to plant cotton, and untold thousands of children, elders, and migrant laborers worked beside them in the fields for all or part of the year. The cotton scheme was not simply a labor regime, however. The colonial state sought to impose limits and boundaries on nearly every aspect of peasant life. Growers were told not only what they should produce, but where they should live, how they should organize their day, with whom they should trade, and how to behave as "rational economic beings." But try as it might, the colonial state could only partially subordinate the rural population. Precisely because it lacked sufficient manpower to impose labor discipline, it had to rely on public acts of coercion and brutality to maintain its grip on the land. The cotton concessionary companies also adopted these tactics. To minimize costs and maximize output, they squeezed the African growers at every phase in the production and marketing process. This book explores the lives of the cotton producers of Mozambique—their pain and suffering, their hopes and aspirations, their creative adaptations, and their struggles to survive.

For much of Africa cotton was the premier colonial crop. British, French, German, Italian, Belgian, and Portuguese planners wrongly assumed that an unlimited supply of labor and the continent's tropical climate offered an ideal environment in which to produce the fiber. Colonial proponents of the "idle labor" thesis defined work in very narrow terms. For example, despite the fact that most cotton growers in Mozambique

1

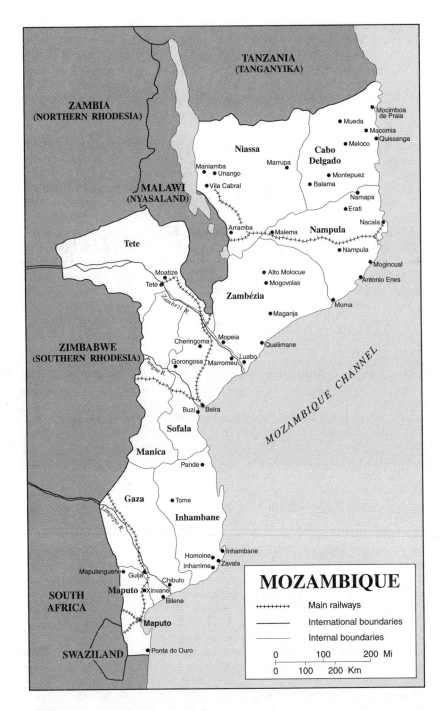

MAP 1. Mozambique and Its Environs

were women, colonial authorities assumed "real" producers to be male, just as they understood "real" work to exclude a wide range of essential tasks they dismissed as women's "domestic chores." Moreover, colonial planners ignored the already heavy labor demands of local agrarian systems, and failed to comprehend that adding a new cash crop—particularly one such as cotton, which is both labor-intensive and inedible—would cause real hardships across the continent.

Ironically, while cotton can be grown under a fairly wide range of agro-ecological conditions, the inadequate rainfall, weak soils, pests, and plant diseases that characterize much of tropical Africa make it a poor growing environment for this crop.[1] Even under the most favorable conditions, yields per hectare are appreciably lower in the tropics than in mid-latitude zones, whose higher potential rates of photosynthesis confer a natural advantage for cotton cultivation.[2] Nonetheless, colonial authorities held out the hope that African cotton would fuel robust metropolitan textile industries and alleviate Europe's unhealthy dependence on the American South.

The search for new sources of cotton coincided with the intensification of colonialism in Africa, a point that Isaacman and Roberts stress in their recent edited volume.[3] Cotton and colonialism were thus intimately associated throughout much of the continent, and the language of cotton became inextricably intertwined with the language of colonialism. In the first instance, colonial governments stressed the use of force to compel "lazy, shiftless Africans" to work. Race became a powerful organizing principle and rhetorical device to legitimate forced cotton cultivation. This was as true in Chad as it was in Tanganyika or Zaire.[4] Over time, European authorities adopted the language and principles of neoclassical economic theory, which stressed the work ethic, "scientific" farming, and "development." This interrelated shift in language and practice occurred somewhat later in the Portuguese territories than in most other parts of the continent. Until the early fifties, Lisbon and the Portuguese cotton companies sought to minimize capital expenditures and, as a result, relied on force rather than any notion of "rational planning" to maximize cotton output.

Because of its economic impact, the expansion of cotton production in colonial Mozambique has attracted the attention of a number of scholars. Four books stand out.[5] Nelson Saraiva Bravo's study *A Cultura Algodoeira na Economia do Norte de*

---

[1]   See A. N. Prentice, *Cotton: With Special Reference to Africa* (London, 1972).

[2]   Philip Porter, "A Note on Cotton and Climate: A Colonial Conundrum," in Allen Isaacman and Richard Roberts, eds., *Cotton, Colonialism, and Social History in Sub–Saharan Africa* (Portsmouth, 1995).

[3]   Isaacman and Roberts, *Cotton, Colonialism, and Social History.*

[4]   For a comparative analysis of colonial cotton projects throughout Africa, see the introduction and the various chapters in Isaacman and Roberts, *Cotton, Colonialism, and Social History.*

[5]   In addition to these four monographs, Manuel Lemos has meticulously documented the juridical basis of the cotton regime. See his "Fontes Para O Estudo do Algodão em Moçambique: Documentos de Arquivo, 1938–1974" (M.A. thesis, Universidade Eduardo Mondlane, 1984). Several studies completed by scholars associated with the Universidade Eduardo Mondlane in Maputo also make an important contribution to the debate on cotton and agrarian change in colonial Mozambique. In 1979 a team of researchers at the Centro de Estudos Africanos (the CEA) launched a broad project on the political economy of cotton in Northern Mozambique. Out of this research came a number of provocative papers that highlight the distorting effects of colonial cotton policy on the rural landscape. See, for example, Christian Geffray and Mogens Pedersen, *Transformação da Organização e do Sistema Agrário do Campesinato no Distrito do Eráti* (Maputo, 1985); CEA, *Cotton Production in Mozambique: A Survey 1936–1979* (Maputo, 1981); CEA, *Já Não Batem: A Transformação da Organização e do Sistema Agrário do Campesinato no Distrito do Eráti: Processo de Socialização Social* (Maputo, 1985).

Moçambique has been the classic work on cotton for three decades. The author, a colonial official, provides a wealth of heretofore inaccessible primary documentation on peasant production, marketing, and price structures that remains indispensable. Inspired by modernization theory, he argues that cotton transformed the countryside and elevated the standard of living of Africans. Carlos Fortuna takes a very different approach.[6] Examining the cotton scheme from a world systems perspective, Fortuna highlights the coordinated efforts of the Portuguese state, metropolitan textile interests, and the cotton concessionary companies to pump wealth out of the colony. As a "semi-core colonial power," he argues, Lisbon lacked the economic resources to stimulate voluntary cotton production or to guarantee that fiber would end up in Lisbon except through political intervention. Anne Pitcher impicitly challenges Fortuna's interpretation.[7] She makes the important point that the notion of a smooth and functional relationship between the state and Portuguese capital obscures a more complex and ambiguous relationship. Lisbon pursued policies that, at times, were at odds with the voracious profit-maximizing strategies of the concessionary companies and the metropolitan textile industry, which in turn did not necessarily speak in one voice. Of these four studies, only Leroy Vail and Landeg White's monograph[8] offers a detailed account of the impact of cotton on the ground. Their path-breaking analysis of peasant songs and use of oral data enabled them to capture the coercive nature of the cotton system and to link it to a broader discussion of the competition for African labor in the district of Zambézia.

This book builds upon the prior scholarship on Mozambique as well as upon the broader literature on agrarian change in colonial Africa. It underscores the important insights of Paul Richard on how peasant science and local systems of knowledge enabled growers to cope and survive in a hostile world.[9] It highlights the social basis of hunger and disease, as well as the notion of entitlements. Writing about very different colonial contexts Steve Feierman, John Iliffe, Megan Vaughan, and Michael Watts reached similar conclusions.[10] This study also extends the significant writing on rural protest of William Beinart and Colin Bundy, Helen Bradford, and Terence Ranger, both by exploring the interrelationship between mental resistance and acts of defiance and by examining less visible conflicts within rural households and communities.[11] Finally, by drawing on the new literature on the social history of cotton, particularly the work of Tom Bassett, Victoria Bernal, Elias Mandala, Osumaka Likaka, Richard Roberts, and Thaddeus Sunseri, the study demonstrates that it was the politics of production, not the technical requirements of

---

[6]   Carlos Fortuna, *O Fio da Meada: O Algodão da Moçambique, Portugal e a Economia–Mundo, 1860–1960* (Porto, 1993).

[7]   M. Anne Pitcher, *Politics in the Portuguese Empire* (Oxford, 1993).

[8]   Leroy Vail and Landeg White, *Capitalism and Colonialism in Mozambique* (Minneapolis, 1980).

[9]   Paul Richards, "Ecological Change and the Politics of African Land Use," *ASR* 26(1983), 1–72.

[10]   Steven Feierman, *Peasant Intellectuals* (Madison, 1980); John Iliffe, *The African Poor: A History* (Cambridge, 1987); Megan Vaughan, *The Story of an African Famine* (Cambridge, 1987); Michael Watts, *Silent Violence: Food, Famine and Peasantry in Northern Nigeria* (Berkeley, 1983).

[11]   William Beinart and Colin Bundy, *Hidden Struggles in Rural South Africa* (Berkeley, 1987); Helen Bradford, *A Taste of Freedom* (New Haven, 1987); Terence Ranger, "Resistance in Africa: From Nationalist Revolt to Agrarian Protest," in Gary Okihiro, ed., *In Resistance* (Amherst, 1986).

the staple, that differentiated the Mozambican cotton scheme from its colonial counterparts.[12]

By highlighting the organization of rural work, this study departs from much of the literature on agrarian change in Africa. Although the practices of local administrators and labor overseers and the vagaries of the market figure prominently in this study, they are not at its center. Instead, I have shifted the focus to the peasant producers, particularly women, who in many parts of the colony were the principal cotton growers. I have placed work at the heart of this study. Work was critical in structuring the rhythm of rural life. In sharp contrast to the colonial image of African laziness, most peasants toiled from dawn until nightfall to meet their daily needs. Labor demands helped to shape the ways in which different groups organized production, consumption, and long-term social reproduction strategies.[13]

Production and control of scarce resources were also integrally bound up with the cultural understanding of how work should be defined and valued. When southern Mozambican women organized labor exchanges (*mafunana*) to alleviate the heavy demands of cotton production or when northern Mozambican households organized work parties (*mukume*) followed by copious amounts of beer, food, dance, and gossip, they were drawing on a repertoire of cultural resources that antedated both the cotton regime and the colonial period. Similarly, when Amélia Novane of Manjacaze observed that "cotton was our *chibalo*," she was making a distinction between different types of work. The work of cotton was associated with *chibalo*—forced labor for the colonial economy—and was understood to be very different from work to sustain the household. In much the same vein, men across the colony complained that they were humiliated by cotton overseers who not only forced them to weed, which they considered "women's work," but then beat them in front of their wives and children.[14] Thus, the onslaught of cotton had a profound impact on the material as well as the cultural universe of Mozambican peasants. The inextricable relationship among culture, power, and work was hardly unique to colonial Mozambique. In her far-reaching analysis of the dynamics of African agrarian change, Sara Berry demonstrates that culture and politics are not exogenous or subordinate to economic forces, but rather that all three factors act "in mutually constitutive ways to shape the course of economic and social change."[15]

Work was also the most important determinant of the relationship between growers and the colonial state. Unlike other forced cultivation schemes, such as in Java, where land shortages were critical,[16] in Mozambique the organization of and access to labor was the constraining factor. Thus, an examination of how

---

[12] See the chapters by these various authors in Isaacman and Roberts, *Cotton, Colonialism, and Social History*. See also Elias Mandala, *Work and Control in a Peasant Economy: A History of the Lower Tchiri Valley, 1859–1960* (Madison, 1990).

[13] By "social reproduction" I mean those ongoing activities, responsibilities, and relationships that are critical for the maintenance of the daily and intergenerational life of rural society. See Barbara Laslett and Johanna Brenner, "Gender and Social Reproduction: Historical Perspectives," *Annual Review of Sociology* 15(1989), 381–404.

[14] Interview with Bishop João Somane Machado, Maputo, 23 July 1992.

[15] Sara Berry, *No Condition Is Permanent* (Madison, 1993), 13.

[16] Clifford Gertz, *Agricultural Involution: The Processes of Ecological Change in Indonesia* (Berkeley, 1963); J. S. Furnival, *Netherlands India: A Study of a Plural Economy* (Cambridge, 1939).

the Portuguese colonial state sought to organize peasant labor and how peasants sought to organize themselves can reveal the complexity of relations between colonizers and colonized. Moreover, unlike workers in capitalist or colonial capitalist societies, peasants neither sell their labor power nor entirely surrender their interest in or control over the labor process.[17] As a result, even in the tightly regimented cotton scheme, Mozambican growers maintained a small measure of control over what they produced and for whom. The core of this book is about this complex relationship between the peasant labor process and the colonial state.

For the purposes of this analysis, I understand the constituent elements of the peasant labor process to include (1) the composition and organization of the rural work force; (2) the ways in which growers interacted with nature; (3) the degree to which their necessary labor and surplus labor were separated in time and space; (4) the degree to which growers were able to set in motion the instruments of production independently of landlords, the state, or the ruling class; (5) the manner in which their labor was supervised by outside agents and work obligations were secured through political or legal institutions; and (6) the degree to which growers were forced to assume the risks of production. Viewing the "labor process" in this way opens up a number of areas of inquiry. It highlights, for example, the fact that environmental conditions were not mere backdrop against which growers made crop management decisions. More than a decade ago John Tosh admonished Africanists for "strangely detaching peasants from their environment."[18] Farming, after all, is an interactive process between people and nature. In the process of altering nature, growers transform themselves and alter their daily lives. When Celeste Cossa of southern Mozambique began to cultivate cotton in the early 1940s with an ox-drawn plow rather than with a hoe, she did so not only with the knowledge of how difficult it was to work the heavy clay soils of Gaza by hand, but also with the understanding that she was challenging deeply held cultural taboos prohibiting women from tending cattle herds. Her story (see Chapter 4) reveals that paying greater attention to the complex ways in which peasants interacted with their environment opens up a wide range of related questions about soil structure, agricultural technologies, and gender relations—questions that have escaped the attention of most historians of rural Africa.

An exploration of the labor process also connects the technical requirements of cotton to the risks that growers were forced to assume. Peasants who were forced to cultivate cotton under unfavorable ecological conditions faced the risk of losing all they had worked for. Even where environmental factors were satisfactory for cotton cultivation, the technical requirements imposed serious constraints on the organization of work. Cotton is extremely labor-intensive. In Mozambique, colonial officials estimated that rural households had to spend between 140 and 180

---

[17] For a discussion of the labor process in capitalist societies, see Karl Marx, *Capital: A Critique of Political Economy*, vol. 2 (Harmondsworth, 1976), 283; Harry Braverman, *Labour and Monopoly Capital: The Degradation of Work in the Twentieth Century* (New York, 1975); Michael Buraway, *The Politics of Production* (London, 1985), 21–84; Sheila Cohen, "A Labour Process to Nowhere?," *New Left Review* 168(1987), 34–50.

[18] John Tosh, "The Cash Crop Revolution in Tropical Africa: An Agricultural Reappraisal," *African Affairs* 79(1980), 415–39.

days[19] cultivating a single hectare of pure-standing cotton. Whether cotton was grown in grassland savanna, in the forest, or on previously fallowed lands had a bearing on total labor input. Yet regardless of plot type, colonial planners demanded that peasants accomplish an elaborate set of interrelated tasks in a timely fashion in order to achieve the maximum yield of good-quality cotton. The sequence included (1) preparing the land and seed bed, (2) ridging, (3) planting and spacing seeds at the appropriate depth, (4) reseeding in areas of poor germination, (5) thinning seed beds, (6) performing three to four weedings, (7) picking the crop, (8) drying the fiber, (9) preparing and sorting it for the market, (10) transporting it to the market, and (11) destroying the plant residue. All of these tasks had to be done on a strict schedule. Failure to clear the fields before the rains meant that the crop would germinate late under less favorable conditions. Repeated weeding was essential to prevent young plants from being overshadowed and strangled by faster-growing vegetation. Burning the stalks after the harvest robbed cotton parasites of their natural habitat. Since these activities were extremely time-consuming, they interfered regularly with food production, posing problems of diet and nutrition for growers and their families. The challenge to producers was to develop strategies for circumventing or overcoming production bottlenecks—a daunting task given the highly regimented colonial labor regime.

Focusing on the peasant labor process also allows us to redefine what "counts" as work. The colonial regime in Mozambique conceptualized work narrowly. It excluded from the definition such activities as foraging, collecting firewood, preparing food, caring for children, and a variety of other domestic chores typically performed by women and children. Although these tasks were critical for the social reproduction of rural households and communities, Portuguese colonial authorities acknowledged as "work" only those activities that took place within the capitalist and export sectors of the economy. Incorporating all of this "domestic" labor into the definition of work makes it possible to explore the ways in which the allocation of work according to gender has been historically constructed. This line of inquiry has led me to focus on the household as a principal unit of analysis. As used in this study, "the household" refers to "a domestic unit with decision-making autonomy about production and consumption,"[20] embedded within a wider, power-laden economic and political system. Household dynamics are characterized by both cooperation and conflict. In rural Mozambique, disputes often arose between spouses over the allocation of labor, the distribution of cotton income and other scarce resources, and a host of other economic and social issues. To highlight the household is not to overlook the fact that household membership is fluid or that labor obligations and resource allocations often extend to social networks beyond residential units.[21] Through these networks, peasants gained access to labor,

---

[19]   These figures are rough estimates with no explicit agreement on what constituted a "working day." See Nelson Saraiva Bravo, *A Cultura Algodeira na Economia do Norte de Moçambique* (Lisbon, 1963), 201; Arquivo de Instituto de Algodão, Junta de Exportação de Algodão Colonial (AIA, JEAC), Delegação de Moçambique (Del. de Moç.), Brigada Técnica (BT) de Nampula, "Relatório do Campo Experimental de Nacarôa, Campanha de 1942/43," Augusto Guilhermo Alves, Agente da Fiscalização (Ag. Fisc.), n.d.

[20]   Jane Guyer, "Household and Community in African Studies," *ASR* 24, nos. 2/3(1981), 89.

[21]   Ibid.; Jane Guyer and Pauline Peters, "Conceptualizing the Household: Issues of Theory, Method and Application," *Development and Change* 18(1987), 197–214; Pauline Peters, "Gender, Developmental Cycles and Historical Process: A Critique of Recent Research on Women in Botswana," *JSAS* 10, 1(1983), 100–122.

various forms of agricultural capital, and food that they were unable to obtain through impersonal commercial transactions.[22] Most cotton growers stressed the important role of nonhousehold members at critical junctures in the production process. Their reliance on labor exchanges, work parties, and occasionally, casual laborers underscores the fact that households were not autonomous units. Nevertheless, in rural Mozambique, the household in its varied forms was the principal site for production and social reproduction. Under the cotton regime, its central role was mandated by law and confirmed by practice.[23] Old and young, whether registered in the cotton scheme or not, could be found working in the cotton fields assigned to their household throughout much of the year.

Expanding the concept of the labor process makes it possible to view peasants as an integral part of a larger social order in which ruling class agendas, state politics, and international markets impinge on their daily lives and determine how they will allocate a substantial portion of their labor. These structural relationships are particularly critical in this study because no cotton scheme was built on a more repressive or sustained work regime, no system was more completely predicated on political intervention at the point of production, and no peasant economy experienced more effective government control over the terms of exchange than the Mozambican one.

This concept of the peasant labor process also provides a way to explore the varied opportunities available to cotton growers who were willing to take risks in structuring their work day. This approach thus offers analytical space from which peasants might emerge as agents of sustained historical change, while at the same time it recognizes the extraordinary constraints under which they lived. The story of Mozambican cotton growers becomes far more complex than if they were reduced to passive victims of surplus extraction.

In fact, it is one of the central premises of this study that Mozambican cotton growers were able to retain a degree of autonomy from the colonial state and from the cotton concessionary companies. This partial autonomy stemmed partly from their role as peasants and partly from the limits of state power. Peasants' ability to mobilize their own labor through the household, together with their access to land, gave them some measure of control over work and subsistence. Precisely because of the nature of the labor process, cotton growers enjoyed much greater autonomy than did plantation laborers or urban workers. Cotton growers were never entirely divorced from the means of production, nor were they entirely locked into the market. They could, and often did, draw on a repertoire of social practices, ranging from beer parties to bride-service, to deflect some of the onerous demands of the colonial state. Moreover, they were not subject to the same degree of surveillance and labor control as their counterparts in other work endeavors. For both the state and its merchant allies, the cost of effective labor control was prohibitive. Neither had sufficient manpower to enforce labor discipline over mobile peasants scattered over several thousand square kilometers. The colonial administration and the cotton concessionary companies tried to compensate for the small number of Euro-

---

[22] For an insightful discussion of the role of social networks, see Berry, *No Condition Is Permanent,* 161–67.

[23] For an important study of the rural household as an analytical category, see Guyer, "Household and Community."

pean officials in the Mozambican interior by relying on fairly massive African involvement in overseeing cotton cultivation and marketing. African police (*sipais*), chiefs (*régulos*), and local headmen played a critical role in perpetuating the cotton regime. However, there were not enough African functionaries to saturate the countryside, and few expressed unwavering or consistent allegiance to the colonial regime.

That state power was mediated through local political institutions and that cotton growers retained their own language, their own historical memories, and their own expressive culture made it very difficult for the colonial regime to control peasants' attitudes toward cotton. To complicate matters, peasant ideas and actions often remained hidden from public view or fell beyond the gaze of state officials, cotton company overseers, and their African subordinates. Try as they might to promote the virtues of cotton, colonial authorities failed to persuade most growers.

The material and ideological weakness of the alliance was fundamentally at odds with Lisbon's effort to impose a highly controlled labor regime in Mozambique. The reality on the ground compelled most state and cotton company officials to rely on intimidation and periodic acts of terror to try to accomplish what they could not do through supervision or persuasion. Thus I argue that the Portuguese colonial state was weak and brutal at the same time. Its capacity to intervene in the daily lives of most growers was circumscribed. At certain points the state could come down hard on growers. At others it was almost powerless to act. The state could dictate the size of the cotton fields, register hundreds of thousands of peasants, and intimidate recalcitrant growers, but it could not guarantee that these same growers would get up at the break of dawn and head for their cotton fields or that they would not sneak off later in the day to work their food gardens. Similarly, colonial authorities could set the price for cotton and beat growers who did not bring an appropriate amount to the markets, but they had little recourse if peasants chose not to harvest their entire crop. State power was even more problematic, since a shortage of Portuguese officials meant that a good number of local administrative posts, particularly in more remote cotton zones, were vacant at any given time.

For their part, cotton growers were not passive recipients of a colonial mandate. Nor were they the helpless victims of capital accumulation or state oppression. It is true that peasants rarely acted openly or fully against their domination and that there were no great cotton revolts in colonial Mozambique. The partial subordination of the peasants as well as their awareness of their limited power helps to explain why cotton producers were prone to engage in hidden forms of protest rather than in broader social movements (see Chapter 10). Illegal intercropping, sabotage, dissimulation, and flight were typically the "weapons of the weak."[24] Through these acts peasants sought to shield critical resources and to minimize colonial exploitation. In the process they also engaged in a type of mental resistance, a struggle over meaning in which defiant expressions about work, justice, and a world free from cotton were articulated in songs, sculpture, rumor, and gossip. No less than insurgent action, these rebellious visions were derived from lived

---

[24] The term comes from *Weapons of the Weak: Everyday Forms of Peasant Resistance* (New Haven, 1985), James Scott's pioneering study of Malaysian peasants.

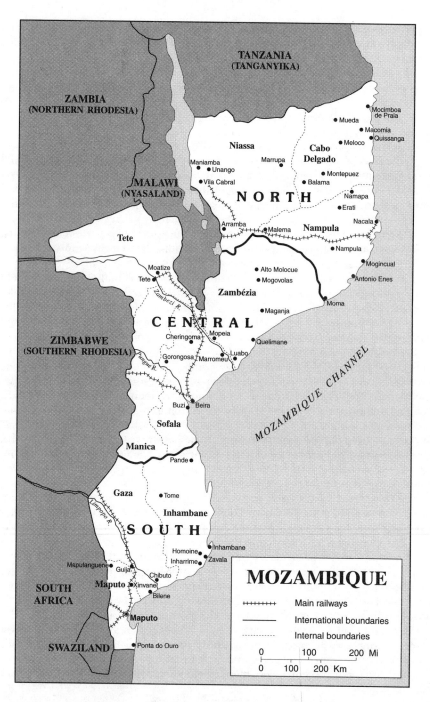

MAP 2. Northern, Central, and Southern Mozambique

experiences inside the cotton regime. The sum total of such seemingly insignificant material and cultural acts of defiance could, and at times did, have far-reaching consequences.

The cotton regime exacerbated conflict within rural households and communities, a terrain that most scholars of rural protest have tended to ignore. By examining who actually performed the labor, who assumed the risks of production, and who controlled cotton income, we can gain a clearer picture of what actually went on inside households.

An examination of the labor process also opens up ways to explore changes across time and space and demonstrates that the effects of cotton production on rural Mozambique were not uniform. There were important variations in the ways work was organized in different parts of the colony, variations stemming in part from local and regional agro-ecological factors. Mozambique's 800,000 square kilometers of territory run the gamut from coastal marshes along the wind-swept Indian Ocean shoreline to plateaus and highlands in the western parts of the country. The diverse and ever-changing character of so large a land mass produced widely fluctuating patterns of rainfall, temperature, soil types, and vegetation, and geographically proximate areas often exhibited widely divergent agricultural qualities. These environmental factors had a direct bearing on the relative hardships associated with cotton production. The critical variable for understanding the differential impact of the cotton regime, however, was the preexisting political economy onto which it was imposed. The political economies of southern Mozambique (Gaza and Inhambane), the central provinces (Zambézia and Manica e Sofala), and the north (Nampula, Cabo Delgado, and Niassa) were quite distinct (see Map 1). I have therefore divided the production of cotton in colonial Mozambique into these three regions (see Map 2).

Well before the introduction of cotton the southern provinces had been transformed into a labor reserve for South Africa, each year sending thousands of male migrants to the gold mines of the Witwatersrand. As a result, when cotton growing was imposed, production fell disproportionately to African women. In central Mozambique, men labored for shorter periods of time on nearby European-owned plantations, often working part of the year in the cotton fields; in the north, rural households remained relatively intact, cultivating the staple year-round. To complicate matters, in each of the three regions some households were forced to grow rice in addition to or instead of cotton.[25] As a result, the labor process varied markedly from one part of the colony to another, as did the subsequent process of differentiation. The cotton regime impoverished unevenly by region, by household, and by gender. Moreover, despite the arduousness of the work, many men preferred toiling side by side with family members in the cotton fields to working on the European plantations. At the same time, a small but powerful group of chiefs and African entrepreneurs prospered from cotton.

Just as an exploration of the complex relationship between the labor process and the colonial state offers a strategic entry into the Mozambican cotton regime,

---

[25] For an important discussion of forced rice production, see Otto Roesch, "Migrant Labour and Forced Rice Production in Southern Mozambique," *Journal of Southern African Studies* 17, no. 2(1991), 239–70. See also Leroy Vail and Landeg White, "Tawani Machambero!: Forced Rice and Cotton Cultivation on the Zambezi, 1938–1961," *JAH* 19(1978), 1–16.

so it provides a way to compare colonial cotton schemes over time and space. Because the technical requirements of cotton did not favor one system of production over another,[26] colonial authorities experimented with a variety of cotton systems. The unsuccessful imposition of large cotton plantations in East Africa that combined slavery and other forms of conscripted labor with modern agricultural equipment[27] stands in sharp contrast to the peasant models of colonial cotton development that ultimately became the backbone of the cotton revolution in Africa. That colonial planners adopted a peasant option should not obscure the fact that different peasantries became enmeshed in different labor regimes. Petty commodity producers in the Gold Coast, the French Soudan, Northern Nigeria, and Nyasaland controlled their own labor and means of production and could decide if and when to cultivate cotton, although they could rarely determine the terms of exchange.[28] Their situation was very different from tenant farmers and sharecroppers in Sudan or in Swaziland, whose conditional access to land was predicated on their willingness to cultivate cotton.[29] The constraints on tenant farmers and sharecroppers, however, were not nearly as acute as they were on forced peasant producers in the Congo, in the Oubangi-Shari region of French Equatorial Africa, or in Angola and Mozambique, who were trapped inside a highly repressive labor regime.[30]

This study focuses on the period from 1938, when the Salazar government established the Cotton Board to oversee the system of forced cultivation, to 1961, when the regime was abolished. The early 1950s mark a point of transition, when the state made serious although not necessarily successful efforts to rationalize the cotton scheme. The chronology of the cotton regime highlights the anachronistic nature of Portuguese colonialism. The fully developed forced cotton system was imposed at a time when virtually all other colonial regimes had abandoned coerced cultivation as inefficient. Even in the Congo, whose cotton scheme had served as a model for Lisbon, Belgium had shifted, to an incentive-based system by 1937.[31] Lisbon's abolition of the cotton regime in 1961 was part of a reform effort designed to strengthen Portugal's hold on its colonies at the very time when other European nations were in the process of withdrawing from the African continent and substituting neocolonial for colonial arrangements.

---

[26] For a discussion of the way the technical requirements of sugar and cotton structure the systems of production, see Ralph Schlomowitz, "Plantation and Smallholder: Comparative Perspectives from the World of Cotton and Sugar Cane Economics 1865–1939," *Agricultural History* 58(1984), 1–16.

[27] W. W. A. Fitzgerald, *Travels in British East Africa, Zanzibar and Pemba* (London, 1897), 639; Thaddeus Sunseri, "Peasants and the Struggle for Labor in Cotton Regimes of the Rufiji Basin (Tanzania), 1885–1918," in Isaacman and Roberts, *Cotton, Colonialism, and Social History*.

[28] Raymond E. Dumett, "Obstacles to Government–Assisted Agricultural Development in West Africa," *Agricultural History Review* 13(1975), 167; Roberts, "The Coercion of Free Markets"; Jan Hogendorn, "The Cotton Campaign in Northern Nigeria, 1902–1914," in Isaacman and Roberts, *Cotton, Colonialism, and Social History*; Mandala, *Work and Control*.

[29] Bernal, "Cotton and Colonial Order in Sudan"; B. A. B. Sikhondze, "The Development of Swazi Cotton Cultivation," *Mohlomi* 6(1990), 117–38.

[30] Eric de Dampierre, "Coton Noire, Café Blanc: Deux cultures du Haut–Oubangui à la veille de la loi–cadre," *CEA* 2(1960), 128–46; Osumaka Likaka, "Forced Cotton Cultivation and Social Control in the Belgian Congo" and M. Anne Pitcher, "From Coercion to Incentives: The Portuguese Cotton Regime in Angola and Mozambique, 1946–1974," in Isaacman and Roberts, *Cotton, Colonialism, and Social History*.

[31] Osumaka Likaka, "Forced Cotton Cultivation and the Colonial Work Ethic, 1936–1960," *CJAS* (forthcoming).

The structure of this book closely adheres to the spatial and temporal dimensions I have just outlined. Parts 1 and 2 analyze the work of cotton in different parts of the colony during the first decade or so of the cotton regime. Parts 3 and 4 move away from the cotton fields, markets, and ginning mills to explore the impact of cotton on the growers and the ways in which the colonizers and the colonized jockeyed and negotiated to adjust the cotton regime to suit their own interests. State initiatives to rationalize the system and peasant adaptations and struggles to make life inside the regime more bearable are the twin themes that unify these sections.

Although the study focuses on the cotton scheme over a twenty-three-year period from 1938 to 1961, the temporal divisions vary from one part of the book to another, and the story moves back and forth over time in an effort to capture the dynamics of the cotton regime. Part 2 (Chapters 3–5) examines the various dimensions of the labor process from 1938 to 1951. Part 3 (Chapter 6) explores colonial policies designed to revamp the regime during the next decade, concluding with a discussion of why Lisbon opted to abolish the system in 1961. The chronological divisions used to organize these two sections are less useful as a way to frame the social and political consequences of cotton production, the subject of the final part of this study. Whereas the colonial reforms of the 1950s did have a real, if limited, impact on the working conditions of thousands of growers, they did little to reverse the deleterious social consequences of the cotton regime and even less to mute rural opposition, which form the subject matter of Part 4. Thus, the periodization used in the previous sections makes little sense for the final portion of the book. Finally, it is important to reiterate that the study focuses on the dynamics taking place inside the cotton regime and that the temporal divisions I have used are necessarily only rough markers of the changes taking place on the ground.

One of the consequences of the book's design is that although its focus is on peasants as historical actors, much of the discussion of peasant agency is located in the final two chapters. The reason is clear. Before it is possible to explore the ways in which peasant producers creatively adapted to and helped to reshape the cotton regime, it is necessary to examine the colonial policies and practices that structured the regime and the variations in their implementation. To underscore the point that in ways growers tried to make their lives more bearable inside the brutal regime, I have woven evidence of peasants' coping with and struggling against colonial cotton policies into the earlier discussions of production, marketing, and food security.

Much of this study is based on archival sources. The Cotton Board archive is the single most important repository of material about this period. It contains an array of uncatalogued documents touching on almost every aspect of the cotton regime. Board inspectors chronicled in detail the difficulties involved in trying to implement cotton legislation and identified those localities where projects fared reasonably well. Agricultural technicians wrote surveys of environmental conditions and monitored the progress of annual cotton campaigns. Agronomists left detailed reports on seed experiments, soil types, and local farming practices. These Cotton Board officials compiled massive amounts of quantifiable data that they used to demonstrate the sharp increase in output and the rise in producers' income during the 1950s. Taken together these accounts tell a story of success. To be sure, there were occasional dissenting reports from critical inspectors, but these skeptical voices were few; even so, they are a critical part of the dominant colonial representation of the cotton regime.[32]

Shortly after independence these records were incorporated into the national archives (the Arquivo Histórico de Moçambique) and are currently being reclassified and integrated into the larger collection. The national archives house two other important collections. The reports of inspectors working for the Department of Native Affairs (ISANI)[33] provide an unusually rich and critical view of economic and social changes taking place in the Mozambican countryside, and the correspondence from local administrators and from provincial governors describes conditions in their respective domains.[34] Archives in Malawi, Tanzania, Portugal, Britain, Switzerland, and the United States also house valuable material written by missionaries, anthropologists, and colonial officials.

For all the valuable detail of this written documentation, it lies embedded within a colonial discourse that masks and disguises the social realities of peasant life. Even the richest of these documents is a colonial artifact. As such, peasants' words, ideas, and ideologies have been mediated through the eyes and ears of nonpeasant chroniclers whose agendas were shaped by their own race, nationality, class, gender, and position within the colonial order.

One example will suffice. Colonial accounts—and scholarship grounded in this documentary evidence—describe a dismal picture of deepening rural impoverishment in southern Mozambique over the course of the twentieth century. Attributing this process to the combined impact of male labor migration, forced labor (*chibalo*), a coercive cotton regime, and repeated ecological crises, scholars portray the very old, the very young, and particularly the women of the south as powerless victims of the exploitative forces of Portuguese and South African colonial capitalism. With so many men absent, for instance, women often bore the brunt of *chibalo* and were singled out to work on the chiefs' fields and on European farms. Women had to balance these additional labor demands with their normal daily tasks—cultivating the family food garden, gathering wood, grinding corn, cooking, and performing other household chores. Scholarly formulations of the far-reaching impact of male labor migration correctly highlight the suffering of many women in this situation.[35] And yet for all of its richness and drama, this story remains incomplete. By focusing on the ways in which the withdrawal of able-bodied men from the countryside precipitated the underdevelopment of peasant agriculture and impoverished female-headed households, those individuals "left behind" are seen as little more than history's victims. Women's own stories, on the other hand, while

---

[32] Dominant historical representations, or "dominant memory," are produced in the course of struggles over competing constructions of the past. Out of these struggles certain representations achieve centrality and others are marginalized or rendered invisible. See Popular Memory Group, "Popular Memory: Theory, Politics, Method," in Richard Johnson, Gregor McLennan, Bill Schwartz, and David Sutton, eds., *Making Histories: Studies in History Writing and Politics* (Minneapolis, 1982), 207–8.

[33] For a discussion of this collection see Michael Cahen, "O Fundo ISANI do Arquivo Histórico de Moçambique: Uma Fonte Importante da História Social Contemporânea do Colonialismo Português," *Arquivo* 7(1990), 63–82.

[34] As of 1992, most of this material was still being classified and only a small portion was available to the general public. Mozambican scholars and those working for the archives have used some of this material with very fruitful results.

[35] See, for example, Otto Roesch's important article, "Migrant Labour and Forced Rice Production."

acknowledging their bleak situation, provide evidence of agency, proactive struggle, and creative adaptation even under difficult circumstances. These oral accounts present a very different kind of narrative in which women's efforts to cope and to construct acceptable lives for themselves and their families stand at the foreground of processes of historical change.[36]

Because this study is concerned, above all else, with the lived experiences of the cotton growers, their stories figure prominently. The documentation for critical parts of this book rests primarily on more than 160 interviews, usually with former growers and their families, but also with African police and overseers, local settlers, merchants and missionaries, and concessionary company and state employees. I began fieldwork in 1978 as part of a project being conducted by the African Studies Center at Eduardo Mondlane University on peasant resistance to forced cotton cultivation in colonial Mozambique.[37] It took more than a decade to complete my research. The brutal war in Mozambique often made it difficult and dangerous to get to critical cotton areas in the countryside. Trips had to be deferred for long periods. Such inconveniences, however, were inconsequential compared with the suffering and dislocation that had become a way of life for so many of the men and women whose lives are chronicled in these pages. The women, especially, were reticent at first to share their stories with outsiders. When they agreed to be interviewed they spoke poignantly about what life was like for them and their families inside the cotton regime. The willingness of both men and women to share their memories increased dramatically when I indicated that tapes of our conversations would be deposited in the national archives so that their children and grandchildren could hear their stories in their own voices.

The uncertain conditions in the countryside are only part of the explanation for this book's long gestation period. The more I listened to the experiences of cotton growers, the more I came to realize that a study of rural social protest could not be separated from the study of rural life in its fullest expression. I became increasingly aware that the question of peasant resistance was inextricably linked to such issues as work, food security, and rural differentiation. I also came to comprehend the less visible but equally important conflicts within peasant communities and households. Altering the angle of vision through which I viewed the cotton regime required me to return to the countryside and conduct additional research in the three major cotton zones. I began this second phase of my research in 1986 and spent parts of four of the following five years in the field.

The oral testimonies of former cotton growers challenge colonial representations of the cotton scheme and provide a detailed interior view of the regime at work. Similarly, many songs that they still sing offer a rich historical "map of peasant experiences," to paraphrase Vail and White.[38] These oral accounts not only flesh out the real lives of real people, but they also open up new areas of inquiry. My discussions of intrahousehold and intracommunity conflict, for example, rest almost entirely on the recollections of former cotton growers. Like

---

[36] This point has been made most powerfully by Heidi Gengenbach, who is currently doing research on southern Mozambique.

[37] The other members of this team were Yusuf Adam, Maria João Homes, Eugénio Macamo, Alpheus Manghezi, Augustinho Pililão, and Michael Stephen.

[38] Leroy Vail and Landeg White, *Power and the Praise Poem* (Charlottesville, 1991), 40–82.

all oral testimonies, however, these accounts benefit from, but are also constrained by, their interior position. They are only partial accounts. Moreover, like the colonial texts, these narratives have a self-serving character. With this in mind, I tried to conduct a broad range of interviews not only with male elders, who were anxious to tell their stories, but particularly with women, who on such public occasions typically hovered in the background. Since women were the principal cotton growers, the primary victims of colonial terror, and the major architects of coping and resisting strategies—and since the colonial record tended to obscure their activities—women's memories of their experiences were essential to this study. A few African police and overseers also shared their experiences of the cotton era. Many initially wished to remain anonymous, but as they told their stories it became clear that their activities were far more ambiguous than the stereotype of "collaborator" would suggest. All of these, then, are facets of the story of cotton production in colonial Mozambique, because there is no single authentic peasant voice or transcending unity that structures the diverse experiences of cotton growers and their families. These oral documents are significant social texts with hidden, multiple, and often contradictory meanings.

The issue of violence, which figures prominently in all of the oral testimonies and which lies at the very heart of the cotton regime, exposes the difficulties of interpretation. There are several possible reasons for the arresting similarity with which violence is reported in oral testimony. These texts could be part of an explicitly motivated postcolonial narrative, perhaps an ongoing revision of popular historical memory.[39] After all, this research began just three years after independence, when discussions of coercion, terror, and resistance no longer had to be submerged. Indeed, throughout the armed struggle that preceded independence, the Front for the Liberation of Mozambique (FRELIMO) used the Portuguese cotton regime as a metaphor for colonial oppression.[40] From this perspective, we might interpret the testimonies as part of an authorized text within the broader political agenda of an independent FRELIMO state. Highlighting the common experience of violence and degradation during the colonial period may have helped to foster a new sense of national unity that cut across ethnic and regional boundaries. The national government's desire to discredit the opposition group RENAMO (Mozambique National Resistance), which had close ties to loyalist chiefs and leading figures in the colonial regime, may have provided an additional incentive to highlight colonial oppression.

The oral accounts may also be interpreted as having important contemporary meaning. Since independence, the FRELIMO government has sought to stimulate cotton production as part of its larger economic development strategy. It is not surprising that peasants in the former cotton zones have not responded enthusiastically to this state initiative. On occasion, government officials have reacted to peasant reluctance with threats of force and draconian pronouncements reminis-

---

[39] Otto Roesch, who did extensive research on agrarian change in southern Mozambique, indicated that "some of my interviews, I felt, were indeed part of an authorized text which fit within the broader political discourse of FRELIMO" (personal communication, 15 January 1994).

[40] See, for example, Eduardo Mondlane, *The Struggle for Mozambique* (Harmondsworth, 1969), 83–86; and "The Cotton Regime," *Mozambique Revolution* 46(1971), 18–23.

cent of the worst days of the cotton regime.[41] Set within this contemporary context, oral historical narratives may very well be offering a commentary about the present and may reflect fears that peasants will once again suffer a state assault on their autonomy.

Whatever their metaphorical and contemporary overtones, I am confident of the power of these oral testimonies as historical texts, which, like other forms of historical evidence, require a critical reading. This, after all, is the historian's craft. In the case of Mozambique, the broad outlines of state violence are corroborated in colonial documents, as well as in the memoirs of a number of Portuguese officials, settlers, and missionaries. The veracity of the oral testimonies is also suggested by their similarities to oral accounts of colonial violence collected by a number of scholars who have conducted fieldwork in Mozambique since independence.[42]

It is equally essential to address the silences in the oral texts.[43] At the outset of my research I was very interested in hidden forms of peasant struggle. For such acts to be successful, they had to be disguised or completely outside the view of the colonial authorities, and therefore they do not normally appear in written records. Naively, I believed that cotton growers, freed from the terror of colonialism, would be anxious to discuss their heroic exploits in great detail. I traveled with a group of researchers from the university's African Studies Center to Serra Nkanyavane, a fairly remote area in the Gaza province, which had a reputation as a hotbed of rural insurgency. It was common knowledge throughout Gaza that peasants in Serra Nkanyavane had covertly boiled cotton seeds before planting them in order to persuade the Portuguese that the terrain was not appropriate for cotton cultivation and that they had subsequently been freed from the scheme. After a fruitful discussion about various aspects of the cotton regime with a number of elders, I confidently broached the subject of boiling the seeds. Ex-cotton growers who had been forthcoming on other topics suddenly became silent. Others mumbled uncomfortably or adamantly denied that they or anyone else in their community had engaged in such activity. "Cotton was cultivated and it grew but did not flower—it died. But we have no knowledge that some people boiled the seeds," was a common retort. Only after an African researcher in our group intervened and assured the elders that although I was white, I was not a "*colono*" and was not there to arrest them, did an elder admit that he had "boiled the seeds . . . because he did not want to cultivate cotton since it brought no benefit." Other men and women subsequently told similar stories. After we left, my colleague tactfully suggested that it made no sense to try to get at hidden forms of resistance in the past from peasants who were engaged in similar forms of subterfuge in the present.[44]

---

[41]   João Moyana, "Produzir Algodão e Castanha de Caju Não é Favor é Ordem do Estado," *Tempo* 836 (16 October 1986), 12–15.

[42]   See Judith Head, "State, Capital and Migrant Labour in Zambézia, Mozambique: A Study of the Labour Force of Sena Sugar Estates Limited" (Ph.D. thesis, University of Durham, 1980); Kurt Habermeir, "Algodão: Das Concentrações á Produção Colectiva," *EM* 2(1981), 37–58; Alpheus Manghezi, "A Mulher e O Trabalho," *EM* 3(1981), 45–56; Geffray and Pederson, *Transformação*; Vail and White, *Capitalism and Colonialism*.

[43]   For a discussion of the problem of silences, see Richard Roberts, "Reversible Social Processes, Historical Memory, and the Production of History," *History in Africa* 17(1990), 341–49.

[44]   Group interview, Serra Nkanyavane, 2 February 1979.

This dialogue was particularly instructive for several reasons. First, it high-lighted the politics of memory.[45] How people reconstruct, interpret, and use the past is preeminently a political act. In this case, a discussion in the present of events that had taken place thirty years ago was framed by perceptions of contemporary social and political realities. And at one point my own identity became the issue. I was, after all, a white researcher from the university, conducting research that had the at least tacit approval of the Mozambican government. Second, the initial re-luctance of former cotton growers to discuss seed boiling despite my prodding, and my African colleague's ability to convince them to take this risk, suggest that surrounding these interviews was a set of power relations that affected the pro-duction of historical knowledge. Finally, the astute admonition of my colleague after we left reminded me that I needed to be more attentive to possible asymme-tries of power, to listen more carefully during interviews, and to try to understand the significance not only of voices but of silences.

For all their potential difficulties, however, interviews provide indispensable material for the social history of cotton. Oral accounts contain invaluable firsthand experiences and, perhaps more important, the critical subjective elements that his-torians often find so difficult to capture. Personal testimonies vividly describe the anguish faced by growers when they had to choose between cotton and food crops. They recall the fear that labor overseers inspired and the disdain heaped on loyal-ist chiefs who vigorously enforced colonial work obligations. And they depict the mixed feelings of courage and apprehension with which peasants—at great per-sonal risk—tried to circumvent the state's labor demands. But above all else, oral testimonies provide researchers with the possibility of understanding the complexi-ties of rural life by eliciting peasant self-perceptions and deciphering their mean-ing. Their understanding and construction of their experiences offer a strategic entry into the social history of the Mozambican countryside.

This study attempts to probe the inner world of the cotton growers. It explores the ways in which forced cotton cultivation affected the rhythm of peasants' daily lives, the extent to which the cotton regime restructured the organization of rural work, the repercussions of cotton production for food security and rural differen-tiation, and finally, how peasants developed a repertoire of skills to make their lives more bearable. Questions of power, differentiation, negotiation, coping, and struggle are discussed not just as abstractions but as issues deeply rooted in the daily practices and experiences of the women and men, young and old, who were trapped within the cotton regime. Although this book focuses on peasant produc-tion of a single crop in a specific colonial context, it addresses issues that transcend the Mozambican experience. The uneven and varied impact of commodity produc-tion on agrarian communities, the organization of work in the countryside, the relationship between peasant thought and peasant action, and the daily struggles of the rural poor are the very stuff of social history.

---

[45] For a theoretical discussion of the politics of memory, see Popular Memory Group, "Popular Memory."

2

The Antecedents and Formation of the Mozambican Cotton Regime, 1800–1938

The history of early cotton cultivation in Mozambique is a story of unrealized Portuguese dreams and unfulfilled legislative proclamations. Lisbon's initial cotton efforts fall roughly into three periods. The first, from the end of the eighteenth century until the imposition of formal colonial rule in the early 1900s, was limited to ineffectual policy directives and sporadic proposals alternately promoting a plantation strategy and calling for increased peasant production. The second began with the establishment of Portuguese control around the turn of the twentieth century and the expansion of the metropolitan textile industry, which precipitated a sharp increase in interest in Mozambique as a source of cotton. Nevertheless, neither the monarchy nor the republican government, which came to power in Portugal in 1910, coupled their rhetoric with action. Lisbon was unwilling or unable to promote cotton production. Its highest priority was to secure income by renting male labor to South Africa and by ceding large tracts of land to foreign-owned concessionary companies with little interest in cotton. To the extent that cotton was grown, it was limited to a handful of plantations. Only in the aftermath of the 1926 right-wing coup in Portugal did the state seek to regulate and restructure production of the staple as part of its new neomercantile agenda. During this third period, from 1926 to 1938, Lisbon tried to impose highly regimented peasant labor policies in Mozambique in an effort to satisfy the increasing demands of the metropolitan textile industry. Although there was some growth in cotton production after 1932, this scheme failed.

From these flawed projects the Salazar regime drew a number of lessons in its formulation of the post–1938 cotton scheme. If cotton was to be grown across the colony, peasants would have to be forced to cultivate it, concessionary companies would have to be guaranteed a profitable return on their investments, and the colonial state would have to regulate all aspects of production and marketing. This chapter explores Lisbon's initial efforts to promote cotton in the Mozambican countryside.

The Dream of Cotton, 1800–1900

By the end of the eighteenth century, colonial planners had a vision of Mozambique as a cotton-producing colony. The highly influential Governor Lacerda e Almeida noted in 1797 that the colony's potential for the "cultivation of cotton is unlimited."[1] His words were echoed by the governor general of Mozambique, Sebastião Botelho, three decades later: "Cotton blooms everywhere; it is as high in quality as anywhere and it grows either wild or sown."[2] In the middle of the nineteenth century, David Livingstone and his companions stressed the region's potential as a source of raw cotton, even entertaining the hope that it might reduce the British textile industry's dependence on the cotton exports of the American South.[3]

Despite their optimism, however, nineteenth-century Portuguese officials were forced to concede that there was virtually no systematic cultivation of cotton in the colony. "Whites leave this activity for the natives," admitted Governor General Botelho, "and the natives do not sow a single seed of it."[4] His observation reveals one of the paradoxes of Mozambican agrarian history. On the one hand, there is ample evidence that cotton, either growing wild or cultivated as a semiperennial crop,[5] was an important commodity in at least some parts of Mozambique.[6] The trade in locally woven cotton piece goods known as *manxillas* (or *machira*) flourished in Zambézia and the surrounding region from at least the seventeenth century onward.[7] On the other hand, despite the efforts of resident Portuguese officials to stimulate settler cotton production, during this period Mozambican cotton never became a major export commodity. Throughout the eighteenth and first half of the nineteenth centuries, trade in ivory and slaves dominated the region's export economy.[8]

Several factors help to explain the insignificance of cotton as an export commodity. Neither the small number of Portuguese settlers located on the coast nor the inland estate-holders of the Zambezi Valley (the *prazeiros*) exhibited any real

---

[1]   Quoted in Direcção dos Serviços de Agricultura (DSA), *Algodão* (Lourenço Marques, 1934), 1.

[2]   Sebastião Xavier Botelho, *Memória Estatística sobre os Domínios Portugueses na África Oriental* (Lisbon, 1935), 272. In parts of Mozambique, particularly the Zambezi Valley, wild cotton was spun into a coarse cloth that was the principal item of dress and an important trading commodity.

[3]   J. P. R. Wallis, ed., *The Zambezi Expedition of David Livingstone*, vol. 1 (London, 1956), 50–53, 80–84, 126–37.

[4]   Botelho, *Memória*, 272.

[5]   Mandala notes that in the Shire Valley indigenous cotton was a semiperennial (*Work and Control*, 55).

[6]   Allen Isaacman, *Mozambique: The Africanization of a European Institution, the Zambezi Prazos, 1750–1902* (Madison, 1972), 66, 73, 75; M. D. D. Newitt, *Portuguese Settlement on the Zambezi: Exploration, Land Tenure and Colonial Rule in East Africa* (New York, 1973), 180–82.

[7]   See Isaacman, *The Africanization of a European Institution*, Newitt, *Portuguese Settlement*; S. I. G. Mudenge, *A Political History of the Munhumutapa c. 1400–1902* (Harare, 1988), 29, 36–37.

[8]   See Edward Alpers, *Ivory and Slaves in East Central Africa* (London, 1975).

interest in the staple, although many did profit from commerce in locally woven cloth. Their lack of experience in cultivating cotton and their unfamiliarity with local agro-environmental conditions were powerful deterrents.[9] To the extent that the settlers farmed themselves or organized plantations, they preferred more traditional European staples such as grains, coffee, and sugar. But lack of settler interest is only part of the explanation. In a recent study, Carlos Fortuna argues persuasively that as far back as the eighteenth century local merchant interests had actually sabotaged the development of cotton production in northern Mozambique because they were afraid that European-organized plantations would divert African labor from the ivory-hunting, slave-trading, and mining activities on which their lucrative commerce depended. Under pressure from this powerful community, Lisbon's Board of Trade banned production of the staple in 1751.[10]

Fortuna's suggestion that merchant capital possessed the capacity to undermine northern Mozambican cotton production requires further study. There is no question, however, that over the next century most state attempts to promote cotton were badly conceived and poorly implemented. Examples of these ill-fated initiatives range from a compulsory peasant production scheme in the Tete province in 1770 to the distribution of free seeds to European farmers in 1858.[11] Even the efforts of the liberal government to promote cotton production as part of its midcentury abolitionist agenda yielded few tangible results.[12] Export statistics from 1863 are the clearest indicator of the failure of these policies. In that year Portuguese settlers produced under 2,000 kilograms of cotton, less than a quarter of which was exported to the metropole.[13]

Despite the flow of rhetoric and the number of government schemes involving cotton, until the second half of the nineteenth century there was not a great demand in Portugal for raw fiber.[14] Imports from Brazil easily satisfied the nascent Portuguese textile industry, which was still dominated by small household units of production. Unlike the large textile factories in Britain or France, textile production in Portugal at this time remained a cottage industry.[15]

The gradual expansion of the Portuguese textile industry during the late 1860s, combined with Lisbon's search for alternatives to American cotton in the aftermath of the U.S. Civil War, elevated interest in Mozambique's cotton potential. The decline of Britain's international textile monopoly raised the possibility that Portuguese metropolitan interests might gain a share of this market. Toward this end, Portuguese officials offered subsidies, special allocations, and bonuses to settlers who agreed to cultivate the staple in Mozambique. At the same time, the governor general of Mozambique ordered that cotton seeds be distributed to Africans. The

---

[9]   Botelho, *Memória*, 286.

[10] Carlos Fortuna, "Threading Through: Cotton Production, Colonial Mozambique, and Semiperipheral Portugal in the World Economy" (Ph.D. thesis, State University of New York at Binghamton, 1988), 126.

[11] Ibid., 127; M. Anne Pitcher, "Sowing the Seeds of Failure: Early Portuguese Cotton Cultivation in Angola and Mozambique, 1820–1926," *JSAS* 17, no. 1(1991), 45.

[12] For a discussion of Sá Da Bandeira's policies, see Gerald Bender, *Angola Under the Portuguese, Myth and Reality* (Berkeley, 1978), 63–64.

[13] Fortuna, "Threading Through," 127; Pitcher, "Sowing the Seeds of Failure," 45.

[14] See Carlos Bastos, *O Algodão no Comércio e na Indústria Portuguesa* (Porto, 1947).

[15] Carlos Bastos, *Indústria e Arte Textil* (Porto, 1960), 273–74; Fortuna, "Threading Through," 132–34.

governor of Tete went one step further, demanding that all peasants and ex-slaves cultivate "fifty feet of cotton per hut."[16]

Both settler- and peasant-oriented cotton strategies failed miserably. Declining world prices in the aftermath of the post–1873 depression, labor shortages, poor-quality seeds, and recurring crop diseases quickly soured planter interest. Peasants preferred to produce foodstuffs and, where conditions permitted, more lucrative cash crops, such as sesame seeds and peanuts.[17] Extant documentation makes no reference to cotton production in the colony during the later nineteenth or early twentieth centuries.[18]

Portugal's formal annexation of Mozambique after the Congress of Berlin in 1884 theoretically positioned Lisbon to strengthen its fragile hold over the colony and to exploit more effectively the region's cotton potential. In reality, Lisbon could do neither. In the face of sustained African resistance, it took Lisbon more than thirty years to conquer the entire colony.[19] Even after the conquest, Portugal imposed only a skeletal administrative structure over much of the interior.[20] Portugal's subordinate role within the world economy belied its status as a colonial power. For Lisbon, "cotton imperialism" was a dream rather than a reality. Unlike its British, French, German, or even Belgian rivals, Portugal lacked the capability to initiate or implement an aggressive cotton policy.[21]

Cotton Production: Fits and Starts, 1900–1926

To understand why cotton in Mozambique production got off to such a slow start, it is necessary to review briefly the political economy of early colonial Mozambique. Lisbon formulated its economic policy when its hold on Mozambique was precarious. In the 1890s Portugal was faced with widespread African resistance, the need to develop a colonial infrastructure, and a growing fiscal deficit. To compound its problems, Portuguese capitalists were unwilling to invest in Mozambique on any appreciable scale. Policymakers tried to overcome this financial burden in two quite different ways: first, by transforming thousands of African men into "cheap" migrant laborers, some of whom were to be "rented" to neighboring colonies; and second, by ceding large chunks of its territory to foreign concessionary companies. Although neither strategy necessarily precluded cotton production, in practice both had precisely that effect.

---

[16]   *Boletim Oficial do Governo Geral da Província de Moçambique (BOM)*, 19 April 1862, 61; Pitcher, "Sowing the Seeds of Failure," 47.

[17]   Arlindo Chilundo, "Quando Começou o Comércio das Oleaginosas em Moçambique," *Relação Europa–Africa*, no. 3, Quartel do Séc. 19 (Lisbon, 1988), 511–23.

[18]   DSA, *Algodão*, 1; Pitcher, "Sowing the Seeds of Failure," 46.

[19]   For a discussion of African resistance, see Nancy Hafkin, "Trade, Society and Politics in Northern Mozambique, 1753–1913" (Ph.D. thesis, Boston University, 1973); Isaacman, *The Tradition of Resistance*; René Pelissier, *História de Moçambique*, 2 vols. (Lisbon, 1987, 1988).

[20]   The basic administrative units were the localities (*postos*). A number of localities were grouped together into rural subdistricts (*circunscrições*). A Portuguese administrator was theoretically assigned to each of these subdistricts and localities. In practice, many positions were vacant. The *circunscrições* were joined into districts, each of which had its own governor who ultimately reported to the governor general of Mozambique.

[21]   Isaacman and Roberts, *Cotton, Colonialism, and Social History*.

The proposition that the only way to make Mozambique profitable was by exploiting "idle" African male labor quickly became an article of faith among colonial planners. The 1899 government commission, whose task it was to analyze the prospects for economic development in the Portuguese colonies, was unequivocal on this point.[22] The commission, which drafted the colony's most important pieces of labor legislation, declared that

> the state, not only as a sovereign of semi-barbarous populations, but also as a repository of social authority, should have no scruples in obliging and if necessary forcing these rude Negroes in Africa . . . to better themselves by work to acquire through work the happiest means of existence, to civilize themselves through work.[23]

Thus, from the outset, Lisbon claimed an identity of interests between the paternalistic notion of its "civilizing" mission in Africa and the economic development of the colony. In this regard Portugal was hardly unique; other colonial powers were pursing similar agendas.

Despite new tax laws designed to create a pool of cheap African labor and policies to transform peasants into workers,[24] labor shortages persisted in the capitalist sectors of the colonial economy. Given the depressed wage structure and the fact that salaries were not competitive with those paid in the neighboring colonies, it is hardly surprising that thousands of rural Mozambican men sought employment outside Portuguese territory, particularly in South Africa and Southern Rhodesia.[25] To stem this flight and meet growing internal labor demands, colonial officials increasingly resorted to undisguised coercion, known locally as *chibalo*.

The system of *chibalo*, which continued in various guises throughout much of the colonial period, worked in the following manner. European planters, agricultural companies, factory owners, and local merchants who were unable to meet their labor needs through volunteers, as well as state officials overseeing public works projects, would petition the Department of Native Affairs, which in turn would notify regional administrators. They would then order local administrators (*chefes de posto*) to conscript men for six-month periods. Each *chefe de posto* would then send out African police (*sipais*) to contact designated chiefs, who used either the *sipais* or their own local retainers to round up peasant recruits. *Sipais* entered communities at night, seized men from their homes, beat and bound them, and marched them off to the local or regional administrator who would distribute the recruits to their new employers. Local administrators and their subordinates were given complete discretion to determine who was "idle," and many *chefes de posto* supplemented their modest salaries with gifts and favors from the Europeans for whom they recruited labor.

In this way, the rural areas of the colony were transformed into labor reserves. When male workers were needed to plant sisal, sugar, tea, or copra on European plantations or to build roads, lay railroad lines, to construct bridges, or to perform any other private or public task, local administrators readily provided them. It did

---

[22] Quoted in J. M. da Silva Cunha, *O Trabalho Indígena: Estudo do Direito Colonial* (Lisbon, 1949), 3–4.

[23] Quoted in James Duffy, *A Question of Slavery* (London, 1967), 139–40.

[24] Vail and White, *Capitalism and Colonialism*, 132–33; Chilundo, "Quando Começou O Comércio."

[25] Patrick Harries, *Work, Culture, and Identity: Migrant Laborers in Mozambique and South Africa, 1860–1910* (Portsmouth, 1994), 18–42, 81–108; Charles Van Onselen, *Chibaro: African Mine Labour in Southern Rhodesia, 1900–1933* (London, 1976), 86–91.

not matter whether conscripts were successful farmers or whether their absence would jeopardize the economic security of their families.

Men could expect to be conscripted and forced to work under grueling conditions many times in the course of their lives. They were subjected to physical abuse and received little or no remuneration and only minimal amounts of food during the period of their *chibalo*. Peasants who failed to pay taxes or who were charged with crimes were also subject to conscripted labor. Sabino Joni from Gilé in Zambézia province was one such victim:

> After World War I, Portuguese settlers arrived here. We were taken from the jails to work on their cotton and tobacco fields for a minimum of six months. For our labor some of us received ten *escudos* [fifty cents], others fifteen, and some as little as seven and a half.[26]

Women and children, although legally exempt from *chibalo*, often suffered a similar fate. In 1924 an American sociologist studying labor conditions in Mozambique reported:

> Women, even pregnant or with a nursling, are taken for road work by *sipais*. In out-of-the-way places the Government builds little barracks to house them. No pay nor food. According to the circumscription the term is from one week to five but women may be called out again in the same year. Others in the village bring food to them, in some cases a day's journey away. Girls as young as fifteen are taken and some are made to submit sexually to those in charge. They work under a black foreman who uses a stick. They begin work at six, stop for an hour at noon and work until sunset. There are some miscarriages from heavy work.[27]

This combination of forced labor, terror, and sexual abuse would become a hallmark of the forced cotton regime twenty years later (see Chapter 3.)

Instead of satisfying the labor needs of the emerging capitalist sectors, however, *chibalo* often produced the opposite effect. Thousands of men anxious to avoid conscription and to provide for their families fled across the border to work in the mines and plantations of South Africa.[28] The Portuguese colonial government, anxious to reap some benefit from this migration, signed a number of formal agreements with the Witwatersrand Native Labor Association (WNLA), the official representative of the South African mining industry. Concluded around the turn of the century, these agreements codified the "rent" to be paid by South African employers to the colonial government for Mozambican workers lost to the local labor market. By 1904 more than 50,000 Mozambican men, primarily from the southern provinces of Gaza and Inhambane, were working on the South African mines. Two decades later the number had doubled. Moreover, legal accords failed to curtail clandestine migration to South Africa.[29] Thousands of Mozambican men also found employment for themselves in Southern Rhodesia. In 1914 Lisbon acknowledged this reality and signed the Tete Agreement, stipulating that labor recruiters from

---

[26] Interview with Sabino Joni et al., Gilé, 15 July 1976 (Head Collection).

[27] Edward Alsworth Ross, *Report on Employment of Native Labor in Portuguese Africa* (New York, 1925), 40.

[28] See Harries, *Work, Culture, and Identity*, 7–13; David Webster, "Migrant Labour, Social Formations and the Proletarianisation of the Chopi of Southern Mozambique," *African Perspectives* 1(1978), 157–74.

[29] Harries, *Work, Culture, and Identity*, 81–108.

the British colony could enlist up to 25,000 Mozambicans per year in return for fees and a preferential trading agreement.[30]

These treaties, combined with the colonial state's continuing inability to contain clandestine African flight from the colony, stifled commodity production in southern Mozambique. European planters found it difficult to recruit sufficient labor to work their fields. The loss of male labor through out-migration, together with *chibalo*, also left many peasant households in a precarious economic position, because men were responsible for clearing the fields and helping to plant and harvest household crops. Their absence increased this burden on rural women, many of whom were already overworked. In such an uncertain environment, experimenting with cotton made little sense for either Europeans or Africans.

Economic conditions in central and northern Mozambique were no more conducive to cotton production than they were in the south. The shortage of investment capital compelled Lisbon to turn the direct administration and exploitation of much of central and northern Mozambique over to foreign-owned concessionary companies. The three most significant were the British-dominated Companhia de Moçambique (Mozambique Company), founded in 1888,[31] which received control of the central regions of Manica e Sofala; the Companhia da Zambézia (Zambezi Company), which in 1892 acquired the decaying *prazo* system in the districts of Zambézia and Tete;[32] and the Companhia do Niassa (Niassa Company), which governed the "backwater" northern regions of Cabo Delgado and Niassa from 1894 until 1929.[33] While all of these undercapitalized and poorly managed firms experimented with cotton at one time or another, none exhibited any interest in promoting the production of the staple on any appreciable scale.[34]

While conditions in Mozambique precluded any serious consideration of cotton cultivation and while colonial planners in Lisbon failed to develop a coherent cotton strategy, metropolitan demand for the fiber increased dramatically. During the last quarter of the nineteenth century the metropolitan textile industry had experienced rapid mechanization and growth. In 1880 there were 108,000 spindles and 1,000 looms in production; by 1901 this number had grown to 230,000 spindles, and six years later there were more than 11,000 looms. While this growth in industrial capacity was small compared with even minor textile producers such as Belgium, Holland, Sweden, or Brazil,[35] it nonetheless created a new demand for raw cotton in Portugal. Between 1887 and 1912, imports of raw cotton increased more than threefold.[36] Increased urbanization in and around Lisbon and Porto led to a

---

[30] For an examination of the Tete Agreement, see P. R. Warhurst, "The Tete Agreement," *Rhodesian History* 7(1970) 32–42.

[31] For a discussion of the Mozambique company, see Barry Neil–Tomlinson, "The Growth of a Colonial Economy and the Development of African Labour: Manica and Sofala and the Mozambique Chartered Company, 1892–1934," in *Mozambique* (Proceedings of a Seminar at the Center of African Studies, University of Edinburgh, 1979); Leroy Vail, "Mozambique's Chartered Companies: The Rule of the Feeble," *JAH* 17(1976), 389–416.

[32] Vail and White, *Capitalism and Colonialism*, 115.

[33] Ibid., 401.

[34] DSA, *Algodão*, 5–6.

[35] S. J. Chapman, *The Cotton Industry and Trade* (London, 1905), 170.

[36] José Henriques de Azevedo Peridigão, "A Industria em Portugal: Para Um Inquerito," *Arquivo Universidade de Lisboa* 3(1916).

further expansion of domestic textile markets, while newly acquired African colonies offered additional outlets for Portuguese cloth.[37]

Rising international prices intensified metropolitan interest in the colonies as a source of cotton. The Portuguese Industrial Association and the influential Lisbon Geographical Society supported efforts by the textile capitalists and their commercial allies to promote colonial cotton.[38] In the same year the Portuguese state gave special concessions to companies promoting cotton, granted duty and tax exemptions on any cotton exported from the colonies, and allowed a similar tax exemption on machinery and seeds imported into the colonies. Shortly thereafter, cotton interests organized the Sociedade Fomentadora da Cultura do Algodão Colonial (Colonial Cotton Development Society), modeled after the highly successful British Cotton Growing Association, an organization of English textile, commercial, and shipping interests.[39]

In Mozambique, as in most of East and Central Africa, colonial planners initially assumed that cotton had to be a "white man's crop." There was a general consensus that plantations worked by Africans under the immediate supervision of Europeans would yield the highest returns. During the first decade of this century a number of companies organized cotton plantations.[40] All of these early cotton ventures failed. Underfinanced companies were reluctant to invest in plantation infrastructure or in mechanized agricultural equipment or to undertake the expensive scientific research necessary to determine the most appropriate ecological zones or seed types for cotton cultivation in Mozambique. For all the pseudoscientific rhetoric about European managerial skills, most cotton projects were organized in a rather haphazard manner.[41] A British agricultural officer traveling through Mozambique concluded in 1913 that "cotton has as yet not made headway in Portuguese East Africa . . . [and] it is impossible as yet to say where, if anywhere, cotton can be grown successfully."[42]

The fledgling Mozambican cotton economy received a big boost during the war years. Between 1913 and 1918 European demand increased, both because of the onset of the war and because American cotton supplies were erratic because of a boll weevil epidemic. Prices soared, jumping more than tenfold between 1915 and 1922 and quadrupling over the next two years. Even discounting for the rampant inflation in Portugal, the real price of cotton doubled between 1915 and 1924.[43]

The high price intensified interest in the colony as a potential cotton producer. In 1920, for the first time, Portuguese textile interests invested in Mozambican cotton production.[44] The Mozambique Company expanded production in Manica e

---

[37]   For a discussion of the growth of the Portuguese textile industry, see Bastos, *Algodão*; Bastos, *Indústria*; Carlos Fortuna, *O Fio da Meada: O Algodão da Moçambique, Portugal e a Economia–Mundo, 1860–1960* (Porto, 1993); Maria Filomena Mónica, *Artesãos e Operários: Indústria, Capitalismo e Classe Operária em Portugal 1870–1934* (Lisbon, 1986); Pitcher, *Politics in the Portuguese Empire*.

[38]   Quoted in Fortuna, "Threading Through," 160.

[39]   This information is derived from Pitcher, "Sowing the Seeds of Failure," 52–54.

[40]   Ibid.; *Anexo Ao BOM*, 1908, 38–39, 54–55.

[41]   Lynes, "The Agriculture of Moçambique," 102–10.

[42]   Quoted in Pitcher, "Sowing the Seeds of Failure," 57.

[43]   Pitcher, "Sowing the Seeds of Failure," 69.

[44]   Porto Colonial Ltd., founded by João Guimarães, a Portuguese industrialist, and Ismael Alves da Costa, a local settler, established a cotton plantation at Mugeba. Their experiment was short–lived (Fortuna, "Threading Through," 175–77).

Sofala and exported 742 tons in 1924.[45] The Niassa Company, hopelessly disorganized, managed to market only 124 tons in the same year. A handful of European planters in Zambézia used state-commandeered African labor and recruited low-paid youth groups (*nomi*) to cultivate the staple.[46] In a few regions, such as Mogovolas, the state even began to encourage men as well as women to produce the fiber.[47]

For all this renewed activity in the northern and central parts of the colony, the center for cotton cultivation had already shifted southward. By the mid–1920s more than 70 percent of the cotton-producing land was in the southern part of the colony.[48] "All of the land within reach of transportation to the railways or rivers is being taken up [by cotton]," wrote one observer in 1923.[49]

As has so often been the case in Mozambican history, foreign investment, rather than initiatives from the Portuguese state or from Portuguese capital, stimulated the cotton resurgence in the south. In 1922, representatives of the British Cotton Growing Association targeted British farmers in the Lourenço Marques and Beira hinterlands. It offered to purchase any cotton they grew and to pay for ginning, bailing, and shipping.[50] Not only did a number of British farmers shift from maize, sugar, and tobacco to cotton production, but many recent Portuguese immigrants adopted the crop in the hope of making a quick profit.[51] Despite their lack of experience and the absence of technical and financial support from the state, these settlers prospered as long as cotton prices remained high. According to an American consular officer:

> In the vicinity of Lourenço Marques, interest has been greatly stimulated by the very satisfactory returns of this year's experiments. Because of the forced labor system, abundant labor is available for picking and other work at the time it is needed and its cost is such that at present a return for raw cotton of over $50.00 per acre is generally being realized.[52]

To stimulate output still further, British and South African interests invested directly in cotton production. In 1924 Premier Cotton Estates, Ltd., of South Africa acquired 30,350 hectares of choice farm land in Moamba, fifty kilometers from Lourenço Marques. Raul Honwana, who was a young man living in the region at that time, recalled how the company acquired its substantial holdings:

---

[45] DSA, *Algodão*, 5–6.

[46] See Pitcher, "Sowing the Seeds of Failure," 62; Vail and White, *Capitalism and Colonialism*, 172–74. For a fuller discussion of *nomi* labor in the adjacent cotton regions of Malawi, see Mandala, *Work and Control*, 156–57.

[47] José Torres, "A Agricultura no Distrito de Moçambique," *Boletim da Sociedade de Estudos da Colónia de Moçambique (BSE)* (1932), 74.

[48] F. Monteiro Grilo, *Relatório do Chefe dos Serviços de Agricultura, 1940–1944* (Lourenço Marques, 1946), 136.

[49] United States Naval Archive (USNA), Collection 705, "Cotton Report No. 3," Cecil M. P. Cross, 17 June 1923.

[50] USNA, Collection 705, "Activities of the British Empire Cotton Growing Association Affecting Portuguese East Africa," Cecil M. P. Cross, 8 March 1923.

[51] USNA, Collection 705, "Cotton Report No. 4: For Information at Close of Harvest," Cecil M. P. Cross, 1 September 1924.

[52] USNA, Collection 705, "Cotton Report No. 3," Cecil M. P. Cross, 27 June 1924.

Premier Cotton was established around 1924, when the Portuguese were strongly pushing cotton. At the time it was very easy for Portuguese settlers and large foreign companies to get titles to farmland. . . . [Africans] were chased off the best lands, where they and their families had lived for generations, in order to provide farmland.[53]

Premier Cotton's ambitious project would have required more than 30,000 workers to weed and harvest the crop, plus a large fleet of tractors. Reality quickly set in. In its first year of operation the company planted barely over 1,000 hectares,[54] and production never dramatically increased. At approximately the same time Portugal granted a 24,000-hectare cotton concession to African Agricultural Estates, Ltd., and the chairman of the London-based Anglo-East African Cotton Company announced that his firm had obtained more than 30,000 hectares along the Inharrime River in the Inhambane province.

To maximize output and minimize costs, these British and South African agricultural firms combined mechanized modern technology with bound labor. They introduced tractors into a region where the short hoe had been the principal agricultural implement and where ox-driven plows were not yet widely in use.[55] Premier Cotton Estates, for example, operated several tractors and three large steam plows. The demand for the machinery was so great that "ploughing by night has been resorted to and the tractors kept working twenty out of twenty-four hours."[56]

The back-breaking work of cotton production was done by conscripted Africans. Although most of the workers were men, women and older children also labored in the cotton fields. Organized in gangs under European supervision, they sowed large tracts of land by hand, spent long hours weeding, handpicked the crop, and carried it in fifty-kilogram sacks on their heads to market. For the chairman of Anglo-East African Cotton Company it was this pool of bound laborers that made Mozambique so attractive:

> With regard to labor, our company is exceptionally favorably situated. . . . The Inharrime district being one of the most fertile in East Africa, the natives have settled there in large numbers. It is estimated that there are today over 25,000 people living on our property. The quality of the labor is very good. Under Portuguese law, no labor is permitted to migrate until the requirements of the local district have been supplied.[57]

Despite this flurry of activity in the south, production never reached the levels that cotton advocates predicted. Even if the entire crop had been exported to Lisbon, it would have been equivalent to just one-twentieth of Portugal's burgeoning do-

---

[53]   Raul Honwana, *The Life History of Raul Honwana: An Inside View of Mozambique from Colonialism to Independence*, trans. Tamara L. Bender, ed. Allen Isaacman (Boulder, 1988), 123.

[54]   USNA, Collection 705, "Cotton in Portuguese East Africa: Changing the Face of the Veldt," n.d.

[55]   USNA, Collection 705, "Cotton Prospects in Portuguese East Africa for 1925," Cecil M. P. Cross, 21 November 1924.

[56]   Ibid.

[57]   USNA, Collection 705, "Anglo–American Cotton Growing Programme," Alfred Nutting, Clerk, American Consulate, London, 18 June 1925.

[58]   A. Quintanilha, "The Problem of Cotton Production in Portuguese Africa," *SAJS* 44(1948), 5–6.

mestic requirement.[58] Beginning around 1926 international prices commenced a long downward spiral, reaching a low point during the Great Depression. Cotton production, married as it was to international market fluctuations, declined as well.[59] The lack of promised state aid, an inefficient transportation system, unpredictable rains, and pest invasions further discouraged European producers.

To reassure investors, in 1926 Lisbon commissioned James Evans, a highly regarded American extension officer with substantial experience in the cotton states of the American South, to undertake a yearlong study of Mozambique's cotton potential. Even before he completed his report, however, the management of Moamba Cotton Estates announced that it was shifting from cotton to tobacco and peanut production, and other British agricultural firms quickly followed suit.[60] Against a backdrop of growing despair in Portugal, Evans's widely circulated report confirmed Lisbon's worst fears. Evans concluded that the combination of erratic rains in the south, numerous fungal and bacterial diseases, and a wide variety of uncontrolled insects "made it highly unlikely that the stable development of cotton can take place in Mozambique."[61] The Salazar regime was determined to prove Evans wrong.

Changing the Color of Cotton, 1926–1938

Successive Republican governments in Portugal (1910–1926) had failed to implement a coherent cotton policy. This failure carried important consequences for the metropolitan economy.[62] Between 1900 and 1924 the Portuguese textile industry nearly quadrupled.[63] This boom, combined with low cotton production in the colonies, required Portugal to increase the amount of ginned cotton it purchased on the world market. In 1926 only about 5 percent of the 14.6 million kilograms of cotton that Portugal imported came from its colonies, and only a third of that amount was Mozambican. The remaining 95 percent cost almost 178 million *escudos* (roughly U.S. $8.7 million), exacerbating a growing balance-of-payments deficit.[64] Portugal's annual trade deficit grew by 250 percent, jumping from an average of thirty million *escudos* in the 1905–1915 period to seventy-five million *escudos* one decade later.[65] To make matters worse, only about one-fifth of the textiles imported into the colonies came from Portugal.[66] Self-sufficiency remained illusory for the struggling colonial power, and the metropolitan economy was in shambles.

---

[59] AIA, JEAC, "Propaganda Moçambique" (PM), 720/0/6/34, nd.

[60] USNA, Collection 705, "Cotton in Portuguese East Africa," J. P. Moffit, American Consul, 25 January 1927.

[61] Mánuel Guerreiro Beatriz, "A Classificação e os Preços do Algodão–Caroço em Moçambique de 1930 a 1962," *Gazeta do Algodão* 14(1962), 21–22; USNA, Collection 705, Department of Agriculture, Official Record, 13 October 1926.

[62] Lisbon had zeroed in on cotton because it was one of the few commodities that the colonies could provide to the metropolitan economy. I am grateful to M. Anne Pitcher for highlighting this point.

[63] Armando Castro, *A Economia Portuguesa do Século xx 1900–1925* (Lisbon, 1973), 68.

[64] AIA, JEAC, "PM: Elementos Para o Século," Gastão de Mello Furtado, 15 June 1954.

[65] Pitcher, *Politics in the Portuguese Empire*, 15.

[66] *Ibid.*, 53.

Portugal's inability to exploit the colonies' resources and thereby reduce the national debt was one of the factors precipitating a right-wing coup in May 1926. The coup leaders adopted a vigorous nationalist stance, emphasizing Portugal's imperial heritage and the ties binding the colonies to Lisbon. Just two months after seizing power, the new government set out to restructure and regulate cotton production in colonial territories by promulgating Decree 11.994. The new leadership discarded the previous plantation strategy in favor of a highly disciplined peasant labor regime, thereby shifting the risks of production from European investors to African producers. As Fortuna so aptly put it, this new policy quite intentionally "changed the color of cotton."[67]

The state project was modeled on the highly regimented Belgian Congo cotton scheme, which, as Mozambique's colonial officials noted enviously if not entirely accurately, "had achieved brilliant results."[68] The compulsory cotton system was straightforward. The colonial government would grant concessions in Mozambique and Angola to foreign commercial interests with the exclusive right to purchase the fiber at low fixed prices from the peasants who would be forced to grow it. The concessionary companies would then sort and gin the cotton and sell it overseas, preferably to the Portuguese textile industry. As an inducement to attract Portuguese investors, the state offered choice lands, reduced taxes and tariffs, and the promise that it would strengthen agricultural extension services in the colonies.[69] The new legislation required the colonial state to be more interventionist than in the past, overseeing the entire production process from cultivation to shipping.

This new cotton initiative enjoyed enthusiastic support from António Salazar, who became finance minister in 1928, prime minister four years later, and subsequently ruled Portugal with an iron hand until 1967. Fiercely nationalistic, Salazar declared the colonies to be the preserve of the nascent Portuguese capitalist class and the source of raw materials and markets for the metropole.[70] These two principles were embodied in the 1930 Acto Colonial, which defined Lisbon's overseas policy. The expansion of cotton production became one of the cornerstones of this neomercantile project.

Because of its tropical climate, accessible ports, and previously minimal contribution to the colonial economy, Portuguese officials assumed that Mozambique would be the center of colonial cotton production. The first years of the new cotton regime, however, were an unmitigated disaster. Falling prices, the vagaries of nature, the lack of infrastructure, and the inability of the colonial state to oversee peasant production created an inhospitable investment climate. Try as it might, Lisbon was unable to attract prospective concessionaires or to convince companies already in Mozambique to switch to cotton. By 1931 production had dropped to less than half the 1926 level.[71]

---

[67]   This notion of "changing the color of cotton" is derived from Fortuna, "Threading Through," 196.

[68]   See *BOM*, Series 1, no. 37, 11 September 1926.

[69]   AIA, JEAC, "Dossier VZS, 1941–1945," Sousa Barreto, November 1942; Quintanilha, "The Problem of Cotton Production," 45–46.

[70]   A. de Oliveira Salazar, *Doctrine and Action: Internal and Foreign Policy of the New Portugal, 1928–1939* (London, 1939), 303–4.

[71]   AIA, JEAC, "PM," 720/0-6/34, n.d.

Complicating matters, different fractions of Portuguese capital were divided on the question of colonial cotton. When international prices were high, as in the early 1920s, metropolitan industrialists had lobbied for state-sponsored cotton schemes in order to secure cheap cotton. But with prices low, they argued that there was no pressing need for the state to act. Pitcher's recent book demonstrates that industrialists actually preferred foreign cotton because they had established good relations with international suppliers and because Mozambican fiber was considered to be of poorer quality.[72] In fact, in 1931 Lisbon purchased 99 percent of its ginned cotton abroad.[73] Shippers and merchant capitalists with ties to Mozambique, on the other hand, as well as concessionaires and settler producers, argued for the promotion of a colonial cotton scheme. For its part, the Salazar regime remained committed to cotton self-sufficiency. Pulled in such opposing directions by Portuguese merchant capitalists, textile interests, and colonial settler-producers and determined to increase colonial exports to Portugal, the government in 1932 set a price well above the depressed international level for all colonial cotton shipped to the metropole on Portuguese vessels. The differential was paid to concessionaires by the state as an export bonus so that the textile industry would not have to bear the cost.[74] Little or none of the price hike was passed on to African growers. This fiscal policy did stimulate some new investment and helped to redirect exports to Portugal. By 1934 the number of cotton concessionary companies in Mozambique had jumped from two to nine, and some of the most suitable land for cultivation, previously held by the now-defunct Niassa Company, was parceled out to these new firms. But prospective investors exhibited no interest in large areas of the colony, including Manica e Sofala, Tete, and Niassa. Forced cotton cultivation was essentially limited to the old cotton zones in the far south and in parts of Zambézia, Cabo Delgado, and Nampula.[75] Even in these regions, undercapitalized firms remained content to plunder the peasants who lived within the immediate vicinity of the few markets and primitive ginning mills the companies had constructed.

Such was the case with the Societé Coloniale Luso-Luxembourgoise, known more commonly as GRANDUCOL. This agricultural corporation began in 1929 with one hundred million *escudos* worth of start-up capital from investors in Portugal and Luxemburg. The GRANDUCOL concession covered the densely populated northern Mozambique regions of Nampula, Ribáuè, and Murrupula to Alto Molócuè, Ile, Lugela, and Pebane (see Map 2).[76] Company officials made little effort to select the most appropriate seeds or land. On the contrary, women and men were often forced to cultivate the staple on inhospitable terrain. Production in these areas averaged between five and twelve kilograms per producer for one year's labor. It was "the worst native policy possible," reported one colonial official.[77] By the late

---

[72] Pitcher, *Politics in the Portuguese Empire*, 70–71.

[73] In 1931 Portugal imported 15,884,841 kilograms of cotton, of which only 150,251 came from Mozambique; AIA, JEAC, "Prop. Moç.," 720/0–6/34, n.d.

[74] Pitcher, *Politics in the Portuguese Empire*, 75.

[75] DSA, *Algodão*, 8.

[76] AIA, JEAC, 13/2, GRANDUCOL Companhia dos Algodões de Moçambique (CAM), "Matrícula," Alves Barbosa, 23 August 1938.

[77] Quoted in Fortuna, "Threading Through," 222.

1930s GRANDUCOL was insolvent, with a public debt of forty million *escudos* (U.S. $1.6 million)[78] and had come under attack from Portuguese stockholders who, impelled by nationalist sentiment, wanted the foreign directors removed.

The other major northern company, the Sociedade Agrícola Algodoeira (SAGAL), fared somewhat better. In 1934 SAGAL received a 45,000-hectare concession in the fertile and densely populated region of Montepuez. With the aid of local administrators and their African police force, the company's overseers compelled peasants living in more accessible areas to restructure household production. Both female and male agriculturalists were forced to privilege cotton over food and other cash crops. By the end of the 1935 agricultural campaign, SAGAL had collected almost 1.5 million kilograms of cotton valued at 4,356 *contos* (4.356 million *escudos*), or approximately ten times the company's initial investment. Between 1934 and 1937 production in the Montepuez region increased twentyfold, from 189,000 to more than 4,000,000 kilograms.[79] By the end of the decade, yields per hectare ranged from a modest 190 kilograms in Montepuez to a mere thirty-five kilograms in the Makonde highlands. Despite gains in production volumes, peasants often received less than twenty-five *escudos* (U.S. $1) for their entire crop and engaged in a variety of activities, including flight and sabotage, to express their displeasure.[80]

SAGAL made monumental strides compared with the concessionary companies in southern Mozambique. The Department of Agriculture, anxious to stimulate production in the south, awarded a concession to Raphael Agapito Guerreiro, a Portuguese farmer and small-time trader, in 1935, despite the fact that he was already deeply in debt. Guerreiro's holdings included much of the area from Guijá to Morrumbene. He purchased a run-down cotton gin from a Greek planter and hired two overseers to distribute the seeds and supervise production. From the outset the situation on Guerreiro's land was chaotic. His overseers could not possibly patrol such a vast area, and the rural population, which had little or no experience with cotton, was totally disinterested in the low-paying crop. That many of the intended growers were overworked women whose husbands labored in South Africa made the situation all the more problematic. Poor rains and an invasion of pests in 1936 undercut production, increasing peasant antipathy toward cotton.[81]

Across the colony, most of the other concessionary companies just managed to limp along. Generally undercapitalized, they suffered from many of the same problems that had plagued their predecessors. The paucity of scientific data on rainfall and soil types, poor choice of lands, and the failure to control pests and plant diseases all contributed to low output. So did peasant antipathy. Many refused to grow cotton at all or did so halfheartedly; others fled to South Africa, Tanganyika,

---

[78]   This discussion of the Societé is drawn from Fortuna, "Threading Through," 220–23. Also see Torres, "A Agricultura," 73.

[79]   AIA, JEAC, 12/1, Sociedade Agrícola Algodoeira (SAGAL), Pedro Augusto Vieira da Fonseca to Governador Geral (GG), 23 July 1945.

[80]   AIA, JEAC, 12/1, Dir. of SAGAL to Pres. da JEAC, 19 August 1938; AIA, JEAC, 12/1, Dir.of SAGAL to Pres. da JEAC, 8 November 1938; AIA, JEAC, 12/1, SAGAL, Delegação (Del.) Aduaneira de Porto Amélia to CD (CD) Aduaneira de Porto Amélia, 16 August 1938; Bravo, *Cultura Algodoeira*, 145–48.

[81]   AIA, JEAC, "Notas Recebidas," Palma Gallão to CD de JEAC, 12 May 1939.

and Nyasaland.[82] By 1937 only approximately 80,000 peasants out of a rural population of more than four million were growing cotton.[83]

This modest figure included a relatively small number of peasants forced to work under the supervision of local administrators rather than for the concessionary companies. In some regions where Lisbon was unable to attract concessionaires, Portuguese *chefes de posto* assumed direct responsibility for organizing production. One such area was Bela Vista in southern Mozambique. In 1932 the local administrator, Serra Cardoso, received orders to promote cotton within his domain. Raúl Honwana, an interpreter for Serra Cardoso, recounted this episode in some detail:

> The administrator decided that all the peasants should include one hectare of cotton in their fields. . . . At a meeting called by local chiefs, the peasants were instructed on how to plant cotton and how to take care of it. Then the administrator distributed the seeds. When the cotton was ready for harvesting, the administrator supplied the sacks, and both the peasants and the settlers brought their cotton to the administrator to be classified, weighed, and paid for before a designated agricultural officer. . . . [T]he settler's cotton was given a first-class designation, but the peasant's cotton was nearly always given a third-class designation and only rarely a second-class one. The price for third-class cotton was twenty *centavos* per kilogram.[84]

The following year the rural population refused to grow cotton. Honwana remembers that they demanded to present their case to Cardoso:

> More than five hundred people came, more women than men, and they were all chanting and singing in unison. . . . Translator, tell the administrator that we haven't paid our taxes; tell him that no matter how many sacks of cotton we sell, we still won't have enough to pay even one hut tax, and one family household usually has five or six huts. Tell him that we don't have time to grow food and that we're hungry.[85]

Honwana transmitted their complaints and Cardoso responded. Honwana continues,

> I talked so much I was exhausted. But then something happened. Two of the peasants suddenly leaped up to where the adminsitrator was standing and began to dance and gesture defiantly in front of him. Scandalized and incredulous at the same time, the administrator called for two African policemen to seize them and take them to the jailhouse. But to do so, the policeman had to walk the two peasants through the crowd, which then attacked the policemen and the prisoners got away. The police panicked,

---

[82] MNA, LSDA, PHDAR for 1934 in S1/88/35. For corroborating evidence, see MNA, LSDB, E. Lawrence, District Agricultural Officer, Zomba to Dir. of Agriculture, 30 January 1934; and Mandala, *Work and Control*, passim.

[83] The figure of 80,000 is based on the assumption that productivity per peasant in the middle 1930s was roughly equivalent to the 1940–1943 average of about ninety kilograms per producer. Using slightly different production figures, Fortuna estimates that there were approximately 97,000 growers in 1937 (Fortuna, "Threading Through," 198).

[84] Honwana, *Life History*, 88.

[85] Ibid.

and the crowd started yelling and throwing tax bills at the administrator and all over the porch where he was standing. The noise became deafening. People were shouting, "You can have your cotton, we're going to Zululand."

And they did.

Despite such public hostility toward cotton, in the northern district of Nampula local authorities also organized state-run cotton farms wherever the concessionary companies were either ineffectual or totally absent. In the circumscription of Corrane the *chefe de posto* compelled two hundred single women to work side by side growing cotton through the entire 1937–38 agricultural season. For their labor, each woman received a daily food ration, a tax exemption, and a small amount of cloth after the harvest.[86] Their neighbors in Mocubene did not fare nearly as well. There both men and women had to work on a collective cotton plot. The Portuguese administrator sold the fiber to GRANDUCOL, paid the taxes of those who labored in the field, and pocketed the rest.[87]

Roughly fifty European settlers and a handful of small firms using conscripted labor also cultivated cotton. The crop was a relatively insignificant part of their agricultural operations. Most settlers devoted under ten hectares to the staple and some as little as two. To be sure, there was a handful of fairly large cotton estates, particularly in the districts of Manica e Sofala, but these were the exceptions. Production from these estates was minimal.[88]

Although Mozambican exports to the metropole had increased dramatically from 1932 to 1937, the shortfall in the colonial cotton supply was still 19.6 million kilograms—virtually the same amount that the Portuguese textile industry had imported in 1932. With increased international demand and with World War II looming, powerful voices within the metropolitan textile industry began once again to call for intensified state intervention to assure future cotton surpluses.

The Cotton Board: Restructuring the Cotton Regime, 1938

The Salazar regime's decision in 1938 to restructure colonial cotton production had a far-reaching impact on Mozambique. It removed the coordination and supervision of cotton cultivation from the hands of the inept Department of Agriculture and placed the full power of the state behind the newly formed Junta de Exportação de Algodão Colonial (Colonial Cotton Board, or JEAC). The Board's mandate was clear—increase production, increase it exponentially!

The five-member Cotton Board, chosen by the minister of the colonies, represented the metropolitan textile industry, commercial and shipping interests, and advocates of colonial cotton. Its technical capacity was enhanced by the establishment of the Centro de Investigação Algodoeira (Center for Cotton Research, or

---

[86] AHM, Secção Reserva (SR), Cx. 76, Inspecção dos Serviços Administrativos e dos Negócios Indígenas (ISANI), "Relatório . . . de Moçambique (1936–1937)," vol. 2, A. Pinto Correa, Inspector Administrativo (Insp. Admin.), 5 April 1938.

[87] Ibid.

[88] In 1940 the northern settler estates produced approximately sixty tons. Repartição Técnica de Estatística (RTE), *Recenseamento Agrícola de 1939–1940* (Lourenço Marques, 1944), 22.

CICA) five years later. CICA quickly became the scientific arm of the Cotton Board. Working in concert with the Commissão Reguladora do Comércio do Algodão em Rama (Cotton Regulatory Commission, or CRCAR), which regulated cotton imports and exports, the Board set cotton policy.

Responsibility for executing the Cotton Board's program lay with the field staff located in the colonies. In Lourenço Marques, the director presided over a network of five regional offices in Beira, Chinde, Quelimane, Nampula, and Porto Amélia. A small number of inspectors, agricultural technicians, and agronomists traversed the countryside supervising production and collecting scientific data. Relying on their field reports, the head of the Mozambican delegation recommended policies for improving cotton output and marketing to the governor general.

Unlike the Department of Agriculture, the Cotton Board was empowered to intervene vigorously at the point of production. It did so by defining vast zones where peasants would be forced to cultivate cotton; by fixing mandatory dates by which rural communities had to plant, reseed, and harvest their cotton crops; by determining the number of times fields must be weeded; by defining the various qualities of the cotton produced; and by playing a major role in setting the prices paid to peasants and to concessionary companies. The Board also had the authority to resolve conflicts between concessionary companies, to regulate relations between them and the metropolitan textile industry, and to ensure that all Mozambican cotton went to Portugal. In short, the Cotton Board became the vehicle through which an economically rational and highly repressive system of production and marketing was to supersede the chaotic arrangements of previous years.

JEAC's first priorities were to restructure existing concessionary arrangements and to attract new Portuguese investors. In order to weed out undercapitalized or speculative firms, it established specific financial and technical requirements for each grantee. As an inducement to investors, it offered low-interest loans, cash advances, preferential tariffs, and other financial incentives.[89]

Thirteen concessionaires were initially incorporated into the new regime. They represented different interest groups and fractions of capital. Broadly speaking, the concessionaires fell into four categories: the settler community, large agricultural firms only marginally interested in cotton, commercial firms that diversified into cotton, and large corporations whose *raison d'être* was the fiber.

Several of the initial concessionaires came from the settler community, which was already marginally involved in cotton production. Alberto Pereira was awarded a monopoly in the far northern regions of Nangade, Mocímboa de Rovuma, and Mueda. António Mendes's territory extended through the circumscriptions of Homoine, Inharrime, and Zavala in Inhambane, adjacent to the Morrumbene holdings of Rafael Agapito Guerreiro. All three planters were also engaged in a variety of other agricultural and commercial activities. Each went through the motions of stimulating peasant output without making any serious investments in cotton production. Instead they sought to impose a commercial monopoly within their domain, forcing peasants to sell them whatever cash crops they produced. Cotton Board officials characterized these settlers as "poor imitations of concessionaires whose actions have done serious damage to the develop-

[89]   AIA, JEAC, "Relatório da Inspecção de JEAC," João Contreiras to Pres. de JEAC, 31 January 1941.

ment of peasant cotton production."[90] The Board quickly put pressure on them either to expand cotton cultivation or to cease their activities. All abandoned their concessions. The Board awarded António Pereira's holdings to SAGAL. It negotiated an agreement with a new firm, Algodoeira do Sul do Save (Sul do Save Cotton), which absorbed the former territories of Guerreiro and Mendes and received additional holdings in the Gaza province. Algodoeira do Sul do Save, backed by local commercial and agricultural interests, was to be the only cotton company operating in the south.[91]

The second set of concessionaires were the large agricultural firms located in central Mozambique that agreed to promote peasant cotton production but whose principal commitment was to their plantation holdings. The concessions offered them a convenient way to shield the labor under their control from other agricultural interests and to make a modest profit as well. The policies of Sena Sugar were typical of this group. In response to earlier government legislation, the British-owned firm had already taken out a cotton concession in 1936, but it was never serious about cotton, which it defined as a "women's crop." Forcing women alone to cultivate cotton was a way to preserve male workers for company plantations and to prevent rival firms from acquiring laborers for their own estates (see Chapter 4). Although Board officials complained about Sena Sugar's indifference to cotton, they never seriously challenged the British company. Unlike the settlers, whom the Board forced to forfeit their holdings, Sena Sugar was too powerful a player in the colonial economy.

The Zambezi Company, which had substantial sisal, tea, and copra plantations, and the Companhia de Búzi (Buzi Company), with its large sugar estates, were drawn into the cotton scheme for much the same reason. However, these companies were more committed to stimulating cotton cultivation than their British rival. In Zambézia province, somewhat smaller family-run firms, including Lopes & Irmão, Monteiro & Giro, and João Ferreira dos Santos, all promoted cotton production as part of their larger agricultural and commercial empires (see Map 4, next chapter).

Finally, there were the large corporations focused on cotton. The Companhia Algodões de Moçambique (Cotton Company of Mozambique, or CAM) was the most significant. With holdings extending from Nampula north into Cabo Delgado and south into Zambézia and with six factories serving this vast area, this company quickly came to dominate the colonial cotton market. By the early 1940s, territory under CAM control accounted for almost 50 percent of all cotton grown in Mozambique.[92]

CAM was the successor to the financially crippled firm GRANDUCOL, which had promoted cotton in the north since 1930. Dominated by capital from Luxemburg, GRANDUCOL's frail position left it vulnerable to Portuguese nationalists who wanted to free the colony from foreign domination. In 1942 Portuguese and colonial investors purchased the debt of GRANDUCOL from the Banco Nacional Ultramarino (Overseas National Bank) and, with the approval of the Cotton Board,

---

[90] Quoted in AIA, JEAC, "Relatório da Inspecção de JEAC, 1940–1945," João Contreiras, Inspector dos Servicos Algodoeiros Ultramarinos de JEAC (Insp. dos SAU) to Pres. de JEAC, May 1945.

[91] Fortuna, "Threading Through," 213–15.

[92] AIA, JEAC, CAM, 31/2, 1941, Direcção da Societé Luso–Luxembourgeoise to Del. da JEAC, 10 September 1941.

took over operation of the concession and began an aggressive campaign to expand CAM's large holdings.[93]

The other major cotton company in the north was SAGAL. With the new cotton regime in place, SAGAL moved quickly to gain control of all of Cabo Delgado and to exploit the labor of thousands of additional growers. By the middle of the decade it had obtained concessions for all of Cabo Delgado with the exception of the southern tip, which belonged to its rival CAM. SAGAL also controlled a small part of eastern Niassa. The only other company in the north, the Sociedade Algodoeira do Niassa (Niassa Cotton Society), began with a small operation centered around Amaramba.[94]

From the Cotton Board's perspective, none of these firms was nearly as successful as the Companhia Nacional Algodoeira (National Cotton Company, or CNA). This firm had obtained nine cotton zones in Manica e Sofala, in areas formerly belonging to the defunct Mozambique Company. Portuguese officials proclaimed CNA the model firm. It spent more money on machinery and equipment than any of its competitors, and its management introduced a number of labor and marketing reforms designed to encourage, rather than force, peasants to grow cotton (see Chapter 6).[95]

By the early 1940s the Cotton Board had woven together an amalgam of very different companies. Some were family firms; most were corporations. Eight were Portuguese-owned and -operated; three had appreciable foreign investments. For some, cotton was their lifeblood; for others, it was a necessary evil; and for a third group, it was a tangential activity (see Appendix A). But despite their differences, the companies shared two common features. All exercised de facto political power over the African populations living within their domains, and all used force to compel peasants to cultivate the staple.

---

[93] AIA, JEAC, "Província (Prov.) do Niassa," João Contreiras, Insp. dos SAU, 1945.

[94] Fortuna, "Threading Through," 226.

[95] Ibid., 226–27.

3

Cotton, Colonialism, and Work

The revitalized cotton regime posed an unprecedented threat to the way peasants across the colony organized their daily lives. From the southern district of Gaza to the far reaches of the north, thousands of growers were trapped within a highly regimented work scheme. Officials of both the state and the concessionary companies cajoled, intimidated, and at times coerced peasants to make sure that they performed the laborious tasks of cotton production punctually and in the prescribed way. These same officials, however, were basically ignorant of both conditions in the Mozambican countryside and the technical requirements of cotton cultivation. Their unfamiliarity with the rural landscape, their contempt for local systems of agricultural knowledge and risk-management strategies, and the reluctance of concessionary companies to invest in improved technologies greatly increased the risks of failure, which fell squarely on the shoulders of the cotton growers. This chapter explores the strategies the colonial state used to try to control the peasant labor process. It argues that because the state was so thin on the ground and its capacity to intervene in the daily lives of growers was limited, it had to rely on periodic but highly visible acts of violence. As a result cotton production became enveloped in a culture of terror.

Cotton Requirements and the Constraints of Mozambique's Natural Environment

Before discussing the imposition of the cotton regime it is necessary to examine briefly local environmental factors that constrained the colonial project. While cotton can tolerate a fairly high range of soil types,[1] the crop will flourish only under a particular combination of climatic conditions. To thrive, cotton requires abundant sunlight and high summer temperatures (25° to 32° Celsius). When cultivated without adequate heat or sunlight, cotton is slow to germinate and grow, is susceptible to seed damage, and tends to be low yielding.

---

[1] See Prentice, *Cotton*, 148–49.

Even more important than warm temperature is the need for regular and un-interrupted rainfall spread over a five-month period. Rain must come early in the agricultural cycle, must not be too intense, and must taper off well before harvest. The staple needs a preplanting rain sufficient to allow producers to prepare the seed bed, followed by a minimum of 90 to 120 millimeters of rainfall in the subsequent two months to nourish the seedlings. Since cotton matures slowly, even a two-week delay in sowing can reduce output by 10 to 15 percent. During the next sixty days the small plants must have no less than 100 millimeters and no more than 300 millimeters of rain per month if they are to flower fully, and there must be approximately 200 millimeters of rain in the third month when the cotton capsules are beginning to open. Any extensive rainfall or intense downpours after this period will damage the crop. The optimal precipitation pattern is between 700 and 1,100 millimeters of regular rainfall with about 75 percent of the total falling during the three months after sowing.[2]

If seasonal rains are late, irregular, or insufficient, growers face poor germination or total crop failure. Late rains can wreak havoc at harvest time as well, damaging cotton on the boll and ruining the crop. Too much rain, on the other hand, can cause flooding. Excessive precipitation also poses problems of drainage and waterlogging, especially in soils with a heavy clay content where filtration rates are slow.

Mozambique was not well suited for cotton cultivation. Whereas none of the three regions were ideal, on the whole the north was better endowed than either the central or southern part of the colony. A preliminary colonial survey of climatic factors and soils types, published in 1948, found that favorable conditions for cotton agriculture existed in less than one-third of the north; but even this low proportion was appreciably higher than elsewhere in Mozambique (see Map 3).[3]

Annual precipitation in the north fell within the 700 to 1,100 millimeter range. The region rarely suffered from a lack of precipitation, and excessive rainfall was a recurring problem only in a few areas, such as Mogincual and Maniamba (see Table 3–1). Nevertheless, cotton cultivation in the north was somewhat risky because of the short and rather unpredictable rainy season. Irregular rainfall was the most important cause of variation in cotton yields.[4]

Cotton can grow well in many different types of soil, including the deep ferralitic and feral soils found in northern Mozambique. However, certain characteristics of these soils pose short- and long-term problems for cotton agriculture. Because of their high clay content, these soils are hard and heavy, making tilling without plows or tractors extremely strenuous. Since clay soils become even more difficult to turn when they are wet, cultivators must prepare their lands for planting before the first rains arrive. Clay soils are also prone to waterlogging.[5] A longer-

[2] Ibid., 141–47; Mário de Carvalho, "Resultados da Experimentação Algodoeira em Moçambique (1942/43–1945/6) Análise Estatística e Redacção," *Trabalhos do CICA* 2 (1951), 372–74; AIA, JEAC, "Relatório a Brigada de Divulgação Técnica" (1956), Domingos H. Godinho Gouveia, Elias Gonçalves Valente, Armando Antunes de Almeida.

[3] J. Gomes Pedro, "Fito Ecologia na Zonagem Algodoeira," *Trabalho do CICA* 1(1948), 1–26.

[4] Ibid.

[5] D. H. Godinho Gouveia and Ário Lobo Azevedo, "Os Solos," in *Esboço do Reconhecimento Ecológico–Agrícola de Moçambique*, vol. II, ed. Centro de Investigação Científica Algodoeira (CICA) (Lourenço Marques, 1955).

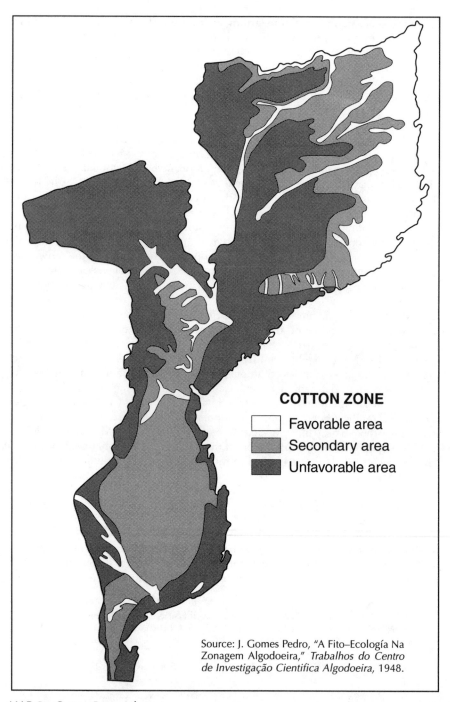

COTTON ZONE

☐ Favorable area
▨ Secondary area
■ Unfavorable area

Source: J. Gomes Pedro, "A Fito–Ecología Na
Zonagem Algodoeira," *Trabalhos do Centro
de Investigação Cientifica Algodoeira*, 1948.

MAP 3. Cotton Potential

TABLE 3–1 Average Rainfall in Select Regions of Mozambique

Northern Mozambique	Average Rainfall (mm)			Range (95% prob.)
Memba	724.9	±	60.8	589–860
Montepuez	846.1	±	75.8	667–1025
Namapa	928.6	±	64.2	783–1074
Mocímboa de Praia	953.0	±	69.4	783–1123
Nampula	1026.9	±	89.0	798–1256
Macomia	1087.1	±	70.8	920–1254
Moma	1115.7	±	60.8	959–1272
Mueda	1179.7	±	111.6	916–1444
Moguincual	1393.5	±	158.4	1045–1742
Central Mozambique (Zambezia)				
Morrumbala	927.3	—		
Mopeia	992.0	—		
Chinde	1099.6	±	84.5	908–1291
Pebane	1208.8	±	149.9	852–1549
Maganja da Costa	1303.7	±	127.3	1028–1580
Alto Molócuè	1448.8	±	101.5	1236–1662
Ile	1599.1	±	155.1	1241–1957
Namarroi	1823.4	±	27.2	1796–1851
Southern Mozambique				
Magude	645.9	±	57.1	570–772
Manjacaze	695.9	±	61.0	762–828
Chibuto	702.1	±	76.3	526–878
Macia	755.3	±	155.2	631–1308
Inharrime	861.8	±	52.5	753–971
Morrumbene	869.9	±	42.0	782–958

Source: Derived from CICA, *Esboço do Reconhecimento Ecológico–Agrícola de Moçambique*, 160.

term disadvantage of ferralitic soils lies in their poor capacity for retaining nitrogen, sodium, and other nutrients. Cotton is a very demanding crop and quickly saps these soils of nutrients and speeds the process of erosion.[6] Soil conditions become more problematic within the narrow northern coastal belt that stretches about thirty kilometers into the interior, where soils are excessively sandy and shallow and contain little rich organic material. Peasants forced by the colonial regime to grow cotton in Mocímboa de Praia or Palma typically had among the lowest yields per hectare in the north.[7]

Variations in temperature posed much less of a problem. The north's tropical climate, with average summer temperatures hovering around 25° to 27° Celsius (77° to 81° Fahrenheit) and long hours of sunlight, provided the warmth and sunshine that cotton required for good growth. The principal exception was in the eastern highland regions, particularly in the Niassa district. Here, daytime tem-

---

[6] Interview with Daniel de Sousa, Maputo, 21 July 1993.

[7] Bravo, *Cultura Algodoeira*, 147–50.

peratures often fell below 15° Celsius (58° Fahrenheit) and cold snaps occurred with some regularity in the preharvest months of June and July.[8]

By contrast, in central Mozambique the principal obstacle to cotton cultivation was excessive rainfall. In the western upland areas of Zambézia, annual precipitation was often as high as 1,600 millimeters.[9] Annual rainfalls of well over 1,100 millimeters were quite common for Zambézia as a whole, including the districts of Alto Molócuè, Namarrói, Ile, and Maganja de Costa, all of which were designated as cotton zones (see Table 3–1). Other areas, such as Mocuba and Pebane, were perilously close to the upper rainfall limits. Torrential rains posed problems of flooding and poor drainage, which rotted the roots of the cotton plants.[10] In the lowland riverine areas, especially adjacent to the Zambezi, Shire, and Punguè Rivers, extensive flooding in late January and February often destroyed substantial portions of the cotton crop.[11] Recurring precipitation and the large number of overcast days also meant a shortage of sunlight. Excessive rainfall was also a problem in much of Manica e Sofala, while in vast areas of Tete there was too little rain.[12]

The soils and temperatures characteristic of central Mozambique posed few problems for cotton cultivation. Like the soils of the north, the "black earth" and red soils had a high clay content. While cotton could flourish in such terrains, the soil was heavy and hard to work, particularly during the intense rainy period. With the exception of the cooler Manica highlands, temperatures fell well within the acceptable range.

Unlike central Mozambique and parts of the north, the problem facing cotton growers in the south was the severe lack of rainfall. Annual rainfall in key portions of the cotton zone was either below or perilously close to 700 millimeters, the minimum level that cotton plants require. In Manjacaze, for example, rainfall throughout the 1940s hovered at around 500 millimeters (see Table 3–1); in Chibuto the situation was only marginally better. Between 1936 and 1946 there were six major droughts in this region (1936, 1938, 1941, 1945, 1946). The precipitation problem was compounded by the variability of rainfall from year to year and from one part of the region to another, which created seasonal microclimatic environments. High evaporation rates exacerbated the effects of low and irregular rainfall.[13] Colonial authorities acknowledged the troubling problems of rainfall, but believed that the rich terrain, particularly the alluvial soils of the Limpopo Valley in the Gaza district, could support a vibrant cotton economy.[14]

The fluctuations in rainfall and temperature and the uneven soil quality that made cotton cultivation problematic in parts of the colony had long posed similar

---

[8]   CICA, *Esboço do Reconhecimento.*

[9]   Ibid.; Pedro, "Fito-Ecologia"; S. Gregory, "Annual, Seasonal and Monthly Rainfall over Moçambique," in *Geographers and the Tropics: Liverpool Essays*, ed. Robert Steel and R. Mansell Prothero (London, 1964).

[10]   Bravo, *Cultura Algodoeira*, 96.

[11]   Sena Sugar Estates Ltd. (SSE), File 44, "Final Cotton Report 1940," Luabo, 27 March 1940; AIA, JEAC, "Relatório (Rel.) da Inspecção (Insp.) de JEAC 1940," João Contreiras, Adjunto (Adj.) da Del. JEAC to Pres. de JEAC, 31 January 1941; AIA, JEAC, 660/55 (1), 1952.

[12]   CICA, *Esboço do Reconhecimento.*

[13]   Ário Lobo Azevedo, "Clima, Estudo de Alguns Factores Climáticos," in JEAC, *Esboço do Reconhecimento.*

[14]   AIA, JEAC, "Papeis Diversos 1939–1941," J. Anachoreta to Chefe da Sub–Delegação (CSD) do Sul do Save to Del. da JEAC, 11 September 1941.

problems for agriculture in general. To minimize the effect of these environmental factors on food security, rural Mozambicans had developed a number of creative coping mechanisms. Peasants often had two or three food fields strategically located in different ecological zones to take advantage of variations in soil, sunlight, and moisture availability and to minimize risks. The agricultural practices of the Makonde offer a good example of multiple fields and crop rotation. Jorge Dias, Portugal's preeminent colonial anthropologist, described this complex historical system in great detail:

> The harvesting of various foodstuffs is done gradually. During the liala or second stage [year] of the plot's production, they sow the same seeds as in the first year, as the earth still produces good cereal; and if it yields a good harvest, they may sow a third time. . . . When the crop becomes smaller, and this depends on the area of the plateau and the degree of the exhaustion of the soil, the Makonde sows for the last time, this being called *indima*. In the *indima* they never sow cereals, but normally sow only one foodstuff; groundnuts, beans or manioc. . . . When the Makonde has one *machamba* in the first phase of cultivation, he has another in the second and still another in the third; while several others are fallowing until complete regeneration.[15]

Dias's account highlights four important points about peasant agricultural principles. First, Makonde growers were acutely aware that the carrying capacity of the land changed over time. Shifting cultivation was a coping strategy developed to deal with the rapid depletion of the soil's nutrients. Second, intercropping was an effective labor-saving device, since several crops could be tended simultaneously. Third, households were occupied most of the year with agricultural production in order to minimize labor bottlenecks and to ensure an adequate annual food supply. Finally, leaving most of the land to lie fallow for several years allowed the soil to regain some of its lost fertility; during this regenerative process a cover of natural vegetation protected the soil against erosion. Although the details varied, Mozambican producers elsewhere developed similar practices of crop rotation, born out of years of trial and error and a deep understanding of the physical environment.[16]

Cultivating manioc was another important adaptation to cope with the threat of hunger, since it could be grown on marginal lands and in sandy soil, was drought-resistant, and could withstand the attacks of most pests.[17] In moist areas, Mozambicans grew sweet potatoes as well. Sweet potatoes offered many of the same advantages as manioc, although their cultivation was more labor-intensive.[18]

Intercropping was also a time-tested technology throughout Mozambique.[19] Planting several crops, such as maize, sorghum, beans, and peas, in a common

---

[15] A. Jorge Dias, *Portuguese Contribution to Cultural Anthropology* (Johannesburg, 1961), 41–42.

[16] See, for example, Pedro Massano de Amorim, *Relatório do Governador 1906–1907* (Lourenço Marques, 1908), 96–97; José Fialho Feliciano, "Antropologia Económica dos Thonga do Sul de Moçambique" (Ph.D thesis, Universidade Técnica de Lisboa, 1989), 172–73.

[17] Robert Nunez Lyne, *Mozambique, Its Agricultural Development* (London, 1913), 36; Henri A. Junod, *The Life of a South African Tribe*, vol. 2 (New York, 1962), 15.

[18] Lyne, *Mozambique*, 36; Junod, *Life of a South African Tribe*, vol. 2, 13.

[19] Junod, *Life of a South African Tribe*, vol. 2, 23.

field offered several advantages. Mixing crops tended to retard parasitic diseases. The dense plant cover of intercropped mounds also helped to retain soil humidity, which was particularly important in regions with sandy terrains. Intercropping restored depleted nutrients to the soil because peasants regularly mixed nitrogen-fixing leguminous crops, such as beans and peas, with sorghum, maize, and millet.[20] Placing different crops in the same mound also reduced the amount of labor needed in the production process.

Finally, rural Mozambicans relied on a number of cultural practices to expand their labor pool beyond the household or localized lineage. At critical times in the production process, such as weeding or harvesting, additional hands were often needed. Across the colony agriculturalists organized labor exchanges and beer parties to meet these demands. In the matrilineal northern belt, bride-service was an effective way to command additional labor. The ability to call upon extra-household labor was particularly important in those areas of central and southern Mozambique where large numbers of men were gone for much of the year, either on the plantations located in Zambézia or in the mines of South Africa.

All of these practices derived from indigenous systems of knowledge about local ecosystems. They were designed to minimize the risks of crop failure. They did not always prevent hunger, but they did blunt the effects of the vagaries of nature most of the time. Almost all of these practices came under vigorous attack with the imposition of the cotton regime.

The Cotton Regime in Practice:
Imposing the System 1938–1941

Given the considerable obstacles to voluntary peasant production, the simplest way for the Cotton Board to maximize the number of rural households in the regime was to designate vast regions of the colony as potential cotton zones and then to distribute concessions en masse. Within five years, much of the north had been divided up among SAN, SAGAL, João Ferreira dos Santos, and CAM, with the latter dominating the region (see Map 4). Seven other companies located throughout central and southern Mozambique received large tracts as well, although limited investor interest meant that substantial portions of both regions remained outside the cotton regime.

One effect of this land policy was the creation of a dynamic cotton frontier. As new areas were rapidly incorporated into the system, local state and company officials registered the African inhabitants as cotton producers. Each grower received a production card that he or she carried through the growing cycle and that had to be presented when the cotton was marketed.[21] This card documented name, age, place of residence, size of cotton field, type and quality of seeds received, number of times the field had been weeded, when planting had begun, when crop collec-

---

[20]   For a discussion of the advantages of intercropping, see Paul Richards, "Ecological Change and the Politics of African Land Use," *ASR*, 26(1983), 1–72.

[21]   The only exception were the senior wives of *agricultores*, who were listed on their husbands' cards. *Agricultores* were a legal category that referred to cotton producers who agreed to cultivate a minimum of a hectare of cotton and met other state-imposed criteria (see Chapter 6).

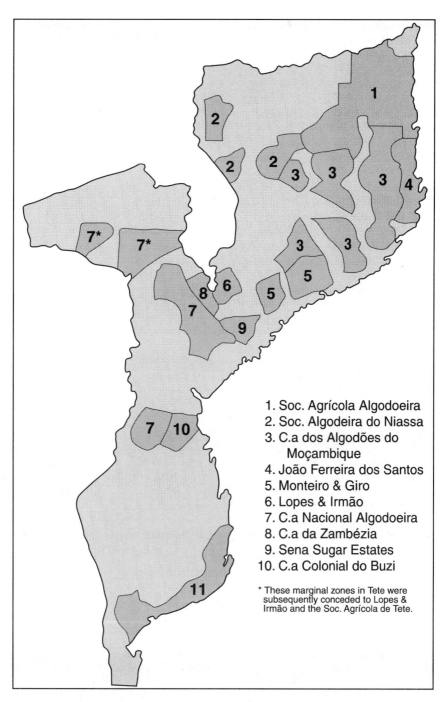

1. Soc. Agrícola Algodoeira
2. Soc. Algodeira do Niassa
3. C.a dos Algodões do Moçambique
4. João Ferreira dos Santos
5. Monteiro & Giro
6. Lopes & Irmão
7. C.a Nacional Algodoeira
8. C.a da Zambézia
9. Sena Sugar Estates
10. C.a Colonial do Buzi

* These marginal zones in Tete were subsequently conceded to Lopes & Irmão and the Soc. Agrícola de Tete.

MAP 4. Principal Cotton Concessionary Companies, 1946

tion had been completed, and the quantity and quality of the crop produced—all the vital statistics the state needed to determine individual productivity and to identify recalcitrant growers.

Since expanded crop production was the primary objective, there was a strong tendency to incorporate more marginal areas into the cotton scheme. In the northern circumscription of Maniamba in the Niassa province, for example, cool highland temperatures and inadequate sunlight made cotton cultivation particularly inappropriate, almost impossible. Yet, between 1940 and 1941, the number of peasants forced to grow the crop increased from 2,934 to 7,926—even as annual income dropped from four to two *escudos* (U.S. $0.15 to $0.08) per producer.[22] For aggressive companies, ever more territory meant more cultivators and more cotton. This strategy allowed the firms to increase total output without having to make costly investments to improve productivity. As one colonial authority lamented in 1940, "Without an infusion of new technology or sufficient knowledge of rainfall and soils, the only way to increase total output is by increasing the area under cultivation since we will not be able to increase output per hectare."[23]

To entice the rural population to take up cotton cultivation, many state and company officials concealed the risks involved and painted an excessively attractive picture of the possibilities that cotton offered. Former growers living in the central region of Alto Molócuè remembered how "our most prestigious Tawa, Chapala, and Mugera chiefs . . . assured us that we could grow as much cotton as we wanted and we would earn a good deal of money. When we heard their stories we agreed to grow cotton."[24]

Some enterprising administrators offered salt, cloth, and other prizes to demonstrate that hard work would yield material rewards.[25] Loyalist chiefs appointed by the colonial state echoed the promises of the European authorities. Former growers in Montepuez stressed that the indigenous authorities often took the lead in becoming model cotton farmers:[26] "Cotton came first to Montepuez. The following year [SAGAL] brought several chiefs from Montepuez here to Balama where they explained to us the advantages of cotton and how much money they had earned. When we heard their stories we agreed to grow cotton."[27] Not all of these initial encounters were so cordial. Many state and company officials lacked the time or interest to cajole prospective growers and relied on coercion from the outset.[28]

Many Roman Catholic and Protestant missionaries actively promoted cotton as well. Seeking to instill their notion of the "work ethic," they reiterated the message that cotton represented progress and a Christian way of life. Indeed, many missionaries saw no contradiction between evangelizing and forcing African stu-

---

[22] From 1940 to 1950 producers' income jumped to barely fifty *escudos* (U.S. $1.70) for one year's labor. Bravo, *Cultura Algodoeira*, 141.

[23] AIA, JEAC, "Rel. An. 1939–1941," Rel. de Posto de Porto Amélia, Faria Leal, 30 November 1940.

[24] Interview with Rafael Naxtaro et al., Alto Molócuè, 16–17 July 1976 (Head Collection).

[25] Interview with Maulana Samate et al., Balama, 23 July 1979.

[26] Group interview, CV Nawawane, Montepuez, 10 July 1979; interview with Chico Nhulialia and Costa Gaio Nampire, Namapa, 2 May 1979; Interview with Romeu Mataquenha, Tirani Ntuka, and Mussa Vaquina, Montepuez, 19 July 1979.

[27] Interview with Aridhi Mahanda et al.

[28] Interview with Sona Kendamale and Divarasone Watebo, Nicoadala/Morrumbala, 17 July 1991.

dents and teachers to work on church-owned cotton fields.[29] Eduardo José Macore recalled that at the Catholic Mission at Cuamba "all the students had to work in the cotton fields for the Padres."[30] Ten missionary schools in the north participated in the 1939–1940 cotton campaign; the Namumo Mission alone produced 20,000 kilograms of cotton.[31] The story was the same throughout central and southern Mozambique. Catarina Bendane, who taught with her husband at the Missão Nossa Senhora do Amparo (Mission of Our Lady of Amparo) near Chókwè in the south, explained:

> Padre António da Silva and Padre Lopes convened all the students and teachers and ordered them to cultivate cotton. They said that if we did not, there would not be any money to buy books and other essentials for the schools. The students worked in the fields and did not receive any payments. [The teachers] received a bit after the harvest. No one dared to refuse. Every Sunday at mass the Padres exhorted us to work harder.[32]

Missionaries adopted the same tactics even when they privately disagreed with the coercive nature of the colonial regime. The complementary themes of evangelization and disciplined work were stressed in daily sermons, in church pedagogy, and in Christian cultural activities. Consider the popular agricultural play *The Court Trial of Mr. Year*, which African converts practiced and performed at the Cambine mission station, a major center of cotton production. The play features two protagonists, Mr. Set-in-His-Ways and Mr. Goodfarmer. The former lives "in a dilapidated hut, . . . [is married to] Lazy, . . . [and complains] that the year is evil [and] that corn refused to grow and the cassava got itself eaten by the grasshoppers." The latter, by contrast, "busies himself in his garden and reports a fine crop." In the play the two tell their stories before a tribunal of their peers, who celebrate the success of Goodfarmer and condemn Set-in-His-Ways and Lazy in a parody of a popular local song:

> You say the year is evil, but that is not so
> That is bad, bad, bad;
> You say the year is evil, but you do not plant
> That is bad, bad, bad;
> You say that the year is evil,
> but you are stupid and lazy
> that is bad, bad, bad.[33]

What is missing from the colonial record, of course, is how cotton growers actually responded to this message in the privacy of their own homes and villages. Whether most parishioners believed the colonizers' message is unclear, although a number of prosperous cotton growers did come from this region.

In an effort to make cotton more palatable, local officials made a number of compromises. Initially, to ease peasant concerns that cotton production would take valuable time away from food production, they permitted cotton to be planted in

---

[29] Interview with Maulane Samate et al.

[30] Interview with Eduardo José Macore, Unango, 19 August 1980.

[31] AHM, "Fundo Algodão."

[32] Interview with Catarina Bendane and Esina Johane Mulhue, CV Mulanguene, Guijá, 17 February 1979.

[33] "The Court Trial of Mr. Year," *South African Missionary Advocate*, 22(1941), 4–5.

fields near their food gardens.[34] Many concessionary employees and state officials also compromised on the requirement that each adult in every household cultivate a specified amount of cotton. Some closed their eyes when households cultivated less than the minimum number of hectares, while others did not compel both members of husband-wife teams to labor in the cotton fields. Still others experimented with collective plots. In Montepuez, for example, peasants spent a designated number of days working on a large village cotton field and were free to work on their household plots for the rest of the month. Romeu Mataquenha, a Montepuez cotton grower, explained why officials changed their strategy:

> I cannot recall the exact year that we began to grow cotton. But I do remember that in the beginning we all worked in a common field. But when the Portuguese realized some people did not work hard and that others did not even show up, they decided that we each had to work our own plots. The *capataz* marked off a plot of three cords for a couple and two cords for a single adult. Later they increased the size to four cords and three cords.[35]

The limitations of colonial state power notwithstanding, from the outset Portuguese policymakers sought to establish control over cotton agriculture quite literally at the roots of the production process. Their efforts to transform African farming practices were most physically obtrusive, and perhaps most misguided, in the case of the colonial ban on intercropping cotton with household food crops.

The overarching concern of colonial agronomists was to protect cotton from having to compete with other crops for available moisture, sunlight, and soil nutrients. Mound intercropping violated Portuguese norms of scientific farming and, in some cases, offended the sensibilities of European-trained agronomists. Colonial officials adhered to a kind of visual ideology: intercropped fields look like a backward mess, hence the people who intercrop must also be a backward mess. The official position was that peasants had to monocrop cotton in uniform rows, ideally in fields separate from those in which food crops were planted, a sharp break with the local preference for growing cotton together with food crops such as sorghum, beans, and peanuts in elevated mounds. Even while Portuguese officials required peasants to plant cotton in inhospitable regions, they enforced a "scientific" method of cultivation in order to increase cotton yields and to improve lint quality.

These notions of "scientific farming" were not only of dubious agronomic value,[36] but had dire results for the peasants forced to conform to them. By disregarding peasants' own experience-based knowledge of ecosystems and by disrupting local farming methods, colonial policy inadvertently exposed cotton growers to great environmental and economic vulnerability, often making it difficult for producers to meet both their food crop and cash crop requirements. There were just not enough hours in the day for peasants to work in their cotton field and care for their food gardens. The irrationality and deleterious consequences of Portuguese cropping regulations led many growers covertly to defy the prohibition

---

[34] Interview with Faria Lobo, Nampula, 26 May 1987.

[35] Interview with Romeu Mataquenha et al.

[36] For a powerful critique of colonial agrarian policy, see Richards, "Ecological Change."

Thousands of Producers

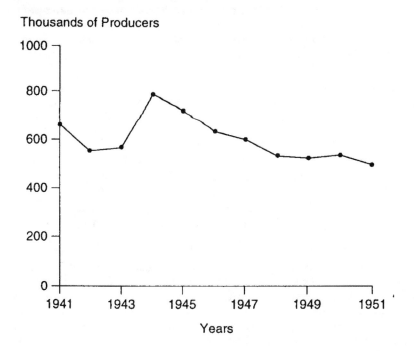

GRAPH 3-1. Number of Peasants Cultivating Cotton in Mozambique, 1941–1951

Sources: Bravo, *A Cultura Algodoeira*, 81; RTE, *Recenseamento Agrícola* (Lourenço Marques), 1940–1941; RTE, *Estatística Agrícola* (Lourenço Marques), 1941–1951.

against intercropping, despite the very real personal risks such defiance involved (see Chapter 10).[37]

By 1940 the state-concessionary company alliance had achieved its first objective. The number of peasants brought into the system had jumped from under 80,000 in 1937 to approximately half a million in 1940. By 1944 the number had increased to almost 791,000 (see Graph 3–1).[38] This figure did not include the large number of children and elders who, while not formally registered in the cotton scheme, regularly aided family members.[39] Colonial authorities stressed that husband-wife teams working together on conjugal plots should be the basic unit of production. This stipulation was deeply ideological, reflecting the Salazar regime's rhetorical commitment to preserving the nuclear family and promoting Christian values in Por-

---

[37] Interview with Makwati Simba et al., Chibuto, 13 February 13; group interview, CV Imbou, Mueda, 31 July 1979.

[38] Bravo, *Cultura Algodoeira*, 81.

[39] AIA, JEAC, "Esboço Estatística Referente à 1941 (EE 1941)," vol. 1, João Contreiras, 1942. Statistics collected by Bravo indicate that the rise was somewhat more gradual, with 496,000 registered in the system by 1940; only in 1944 did the number reach 660,000. Bravo, *Cultura Algodoeira*, 135.

tuguese territories rather than being dictated by the exigencies of cotton production.[40]

From the outset most growers were skeptical about the benefits of cotton. In the words of Manuel Sitói, who planted cotton in southern Mozambique for much of his adult life,

> [State officials] forced us to seed. We did not want to. But we did not want to be beaten. The chiefs ordered us to work and assured us that we would have money for cloth and cooking oil. The *capatazes* Dinis Tembe and Vasco and their African assistants Mbelhe, Mazivila, Chigadane, and Paulo Macamo threatened us. So we planted cotton. But not much grew.[41]

Other producers were equally cynical. "We did not like cultivating cotton," stressed one of Sitói's neighbors, "because we knew this soil is not suitable. . . . We cultivated cotton only because we were forced to do so: they said 'Work!' and you had to work."[42]

Peasants had every reason to be distrustful. Instead of the promised economic opportunities, low yields and artificially depressed prices left many rural households impoverished. The average northern producer in 1940 received approximately sixty *escudos* (slightly more than U.S. $2) for his or her entire crop.[43] The story was the same in much of central Mozambique and was equally dismal in most parts of the south.[44] In some of the more marginal regions, income for one year of labor was less than twenty-five cents per capita.[45]

Peasant skepticism rapidly turned to hostility. Experience quickly taught them that cotton demanded a great deal and offered little in return. As a result, many peasants withdrew land and covertly diverted labor from cotton to food and other cash crops (see Chapter 10). For colonial authorities, these tactics reinforced racist assumptions that Africans were indolent and short-sighted. "You are no doubt familiar," wrote one local administrator, "with the indolence of the blacks. . . . They have the habit of waiting to the last moment which reflects their laziness and bad will—which in this case prejudices cotton production."[46] Between 1939 and 1940 the number of hectares per capita dedicated to cotton production declined by 40 percent in northern Mozambique.[47] Peasants in central Mozambique reacted in similar fashion. One local official summed up the response of growers living in Maganja:

> Last year [1940] excess rains and cold destroyed their crop. As a result this year many Africans have begun to abandon their cotton fields. Others are only making a half-hearted effort at weeding with the effect that many plants have died or atrophied. Each day the situation deteriorates more.[48]

---

[40] State–sanctioned labor migration in southern Mozambique suggests how hollow this ideology was.

[41] Interview with Manuel Sitói et al., Guijá, 16 February 1979.

[42] Group interview, Serra Nkanyavane, 17 February 1979.

[43] Bravo, *Cultura Algodoeira*, 140–65.

[44] Ibid., AIA, JEAC, "EE 1941," João Contreiras, 1942.

[45] Bravo, *Cultura Algodoeira*, 138–45.

[46] Ibid., 120.

[47] According to Contreiras, the number of hectares of cotton increased minimally from 142,289 to 155,925, while the number of peasants nearly doubled from 345,581 to 636,481. Thus, although peasants could not avoid cotton, they cultivated dramatically less (AIA, JEAC, "EE 1941," vol. 1, João Contreiras, 1942).

[48] AIA, JEAC, "Dossiers Diversos 1939–1941," 13 January 1940.

Peasant antipathy toward cotton was even stronger in the south.[49]

These colonial accounts reveal the contradiction inherent in the system. The state could mandate that all peasants cultivate cotton, but it could not oversee the daily labor of thousands of peasants throughout the countryside. That local administrators bent some rules and that peasants reluctantly cultivated some cotton must be seen as part of an ongoing process of negotiating for power. Although under siege, peasants managed to retain a degree of autonomy. Indeed, in the most remote and inhospitable cotton zones, many peasants escaped the regime entirely. Less than 4 percent of the adult population in the Makonde highlands, for instance, cultivated cotton during the 1941–42 campaign.[50] Portugal's goal of cotton self-sufficiency remained illusory.

Restructuring the Labor Process, 1941–1951

From Lisbon's perspective the partial autonomy of peasants in the cotton zones had to be narrowed, both in order to boost cotton production and to prevent rural dissatisfaction from erupting into open protest. It was not enough simply to incorporate thousands of new producers into the system. The cotton regime required a more intensive utilization of peasant labor, which for the colonial state involved defining more precisely the composition and organization of the rural labor force, attempting to restructure the peasants' workday and work space, and more vigorously enforcing labor obligations. Portugal's campaign to control the peasant labor process more effectively began in earnest in the early 1940s.

With more than 791,000 growers already registered in the cotton scheme, the immediate problem confronting colonial planners was how to ensure that cultivators legally required to plant cotton actually did so. State and company officials ordered all men and women living within the concessionary zones to cultivate cotton. The only exceptions to this rule were adults with severe physical disabilities, elders over the age of fifty-five, men conscripted to work on state projects or on European plantations, prosperous farmers, men legally registered to work in South Africa or Southern Rhodesia, and men involved in specialized tasks such as fishing.[51] Peasants were responsible for proving that their special circumstances warranted an exemption. The decision rested ultimately with local administrators, who often refused even to exempt women who were in the final stages of pregnancy. "Women worked right up until they gave birth," sighed Rosa Ernesto who lived in Nampula, "and a week later they had to be back in the fields."[52] Women throughout Mozambique reiterated variants of Rosa Ernesto's account.[53]

---

[49]　AIA, JEAC, "Prov. do Sul do Save, Prov. da Zambézia e Prov. do Niassa," João Contreiras, Insp. dos SAU, May 1945.

[50]　AIA, JEAC, "Rel. An. 1945," João Contreiras, Insp. dos SAU, May 1945.

[51]　They based their more stringent demands on the October 1942 decree (Circular 818/D–4) of Gov.–Gen. Tristão de Bettencourt redefining African obligations to work. José Tristão de Bettencourt, *Relatório do Governador–Geral de Moçambique, 1940–1942*, vol. 2 (Lisbon, 1949), 78–79.

[52]　Interview with Rosa Maria Ernesto, Nampula, 11 July 1991.

[53]　Interview with Catarina Jossias Simbine and Nely Simbine, Maputo, August 8, 1991; interview with Catarina Bendane and Esuba Johane Mulhue, Guijá, February 19, 1979; interview with Maria Fijamo, Morrumbala, July 18, 1991.

By the mid–1940s every adult was also legally obligated to put a certain amount of land under cotton cultivation. Across most of the colony, a husband and his first wife were required to grow one hectare of cotton between them. In polygynous households, each junior wife was responsible for her own half-hectare of cotton, as were single women and widows. It is difficult to know how the colonial regime arrived at these apparently arbitrary figures; other colonial regimes assigned much smaller plots to African growers.[54] To increase output still further, the Cotton Board in 1946 declared that male elders between the ages of fifty-five and sixty-five would be required to grow cotton as well.[55]

Despite the Board's quest for uniformity, local authorities often modified the labor requirements to conform with their perceptions of how to maximize output. In Niassa, for example, the adult population between eighteen and fifty-five was divided into five age and gender categories, with men from eighteen to thirty years of age, considered most productive, made to plant fields measuring 110 meters square, or slightly more than a hectare.[56] In other regions zealous local officials, such as the administrator of Namapa in the Nampula district, forced peasants to plant more than the legal requirement.[57] This practice was particularly common in the southern districts, where many peasants had access to plows.[58] At a meeting organized by an inspector from the Native Affairs Department, Elija Mutombena complained that "the overseer marks cotton plots that are very large and even with oxen and plow it is impossible to maintain them."[59]

Whatever the legal requirements, most growers failed to satisfy them. In 1944, the 630,000 peasants registered in the northern and central districts cultivated only 214,000 hectares, slightly more than one-third of a hectare per grower.[60] As late as 1950, defiant growers continued to frustrate land-under-production targets.[61] But the fact that many people did not fulfill cotton production requirements should not obscure the extent to which the colonial cotton regime was able to transform the rural labor process and the existing gender division of labor. This transformation occurred in complex and contradictory ways, and not always in the manner anticipated by Portuguese officials.

In the first instance, state pressure to maximize cotton output made it impossible for tasks such as sowing, thinning, and weeding to remain women's responsibility, as they had been defined across much of the colony before the cotton era.[62] According to one anthropologist, "it was at this time that the sexual division of labor was substantially altered."[63] Similarly, women were forced to help their hus-

[54]   Isaacman and Roberts, *Cotton, Colonialism, and Social History.*

[55]   AHM, Fundo Governo Geral (FGG), Table 4, Cota 294, "Algodão Cultura, Medidas da Protecção, Direitos Transportes, 1934 à 1945," M. C. Agrélios, CD de JEAC to J. Bettencourt, Gov. Ger., 22 October 1946.

[56]   Bravo, *Cultura Algodoeira*, 116.

[57]   AIA, JEAC, 605/8, Pasta 48, 1946, "Rel. Mensal," Augusto Guilherme Alves, Ag. Fisc., October 1946.

[58]   Interviews with Manuel Sitói et al.; Benjamin Mavunja, Chibuto, 12 February 1979.

[59]   AHM, Cx. 26, ISANI, "Insp. à Circ. de Guijá," António Policarpo de Sousa Santos, Insp. Admin., 1957.

[60]   Bravo, *Cultura Algodoeira*, 135.

[61]   Ibid.

[62]   Only among the Chopi of Inhambane was there a long history of male farming that antedated the colonial period. In most of Mozambique women performed most of the agricultural labor, although the actual division of labor varied somewhat and changed over time. See for example, Junod, *Life of a South*

bands clear new fields and, in men's absence, to cut trees and remove heavy stumps and even plow—strenuous tasks that in the past had been performed almost exclusively by men. Blurring these gendered labor divisions not only redistributed work loads, but altered cultural understanding of how work was defined and valued. Men felt humiliated because they were forced to perform what they believed to be "women's work." Bishop Machado remembered when he was growing up in Inhambane the "humiliations that our fathers experienced when the Portuguese overseers forced them to do a woman's work [weed and clean the cotton plants] and then beat them up in front of their wives."[64] A number of other males expressed similar sentiments.[65] For their part, many women spoke with pride about their ability to perform male tasks, even as they acknowledged that the additional burdens were exhausting.[66]

The physical burdens of the cotton regime fell disproportionately on women's shoulders. This harsh reality was most obvious in the labor-exporting zones of central and southern Mozambique (see Chapter 4). In those regions where their husbands were present, women often still shouldered a disproportionate share of the expanded work load. While the cotton regime required men to help weed and thin the cotton, women typically continued to perform most of this backbreaking work. They also maintained principal responsibility for the food gardens and other household obligations. Manuel Pacheleque's recollection of a "typical day" is quite revealing:

> I went off to our cotton field early in the morning shortly after I awoke. I did not even have a chance to eat breakfast. My wife remained at home and arranged water and prepared porridge which she brought with her to the field. We worked cotton until the early afternoon. Then we went to clean our peanut field. When we returned home, my wife gathered wood, took care of the children and prepared food. I rested in order to recuperate and to gain strength for another hard day of work.[67]

As part of their strategy to increase control over the rural labor process, colonial officials throughout Mozambique tried to divide the workday of cotton producers in both time and space. Hoping to channel peasant labor further away from food crops and into cotton agriculture, administrators in most regions of the colony imposed a fixed work schedule on African farmers. Peasants were expected to spend their mornings in the cotton fields; but at peak periods, particularly during weeding, they were required to work on cotton throughout the afternoon as well.[68] Some

---

African Tribe, vol. 2, 20–28; A. J. de Mello Machado, *Entre os Macuas de Angoche* (Lisbon, 1970), 589; Jorge Dias, *Os Macondes de Moçambique* (Lisbon, 1964), 98–111; António J. Pires, *A Grande Guerra em Moçambique* (Porto, 1924), 58; AHM, C1856; Francisco Lerma Martinez, *O Povo Macua e a Sua Cultura* (Lisbon, 1989), 54–55; Feliciano, "Antropologia Económica," 120–25.

63   Feliciano, "Antropologia Económica," 120.

64   Interview with Bishop João Somane Machado, Maputo, 23 July 1993.

65   Interviews with Paulo Roque, Nampula, 27 May 1987; Romeu Mataquenha et al.; Makwati Simba et al.; Manuel Sitói et al.

66   Interviews with Fátima Konkonho, Pemba, 30 May 1987; Rosa Maria Ernesto; Celeste Cossa, Amélia Novana, and Essineta Namuwiango, Maputo, 31 July 1993.

67   Interview with Manuel Paqueleque, Paulo José, and Lwanykea Nyola, Nampula, 10 July 1991.

68   Interviews with Chico Nhulialia and Costa Gaio Nampire; Eugénio Niquaria, Montepuez, 24 July 1979; Pruan Hassan et al., Montepuez, 20 July 20; Daima Magaga Mbela et al., Montepuez, 30 July 1979.

officials lengthened the workday by increasing the size of cotton plots or by establishing minimum production requirements.[69] As a result, many cultivators only had time to tend their food crops in the late afternoons, in the evenings when there was a full moon, and on Sundays when they were not obligated to work on the cotton fields of the local chief.[70]

The concessionary companies also imposed a new system of land distribution, designed to reinforce a more rigid separation of cotton labor from work in food gardens. Whereas Portuguese officials had originally allowed individual households to select cotton plots adjacent to their gardens, after 1940 they increasingly demanded that peasants grow cotton in specifically marked blocks of land far from their villages.[71] Regrouping cultivators into relatively concentrated areas adjacent to bush roads facilitated greater labor supervision. Agricultural technicians working for the Cotton Board were supposed to select these new sites based on soil surveys, but with so few technicians and so much territory to cover, the new plots were rarely assigned in so careful a manner.[72] Aide Matupera, a cotton grower from Macomia in the north, described how "the *capatazes* [company overseers] and *sipais* brought their cords and stakes. They marked out consecutive plots of uncleared land one hundred meters square for each household. We had no choice, even if the land they chose was unsuitable."[73] Because these cotton blocks were often several kilometers from their gardens, peasants could not easily slip away to work their food crops when they were supposed to be cultivating cotton.[74] Growers were acutely aware of the colonial regime's agenda. Miriam Paulo smiled knowingly as she explained that "the blocks were far away because they knew that we would sneak off to our food crops and then the cotton would fall behind schedule."[75] Judging from contemporary Portuguese accounts, separating the fields diminished but did not eliminate this subterfuge.[76]

Preoccupied with minimizing costs, the concessionary companies were unwilling or unable to invest significant capital in new technology to increase productivity, and the Cotton Board was either unwilling or unable to overcome their resistance. On economic grounds, company officials also rejected the possibility of mechanization or the application of costly fertilizers and insecticides.

---

[69]   In Namapa the local administrator expanded the basic plot by 15 percent (AIA, JEAC, 605/8, Pasta 48, 1946, "Relatório Mensal," Augusto Guilherme Alves, Ag. Fisc., October 1946). In the Niassa district, local officials declared in 1951 that any male who failed to produced 400 kilograms of cotton would be sent to work without remuneration on European tea estates—a powerful incentive to spend longer hours in the cotton fields. AIA, JEAC, "Papéis Diversos," A. Figueira e Sousa to Gov. de Niassa, 21 February 1952.

[70]   Interviews with Romeu Mataquenha et al.; Benjamin Mavunja.

[71]   Interview with Faria Lobo, 26 May 1987; Dias, *Os Macondes*, 112.

[72]   Bravo, *Cultura Algodoeira*, 114.

[73]   Interview with Aide Matupera et al., Macomia, 27 July 1979. Similar accounts were provided in group interview, Base Central, Mueda, 25 April 1979, and in an interview with Faria Lobo, 6 May 1987. Colonial officials acknowledged that the land selected was not always appropriate. See AIA, JEAC, 601/8, "Relatório," António Marques, Enc. da Circ. de Ile, 30 January 1946; AIA, JEAC, 601/8, "Relatório," Pedro João Francisco Lopes, Admin. da Circ. de Maganja da Costa, 30 December 1945.

[74]   AIA, JEAC, 901, "Despacho", n.d.; interviews with Paulo Roque; Fátima Konkonko.

[75]   Interview with Miriam Paulo, Maputo, 16 May 1987.

[76]   Interview with Faria Lobo, 6 May 1987.

Withholding insecticides was a critical blow to producers, since loss from pests could amount to as much as two-thirds of the cotton crop.[77] According to a 1947 report,

> the destruction caused by insect pests is sometimes enormous. Jassids are so abundant and frequent that it is not economic to cultivate non-resistant varieties [of seeds]. The Red Hook Worm, the Stainers, the Pink Boll Worm and sometimes Hellopeltis cause great damage, and are often very difficult to control.[78]

In much the same way, the failure to breed commercial varieties of seeds that would be resistant to local bacteria left many cotton fields vulnerable. Reflecting on the state of colonial science thirty years later, Professor Quintanilha, director of CICA, acknowledged that "there was just so much that we did not know."[79]

The only input the companies provided to peasant growers was the cotton seed. Even the seeds they supplied were not terribly well suited to the environment, adversely affecting yields.[80] In the mid-1940s the Cotton Board's scientific arm, CICA, took responsibility for breeding and selecting disease-resistant seeds with a better-quality fiber.[81] Disgusted Cotton Board inspectors complained bitterly about the "backward-looking mentality of all our concessionary companies who only know how to expand production by increasing the number of peasants forced to grow cotton."[82] Their reaction is just one indication that the Cotton Board did not always line up with the concessionary companies (see Chapter 6).

With few inducements for peasants, the task of stimulating local production fell to the concessionary company field agents (*propagandistas*) and overseers (*capatazes*), in whom the state vested de facto police power. Most of the men who filled these positions came from humble origins in Portugal. Poorly trained and lacking even minimal technical knowledge, they relied on force. In the words of one colonial official, "Their lack of preparation and their complete ignorance as to how to treat Africans aggravated a difficult situation and often led to a decline in cotton production."[83] Cotton Board inspectors regularly complained that most "*capatazes* were little more than thugs whose actions are destroying our prestige."[84] These commentaries reveal more about the class bias of the observers than they do about the underlying causes for the brutality of the system. Because there was never a sufficient number of company agents to oversee the peasants under their control, *capatazes* used fear as much as violence to instill discipline. Armando Cardoso, who worked as a labor overseer for CAM, recalled that he had had to supervise produc-

---

[77] Prentice, *Cotton*, 230; Ministério da Agricultura, "A Socio–economic Survey in the Province of Nampula: Cotton in the Smallholder Economy," working paper no. 56 (Maputo, 1991), 13.

[78] Quintanilha, "The Problem of Cotton Production," 48.

[79] Interview with A. Quintanilha, Maputo, 12 May 1979.

[80] Quintanilha, "Report," 13.

[81] Ibid.

[82] AIA, JEAC, "Rel. An. 1945," João Contreiras, Insp. dos SAU, May 1945.

[83] AHM, FGG, Tabela 4, Cota 294, "Algodão Cultura, Medidas de Protecção, Direitos Transportes, 1934 à 1945, Admin. da Circ. Civil do Alto Molócuè Campanha Algodoeira de 1942–43 Relatório," José Manuel da Silva, Admin., 4 March 1944.

[84] AHM, Secção Reserva (SR), Cx. 77, ISANI, "Relatório da Insp. Ord. ao Dist. de Nampula da Prov. do Niassa," Imala, U.3, Hortêncio Estevão de Sousa, 1948.

tion on almost five thousand fields.[85] His situation was not unique.[86] Initially most of these *capatazes* were European. Over time the hard-pressed companies employed an ever increasing number of *mestiços* and even brought in some Africans to patrol the fields.[87]

One grower in Nampula summed up the prevailing mentality among overseers this way: "Of course we were physically abused; for the Portuguese *capatazes* we were simply instruments."[88] A male nurse, Manuel Pinto, who treated some of the victims of *capataz* abuse in Zambézia, ascribed the cruelty of the company foremen to their deficient training. "The *capatazes* lacked scientific knowledge. The only thing they knew how to do was to beat and terrorize."[89] Former growers in Namapa in the Nampula district recalled that the overseers might appear at any moment:

> The *capatazes* did not pass by our fields every day. It could be a week or more before they returned. But when they came back the first thing that they did was to identify those fields which were dirty [not properly weeded]. They ordered the local authorities to fetch the growers whom they beat with their *palmatórias* and rhinoceros whips.[90]

Helena Felizma Chirindza from Marracuene in the south described how, for women, such pressure was often highly personalized: "We were always supervised and controlled by the *capatazes*. If they came across a mother breast-feeding her baby they would hit her and order her to leave the baby in the tree. And although the baby cried, the mother had to continue to work."[91] Unwanted sexual advances from company foremen and state police were characteristic of a system that constantly reduced African women to objects. Chirindza's neighbor, Celeste Cossa, angrily reported:

> There was no respect. They treated us all the same—older women, younger women and teenagers. All were called "Maria." "Maria" was always the love that they needed. They did not distinguish between the oldest "mama" and the youngest. There was no respect, they always abused us.[92]

A group of women who worked on the cotton holdings of Sena Sugar vividly recalled:

> If you were told to undress, we undressed. If [the concessionary official] wanted to sleep with you, you let him sleep with you. Then he was happy. After that he would beat you up. If you didn't let him sleep with you, that day you were in trouble; he would beat you up the whole of the time.[93]

---

[85]   Interview with Armando Cardoso, Nampula, 10 July 1991.

[86]   Bravo, *Cultura Algodoeira*, 112.

[87]   Interviews with Faria Lobo, 6 May 1987; Armando Cardoso; Paulo Roque.

[88]   Interview with Armando Nicula, Liassa Lohaninteve, and Murinvona Mpemo, Centro Piloto de Deslocados, Nampula/Gilé, 8 July 1991.

[89]   Interview with Manuel Pinto, Quelimane, 19 July 1991.

[90]   Interview with Nanjaia Tiabo et al., Namapa, 2 May 1979.

[91]   Interview with Helena Jossias Cambane and Helena Felizmina Chirinda, Maputo, 1 August 1991.

[92]   Interview with Celeste Cossa et al.

[93]   Quoted in Vail and White, "*Tawani Machambero!*"

Testimonies from former cotton growers across the colony confirm that these violent acts toward both men and women were not simply random or excessive abuses of power, but were an integral part of the colonial system of labor control.[94] Force was used to stimulate production, to prohibit intercropping, to curtail flight, and to limit the production of more lucrative cash crops, particularly peanuts.[95]

While violence was initially indicative of the weak control of the colonial state and the concessionary companies over the rural population, in many regions the violence of the cotton regime seems to have taken on a life of its own. António Ramalho, who patrolled the central region of Alto Molócuè, was a particularly notorious overseer. "When he came upon a field that was behind schedule, he grabbed the grower and pummeled him. He loved to beat them," remembered Rudolfo Churupa, a grower from Alto Molócuè. "I know, I worked under him."[96] Churupa described how, even when Ramalho was not physically present, his underlings could intimidate entire villages:

> The *capatazes* and the *cabos* . . . identified villagers who had not fin-
> ished cleaning their cotton fields. He ordered that ten to fifteen of the
> worst offenders from each area be brought to the post. And there one
> could see a multitude of growers waiting to be beaten with the
> *palmatória*. The beatings went on throughout the day and into the
> evening. . . Those who had suffered the *palmatória* returned home with
> their hand badly swollen. They could not work for an entire week. As
> a result many were apprehended again and brought to the post be-
> cause they had not fulfilled their tasks.[97]

Churupa's story suggests that brutality, humiliation, and a "culture of terror" became intrinsic to the system of domination even when such abuse was clearly contrary to economic reality.[98] So do the actions of the Sena Sugar overseer Braz Valezim, who hid young babies in a box if he thought that the women were not working hard enough.[99] Kidnapping growers' babies, imprisoning recalcitrant peasants, beating them so harshly that they were unable to grasp a hoe, sending them off as conscripted laborers to European estates, and sexually abusing rural women did little to increase cotton output, and often had exactly the opposite effect. But the message from these rituals of terror was clear: the only way a person could hope to escape the harsh realities of the cotton regime was to work longer and harder in cotton production. Stories of violence that were captured in personal narratives, casual conversation, rumors, gossip, and songs—and perpetuated by cotton officials in such small symbolic acts as slapping someone's face, making a threatening gesture, or addressing a grown man as *"rapaz"* (boy)—constantly reminded

---

[94] Vail and White reached a similar conclusion. Ibid., 252.

[95] For a discussion of the use of force, see Allen Isaacman et al., "'Cotton is the Mother of Poverty': Peasant Resistance to Forced Cotton Production in Mozambique," *IJAHS* 13(1980), 581–615; Vail and White, *Capitalism and Colonialism*, 314–24.

[96] Interview with Manuel Nuitha and Rodolfo Churupa, Nampula/Gilé, 11 July 1991.

[97] Ibid.

[98] For a discussion of the "culture of terror" in the Amazon, see Michael Taussig, "Culture of Terror—Space of Death: Roger Casement's Putumayo Report and the Explanation of Torture," *CSSH* 26, 3(1984), 467–97.

[99] Vail and White, *Capitalism and Colonialism*, 321–22.

growers of their vulnerability. To this day, accounts of the overseers' beatings and sexual assaults evoke a sense of fear among rural Mozambicans.[100]

For all their discretionary power, the individual overseers did not live particularly well. By European standards these men received meager salaries and labored under difficult conditions. Armando Cardoso, then in his mid-twenties, earned five hundred *escudos* (approximately U.S. $17) per month in 1949. CAM provided him with a small house, but Cardoso spent most of his time in the "bush." He had to travel several thousand kilometers every month along small dirt roads, covering most of this distance by jeep and some of it by foot. Much of his traveling took place during the hot rainy season. At the end of a long day's work he slept in a hut provided by the local chief. Yet Cardoso acknowledged that his life was not that bad. Wherever he went, chiefs plied him with food taken from the local population; thus Cardoso was able to save the modest food allowance the company provided. In each of the two locales where he was stationed, Cardoso "arranged" to have an African wife, neither of whom he formally married. Every year he and his European compatriots received a cash bonus, depending on how many tons of cotton the peasants in their jurisdictions had produced. The small number of African *capatazes*, by contrast, did not receive incentives of this kind. They also earned less than one-third the salary paid to European overseers.[101] In our conversations, Cardoso skillfully skirted the issue of coercion, but he admitted that production bonuses enhanced his meager salary and made his life in the bush more bearable. Today, Cardoso is an old man living in extreme poverty in Nampula with his African wife and children.[102]

The firms relied heavily on local and state administrators to help enforce the cotton regime. According to one *chefe de posto* in Zambézia, "Our intervention was sought dozens if not hundreds of times per year. All these efforts were a continuous action, persistent, exhausting and thankless."[103] Local officials cajoled, harangued, and intimidated peasants to register for the cotton scheme. When necessary, they did more. John Paul, a Protestant missionary based in the Niassa province, recalled: "Administrator Cunhal tyrannized the blacks. He was always accompanied by several *sipais* armed with truncheons and kept a *palmatória* and a *chicote* [whip] in his car."[104] Some, such as the administrators of Mocuba and Lugela, received high marks from their superiors for putting so much pressure on the Africans that they "accepted cotton with fatalistic resignation."[105] Other local officials preferred persuasion over brute force; still others organized cotton fairs to extol the crop's virtues, rewarding loyalist chiefs and especially productive peasants with such prizes as salt and hoes.[106] These examples demonstrate both the centrality of

---

[100] Interview with Marcelina Joaquim, Juliana Lias, and Hirondiena Tonia, Mueda, 25 April 1979; interview with Aridhi Mahanda et al.; interview with Daima Magaga Mbela et al. See also AHM, SR, Cx. 77, ISANI, "Rel. da Insp. Ord. ao Dist. de Nampula," vol. 3, Hortêncio Estevão de Sousa, 1948; Vail and White, *Capitalism and Colonialism*, 314–25.

[101] Interview with Paulo Roque.

[102] Interview with Armando Cardoso.

[103] Quoted in Vail and White, *Capitalism and Colonialism*, 315.

[104] John Paul, *Memoirs of a Revolution* (London, 1975), 71.

[105] AIA, JEAC, 601/8, "Relatório," A. Santos Baptista, Sec. da Circ. do Lugela, 31 December 1945; AIA, JEAC, 601/3, Posto 48 (1946), December 1946.

[106] AIA, JEAC, "Rel. An. 1939–1941: Rel. de Posto de Chinde, 1940," António Barreira Silvestre, Chefe de Posto (CP), 31 January 1941.

the administrators and their wide discretionary power, which they exercised in ways that reflected their personalities and their reading of local politics.

Relying on local authorities was hardly a viable solution when most *chefes de posto* were themselves overworked and lacked appropriate support staff. Only 30 percent of the posts in the north, for example, were filled in 1943. Such personnel shortages reflected a characteristic weakness of the Portuguese colonial state.[107] However, given the vast power of the concessionary companies, local officials' desire for promotion, and the monetary rewards they received from the cotton firms, most administrators worked as allies of the cotton companies whenever they could.[108]

Since the limited number of local officials and company *capatazes* could not possibly supervise the labor of thousands of growers under their domain, the cotton regime required fairly substantial African involvement to oversee the rural population. Whatever reservations Portuguese colonizers might have harbored about the competence or loyalty of their African subordinates, racial distrust gave way to demographic realities. To enforce colonial law, colonial authorities often recruited African police, or *sipais*, from the ranks of soldiers, from loyalist chieftaincies, and from "bellicose tribes."[109] When necessary, they press-ganged others into service.[110] *Chefes de posto* throughout the countryside periodically dispatched the dozen or so *sipais* under their command to thrash peasants who were not working sufficiently rapidly or whose fields were not judged to be in appropriate condition. "They were always on our backs, beating with *palmatórias*,"[111] remembered Jonas Nakutepa, a former cotton grower from Macomia in the Nampula district.

These unsupervised visits offered African *sipais* an opportunity to plunder the peasants and to supplement their meager salaries. Sometimes *sipais* made it clear that members of the rural population could avoid the most excessive punishments by supplying them with grain, beer, goats, and sexual favors. In other cases, *sipais* simply seized what they wanted, beating peasants or chiefs who tried to resist. "Many men were sent to Nangororo [the sisal plantation]," remembered Anasse Nuita, "because they had beautiful young wives whom the *sipais* desired, and if they were working *chibalo* the *sipais* could come and get their wives any time they wanted."[112]

Yet, as lowly African functionaries, the *sipais*' position was both ambiguous and contradictory. *Sipais* were not only themselves harangued and abused by European officials, but also subject to scorn from their neighbors and to occasional attacks from disgruntled peasants.[113] Valente Yota, who worked as a sipai in the

---

[107] AHM, SR, Cx. 96, ISANI, "Rel. e Docs. Ref. à Insp. Ord. Feita na Prov. do Niassa," 1943, Carlos Henriques Jones da Silveira, 1943.

[108] A number of administrators refused to enforce the cotton legislation. Their reasons ranged from moral outrage at the naked exploitation to profitable labor recruiting agreements that they made with the planter community.

[109] For a discussion of the origin and role of the *sipais* during the early days of the colonial period, see J. Coutinho, *A Campanha de Barue em 1902* (Lisbon, 1904); A. Martins, *O Soldado Africano de Moçambique* (Lisbon, 1936); Allen Isaacman and Anton Rosenthal, "Slaves, Soldiers and Police: Power and Dependency Among the Chikunda of Mozambique, ca. 1825–1920," in *The End of Slavery in Africa*, ed. Suzanne Miers and Richard Roberts (Madison, 1988).

[110] Interview with Valente Yota, Macia, 19 February 1979.

[111] Interview with Jonas Nakutepa et al., Macomia, 30 July 1979.

[112] Interview with Amasse Nuitha, CV Nawana, Montepuez, 20 July 1979.

[113] Group interview, Likanganu, Macomia, 1 May 1979.

Gaza district from 1940 to 1956, confirmed his own sense of vulnerability in a 1979 conversation at his home in Macia:

> In 1939 I returned home from the mines to work for the railroad at Macia. I then went back to South Africa [the mines] because the pay was better. When I next came home the local administrator ordered me to report for police duty. He beat me three times with the *palmatória* and threatened me with *chibalo* unless I worked as a *sipai*. Twice I asked to resign and on both cases was threatened with *chibalo* and the *palmatória*.[114]

Yota's account reveals the inherent problems for Africans who collaborated with the colonial state.

The loyalist chiefs (*régulos*) and their coterie of headmen played the most critical role in overseeing the rural population on a daily basis. These African authorities traveled with company officials to make certain that all eligible adults under their jurisdiction were registered and had received parcels of land to work. The chiefs distributed government-selected seeds to growers a few weeks before planting and then supervised the subsequent production process. Chiefs and village headmen patrolled the fields to ensure that cotton was being planted, weeded, and harvested at the designated time. Peasants in the southern district of Gaza angrily recounted, "Even as we were on our knees placing seed in the ground, the *régulos* would come and beat us. Then they would warn us that if we did not complete the entire field we would suffer worse punishments."[115] Chiefs also checked village homesteads and food gardens in search of "loiterers" who covertly worked their own fields in order to feed their household. Those whom they discovered were usually beaten, fined, arrested, or forced to work an extra stint in the chief's cotton field.[116] In addition, chiefs were expected to prevent their subjects from fleeing the territory. They sought to dissuade peasants through intimidation, harassing and threatening villagers whom they suspected were contemplating escape. Runaways they caught were often incarcerated. Amasse Nuitha remembered that "when someone escaped, his entire family was arrested. The women were forced to serve the chief and work in his fields. The men were sent to the Nangororo sisal plantation."[117] Indigenous authorities were thus both the eyes and ears of the colonial administration and the first line of defense against peasant resistance. They reported to both the company overseers and to the local administrators what village headmen reported to them. "In our present condition," concluded one inspector in 1943, "the chiefs and their counselors are the critical agents of white authority."[118] The state rewarded effective chiefs in a variety of ways. These rewards brought substantial economic gain to many *régulos* across the colony and provided a strong incentive for most to enforce the cotton regulations (see Chapter 8).[119]

---

[114] Interview with Valente Yota.

[115] Group interview, CV Magul, Bilene, 20 February 1979.

[116] Interviews with Adelino Cedo and Andre Marques da Pinha, Montepuez, 21 July 1979; Romeu Mataquenha et al.; Aridhi Mahanda et al.; Daima Magaga Mbela et al.

[117] Interview with Amasse Nuitha.

[118] AHM, SR, Cx. 99, ISANI, "Rel. e Docs. Ref. à Insp. Ord. Feita na Prov. do Niassa, 1ª parte, 1943," Carlos Henriques Jonas da Silveira, 1943.

[119] Allen Isaacman, "Chiefs, Rural Differentiation, and Peasant Protest: The Mozambican Forced Cotton Regime 1938–61," *AEH* 14(1985), 15–56.

Nevertheless, the relationship between the state and chiefs was full of contradictions. The Portuguese needed strong African chiefs to whom they could shift much of the responsibility for rural social control and for overseeing commodity production. When chiefs who enjoyed popular support and who were perceived as legitimate by their subjects chose to promote the cotton project, their influence could be enormous. This was the case in Montepuez. There "peasants would not plant nor harvest cotton without the secret orders of the chiefs and their councillors."[120] Strong chiefs, however, could also pose a serious threat to state power. As a result, the colonial regime often replaced or bypassed powerful indigenous authorities in favor of more compliant members of the royal family or *sipais* and other state functionaries who had demonstrated their loyalty to the Portuguese. One senior Portuguese official, writing in 1943, acknowledged the disastrous consequences of this policy: "Immediately after we defeated the tribes of this province it was decided to fragment the large chieftaincies and remove those chiefs who were most prestigious and most powerful. We replaced them with '*amigos*.' It is their descendants who govern today without any prestige."[121] Five years later, a Native Affairs official noted contemptuously that "in the majority of cases to call them chiefs makes no sense because they were not born in the areas they govern but were drawn from the ranks of police, overseers, messengers, and state functionaries."[122]

The ambiguous and at times unwieldy relationship between the colonial regime and African chiefs helped to shape an equally ambiguous relationship between the chiefs and their rural subjects. As local representatives of the colonial government, chiefs had the power to protect and reward their closest followers. But as state functionaries, chiefs could also speak out against the government on behalf of their communities. Many did so of their own volition, others in response to pressure from their subjects. *Régulos* complained to local administrators about abuses by *sipais* and company overseers, about price-gouging at the markets, and about the failure of the cotton companies to provide promised technical assistance to African growers. Some chiefs were furious about the indignities their own families suffered under the cotton regime. Outside the gaze of European officials, a number of *régulos* organized covert acts of defiance (see Chapter 10). Ultimately, however, few chiefs were able to mediate successfully between the world of the colonizer and the world of the colonized. In order to perpetuate their own relatively privileged position, most *régulos* opted for the colonial order.[123]

Peasants at Work: Laboring in the Cotton Fields

Peasants felt the full brunt of the intensive labor demands of cotton cultivation, which consumed the bulk of their time for virtually the entire year. Typically, peas-

---

[120] AHM, SR, Cx. 97, ISANI, "Rel. e Docs. Ref. à Insp. Ord. Feita na Prov. do Niassa," 2ª parte, Capitão Carlos Henriques Jones da Silveira, Insp. Admin., 1944.

[121] Ibid., 1ª parte, 1943.

[122] AHM, SR, Cx. 77, ISANI, "Rel. da Insp. Ord. ao Dist. de Nampula," Hortêncio Estevão de Sousa, Insp. Adm., 1948.

[123] For a discussion of the ambiguous and contradictory position of the chiefs, see Isaacman, "Chiefs, Rural Differentiation, and Peasant Protest," passim.

PHOTO 1   Men cutting trees and removing stumps to prepare cotton fields. Courtesy of Arquivo Histórico de Moçambique. Rebelo Júnior, photographer.

ants began to open up new cotton lands in late September or early October.[124] Men, working together in assigned groups, cut down trees and removed the stumps and heavy shrubbery. If husbands had been press-ganged to work for the state or on European farms or were away laboring in the South African gold mines, their wives were forced to perform these tasks themselves.[125] With only machetes, axes, and hoes for tools, land clearing was exhausting work that "almost all the natives detested."[126] It took from four to six weeks to complete this arduous task before the rains came.

Because of the relatively short growing season in Mozambique and because of the tendency for late-sown cotton to be low-yielding and poor in quality, the Cot-

---

[124] This description of the work calendar is based on northern Mozambique; there were modest variations from region to region. See Chapter 4.

[125] Interview with Armando Nicula et al.

[126] Bravo, *Cultura Algodoeira*, 114.

ton Board required all producers to clear their cotton plots by late November so that they could begin seeding promptly after the first rains. Company overseers forced peasants to leave their sorghum, corn, and peanut fields after the initial downpour. Paulo Roque, an overseer for CAM, emphasized that "after the rains came in the end of November or early December, everyone had to go immediately to their fields to sow their cotton,"[127] although he and his colleagues acknowledged that they often lacked the manpower to enforce this rule.[128] Thus in specific instances the shortage of manpower could mean less coercion, although for the system as a whole it had the opposite effect.

For peasants willing to risk retribution there were also sometimes opportunities to take advantage of the manpower shortage. Indeed, the accounts of Cotton Board representatives, local authorities, and company representatives all suggest that throughout the 1940s it was quite common for peasants across the colony to plant their cotton crop after the designated date but before the *sipais* arrived to investigate their fields. In 1947 a senior agricultural officer in central Mozambique complained that "the preparation of the cotton fields is way behind schedule in a number of areas."[129] The same year, his frustrated counterpart in the northern circumscription of António Enes grumbled that "the Africans in this part continually fabricate excuses why they have not seeded any cotton yet."[130]

Seeding generally took four to five full days and was considered the least onerous stage of cotton cultivation. Once the rains had softened the parched earth, men began to mark and prepare seed beds in straight rows, scraping small hollows at prescribed intervals. Women and older children placed several seeds in each hole to reduce the risk of crop failure.[131] "If, however, the rains were insufficient and the plants did not germinate, or if there was excessive rainfall," Roque noted, "we ordered the growers to reseed their fields."[132] Flooding meant that growers regularly had to devote an additional week or two to reseeding washed-out fields. Since rainfall was so unpredictable, reseeding in late December and through the month of January occurred frequently.[133] On occasion, tropical storms inundated entire regions. In 1949, for example, more than 440 millimeters of rain fell over vast parts of the north during January. Fields were flooded, and the water severely damaged the cotton plants. Many households were unable to destroy fast-growing grasses and weeds before they strangled the crops. As a result, cotton yields plummeted.[134] Two years later, over much of the same region, the rains suddenly ceased on December 22. Peasants who had finished planting their crops before that date could turn their attention to saving their food crops, while those who had not finished planting had to spend the next six weeks periodically reseeding in the aftermath of

---

[127] Interview with Paulo Roque.

[128] Ibid.

[129] AIA, JEAC, Conf. 1947, José da Cunha Dias Mendes, Regente Agrícola (Reg. Ag.) ao CP da JEAC, 9 December 1947.

[130] AIA, JEAC, Arquivo Técnico (AT), 9352, Boletins de Informação, CAM, 1946/47, Concelho de António Enes, Posto Administrativo (PA) do Namaponda, 10 April 1947.

[131] Interview with Paulo Roque.

[132] Ibid.

[133] Interview with Paulo Roque.

[134] JEAC, *Esboço do Reconhecimento*, vol. 1.

PHOTO 2   Peasants doing second weeding of cotton plants. Courtesy of Arquivo Histórico de Moçambique. Rebelo Júnior, photographer.

irregular downpours.[135] The delay left them with less time to care for their grains and vegetables. If reseeding took place too late in the agricultural cycle and seedlings did not receive enough sunlight, as often happened in the humid regions of Zambézia, the crop might not have a chance to mature before state officials would order growers to uproot their cotton plants to avoid the spread of diseases.[136]

Within two weeks of planting, rural households began weeding their cotton plots. Cotton could not compete with faster-growing vegetation for nutrients, moisture, and sunlight, and if weeding were delayed or done poorly, the plant became drawn, spindly, and susceptible to a number of diseases.[137] Local officials thus re-

[135]   Prov. de Moç., Gov. do Niassa, Circ. de Mogovolas, "Rel. de Circ. Admin. de Mogovolas, 1953," Manuel Maris Souto e Silva, Admin., 26 February 1954.

[136]   Vail and White, "*Tawani Machambero!*," 144.

[137]   Prentice, *Cotton*, 80.

PHOTO 3 Women in Nampula picking cotton. Allen Isaacman, photographer.

quired the producers to weed a minimum of three times between late January and early April. Since young seedlings were particularly vulnerable, peasants had to spend up to three weeks completing the initial weeding and thinning of the cotton stands. Company overseers in some regions insisted upon a fourth weeding as well. Gabriel Nantimbo remembered that "We didn't have time to look after our other crops. Cotton needs constant attention. You have to keep weeding the field and thinning out the plants."[138]

Cultivators often had to choose between cleaning their food gardens and clearing their cotton plots. If they chose the latter, they jeopardized their food security; if they chose the former, they jeopardized their physical security. Maria Sindique from Zambézia poignantly captured their dilemma:

> There just was not enough time to do both. The *capataz* threatened to whip us with the *chicote* [hippopotamus whip] if we did not spend more time in our cotton fields. The little bit of time that remained we dedicated to the production of manioc. There was never any time for peanuts and beans.[139]

In addition to weeding their cotton, sorghum, and corn during the busy rainy season, growers were called on to repair roads and bridges that had been washed out by the downpours. This extra burden often provoked great resentment, according to the local administrator of Corrane:

> There were some conflicts during the rainy season. The rains had ruined most of the roads and bridges. We gathered peasants working in the fields

---

[138] Quoted in Mondlane, *The Struggle for Mozambique*, 86.

[139] Interview with Maria Sindique et al., Nicoadala/ Morrumbala, 18 July 1991.

PHOTO 4   Drying cotton and preparing it for market. Courtesy of Arquivo Histórico de Moçambique. Rebelo Júnior, photographer.

and forced them to repair the roads. Each village spent three to four days working on the roads. Only then were they allowed to return to their fields.[140]

For a brief period in April, as the plants matured and before the harvest began, demand for adult labor slackened. During this time, however, young children spent their days in the cotton fields protecting the maturing plants from monkeys and other animals. Labor demand intensified again in May when the plants flowered and the harvest began. Handpicking cotton was a difficult task, especially in the hot sun. Men, women, and older children worked from early morning until the middle of the afternoon every day but Sunday. On a good day one adult could pick between thirty and forty pounds of cotton.[141] Deft pickers who were able to empty all the compartments of a cotton boll with one snatch of their fingers could collect appreciably more. Peasants avoided harvesting on rainy or cloudy days whenever possible, since excessive moisture discolored the cotton lint, which reduced its value. After picking the cotton, men and women separated the lint by quality and stacked it into large piles left outside for a month to dry. Since the

---

[140] Interview with Semble Roldão et al., Nicoadala/Morrumbala, 16 July 1991.

[141] See Prentice, *Cotton*, 185; J. D. Acland, *East African Crops: An Introduction to the Production of Field and Plantation Crops in Kenya, Tanzania, and Uganda* (London, 1971), 102.

cotton plants did not flower all at once, growers had to repeat this set of tasks several times.[142] Thus, harvesting took up most of May and June, and often extended into July. Even when household members completed their own fields, they were not necessarily finished with the cotton harvest. According to Fátima Konkonko, who lived near the northern capital of Pemba, "if there was a *machamba* [field] that was behind schedule, the *sipais* rounded up people in the village and ordered them to work in the field until all the cotton had been picked."[143]

During July and August growers had to carry their cotton to market (see Chapter 5). Without trucks or other motorized transport, producers were transformed into conscripted porters. Even after peasants had returned home from the market with their meager earnings, they still had to chop and burn the cotton stalks in their fields to prevent them from becoming the host for parasites that might jeopardize the following year's crop. Shortly after they completed the cycle of clearing, planting, weeding, harvesting, and burning, growers had to begin all over again.

This cursory description highlights the four important ways in which the state-imposed work calendar altered the peasant labor process. Taken together, they reveal the excessive labor demands and enormous production risks imposed on peasants who were caught within the cotton scheme and the adverse effects forced cotton cultivation had on their short-term food security and long-term social reproduction requirements.

First, even under the most salutary conditions, cotton cultivation was a long process. Apart from the brief pause in August and September between one cotton season and another, April was the only month in which peasants were largely free from cotton. Yet, in that month, thousands of rural men and women were conscripted to clear paths and to rebuild the cotton markets.[144]

Second, cotton production was highly labor-intensive. Without the assistance of labor-saving technologies such as plows or pesticides and without trucks or easily accessible markets, cotton imposed a staggering burden on growers. State and cotton concessionary officials estimated that rural households spent between 110 and 175 days cultivating one hectare of cotton properly.[145] Minimum labor requirements varied in practice depending on whether cotton was grown in forests, on savanna, or on fallow lands.[146] Official estimates, however, were not terribly reliable. They tended to be conservative, because officials assumed that growers per-

---

[142] Interview with Manuel Pacheleque et al.

[143] Interview with Fátima Konkonko.

[144] Interview with Paulo Roque; Bravo, *Cultura Algodoeira*, 118.

[145] Bravo, *Cultura Algodoeira*, 201.

[146] A 1943 household survey followed four peasant households in northern Mozambique through an entire cotton cycle. Each household cultivated three–fourths of a hectare but only weeded twice, working between 80 and 109 days for six hours per day. The household that devoted 109 days to carefully cleaning and weeding their field collected 198 kilograms, more than double their counterparts who only worked 80 days. When adjusted to account for the cultivation of a full hectare, a third weeding, marketing, and plant destruction, a figure of approximately 150 days would seem quite reasonable. AIA, JEAC, Del. de Moç., BT de Nampula, "Rel. do Campo Experimental de Nacarôa Campanha de 1942–3," Augusto Guilherme Alves, Ag. Fisc., n.d. A team of researchers who did a survey in Nampula during the 1978–1979 cotton campaign also concluded that peasants spent 150 days to cultivate one hectare of cotton. Postcolonial growers were still using the same hand tools as their predecessors. See CEA, *Transformação da Agricultura Familiar na Província de Nampula* (Maputo, 1980), 21–24.

formed the minimum number of weedings; they did not make adjustments for re-seeding; and most important, they failed to count the labor of unregistered children and elders. The estimates also made no allowance for the additional time peasants had to devote to working in their chief's cotton fields. Regardless of the exact number of days, recent studies suggest that cotton production in Mozambique required between one-third and two-thirds more labor time than cultivation of maize, sorghum, millet, beans, or peanuts.[147] The number of days needed for cotton takes on added significance because environmental factors greatly limited the number of days when work in the cotton fields was actually possible. During the rainy season, heavy downpours and wet fields reduced by as much as one-half the amount of time peasants were able to farm. The rains also meant there were more weeds that had to be destroyed.[148]

Third, the large number of days that peasants had to spend laboring in their fields was made more onerous by the increased length of their workday. It was not uncommon for peasants to work from sunrise to sunset, and sometimes they remained in their fields until well into the night.[149] Since women continued to be responsible for critical domestic chores like cooking, carrying firewood, and caring for infants, they experienced even greater problems. Even after they had completed their stint in the cotton fields, peasants were not necessarily free to return to their food gardens or to perform other deferred tasks, but often had to work the cotton fields of neighbors who had fallen behind the official schedule.[150]

Finally, to the extent that peasants were forced to allocate the bulk of their labor to meet cotton requirements, they jeopardized their own food security (see Chapter 8). Under the best of circumstances it would have been difficult to maintain several fields located far apart. Moreover, peasants spent hours that had been previously allocated to their gardens walking to and from their cotton plots. To complicate matters, the agricultural cycle of cotton production coincided almost identically with the growing schedules of Mozambique's basic cereals and legumes. For most households this conflict created an impossible burden. Pressure on households to furnish labor for public work projects and for European estates exacerbated this subsistence dilemma, as did overseers who burned food crops to punish peasants believed to be neglecting their cotton fields.[151] If this were not enough, the depressed cotton payments they received rarely enabled growers to purchase the food they no longer had time to grow (see Chapter 5).

Conclusion

One of the central features of the peasant labor process under the cotton regime was the extent to which growers were forced to assume the risks of production.

---

[147] See CEA, *Transformação da Agricultura*, 21–23.

[148] I am grateful to Mr. Paulo Zucula, a Mozambican agronomist, for this point.

[149] Interview with Murinvona Mpemo, Nampula/Gilé, 8 July 1991.

[150] Interview with Fátima Konkonko.

[151] AHM, SR, Cx. 77, Prov. do Niassa, ISANI, "Rel. . . . Niassa," 2ª parte, Capitão Carlos Henrique Jones da Silveira, Insp. Admin., 1944; AHM, SR, Cx.77, ISANI, "Rel. . . . Nampula," Hortêncio Estevão de Sousa, Insp., 1948.

Throughout Mozambique, low yields per hectare and depressed cotton prices combined to create rural impoverishment. The eagerness of the state-concessionary alliance to extend cotton production without the necessary scientific data made low productivity almost inevitable. In the words of one official, cotton yields were "low and irregular."[152] By 1945 there were still areas of Mozambique where yields per hectare were a paltry thirty kilograms or less and the average yield per producer in the principal cotton regions of northern and central Mozambique was approximately eighty kilograms.[153] Moreover, households were held hostage to the wide fluctuations in yields from year to year.[154]

The low output and sharp fluctuations in part reflect the impediments and unpredictable conditions that peasant households confronted once they were forced to cultivate cotton. The single greatest hazard they faced were the uncertain climatic conditions. The extent to which peasants were forced to farm on inappropriate lands or in soils exhausted by ill-advised agricultural practices obviously affected output as well. Pest and plant diseases also posed a serious problem. Jassids, stainers, and bollworm wreaked havoc throughout the countryside. Yet until the 1950s colonial agronomists knew little about the entomology of these pests, and the companies showed no interest in investing in pesticides to control them. In much the same way, the failure to develop seeds that were resistant to local bacteria left many cotton fields vulnerable to infestation.

Dismayed colonial officials and contemporary observers saw the ruptures in production caused by pests, disease, and drought as problems intrinsic to the physical environment. For them the issues were irreducibly technical and without political content. In reality, however, these problems were preeminently political, rooted in colonial-capitalist politics of production. The way in which the colonial state organized work was hardly neutral. To achieve its economic agenda, it initially disregarded the locally specific ecological conditions and crop systems onto which it grafted the cotton regime. It prohibited many of the practices that peasants had historically developed to manage the risks of farming in this environment. It assumed that suitable land and underutilized labor were abundant. It relied on force and terror to intimidate reluctant growers. It dismissed African agricultural practices as backward, destructive, and unproductive but failed to introduce even the most basic technological innovations, such as better seeds or more efficient hoes. Finally, it chose to overlook or to minimize the deleterious effects of cotton production on food security, often promoting policies that necessarily exacerbated food shortages. All were intended to increase output to meet the needs of the metropolitan textile industry.

---

[152] Quintanilha, "The Problem of Cotton Production," 48.

[153] These included Macomia, Mocímboa de Praia, Palma, and Namarrói (see Bravo, *Cultura Algodoeira*, 140–74).

[154] For the decade of the 1940s as a whole, average yields increased from approximately forty to almost sixty kilograms per hectare. However, upward trends during this period obscure the enormous annual fluctuations and variations in productivity between regions.

4

Variations in the Cotton Regime

While labor intensification and rural impoverishment accompanied the introduction of forced cotton cultivation throughout the colony, there were important variations between and within regions, from one household to another, and even within households. These differences stemmed from the interplay of regionally specific ecological conditions, the systems of production onto which the cotton scheme was grafted, the different economic strategies of the state and the concessionary companies, and peasants' individual and collective responses to the cotton regime's demands. Cotton became king in the north, but remained subordinate to the plantation economy in central Mozambique and made few inroads in the south.

The Cotton Boom: An Overview

Cotton production increased sharply from approximately 15,000 tons in 1939 to almost 90,000 tons in 1951, a sixfold increase. This sixfold jump did not occur uniformly throughout the colony. There were some districts where cotton had a transforming impact on the rural economy. In other districts the effects of the cotton regime were almost negligible for the majority of peasant households.

From the outset, the northern district of Nampula held a predominant position in the cotton economy. In the 1938–1939 campaign, growers in that region produced 7,433 tons of cotton—almost 50 percent of the total colonial output (see Table 4–1). Nampula retained this preeminent position throughout the subsequent decade, although its relative importance declined somewhat as the state distributed new cotton concessions across the colony. By the early 1950s peasant production in Nampula hovered around 30,000 tons, still accounting for about one-third of the colony's total cotton output.

The adjacent district of Cabo Delgado was initially the second most important cotton region. Peasants here collected 3,925 tons in 1939; a decade later, cotton production in Cabo Delgado had jumped to approximately 15,000 tons. Production similarly skyrocketed in Zambézia during the 1940s, despite momentary reversals in the 1945 and 1946 campaigns. By 1951 growers in Zambézia were marketing

TABLE 4–1 Marketed Cotton by District, 1939–1961 (metric tons)

Year	Nampula	Cabo Delgado	Niassa	Manica/Sofala & Beira	Tete	Quelimane/ Zambézia	Inhambane	Gaza
1939	7,433	3,925	328	1,738	181	985	133	42
1940	8,550	4,559	362	3,275	379	2,617	583	139
1941	23,511	9,501	1,101	6,051	837	7,545	1,809	653
1942	33,276	9,380	1,152	7,528	2,176	14,554	1,336	992
1943	26,148	10,169	2,864	7,477	3,197	2,364	1,992	972
1944	17,902	8,648	2,650	9,464	1,235	11,615	844	1,457
1945	21,173	7,855	3,480	11,198	1,923	5,786	1,793	1,257
1946	26,284	13,598	4,316	7,415	1,593	5,637	2,280	1,635
1947	23,418	7,013	5,719	15,132	3,447	13,061	4,096	3,170
1948	18,874	8,220	3,890	10,723	2,926	13,859	4,081	2,348
1949	30,765	16,213	8,503	12,167	3,657	12,485	2,808	3,367
1950	17,901	6,706	4,951	10,889	3,092	10,358	1,481	3,875
1951	28,301	15,012	10,048	11,009	0	18,477	3,149	3,319
1952	32,677	17,565	10,133	9,538	0	12,611	4,800	6,398
1953	38,162	15,055	9,902	19,015	0	24,355	7,903	11,771
1954	31,728	11,017	7,756	14,613	0	21,936	7,364	8,522
1955	25,510	14,010	5,803	6,691	0	15,495	6,282	9,104
1956	5,132	2,513	5,284	11,814		16,501	6,444	14,408
1957	28,680	15,243	9,830	12,809	3,333	22,808	8,304	7,227
1958	22,756	13,861	4,955	10,375	1,313	21,768	5,282	10,653
1959	33,788	11,405	7,959	16,216	7,181	36,776	9,364	12,211
1960	37,772	15,954	12,154	19,258	5,571	27,742	11,718	9,670

Sources: RTE, *Recenseamento Agrícola* (1940–1941); RTE, *Estatística Agrícola* (1941–1960); Direcção Provinçal dos Serviços de Estatística Geral, *Estatística Agrícola* (1960–1964).

TABLE 4–2   Total Cotton Income by Region, 1943–1961(millions of *escudos*)

Year	South	Central	North	Total
1943	3.6	21.7	45.9	71.1
1944	2.9	26.0	46.6	75.5
1955	3.8	22.3	37.8	64.0
1946	4.9	17.0	52.4	74.4
1947	11.3	48.0	54.4	113.7
1948	9.9	41.5	46.6	98.0
1949	11.4	43.7	99.7	154.8
1950	9.9	38.1	52.9	100.9
1951	17.6	77.7	116.6	211.9
1952	30.4	58.0	160.8	249.2
1953	51.5	113.5	167.0	331.9
1954	43.1	96.1	102.6	241.8
1955	41.5	66.9	116.1	224.5
1956	62.0	86.6	34.1	182.6
1957	46.0	108.4	155.1	309.5
1958	47.8	93.1	119.4	260.2
1959	63.9	175.5	154.3	393.6
1960	62.7	150.8	191.7	405.2
1961	53.1	145.5	181.5	380.0

Sources: RTE, *Recenseamento Agrícola* (1940-1941); RTE, *Estatística Agrícola* (1940-1960); Direcçao Provinçal dos Serviços de Estatística Geral, *Estatística Agrícola* (1960-1964).

more than 18,000 tons—20 percent of the total output in Mozambique (see Table 4–1)—and Zambézia had displaced Cabo Delgado as the second most productive cotton region.

On the other hand, cotton barely took hold in the Tete, Gaza, and Inhambane provinces. Although peasants in Gaza and Inhambane managed to produce only 3,000 tons in 1951, this amount represented a sharp increase over the preceding years. Peasant output in Tete was so erratic that the state declared a temporary moratorium on cotton production there in 1951.

Viewed regionally, a fairly clear pattern emerges. By 1939 northern Mozambique (Nampula, Cabo Delgado, and Niassa) was already the premier cotton zone in the colony. That year northern growers cultivated almost 80 percent of the total colonial output; at no time in the subsequent decade did this figure fall below 50 percent. The 53,000 tons that northern peasants brought to market in 1951 accounted for almost 61 percent of the colony's cotton production. After a rather inauspicious beginning, central Mozambique (Manica e Sofala, Tete,[1] and Zambézia) became an important secondary source of cotton. The region's market share increased from 20 to 31 percent by the early 1950s. Total output in 1951 was almost 30,000 tons. Actual output in the south (Inhambane and Gaza) remained fairly inconsequential, contributing only 8 percent to Mozambique's expanding cotton economy by the early 1950s. Cotton income by region broadly corresponded to this pattern. Table

---

[1] Production in Tete was so inconsequential that throughout this study I make only passing reference to it.

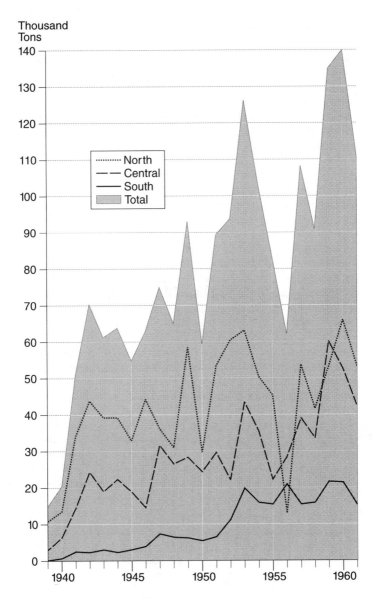

GRAPH 4–1. Cotton Marketed by Region, 1939–1961

Sources: RTE, *Recenseamento Agrícola* (Lourenço Marques), 1940–1941; RTE, *Estatística Agrícola* (Lourenço Marques), 1941–1960; Direcção Provincal dos Serviço de Estatística Geral, *Estatística Agrícola* (Lourenço Marques, 1960–1964).

4–1 and Graph 4–1 reveal the magnitude of these cross-regional variations in production trends over time, the sharp fluctuations in annual output, and the dominant position of the north in the colonial cotton economy.

Cotton Production in the Peasant North

The warm northern climate and favorable rainfall patterns help explain the pre-eminent position of the north in the colonial cotton economy.[2] Only in the eastern highland region of the Niassa district did cool temperatures adversely affect cotton output during the 1940s. Cotton planted in these cooler regions was very slow to germinate and the seedlings were vulnerable to soil fungi. Cold nights in May and June, when temperatures occasionally dropped to near freezing, prevented cotton bolls from developing fully. After a disastrous decade, state officials allowed peasants in Maniamba to withdraw from the cotton regime in 1950.[3] Growers in the Makonde highlands were not so fortunate, although the state temporarily suspended production there during the 1947–1949 campaigns.[4]

If environmental factors were relatively favorable for cotton agriculture in the north, demographic and economic factors, at least at first glance, were not. The region's relatively low population density, which in 1940 hovered around six people per square kilometer (and in the Niassa district was barely one person per square kilometer[5]), posed obvious problems for a work regime predicated on labor-intensive production. To overseers, the prospect of trekking great distances to visit remote communities must have been daunting, as was the idea of controlling population movements along the unmarked boundaries that separated northern Mozambique from Tanganyika and Nyasaland. There was a long tradition, antedating the colonial period, of Mozambicans' migrating across these porous borders often and returning home when conditions seemed better. More recently they were leaving because wages were higher and taxes considerably lower in the British colonies.[6] Migration offered peasants in the north a means to escape the regime's excessive labor demands once the concessions were in place (see Chapter 10).

Indigenous agricultural technology complicated the prospects for cotton production in the north. The overwhelming majority of cultivators depended on hand tools, primarily hoes, machetes, axes, and shovels.[7] These implements were perfectly adequate for cultivating sorghum, maize, manioc, beans, and peanuts,[8] but they limited the amount of additional land that could be opened and cultivated under the cotton regime. A handful of African households in the north acquired plows during the early 1950s; however, the prevalence of tsetse fly in the region meant that most rural communities could not rely on draft animals or manure fertilizers.

---

[2]   Irregular rainfall could still play havoc with the cotton crop, as it did in Macomia in 1948–49, when the rains were both late and short and cotton production plummeted (Bravo, *Cultura Algodoeira*, 144).

[3]   Bravo, *Cultura Algodoeira*, 141.

[4]   Ibid., 145.

[5]   Ibid., 95.

[6]   Edward Alpers, "'To Seek a Better Life': The Implications of Migration from Mozambique to Tanganyika for Class Formation and Political Behavior," *CJAS* 18, 2(1984), 372.

[7]   AIA, JEAC, "Brigada de Mogovolas," Álvaro Martins da Silva, 16 October 1951; AHM, SR, Cx. 97, ISANI, "Rel. Docs. Ref. à Insp. Ord. Feita Na Prov. do Niassa," Part 1, 1943, Carlos Henriques Jones da Silveira, 1943; Dias, *Os Macondes*, 105–106.

[8]   Group interviews, Imala State Farm, 4 May 1979; Balama, 19 July 1979; Likanganu, Macomia, 1 May 1979; interview with Nanjaia Taibo et al., Namapa, 2 May 1979.

The lack of a transportation system connecting prospective cotton producers with scattered inland markets (and these markets with coastal ports) posed additional problems for the northern cotton companies. "People in my village had to walk for several days to get to the nearest market," recalled Manuel Baptista.[9] The Niassa district, which extended over 114,000 square kilometers, had less than 1,000 kilometers of road in the 1930s.[10] Most of these roads were little more than upgraded trails, the best of which were surfaced with fine gravel. In the dry season these arteries were suitable for porterage (foot traffic), *machilas*, and rickshaws; during the rainy season, however, most of these roads were impassable. Compounding these difficulties was the shortage of trucks. Not until the 1950s was there sufficient motorized transport to link the countryside to regional markets and railroad hubs.[11]

The absence of motor transport and all-weather roads helps explain why many northern households were only partially integrated into the colonial economy before the imposition of the cotton regime. In Cabo Delgado, Niassa, and the more remote regions of Nampula, rural Makua and Makonde communities allocated most of their labor to the food economy. They cultivated sorghum, corn, manioc, peanuts, and a variety of beans, some of which they traded in local and regional markets. However, for most rural communities in the north, cash crop production and market exchanges were of only secondary importance.[12] To pay their taxes and to purchase a limited number of consumer goods (such as soap, matches, and cooking oil), many rural producers sold a portion of their agricultural surplus along with wild rubber, gum, and wax to itinerant traders or to scattered Asian and Portuguese *cantineiros* (shopkeepers).[13] In 1937 two million peasants sold only 30,000 tons of produce, less than fifteen kilograms per person, through Portuguese commercial networks.[14]

It was precisely the fact that until the 1930s a large part of the north was only minimally incorporated into the colonial economy—and therefore not contributing its share to accumulation in the metropole—that made the region so attractive for cotton production. From the perspective of the cotton companies, the north offered an opportunity to harness the labor of thousands of "idle" African men and women. Best of all, there were no mines and few European plantations to compete for prospective workers after the demise of German-owned coastal sisal estates just prior to World War II.

Yet because most northern rural communities were not involved to a significant extent in commodity production, state officials could not lure them into the

---

[9]   Interview with Manuel Baptista, Nampula, 9 July 1991.

[10]   Manuel Correia da Silva, "Importância Económica das Principais Culturas e Meios de Transporte na Baixa Zambézia," *Primeiro Congresso de Agricultura Colonial* (Porto, 1934), 49.

[11]   Arlindo Chilundo is currently completing a Ph.D. dissertation on the impact of transportation on rural agriculture in northern Mozambique during the colonial period.

[12]   That a large portion of the rural population wore only bark cloth (*nacoto*), rather than imported textiles, is but one indication of their priorities (interview with Manuel Baptista).

[13]   Interviews with Aridhi Mahanda et al., Balama, 23 July 1979; Romeu Mataquenha, Tirani Ntuka, and Mussa Vaquina, Montepuez, 19 July 1979; Artúro Augusto Dias, Montepuez, 24 July 1979.

[14]   Bravo, *Cultura Algodoeira*, 222. This figure includes sales from the fertile central region of Zambézia where commercial production was probably higher than the adjacent northern regions. AHM, SR, Cx.77, ISANI, "Relatório da . . . Imala," vol. 3, Hortêncio Estevão de Sousa, 1948.

cotton scheme simply by persuading them to switch from another cash crop. The skeletal state apparatus in the north posed additional problems.[15] Because of inadequate transport, colonial administrators were cut off from the rural population each year during the rainy season;[16] even during the remainder of the year, it took them a long time to travel from place to place. Manuel Baptista described the manner in which African chiefs and white officials were often forced to travel before jeeps became commonplace:

> the white overseers used to be carried in *machilas* to supervise the cotton production. Whenever the chiefs wanted to go to the field to supervise or oversee the cotton production they would call eight men to carry the *machilas*. They were divided into two teams of four men each. When the first four became tired, they were immediately relieved by the other four, and so on. [17]

Thus they were effectively unable to oversee what peasants were doing on a day-to-day basis.

Nevertheless, the dramatic increase in cotton production between 1939 and 1951 suggests that the state-concessionary alliance did manage to gain a measure of control over rural producers in the north. Four interrelated factors help to explain both this sharp jump in output and the distinctive character of cotton production in northern Mozambique: (1) the commitment of the concessionary firms to promoting cotton above all other activities, (2) the vast territorial expanse of company holdings, (3) the large number of peasants whom the companies managed to incorporate into the cotton scheme, and (4) the regime's definition of the conjugal work team as the predominant unit of cotton production.

In Chapter 2, I noted that the financial success of the three largest northern firms—CAM, SAGAL, and SAN—depended entirely on their ability to maximize cotton output. Only João Ferreira dos Santos, a fairly small northern firm, engaged in other commercial pursuits. The commitment of northern concessionary companies to cotton was matched by the aggressiveness with which they staked their claims to land. Two of the firms, CAM and SAGAL, expanded their existing territorial base, while SAN and João Ferriera dos Santos each carved out new lands for cotton production; competition among the firms for the best available cotton lands was often fierce. In 1938 SAGAL actively lobbied the colonial government in order to block SAN from acquiring any concessions in the north.[18] One year later, SAGAL attempted to thwart João Ferreira dos Santos's claim to the area of Cumba and Mahua, holding that the region had been part of SAGAL's original concession.[19] The Cotton Board rejected SAGAL's arguments in both cases.

By the early 1940s, the four concessionary companies had managed to carve up much of the north. Only the most remote and least populated portions of Niassa

---

[15]   Large parts of Mozambique's Niassa and Cabo Delgado districts had remained outside formal Portuguese control until the period from 1910 to 1920. Throughout the next two decades Lisbon made some futile gestures to bolster its authority, but in many areas state power was nominal at best.

[16]   For a general description of the rural administrative system, see Allen and Barbara Isaacman, *Mozambique: From Colonialism to Revolution, 1900–1982* (Boulder, 1983), 28–38.

[17]   Interview with Manuel Baptista.

[18]   AIA, JEAC, SAN, 39/181, J. Figuerido, 9 September 1938.

[19]   AIA, JEAC, SAN, 39/181, 1940.

remained totally outside their grasp. CAM, the largest of these giants, enjoyed a virtual monopoly over most of the Nampula province, the prime cotton region. Altogether CAM acquired twenty-three northern cotton zones, putting 100,000 hectares under cultivation. Although their holdings were not quite as large as CAM's, SAGAL and SAN each had substantial domains that dwarfed almost all of their cotton rivals to the south (see Map 4).

The territorial reach of the northern companies compensated for the region's low population. The more land brought into the cotton regime, the greater the number of potential cotton growers. The number of northern producers, estimated at under 80,000 before the imposition of the revitalized cotton regime, skyrocketed to almost 350,000 by 1940, almost 37 percent of the eligible population.[20] By 1945, nearly 450,000 northerners had been inscribed in the system. A government report completed in 1945 calculated that 63 percent of the eligible population in Montepuez had planted cotton in the preceding year, up from 31 percent in 1940. Marrupa had the second highest rate at almost 55 percent.[21] According to one senior inspector, the north "is the Mozambican cotton province par excellence."[22]

The high percentage of cotton growers reflects the fact that both men and women cultivated the staple throughout the north. After the imposition of the cotton scheme, northern cultivators lost much of the room they had had for negotiating their labor responsibilities. Husband-and-wife work teams laboring on conjugal plots became by law the unit of production under the cotton scheme. In areas as diverse as the rich cotton zone of Mogovolas and the marginal Makonde highlands, these conjugal teams initially constituted 90 percent of the cotton labor force.[23] The legal statutes and the imperative to maximize cotton output meant that men as well as women were required to get on their hands and knees to clean, thin, and weed the cotton plants. Although some men no doubt tried to evade these "feminine" tasks, the intense, if sporadic, pressure exerted on them by the regime took its toll.[24] Paulo Roque, an African overseer, was emphatic on this point: "We made sure that both husbands and wives cleaned the field and eliminated the weeds that threatened to strangle the cotton. No adult was exempt."[25] Cotton transformed the peasant labor process and the existing gender division of labor.

Even within the same region the experiences of individual cotton growers were often quite different. Consider the testimonies of Rosa Maria Ernesto, Nanjai Tiabo, and Maria Pera. Their firsthand accounts highlight the most salient features of the cotton regime in ways that capture the human drama and the stresses of daily life. For all the similarities in their personal narratives, there are also important varia-

---

[20] According to the 1940 census, the adult population in the north between the ages of twenty and fifty–five was 905,606. Col. da Moç., RTE, *Censo da População em 1940* (Lourenço Marques, 1942).

[21] AIA, JEAC, João Contreiras, Insp. dos SAU, May 1945.

[22] Ibid.

[23] AIA, JEAC, "Rel. Sobre a Campanha de 1944–1945 na Circ. de Mogovolas," João Esteves de Souza, 12 March 1946; AIA, JEAC, 601/8, Sec. do P.A. do Eráti, 2 November 1945; AHM, SR, Cx. 97, Prov. do Niassa, ISANI, "Relatórios . . . Niassa," Part 2, Capitão Carlos Henriques Jones da Silveira, Insp. Admin., 1944; AHM, Cx. 77, ISANI, "Relatório . . . Nampula," vol. 3, Hortêncio Estevão de Sousa, 1948.

[24] AIA, JEAC, Del. de Moç., BT de Cabo Delgado, "Rel. a Que se Refere a Nota No. 1. 615/0/625/53 Campanha de 1952/53," Vasco de Sousa da Fonseca Libre, Reg. Ag., n.d.

[25] Interview with Paulo Roque, Nampula, 27 May 1987.

tions in emphasis that reflect the gender and age of each speaker, as well as their respective positions within the cotton regime.

Rosa Maria Ernesto was born in Namapa and was the regional secretary for the Organização da Mulher Moçambicana (Mozambican Women's Movement, or OMM) at the time she was interviewed. Rosa was a soft-spoken but determined woman:

> I and the other women in my village left for our cotton fields early in the morning at about six and worked there until midday. The work of cotton was very difficult. Even when I was pregnant I had to hoe the fields and pick the cotton. When I returned home there was no food for my children. So I had to fetch water, gather wood, and cook. I also did all the other household chores. The following day was more of the same. We women never had a chance to rest, never.[26]

Rosa was fortunate in one respect. Through a combination of fortuitous circumstances, her husband managed to avoid both *chibalo* and forced labor on the European sisal estates. As a result Rosa and her husband worked side by side in the cotton fields and performed the same tasks, except that her husband alone chopped the trees and cleared the stumps to prepare the fields for planting.

Rosa and her husband had four children. When each of the children was an infant Rosa labored in the the field with the young one tied onto her back. When the children reached about two years of age Rosa placed them in a piece of cloth that she tied to the branches of a nearby tree. This arrangement eased the physical burden but not the emotional strain. Rosa was always afraid that the overseer or *sipai* would catch her feeding her baby or looking after the older children and punish her. By the time they were seven or eight, Rosa's children were already helping to plant the cotton crop and to keep it clean.

For Rosa and the other women of Namapa, cotton was their mandated task. There were no exemptions, not even for women in the final weeks of pregnancy.

> As you know pregnant women tire easily. . . . But we were forced to clear the fields, work them daily, and even pick the cotton. Weeding was very demanding and we had to do it four times. It was very difficult to remain on our feet for more than an hour or two at a time, but we had to work for five or six hours. We worked right up until we gave birth. We were allowed to rest for a week. Then we had to begin again.[27]

This work regime had potentially dire consequences for both the mother and the fetus she was carrying. Rosa noted that "there were a number of women who had miscarriages in the field."[28] The physical demands made of female cotton growers as well as their poor diets probably helps explain the high level of infant mortality, although detailed comparisons with noncotton regions need to be made before any causal connections can be firmly established.[29] It certainly makes

---

[26] Interview with Rosa Maria Ernesto, Nampula, 11 July 1991.

[27] Ibid.

[28] Ibid.

[29] One study indicated that over 25 percent of all children died before age five. Gillian Walt and Angela Melamed, *Mozambique: Toward a People's Health Service* (London, 1983), 2. See also Carlos Santos Reis, *A Nutrição no Ultramar Português*, vol. 2 (Lisbon, 1973), 187–218; Allison Butler Herrick et al., *Area Handbook for Mozambique* (Washington, 1969), 120.

comprehensible the sense of exhaustion that pervaded the testimonies of these women as they spoke about their experiences under the cotton regime.

That Rosa and her neighbors suffered is beyond doubt, but they adapted creatively to the exigencies of the cotton regime (see Chapter 9). Their unwillingness to rely on the state-mandated conjugal work team as the exclusive unit of production is just one example; Namapa growers drew instead on a broader pool of labor from both within and outside their households. In Rosa's case not only was the labor of her children significant, but so were the contributions of members of her matrilineage and of other neighbors. Rosa and others in her community organized labor exchanges to help alleviate the burdens of cotton: "If a neighbor's cotton field had a particularly large number of weeds, several families would work all day to remove them. The following day they would move to another field."[30] In doing so they drew on deeply held cultural notions and historical practices.

The men of Namapa found cotton a terrible burden as well. But Nanjaia Taibo and his colleagues told a somewhat different story. For them, growing cotton was the lesser of two evils; it was not nearly as objectionable as being forced to work for low wages and in terrible labor conditions on European farms or sisal plantations. The "peasant option," even the cotton option, was preferable to plantation labor. But in the gendered labor structure of colonial Mozambique, the men often did not have this option.

Nanjaia remembered that cotton was introduced gradually into Namapa. At first it was only cultivated on plots belonging to village headmen and chiefs. "They were forced to grow it, but they did not do the actual work. We did." Nanjaia explained that villagers worked on the chief's land in small groups for several days, after which another group would replace them. "We did not even earn a *quinhenta* [a penny] for our labor."[31] After the first year the local administrator decided that Nanjaia and all his neighbors should plant cotton on their own individual plots:

> The *chefe de posto* called us together and told us we had to grow cotton. We followed his instructions. But at the end of the season we almost had nothing. We did not want to plant it anymore. But we were forced. We worked in the fields from early in the morning to five in the afternoon. We were beaten often. We suffered a great deal; it was not a joke.[32]

Nanjaia worked in the cotton field and had very little money to show for his labor. "It was hardly enough to pay the taxes and certainly not enough to buy clothing for our wives."[33]

But worse than working cotton was laboring on the sisal plantations or as *chibalo* laborers on the growing number of European farms and public works projects initiated in the post–World War II period. In the immediate aftermath of the war, the international demand for sisal grew rapidly, pumping new life into the moribund northern plantations. When local labor proved insufficient, European planters began to cast their nets wider. Nanjaia was unable to escape:

---

[30] Interview with Rosa Maria Ernesto.

[31] Interview with Nanjaia Taibo et al., Namapa, 2 May 1979.

[32] Ibid.

[33] Ibid.

The owner of the [Namialo] sisal estate went to Cardoso [the local administrator] and offered him a great deal of money. The administrator then sent out his police. They came to our houses and seized us. Many men in the village were sold. I was forced to work on the sisal plantations three different times. Each time was for six months.[34]

Nanjaia and his colleagues were press-ganged into service. *Sipais* and labor recruiters often raided their villages in the dead of night. During the postwar sisal boom the number of peasants working on the estates jumped from 17,000 in 1946 to more than 28,000 by 1951.[35] Men who failed to pay their taxes, who were found guilty of minor offenses, who defied the regulation of the cotton regime, or who were simply at the wrong place at the wrong time all ended up on the sisal estates.[36]

The journey to the Namialo sisal plantations was arduous. Nanjaia and the other "recruits" were bound together with their hands tied, to prevent them from trying to escape.[37] Work on the sisal plantations was equally gruelling. As in Tanganyika's *kipande* system,[38] on which the sisal plantations were modeled, the conscripts received an assigned task that had to be completed by the end of the day. If they failed to complete their tasks, their production cards were not marked, and the day did not "count" toward meeting their six-month work obligation. A labor inspector reported that some inexperienced conscripts did not even "stop to eat, fearing that they would be beaten and their cards would not be marked."[39]

To keep costs low, the management of the Namialo plantation provided the minimum amount of food required by colonial law. For breakfast workers received a small amount of porridge, which was served again for lunch and dinner (sometimes with a bit of dried fish as relish).[40] Wages were no better. Conscripted laborers in the early 1940s received thirty *escudos* (just over U.S. $1) per month.[41] Salaries doubled by the end of the decade, when Nanjaia was working on the sisal estates. About a third of this sum was withheld for taxes, and nearly thirty *escudos* were discounted to cover the cost of an identity card, travel documents, and the *imposto de estrada* (road tax).[42] If Nanjaia and his village mates were lucky, they brought home 200 *escudos* each (approximately U.S. $7.50), less than what the average cotton grower earned at the time.[43] Given the coercive recruitment, the harsh working

---

[34]   Ibid.

[35]   Álvaro Navarro Soeiro and Francisco Manuel Fernandes, "O Sisal de Moçambique," *Assembleia Técnica da Associação dos Produtores de Sisal da Prov. de Moçambique XIII* (Braga, 1961), 59; Associação dos Produtores de Sisal de Moçambique, IV Assemblia, *Relatório de Direcçao* (Braga, 1951).

[36]   Interview with Paulo Roque.

[37]   Interview with Nanjaia Taibo et al.

[38]   For the *kipande* system, see Walter Rodney, Kapepwa Tambila, and Laurent Sago, *Migrant Labour in Tanzania During the Colonial Period* (Hamburg, 1983), 44–46.

[39]   AHM, SR, Cx. 39, ISANI, "Relatório . . . do Niassa, 1ª parte, 1943," Carlos Henriques Jones de Oliveria, n.d.

[40]   Interview with Nanjaio Taibo et al.

[41]   Ibid.

[42]   AHM, SR, Cx. 39, ISANI, "Relatório . . . do Niassa, 1ª parte, 1943," Carlos Henriques Jones da Oliveira, n.d.

[43]   In 1949 the average producer in Imala received 430 *escudos* (Bravo, *Cultura Algodoeira*, 154).

conditions, the low wages, and the fact that cutting the sharp prickly plant caused numerous injuries, it is little wonder that northern men preferred cotton, despite its arduousness.

Children also suffered the indignities of cotton. In a brief interview, Maria Pera of Murrupula (200 kilometers south of Namapa) recalled that even at five or six years of age she worked side by side with her parents. She seeded and weeded and even picked the cotton. By the time Maria was thirteen she had already worked for several years in her parents' field and had mastered all aspects of cotton production. It was at this time, in the late 1940s, that colonial authorities, searching for new sources of African labor, began to urge teenagers to open their own cotton fields.[44] For teenagers, particularly boys who were eager to get out of their parents' grip or to accumulate capital with which to acquire a wife, this colonial initiative had some appeal. Maria was more reluctant, since it meant more work as well as being subjected to harassment and intimidation. Her parents, however, put a lot of pressure on her: "They told me that it was necessary for the family to survive."[45]

Like other young people her age, Maria received a half-hectare plot. These plots were located in the same general area, making it easier for Maria and her friends to work together. In much the same way as their parents, teenagers quickly learned that labor exchanges were an easy and effective mechanism to cope with the demands of cotton. Sometimes they received help from older single women. With the assistance of her friends Maria managed to chop trees and remove heavy stumps—work customarily done by men. After the harvest she carried her cotton crop to market. Maria gave most of the money she earned to her parents but kept enough to buy two lengths of cloth for herself.

Maria cultivated her own cotton field for two years. During this period she rarely assisted her parents but continued to work with other teenagers. Later she married and registered in the system under the name of her husband. Even though both Maria and her husband labored in the field, it was her husband who received the cotton income, a common arrangement throughout colonial Mozambique. Maria ended her brief story by noting that she and her husband were made to cultivate cotton until 1961, when the state abolished forced cotton production. The recurring theme that runs through her brief narrative is that throughout her formative years, Maria was forced to grow cotton while her parents, her husband, and the concessionary company were the ones who benefited from her labor.

The accounts of Nanjaia Tiabo and Maria Pera suggest some of the ways in which, in the post–World War II period, the northern cotton regime began to take a somewhat different shape. On the one hand, the Cotton Board began to drop some marginal cotton zones and to organize planned communities in an effort to rationalize cotton production (see Chapter 6). On the other hand, the resurgence of the moribund sisal industry, the increased number of settler farms, and a major expansion of state programs to build all-weather roads, bridges, and railroads led to a gradual feminization of cotton production. Whereas in the early years of the regime men and women worked side by side in the cotton fields, many northern families were forced to send husbands and older sons to colonial plantations, European farms, and government public works projects. In 1948, approximately 5,000

---

[44] Geffray and Pedersen, *Transformação da Organização*, 61–62.
[45] Ibid.

of the 5,300 able-bodied men in Malema were compelled to work on tobacco farms in Ribáuè, while in the circumscription of António Enes more than 80 percent of the 24,000 male residents had to work on European plantations.[46] More and more cotton zones were drawn into this migrant labor system over the next decade. This increasingly left women, teenagers, and children shouldering the burdens of cotton. In this respect the organization of work in the north began to resemble the situation in central Mozambique.

Cotton and the Plantation Economy of Central Mozambique

What distinguished central Mozambique from the north were the robust plantations that had long dominated the regional economy. The plantation sector was located primarily on the northern side of the Zambézi River, the great winding waterway that roughly bisects Mozambique and flows into the Indian Ocean (see Map 1). On the northern bank of the river's mouth were the vast holdings of Sena Sugar Company. Along the Indian Ocean coast the Bororo Company and the Madal Society organized some of the world's largest copra plantations around the turn of the century, and European companies established a number of tea plantations in the Milange-Gurué highlands in the late 1920s. South of the Zambézi, the Buzi Company operated a large plantation complex near Beira. Many Portuguese, British, and Greek settlers also had sizeable estates in the Manica highlands.

This vibrant plantation economy required a substantial amount of male labor. The tea industry alone employed more than 25,000 African workers.[47] Because of the low wages and difficult living and working conditions, neither the plantations nor the farms could rely on voluntary labor. Indeed, company officials and planters preferred conscripted migrant laborers because they were "cheaper" and there was no chance they would slip off to work in their own gardens. Companies competed fiercely for workers but were able, with the aid of state, to keep African wages low.[48] By 1938, more than 28 percent of the productive male population of Zambézia worked on the plantations.[49] Most of these were conscripts. To avoid the harsh world of the foreign-owned plantations, thousands of rural Mozambican men migrated to Nyasaland and Southern Rhodesia, where salaries and working conditions were appreciably better.[50]

---

[46]   AHM, SR, Cx. 77, ISANI, "Relatório . . . de Nampula," Hortêncio Estevão de Sousa, 1949.

[47]   Vail and White, Capitalism and Colonialism, 272.

[48]   Ibid.; AIA, JEAC, 601/8, José Maria Marques da Cunha to Admin. de Cheringoma, 7 December 1945.

[49]   AHM, SR, Cx. 62, ISANI, "Relatórios . . . Zambeze e Respectivos P.A.s, 1944," José Francisco Rodrigues, 1944.

[50]   A British district officer in Malawi noted in 1934 that the heavy flow of migrants was not only due to forced labor but to the fact that taxes were seven times higher in Mozambique. Malawi National Archive (MNA), LSDB, E. Lawrence, District Agricultural Officer, Zambia, to Director of Agriculture, 30 January 1934, found in A3/2/65. AIA, JEAC, Prov. de Manica e Sofala, João Contreiras, Insp. dos SAU, May 1945; Wiseman Chirwa, "Nyasaland's Labor Sources and the Anguru/Lomwe Immigration 1890–1945," IJAHS 27, 3 (1994), 525-50. The 1936 census listed 25,215 Mozambicans employed in Southern Rhodesia. This figure does not include the large number who illegally crossed the frontier and were not formally registered. Southern Rhodesia Census 1901–1936 (Salisbury).

In addition to the high rate of male absenteeism in this region, environmental factors made cotton production in central Mozambique somewhat more problematic than in the north. Much of the region was not particularly well suited for cotton. In some areas, such as Alto Molócuè, Ile, Gurue, Espungabera, and Furancungo, summer temperatures were well below the optimal range for cotton.[51] But the principal obstacle, as previously noted, was excessive rainfall, which often rotted the roots of the cotton plants. In riverine areas flooding was also a serious problem.

The distribution of cotton concessions across central Mozambique was also more uneven than in the north. Much of Zambézia was divided among five concessionary companies (see Map 4). By contrast, investors showed no interest in large portions of Tete and Manica e Sofala, which remained outside the cotton regime. This uneven distribution of concessions created sharp variations in the number of peasants enmeshed in the cotton scheme. In Zambézia, 185,000 peasants were planting cotton by 1944, compared to only 45,000 in Manica e Sofala and half that figure in Tete.[52] There were also noticeable differences within each district in the proportion of the eligible population who actually cultivated the fiber. The 1944 figure in Zambézia ranged from under 9 percent in Chinde to almost 34 percent in Pebane, while in Manica e Sofala the number varied between 10 and 28 percent of the population.[53] For central Mozambique as a whole, the 237,000 cotton growers represented approximately half the number in the north.

However, it was the composition of the African work force rather than its size that defined the cotton regime in central Mozambique. Because the state and the concessionary companies effectively deprived rural communities of male labor, cotton responsibilities fell disproportionately to rural women. In the colonial economic blueprint, cotton production, no matter what its potential, had to be grafted on and remain subordinate to the plantation sector. The forced recruitment of male labor for the plantations continued throughout the 1940s, to the dismay of critics such as the Bishop of Beira:

> The tea plantations are veritable gardens. So beautiful, so profitable and so much work made with the blood of slaves, whose humanity is denied. The law says that there is no compulsory labor. But the reality is that all or almost all are forced to work under conditions that do not respect liberty, justice or social conveniences.[54]

A 1949 government report estimated that more than 146,000 men in Zambézia were required to work six-month contracts on the plantations. Another 15,000 were press-ganged into other activities from fishing to public works projects. Although these figures are estimates, they suggest the scale of the labor drain from rural households in this region.[55]

---

[51]   The optimal range was between 25° and 29° Celsius. The average temperature in the critical month of June was less than 19° Celsius. Azevedo, "Clima, Estudos de Alguns Factores Climáticos," 60.

[52]   Bravo, *Cultura Algodoeira*, 139; AIA, JEAC, "Áreas Cultivadas," n.d.

[53]   AIA, JEAC, "Rel. da Insp. da JEAC, 1940–1945," João Contreiras, Insp. dos SAU to Pres. da JEAC, May 1945.

[54]   Quoted in José Capela, *Escravatura: A Empresa de Saque, O Abolicionismo* (Porto, 1974), 13–14.

[55]   Vail and White, *Capitalism and Colonialism*, 305. By comparison, approximately 95,000 peasants, almost all of whom were women, cultivated cotton. A smaller but still significant number were obligated to grow rice.

Company policies reinforced this tendency to rob rural households of male labor. Unlike those in the north, five of the seven cotton companies also owned large plantations growing other products, including cotton, that required a steady supply of labort. Lopes & Irmãos, which had received a cotton concession for the Morrumbala region, also owned large cotton plantations in Mengaza and Chantego; by 1941 African workers on their plantations were producing almost one million kilograms of cotton.[56] Monteiro & Giro operated cotton plantations in addition to its cotton concession in Mocuba and Massingire. The Zambezi Company, which controlled the cotton area around Mutarara and Inhangoma, had substantial tea holdings in Guruè as well as sisal plantations at Metugo and copra plantations along the coast (Anguase, Andonde, and Bajone).[57] Sena Sugar Estates, with its cotton grants in Luabo and Mopeia, and the Búzi Company were the consummate sugar plantation companies.[58] From the outset, these five companies viewed their cotton concessions not only as a means of acquiring cheap cotton, but also as a way to block rival firms from recruiting male laborers from areas under their control. It is important to stress that the concessionary companies had different labor agendas, depending on the significance of peasant production relative to plantation output in their overall economic strategies. To some degree, every company siphoned off male labor from rural communities to work on their plantations. Max Thrunheer of Sena Sugar was perfectly blunt on this point:

> The cotton growing in this colony . . . is a forced cultivation under artificial conditions. However, one thing is sure and that is that the Company must retain its present cotton concessions while there is a government-controlled cotton scheme, profit or no profit, because on its retention depends the control of now so much needed [male] labor for our sugar plantations.[59]

The logic of bifurcating the rural African labor force along gender lines to guarantee an ample supply of male workers for the plantation sector also drove the Zambezi Company and the Búzi Company. Both organized production so that men worked on their sugar estates while "women would continue to be the most important factor of [cotton] production."[60] To help compensate for the loss of male labor, Lopes & Irmão and Monteiro & Giro pressured rural teenagers not yet old enough to be formally enrolled into the regime to grow cotton.[61]

Thus, unlike in the north, where conjugal work teams remained largely intact throughout the 1940s, in central Mozambique women often had to bear the burden of cotton production without the aid of their husbands and teenage sons, who

---

[56]   AIA, JEAC, 11/69, 1938. AIA, JEAC, "EE 1941," vol. 1, João Contreiras, n.d.

[57]   AHM, Cx. 64, ISANI, "Rel. da Insp. Extraordinária Feita à Companhia da Zambézia Sobre a Forma Como Tem Cumprido Os Seus Contratos Com o Estado, 1950," Manuel Metelle R. De Liz Texeira, Intend. de Dist., 29 August 1950.

[58]   The Búzi Company was primarily a sugar company. The CNA (National Cotton Company) was essentially a cotton concessionary company.

[59]   See SSE, File 44, "Final Cotton Report, 1941," Max Thrunheer, General Manager, 30 November 1942.

[60]   AIA, JEAC, "Conf., 1947," Dir. da Companhia Colonial do Búzi (CCB) to Del. da JEAC, 4 December 1947.

[61]   Interview with Justina Joaquim, Nicoadala, 17 July 1991; interview with Maria Fijamo, Quelimane, 19 July 1991.

worked on the plantations for much of the agricultural season. To be sure, women were only required to cultivate a half-hectare of cotton, and their daughters and younger sons often labored with them in the cotton fields.[62] Liassa Pele Lohaninté of Gilé grew cotton for a number of years.

> [Mostly] I had to work in the fields alone. I awoke very early to fetch water for the house. After that, the first job I had to do each day was fulfill the orders of the government and clean my cotton fields. In the late morning I collected some greens from my garden and cooked them for the children. I returned to the cotton fields until midafternoon. It was very difficult work.[63]

Liassa's situation was not unique. Women throughout Zambézia described similar grueling work schedules. João Contreiras, a senior Cotton Board inspector, was clear about the major obstacle impeding increased output:

> The cotton concessionaires [in Zambézia] are without productive males. Nevertheless, they mark off fields in all the localities where they find huts and distribute seeds to all the women, elders and children whom they find. They use any methods they can to acquire whatever quality cotton they can.[64]

The situation was not much different in Cheringoma and other labor-exporting zones on the southern bank of the Zambézi, where "cotton production . . . is done almost exclusively by women."[65]

Like the experiences of northern peasants, there were some striking differences in the experiences of producers across central Mozambique—the combined result of local environmental conditions, the labor policies of the different companies, and the range of coping strategies growers adopted.

Mopeia: Peasants and Sena Sugar

Mopeia was precisely the type of place where it made no sense to cultivate cotton. By the 1930s, virtually all able-bodied men and many women were already employed on Sena Sugar's plantations. The Zambézi River flooded regularly, further complicating cotton production and increasing the risks for peasant farmers.

Yet the story was more complex. Even though Sena Sugar received a concession for the Mopeia circumscription, its principal objective was not to maximize cotton output but to ensure a steady supply of male workers for its sugar estates. The intense competition for labor meant that Sena Sugar could not allow any rival cotton company to obtain the Mopeia concession, which had been an integral part of its economic empire. Nor for that matter could Sena Sugar permit a competitor to gain control over any of the territory on the northern bank of the Zambézi adjacent to its sugar fields. That would have jeopardized the company's core supply of

---

[62] Interviews with Justina Joaquin; Líguene Alberto, Nicoadala/Namacurra, 17 July 1991; Augusto António, Nicoadala/Morrumbala, 18 July 1991.

[63] Interview with Armando Nicula, Liassa Lohaninteve, and Murinvona Mpemo, Centro Piloto de Deslocados, Nampula/Gilé, 8 July 1990.

[64] AIA, JEAC, "Prov. da Zambézia," João Contreiras, Insp. dos SAU, May 1945.

[65] AIA, JEAC, 601/8, José Maria Marques da Cunha, Admin. de Cheringoma, 7 December 1945.

labor and given peasants the option of cultivating cotton on their own. Company officials remained preoccupied with this threat to their labor supply throughout the life of the cotton regime.[66] Likewise, if a rival company siphoned off workers by offering slightly higher wages or if it entered into a labor agreement with one of the Sena Sugar competitors, company officials would have limited recourse. Either eventuality would have been intolerable.

Sena Sugar began cotton operations in 1936, converting an old sugar factory at Mopeia into a ginning mill. The Mopeia cotton campaign began in a fairly chaotic way. Fields were not marked, nor was there a sustained campaign to discuss the purported benefits of cotton. Peasants were simply ordered to plant the seeds that company officials distributed.[67]

Despite Sena Sugar's disinterest in cotton, the extent to which it intervened to shape the composition of the peasant labor force was unprecedented. While other concessionary companies tried to restructure the organization of the rural work force, only Sena Sugar explicitly prohibited men from cultivating cotton. This restrictive policy angered many state officials, who unsuccessfully pressured the management of Sena Sugar to reverse its policy. But company spokesmen insisted that they had no alternative, given the fierce competition for labor and the reluctance of African men to work on the sugar plantations. Max Thurnheer, Sena Sugar's general manager, was adamant on this issue:

> We again and again stressed our policy of distribution of seed to women only as a good one and assuring us of the male population for labour needs in other directions. . . . This control which we now have and exercise in our cotton concession area must always be retained by us and exploited to the full.[68]

Sena Sugar maintained this gendered division of labor throughout the duration of the cotton regime. While many conscripted male workers cultivated the cotton fields with their wives when they returned home, the women and children in this area bore the brunt of the cotton regime. A group of male laborers recalled:

> The men went to work for the company and the women remained alone to grow cotton. They were responsible for every aspect from receiving the seeds to treating the land, collecting the harvest, and selling it at the market. On many occasions they were beaten because they did not produce much. When we got home we aided our wives.[69]

But women in Mopeia could not take much comfort from their husband's aid, since for most it was short-lived. "Our husbands returned home after six months. They helped us in the fields so that we could also work in our food gardens. But then they had to return to the company leaving us once more without help."[70] While many men in central Mozambique returned for longer periods of time and

[66]   Vail and White, "*Tawani Machambero!*," 16–17.
[67]   Interview with Luís Alberto et al., Mopeia, 1–2 August 1976 (Head Collection).
[68]   SSE, File 44, "Final Cotton Report, Season 1942."
[69]   Group interview, Mopeia, 1–2 August 1976 (Head Collection).
[70]   Ibid.

not all "helped" in the cotton fields, the situation of the women of Mopeia was not unique.

Unfavorable ecological conditions intensified the burden of the women in this area. Located on the northern bank of the Zambezi River, Mopeia flooded almost every year. Although Sena Sugar had built earthen walls to protect its sugar fields, it made no effort to do the same for cotton growers. Thus vulnerability to flooding was determined less by the vagaries of nature than by the politics of production. Sena Sugar was not prepared to allocate scarce resources to safeguard peasant cotton output.

Mopeia's wet environment had a profound effect on the timing and organization of work. Cotton production had to be delayed for several months to minimize the adverse impact of flooding during the rainy season. Rather than distribute the seeds in November, concessionary company officials dispensed them in February. Women, aided by their children, did not begin planting until the end of March or early April. Even so they often had to reseed a second or a third time because of late torrential rains.[71] This delayed planting created the risk that their cotton would not mature by November, when all remaining cotton plants were to be destroyed to prevent the spread of diseases and parasites. Wet fields, high rainfalls, and cool weather at the end of the growing season combined to yield low-quality cotton fiber. In 1939, 1940, 1943, and 1945 vast areas were inundated by torrential rains, people were left homeless, crops were destroyed, and cotton production plummeted. In these years average yields per producer ranged from thirty to forty kilograms, less than half the typical cotton yield.[72]

Even without major flooding, cotton productivity and income were quite low. In 1946, 8,500 peasants in Mopeia produced approximately 635 tons, or slightly less than seventy-five kilograms per grower. Average income per capita was ninety-one *escudos* (about U.S. $3.65), somewhat higher than the norm for the decade but still 25 percent below the paltry national average.[73] Only when precipitation was below normal and flooding was not a serious problem did growers earn even enough to pay their taxes.

Throughout the 1940s, Sena Sugar maintained its cotton concession as a way of ensuring male laborers for its other interests, and company officials in general remained convinced that cotton would never prove very profitable. Those who suffered most were the female growers. Given the low price, the opportunity costs of growing cotton instead of food or other cash crops were immense. In 1950 female cotton growers were earning 139 *escudos* (less than U.S. $5).[74] Their husbands' minimal wages, less than sixty *escudos* per month, did little to alleviate this production crisis. What was at stake was their capacity to maintain the daily as well as the intergenerational life of the household.

---

[71]   See, for example, SSE, File 44, "Annual Cotton Report, 1939," 27 March 1940; AIA, JEAC, "Rel. da Insp. de JEAC, 1940," João Contreiras, Adj. da Del. JEAC to Pres. de JEAC, 31 January 1941; SSE, File 44, "Annual Cotton Report, 1943"; AIA, JEAC, AT, 9352, "Boletim de Informação 1946/47: SSE."

[72]   Bravo, *Cultura Algodoeira*, 172.

[73]   In 1946 the average cotton income for growers in northern and central Mozambique was 114 *escudos*; ibid., 114.

[74]   Ibid., 172.

Alto Molócuè: Cotton Producers on CAM's Holdings

The living and working conditions of cotton producers in Alto Molócuè[75] were not quite as precarious as in Mopeia. The environment was not ideal for cotton, but it was certainly less hostile. More often than not, husband and wives were able to farm together, since CAM, unlike Sena Sugar, did not operate plantations and was therefore committed to maximizing cotton production. If the tyranny of the cotton regime proved too great, there was always the possibility of fleeing to nearby Nyasaland, an option that peasants in the heavily policed and centrally located Sena Sugar holdings could not as easily utilize (see Chapter 10).

At first glance, Alto Molócuè looked suitable for cotton production. A number of European planters had cultivated it in the 1930s, and cotton seemed to be suited to local environmental conditions. The average summer temperature of 25° Celsius fell well within the optimal range, and there was plenty of suitable land.[76] The main threat, as in other regions, was excessive rainfall. Average annual precipitation in Alto Molócuè was almost 1,450 millimeters, significantly higher than the plant could tolerate. In the 1942–43 and 1945–46 campaigns, rainfall actually approached 2,000 millimeters, with disastrous consequences for cotton (see Table 3–1). This moist environment also spawned a number of cotton-killing pests. In 1940 and again in 1945 these parasites destroyed most of the crop.[77]

Local ecological conditions, however, did not deter CAM. As in northern Mozambique, the company's principal objective was to acquire as much cheap cotton as possible. Thus, even marginal areas offered possibilities. Furthermore, the Alto Molócuè region straddled valuable CAM holdings in the Nampula district. CAM officials were concerned that peasants would flee south into Alto Molócuè, if it remained a free zone, in order to avoid forced cotton cultivation in Nampula. By taking out the Alto Molócuè concession as well as concessions for the less fertile circumscriptions of Ile and Namarrói, CAM effectively closed off this escape route. In the words of one skeptical official, "The strategy of attempting to lock the peasants on their land by encircling them is similar to convincing a prison inmate that he enjoys being incarcerated by keeping him perpetually in prison."[78]

The story of cotton in Alto Molócuè is a story of two struggles. One struggle pitted the state and company officials against peasants who quickly came to realize that cotton was hard work, fairly risky, and not terribly rewarding. For Murinvona Mpemo, life under the cotton regime was little more than performing one task after another:

> When I woke up, it was dark. Before going to my cotton field I had to fetch water. As soon as I returned home, I had to pound manioc so that it could be made into porridge. I left my oldest daughter in charge of this task. I then went directly to the field for fear of being late. I spent the

---

[75] Included in this discussion is the adjacent region of Gilé.

[76] Interview with Sabine Joni et al., Gilé, 14–15 July 1976 (Head Collection). See also Pedro, "A Fito Ecologia."

[77] AIA, JEAC, Rel. An., "Rel. da Sub–Del. da Zambézia," José da Cunha Dias Mendes, 31 December 1940; AIA, JEAC, 601/8, "Rel.," José Manuel da Silva, Admin. de Alto Molócuè, 26 January 1946.

[78] AIA, JEAC, "Prov. da Zambézia," João Contreiras, Insp. dos SAU, May 1945.

entire morning weeding cotton. Only in the afternoon could I go to my garden, which was far from the cotton field. I was only able to spend a short time there because I had to return home to gather wood and prepare [food] for my children. After eating I went to bed exhausted.[79]

Cotton output per producer in Alto Molócuè was somewhat higher than in Mopeia between 1940 and 1947, but considerably lower than in the drier regions to the north. Average income was roughly one hundred *escudos* per capita here (about U.S. $4); however, in the worst years peasants earned only one-third that amount.[80]

The second struggle in Alto Molócuè took place between CAM and the plantation companies that had historically recruited large numbers of workers in this area. CAM waged a vigorous campaign to block rival companies from conscripting African laborers from its territory. In this respect, CAM's interests were nearly identical to the interests of most peasants, who preferred growing cotton to working on the plantations. Armando Nicula remembered, "After working at Gurué [tea estates], we came home with almost nothing. While here, we could earn some money from our cotton, and we could still grow other crops. As a result we preferred cotton." Murinvona Mpemo, whose husband was forced to work at Sena Sugar, echoed this view: "He earned more when he was at home and worked cotton."[81] Other conscripts stressed the harsh treatment and poor working conditions on the plantations, especially the tea plantations.[82]

Despite its efforts, CAM was unable to block its plantation rivals. Located in the heart of Zambézia, Alto Molócuè had been a major labor reserve for Sena Sugar and the tea estates at Gurué before the introduction of cotton, and it continued to be so afterward. The proportion of the total population in Alto Molócuè who were cultivating cotton declined from 40 percent in 1940 to 30 percent in 1944. Out of one group of twenty-two men interviewed by British researcher Judith Head, seventeen had worked one contract or more on the sugar plantations and six had also labored on the tea plantations. The remainder had had at least one stint on the cotton plantations of Lopes & Irmão, the Bororo copra estates, the coastal sisal plantations, or European tobacco and corn farms. While most of these men were forced to work between two and four six-month contracts, others, such as Alberto Mamalivo, had been conscripted eleven times.[83] A confidential 1943 Cotton Board memorandum suggested that the collective labor history of this group was not atypical. The author complained "about the systematic depopulation of entire regions owing to orders transmitted from the highest levels of government to local administrators requiring them to assist the sugar, tea, copra, sisal and corn plantations to acquire the necessary labor so that they can continue to develop."[84] The state and the concessionary companies wanted cotton, but the plantation sector that had long anchored the region's economy remained preeminent.

---

[79]   Interview with Armando Nicula et al.

[80]   Bravo, *Cultura Algodoeira*, 166.

[81]   Interview with Armando Nicula et al.

[82]   Interview with Manuel Nuitha and Rudolfo Churupa, Nampula/Gilé, 11 July 1991.

[83]   Group interview, Gilé, 7–8 July 1976 (Head Collection).

[84]   AIA, JEAC, "Prov. de Zambézia," João Contreiras, Insp. dos SAU, May 1945.

Morrumbala: Peasants and Lopes & Irmao

In most parts of central Mozambique, cotton brought impoverishment for most peasants. Only in rare cases were growers able to eke out a living or actually to prosper from cotton. The circumscription of Morrumbala was just such a case. A combination of factors made Morrumbala unique. Many peasants in the region had cultivated cotton long before the imposition of the forced cotton regime in 1938, working as agricultural laborers on African-owned farms in the Shire Valley of Nyasaland during the golden age of peasant cotton there (1920–1939).[85] There they witnessed the prosperity cotton had brought to enterprising African farmers.[86] Some of these migrants subsequently acquired cotton land or became tenant farmers on European estates in Nyasaland.[87] When the permanent inundation of the flood plains sharply curtailed cotton production in Nyasaland, many returned home to Morrumbala and, in the words of one British official, "now grow cotton in [Portuguese East Africa] and receive a higher price than they did in Nyasaland in 1938."[88] Thus, for at least a portion of the population, cotton was an attractive option.

Furthermore, growing cotton offered the possibility of protecting peasants from contract labor. Morrumbala had been a major labor reserve for the Zambézia Company's plantations and for Sena Sugar's estates.[89] Among the first actions Lopes & Irmão took after acquiring its cotton concession there in 1936 was to block rival labor recruiters. It sent its agents throughout the countryside informing Africans that "no one would ever again have to work for Sena Sugar since the Governor of the Province has decided that they could cultivate cotton."[90]

Lopes & Irmão's defense of the "peasant option" was well received by the rural population. "We preferred cotton," agreed a number of elders. "The money we earned from Sena Sugar was hardly enough to pay our taxes."[91] While local administrators continued to send Africans who failed to meet their cotton requirements to Sena Sugar or the tea or sisal plantations,[92] and while Lopes & Irmão drafted some men for its own cotton estates,[93] most men in Morrumbala worked cotton with their families.[94] In 1938 approximately 2,400 men out of an eligible population of 11,500 were conscripted. Five years later this ratio had increased somewhat, but it still remained far below those of major labor-exporting zones such as

---

[85]   MNA, Chikwawa District, Annual Report for 1931, NSC 2/1/3; MNA, Chikwawa District AAR, S1/66B/37; MNA, LSBD, PHDAR for 1935 S1/79A/36.

[86]   For a discussion of cotton production during the golden age in Malawi, see Mandala, *Work and Control*, 133–60.

[87]   MNA, Chikwawa District, Annual Report for 1931, NSC 2/1/3; MNA, Chikwawa District AAR, S1/66B/37; MNA, LSBD, PHDAR for 1935 S1/79A/36.

[88]   MNA, LSDB, PHDAR for 1938, NNSP2/1/7.

[89]   Interview with Sajene Kwalima et al., Morrumbala, 30 July 1976 (Head Collection).

[90]   SSE, File 133, "Recruiting Quelimane and Angónia (1930–1939)," Pinto Basto to Manager SSE, Mopeia, 16 April 1936.

[91]   Interview with Joaquim Nsaio et al., Morrumbala, 16 July 1991.

[92]   Interviews with Semble Roldão et al., Nicoadala/Morrumbala, 16 July 1991; Maria Sindique et al., Nicoadala/Morrumbala, 18 July 1991.

[93]   Interview with Fássimo Sangoma, Nicoadala/Namacurra, 18 July 1991.

[94]   Interviews with Colina Kapucha, 18 July 1991; Jaime José Rodrigues da Costa, Quelimane, 19 July 1991.

TABLE 4–3 Number of Men Contracted from Zambézia Cotton Zones

Circumscription	1938			1943		
	Total	By state	By private sector	Total	By state	By private sector
Chinde	15,354	86	5,415	15,280	121	3,443
Ile	16,434	—	44,369	13,296	523	9,048
Lugela	10,300	—	4,114	10,212	—	5,475
Nhamarrói	11,609	20	4,477	8,043	146	4,207
Morrumbala	11,498	27	2,470	18,403	251	4,260

Source: AHM, SR, Cx. 62, ISANI, "Relatórios e Documentos Referentes à Inspecção Ordinária Feitas aos Concelho de Quelimane, e Chinde, as Circunscrições de Gurue, Ile, Lugela, Massingire, Milange Namarrói, Zambeze e Respectivos Postos Administrativos, 1944," José Francisco Rodrigues, 1944.

Ile, Nhamarrói, and Lugela (see Table 4–3). Husband-and-wife work teams that remained intact in Morrumbala were able to cope somewhat better with the conflicting demands of food and cotton production than were single women. Semble Roldão recalled how.

> The men took primary responsibility for the cotton fields and the women for maize and manioc. We would work very hard in the cotton fields so that we would finish early and still have time to help our wives in the food gardens. But we had to be very careful because, if the cotton fields were not finished, we would be sent off as contract laborers.[95]

Of course, the advantages that intact households enjoyed were only relative and, as Roldão stressed, could be eliminated at any moment.

Favorable environmental conditions further reduced the risks of cotton production and increased local interest. Unlike the clay earth of Alto Molócuè, the red savanna soils common to most of Morrumbala were conducive to cotton cultivation. Climatic conditions were almost optimal (see Table 3–2).[96] The only problematic area in Morrumbala was the east bank of the Shire River, where periodic floods and pest infestations threatened cotton production.[97] But Lopes & Irmão, unlike Sena Sugar, agreed to withdraw this vulnerable riverine area from the cotton scheme after the 1945 campaign.[98] Approximately 11,000 peasants were freed from the uncertainties of cotton production as a result.

For those peasants who remained inside the system, cotton proved fairly lucrative. Cotton growers earned an average of 439 *escudos* per capita in 1947, roughly five times that of their counterparts in Alto Molócuè and Mopeia.[99] Throughout the rest of the decade peasant cotton incomes in Morrumbala were among the highest in the colony, without any of the sharp fluctuations in output that were typical elsewhere. Most elders from Morrumbala agreed that "a family with a hectare of cotton could earn good money."[100]

To argue that peasants in Morrumbala were relatively well off compared to their counterparts in Mopeia or Alto Molócuè is not to minimize the coercive nature of the regime or its deleterious impact on many aspects of rural life. Maria Fijamo stressed that the only way to minimize the risk of corporal punishment was to work harder.

> I woke up very early. It was still dark. The first thing I did was to fetch water from the river for the children who remained in the house. Only then did I get to my cotton field. . . . Normally I worked there until one or two in the afternoon, but during time when we were preparing the field I often returned home a little earlier. Afterward I returned home to take care of my youngest children, and then I went to work in our food gardens. At the end of the day I gathered wood and returned home to pound maize and prepare dinner. When we finished, I went back to the river to

---

[95] Interview with Semble Roldão et al.

[96] AHM, SR, Cx. 62, ISANI, "Relatórios . . . Zambeze e Respectivos PAs, 1944," José Francisco Rodrigues, 1944.

[97] Ibid.

[98] AIA, JEAC, "Rel. Técnico," Fonseca George, Eng. Ag., 1945.

[99] Bravo, *Cultura Algodoeira*, 173.

[100] Interviews with Semble Roldão et al.; Manuel Pinto, Quelimane, 19 July 1991; Abdul Satar.

bathe and returned home to prepare the following day's food for the children.[101]

Life was even more difficult for Maria Sindique. Her husband, unlike most of the men of Morrumbala, was regularly press-ganged by the colonial state for plantation work. He was gone four out of the eight years during which Maria grew cotton:

> My husband had two contracts at Lopes & Irmão [cotton plantations] and one at Milange [tea plantations]. He also was recruited by the Camara to work on the roads. Even when he was gone, the *capataz* ordered me to plant a cotton plot 100 by 100. He threatened to beat me with a *chicote* [hippopotamus whip] if I did not spend enough time in the field. I had little time for manioc and even less to grow beans and peanuts.[102]

In order to spare herself the arduous task of clearing the terrain, Maria tried to cope by planting cotton on lands that had been recently farmed in his absence. Because the soils of Morrumbala are quite fertile, Maria claimed that cotton output did not suffer from her shortcut. Maria remembered that in good years her family could earn 1,000 *escudos* (just under U.S. $40) or more from cotton, and there was always money to purchase food and to buy clothing for her four children. But her relative prosperity came at a cost. Maria lived in fear that the "*capataz* would discover her fields behind schedule and would grab her by the ears, pummel her, and stuff dirt into her ear lobes."[103]

Cotton and Migrant Labor in Southern Mozambique

The experience of women who lived inside the southern Mozambican labor reserve was similar to Maria's except that their spouses were regularly absent for longer stretches, working eighteen months at a time in the South African gold mines. Well before the imposition of the cotton scheme, southern Mozambique had been transformed into a labor reserve for the Rand. There was hardly a family in southern Mozambique that had not sent a father or son across the border. The Swiss missionary A. D. Clerc observed in the late 1940s that "the villages of southern Mozambique are empty of men and thousands of hectares lay fallow."[104] Typically, these labor migrants remained on the Rand for eighteen months, returned home for six, and then repeated the cycle.[105] One knowledgeable observer concluded in 1955 that "most men between the ages of seventeen and sixty, only excepting the physically and mentally handicapped, have spent more than half their adult years in the Union of South Africa."[106]

---

[101] Interview with Maria Fijamo.

[102] Interview with Maria Sindique et al.

[103] Ibid.

[104] Swiss Mission Archives (SMA), Box 194/1754 B, "Some Notes About the Agricultural Work Created by the Swiss Mission in Mozambique," A. D. Clerc, n.d. (1947–1950).

[105] For a discussion of this cycle, see First, *Black Gold*.

[106] C. E. Fuller, "An Ethnohistoric Study of Continuity and Change in Gwambe Culture" (Ph.D. thesis, Northwestern University, 1955), 148.

The outflow of male labor was only one constraint on cotton production in the south. Environmental factors were another. As previously noted, droughts and hunger occurred with frightening regularity. In 1938, the year of the new cotton regime, a widespread famine devastated the countryside. As P. W. Keys, a Protestant missionary, noted, "The whole community seems burned up by the drought. Even the very trees in the woods are almost leafless for lack of moisture."[107] These circumstances were hardly propitious for expanding cotton production.

Cotton officials recognized the potential rainfall problem, but they contended that the high quality of the red silicon clay and argyle soils in this region would compensate for the uncertain climatic conditions.[108] There were, however, two factors cotton officials overlooked in their assessment of southern Mozambique's soils. One was the slow but consistent loss of land to Portuguese settlers increasingly attracted by the fertility of the Limpopo Valley and parts of Inhambane.[109] In 1939 a senior government official complained that in Inhambane "the large-scale distribution of rural land to the settlers has had a profound effect since the settlers do not permit peasant cultivation without rent or other indemnities."[110] The second factor was the uneven quality of the soil. In sharp contrast to the Limpopo Valley, the sandy soils that stretched inland from the coast were not terribly rich, nor did they hold rainwater particularly well. Even in such highly prized districts as Zavala there were substantial variations in soil types.[111]

For both the state and company officials concerned about the limitations of hoe agriculture, the south appeared to offer another advantage: many peasants in this region were already using ox-drawn plows. In the late 1920s a small number of migrant laborers began to bring plows back with them from South Africa.[112] Miriam Paulo remembered that other farmers soon began to follow their lead:

> At first only the European farmers owned plows. Much later a few men who worked in South Africa returned home with them. Other people began to buy them in Lourenço Marques and bring them back here, still others purchased them from Portuguese merchants after shops began to open here in Manjacase.[113]

A number of Protestant missionaries also provided plowing classes as a "civilizing" accompaniment to spiritual evangelization. In 1941, colonial officials estimated that peasants in Chibuto and Bilene circumscriptions alone owned more than 5,000

---

[107] P. W. Keys, "Report of the Inhambane and Limpopo District," *Official Report of the South East African Mission Conference of the Episcopal Methodist Mission Conference* 28(1938), 69.

[108] Ibid.

[109] Sherilynn Young, "Fertility and Famine: Women's Agricultural History in Southern Mozambique," in *The Roots of Rural Poverty in Central and Southern Africa*, ed. R. Palmer and Q. N. Parsons (London, 1977), 75.

[110] AIA, JEAC, Notas Recebidas, Palma Galião, CD da JEAC, 12 May 1939.

[111] In the western parts of Zavala adjacent to the Inharrime River, the alluvial soils were quite rich. In the south and central areas the soils were sandy and of poorer quality than on the coast, which also benefited from higher rainfall. In the northern parts of the district, which was less populated, there were large heavily bushy virgin areas with high–quality land (personal communication from Arlindo Chilundo, 23 September 1992).

[112] Interview with Simone Lote Mavie, Nhanombe, 2 February 1982, Archives of the Ministry of Culture, Maputo.

[113] Interview with Miriam Paulo, Maputo, 16 May 1987.

plows.[114] The introduction of the plow coincided with a dramatic increase in the size of Africans' cattle herds, reversing a thirty-year trend.[115] Although ox-driven plows were not nearly as common in Inhambane as in Gaza,[116] colonial officials nurtured the hope that modern technology would transform the entire region into a major cotton zone.[117]

The south offered other advantages as well. Unlike vast regions of northern Mozambique, most southern peasant households were already involved in commodity production. They sold corn, beans, and peanuts at hundreds of small Asian- and European-owned *cantinas*,[118] as well as at local and regional markets.[119] Peanuts were the most important cash crop for the region as a whole, with output jumping from 11,000 to 37,000 tons between 1925 and 1936.[120] Increased commodification and the proliferation of rural shops in turn generated strong consumer demand for a variety of imported goods, particularly cloth and agricultural implements, and further monetized the economy. The challenge facing the colonial Cotton Board in the south was thus not how to bring peasants into the market, but how to ensure that peasants already producing more remunerative cash crops would shift to cotton.

The colonial regime was better able to intervene at the point of production in southern Mozambique than elsewhere because, by any measure, state power in this region was appreciably greater. Not only had this zone been occupied for a much longer period, but loyalist chiefs were more firmly entrenched.[121] Chiefs had already assumed responsibility for registering the population, controlling the movements of their subjects, recruiting large numbers of *chibalo* laborers, and collecting taxes.[122] The colonial infrastructure, although still fragile, was more highly developed here than elsewhere in the colony.

Even the recurring outflow of male migrants for eighteen months at a time did not deter cotton planners. On the contrary, Cotton Board officials argued that the absence of men had already forced women to develop "an independent spirit" that the cotton regime could exploit. Moreover, inspectors for the Department of Native

---

[114]   AIA, JEAC, Rel. An. 1939–1941, "Actividade da Sub–Del. do Sul de Save em 1940," João Contreiras, n.d.

[115]   See Harries, *Work, Culture, and Identity*, 93–94; Otto Roesch, "Socialism and Rural Development in Mozambique: The Case of Aldeia Comunal 24 de Julho" (Ph.D. thesis, University of Toronto, 1986), 37.

[116]   Most informants from Inhambane indicated that plows only became common in the 1950s. Interviews with Helena Jossias Cambane and Helena Felizmina Chirinda, Maputo, 1 August 1991; Cristina Manhique and Esmeralda Candjelo, Maputo, 6 August 1991; Gonçalo Mazungane Chilundo, Maputo, 8 August 1991.

[117]   AIA, JEAC, "Papéis Diversos 1941," J. Anachoreta to CSD do Sul do Save to Del. da JEAC, 11 September 1941.

[118]   In the first decade of the century one knowledgeable observer estimated that there were already more than two thousand *cantinas* in the Gaza province. Daniel da Cruz, *Em Terras de Gaza* (Porto, 1910), 219–20.

[119]   Ira Gillet, "Early Years in Africa" (manuscript, Milwaukee, Oregon, n.d.), 14.

[120]   Young, "Fertility and Famine," 77.

[121]   This is not to imply that the colonial state was terribly strong but only that the state apparatus was stronger than elsewhere. Even here colonial administrators remained dependent on loyalist chiefs. One of the ironies of the cotton regime is that while the state was stronger in the south, the concessionary companies were less well organized and funded.

[122]   AHM, SR, Cx. 21, ISANI, "Relatório . . . de Chibuto e Muchopes," Francisco de Melo e Costa, Insp. Admin., 1941.

Affairs, concerned about the permanent loss of African labor, believed that through cotton they could lure men back from South Africa.[123] The return of men to the countryside, they claimed, would reinvigorate patrilineal family systems and male domination and also help to eradicate such social problems as alcoholism, adultery, and prostitution, all associated with male migration and female abandonment.[124]

In short, cotton planners argued that southern Mozambique was an ideal place to introduce the staple on a large scale as a peasant crop. According to a senior Cotton Board inspector,

> The Province of the Sul de Save brings together, in my opinion, all the necessary prerequisites. Fertile lands, sufficient and efficient indigenous labor, abundant communication networks and a regional transport system, and the area is totally free of any pests that could prove injurious to the cotton plant.[125]

A colleague predicted that on the best soils, cotton yields would reach 800 kilograms per hectare—several times the national average—and that the prospects for cotton in the fertile Limpopo Valley were practically limitless.[126]

Despite the initial optimism, however, cotton failed to live up to colonial expectations; widespread peasant skepticism, inspired by earlier cotton debacles, helps to explain why. Lisbon's inability to lure concessionary companies other than Algodeira do Sul de Save into the south further aggravated the problem.[127] During the 1940s, a much lower percentage of peasant households was enmeshed in the cotton regime in southern Mozambique than in other parts of the colony. In the 1940–41 campaign only 7,300 of the approximately 450,000 cotton growers in Mozambique resided in the south.[128] The number of peasants trapped within the cotton regime increased rapidly after Sul de Save Cotton replaced a number of fly-by-night operations in 1941, and by 1944 more than 100,000 peasants were producing the staple.[129] Despite this dramatic upturn, the south provided only 14 percent of all cotton growers, even though nearly one-quarter of the colony's population resided there.[130] Most of the south remained outside the cotton scheme (see Map 4).

Peasants inside the scheme, however, had to work under the same highly disciplined labor regime as their counterparts elsewhere.[131] But for all the state's interven-

---

[123] Grillo, *Relatório do Chefe dos Serviços de Agricultura*, 231.

[124] On the relationship between cotton, mining, and the end to social evils see AHM, SR, Cx. 20, "Insp. ao Conc. de Gaza e Circs. do Bilene, Manhiça e Magude, 1953," António Policarpo de Sousa Santos, n.d.

[125] AIA, JEAC, "Papéis Diversos 1941," J. Anachoreta, CSD do Sul do Save, to Del. da JEAC, 11 September 1941.

[126] Ibid., 1939.

[127] AIA, JEAC, "Rel. An. 1945," João Contreiras, Insp. dos SAU, May 1945.

[128] AIA, JEAC , "Prov. do Sul do Save, Prov. da Zambézia e Prov. do Niassa," João Contreiras, Insp. dos SAU, May 1945.

[129] AIA, JEAC, "Áreas Cultivadas."

[130] According to the 1940 census the total population was 5,030,179, of which 1,197,535 lived in the Sul do Save. Col. de Moç., RTE, *Censo da População em 1940* (Lourenço Marques, 1942).

[131] Interview with Manuel Sitói et al., Guijá, 16 February 1979; AIA, JEAC, "Papéis Diversos 1941," J. Anachoreta, CD do Sul de Save to Del. da JEAC, 11 September 1941; AIA, JEAC, "Papeis Diversos," Vivaldo Guerreiro to CSD da JEAC, 18 August 1941; AIA, JEAC, "Notas Recebidas," Palma Galião to CD da JEAC 12 May 1939; AIA, JEAC, 601/8, 23 September 1946.

tionist practices, in one critical way it did not seek to alter radically the preexisting labor process: cotton was cultivated almost entirely by women. Because the great number of male migrant workers traveling every year to the gold mines of South Africa guaranteed Lisbon much-needed income, no serious efforts were made to curtail labor migration—despite the Salazar regime's rhetoric about economic nationalism and self-sufficiency and the need to protect the "the African family" by luring workers back from South Africa.[132] If anything, compulsory cotton production made migration more attractive for African males. "Cotton didn't pay," Gonçalo Chilundo stressed. "We could not earn enough to survive. We worked so hard opening up the bush and we didn't receive anything."[133] Throughout the 1940s, cotton income rarely exceeded 200 *escudos* (approximately U.S. $8) anywhere in the south (see Appendices C, D, and E). At the end of his first mine contract Chilundo earned approximately 3,200 *escudos*, several times what his wife had earned from cotton during the same period.[134] Little wonder that he went regularly to the mines from 1942 to 1958. It is important to stress that while women heavily dominated the cotton labor force, the gender composition of cotton production varied somewhat between and within villages in the south and often changed over time. Moreover, the commonly held assumption of a rural labor force completely devoid of men is not entirely supported by the data.[135] The best documented example of men involved in cotton was in southern Inhambane, where many Muchope continued a long tradition of male farming.[136]

With thousands of men absent for nearly two agricultural seasons, the imposition of cotton led to a dramatic increase in women's work loads. If in the past men had taken primary responsibility for felling trees, clearing dense brush, burning vegetation, and helping to prepare soils, these tasks now fell to women. True, men did from time to time return home to help in the cotton fields, but their help was usually irregular and undependable. Unlike the northern and central cotton zones, where women could often rely on matrilineal relatives who resided in the same village, in the patrilineal south female growers often lived far from their families and had to go it alone most of the time.[137] Miriam Paulo explained the problem in personal terms:

---

[132] AIA, JEAC, "Prov. do Sul do Save," João Contreiras, Insp. dos SAU, May 1945.

[133] Interview with Gonçalo Chilundo, 8 August 1991.

[134] Ibid.

[135] According to the 1940 census of Bilene, there were approximately 7,000 able–bodied males between eighteen and fifty–five. Of that number 5,134 worked in the mines and another 1,600 worked on European plantations or on state public work projects. Most of the latter returned home sometime during the year as did perhaps one-third to one-half of the miners. Thus about 3,500 of the 7,000 productive males were gone for all or part of the 1940–1941 cotton campaign. By contrast, in Guijá approximately 15 percent of the able–bodied male population was gone (AHM, SR, Cx. 20, ISANI, "Relatórios . . . de Gaza, Bilene, Sabié, Guijá, Magude," Rui Cândido dos Reis, Insp. Admin., 1942; AIA, JEAC, "Prov. do Sul do Save," João Contreiras, Insp. dos SAU, May 1945). Several years later the number of males who left Guijá to work in the mines had increased to about 25 percent. In some Guijá communities the absentee rate was over 40 percent (AIA, JEAC, RT, "Zona Algodoeira do Guijá: Aspecto Económico–Agrícola," J. Fonseca George, Eng. Ag., 23 July 1947).

[136] AIA, JEAC, "Rel. An. 1945," João Contreiras, Insp. dos SAU, May 1945. For a general discussion of Chopi male involvement in agriculture, see Young, "Fertility and Famine," 76.

[137] Recent research by Ana Loforte suggests that the history of migrations in southern Mozambique has reduced the extent to which patrilineal claims can be successfully exerted. In a number of cases women regularly drew on the support of female relatives. I am grateful to Jeanne Penvenne for this information.

My husband was away most of the time. In September I was ordered to clear one hectare. I had only an axe and a hoe. My oldest children helped. Cutting down large trees and moving heavy stumps was very hard. I also had to take care of my baby, whom I hung in a nearby tree. When she cried I gave her my breast. But I could never stop working.[138]

With so many men regularly gone, state officials were conscripted female laborers to repair roads and to clear paths as well as to work on European farms and plantations. In this regard the south was different from other parts of Mozambique, where women were usually exempt from *chibalo*.[139] To make matters worse, women in this region often had to work in the chief's cotton fields. Women in southern Mozambique thus felt the weight of colonial capitalism perhaps more acutely than those anywhere else. For many of these women, satisfying the competing claims on their time proved to be a wrenching experience.

The labor requirements for men who remained at home and worked cotton in the south were not significantly different from those of most women. "There is nothing as difficult as cotton," stressed Manuel Sitói of the Gaza district. "Neither corn, nor beans—nothing was so demanding."[140] The overseer's whip and *palmatória* were also generally gender-blind, although male cotton growers were not subject to the constant threat of sexual abuse.

While the evidence indicates that the "people left behind" endured terrible hardships as a result of the imposition of the cotton regime on top of the migrant labor system, this is only part of the story. The other part is about initiative and adaptation, about reorganizing work, and about experimenting with new technologies and crop management systems in an effort to survive in this harsh environment. This human drama is brought into sharp focus through an examination of the daily lives of Adelina Penicela, Celeste Cossa, and Simon Mucave.

Adelina Penicela was born in Manjacaze. Like many elderly peasants, she did not remember the exact year of her birth, but she did remember clearly when cotton first came to Manjacaze:

The history of cotton, if I am not wrong, began by the end of the 1930s. Yes. When this work started, the *chefe de posto* ordered Régulo Semende to open up cotton plots. Then the *régulo* instructed people to cultivate these plots, including his own. Semende sent for a number of women who stayed at his home and worked his cotton field. There were some families who slept there and had to bring food with them. After some time the *chefe de posto* learned that there was a good cotton yield so he encouraged village headmen to capture women to work on their cotton fields. Subsequently he ordered that all families must have their own cotton plot. That is when I started mine.[141]

---

[138] Interview with Miriam Paulo.

[139] Interviews with Sarifa Amati, Xai Xai, 21 August 1977; Simone Sitói, Guijá, 16 February 1979; Emília Machava, CV Magul, Gaza, 20 February 1979; AIA, JEAC, Zona de Experimentação do Sul do Save, "Rel. da Viagem a Macholele e Lourenço Marques," António Fernandes de Almeida Matos, Reg. Ag., 29 May 1948.

[140] Interview with Manuel Sitói et al.

[141] Interview with Adelina Penicela, Maputo, 3 July 1986.

It was at about this time that Adelina's husband, a miner, "ran away for Zimbabwe [Southern Rhodesia] and then South Africa." When he came back, "he did not bring a lot of money. Sometimes it was just enough for a cloth or two." Adelina's husband remained at home for about two months and then returned to South Africa. When he left "it was difficult, very, very difficult," she remembers. For many years Adelina cultivated cotton without the help of immediate family. It was relentless work. She remembered feeling completely at the mercy of the African overseer:

> He wore a suit and a hat. He moved from one field to another which were located in one line. And when he reached a particular plot he would drop his hat on the ground and forbid the grower to leave before he returned to pick up his hat. Sometimes we had to be in the field until 7:00 p.m. to take care of the hat. When it became dark, we had to make a fire in order to see and to continue planting.[142]

The cotton season in Manjacaze was as long as it was hard. Adelina's cotton obligations extended beyond her own field. If she failed to pay her taxes, she had to work in the cotton fields of Chief Semende for at least one week. Even when she satisfied her tax requirement, in most years Adelina was still conscripted for a shorter period to weed or to help with the cotton harvest. Both tasks came at the moment when her crops needed the most care. If Adelina managed to finish her plot early, she could not necessarily attend to her food garden, but had to help those who had not yet finished.[143] For all her labor, she rarely produced more than five sacks of cotton per year.[144] Yet Adelina, like so many women of all ages in Manjacaze, figured out how to survive by (1) doing men's tasks, (2) restructuring work, and (3) bending or breaking the rules.

Out of necessity, Adelina assumed responsibility for a set of "male" economic tasks such as felling trees, clearing dense brush, and burning vegetation. She was not alone. According to Miriam Paulo, who came from the same region, "the most difficult task for us was chopping down and removing the heavy trees, which we almost always did alone."[145]

Second, at critical moments in the labor process Adelina and her neighbors restructured the work of cotton to ease their burden. Whereas the cotton regime was predicated on household labor even in male-deficient regions, Adelina stressed that the women of Manjacaze relied heavily on extrafamilial labor pooling. Although she noted that collective work parties and interhousehold mutual aid were not new, these forms of labor sharing took on added importance inside the cotton regime. Mutual aid was the only way for peasant households to survive the double burden of cotton production and subsistence security. For Adelina, these two labor arrangements meant that "I have never cultivated a cotton field alone." Her story, as well as those of other women of Manjacaze, suggests that the widely held assumptions about the destructive impact of male labor migration and commodity production on kinship and community support networks requires serious reexamination.

---

[142] Ibid.

[143] Ibid.

[144] She could not have earned much more than 250 *escudos* (approximately U.S. $7.50). This figure, somewhat higher than the average grower's income, would have been enough either to pay the household tax bill or to buy a piece or two of cloth or a handful of other basic necessities.

[145] Interview with Miriam Paulo.

Finally, Adelina and her neighbors had to manipulate the cotton system and sometimes bend the rules in order to survive. Adelina tried to cultivate the same cotton plot longer than the prescribed period. And, when forced to move, she tried to work a parcel of land that had no large trees or stumps. She covertly farmed a small manioc field adjacent to her cotton plot, even though this was strictly prohibited. Like many women in Manjacaze, Adelina maintained several small fields in the hills to which, with the help of other *tsima* [explain term?]workers, she periodically sneaked off to work. In these fields she grew corn, peanuts, and beans, despite efforts by overseers to curtail production of these food crops when they competed with cotton.[146] Because these food gardens were unsupervised, cultivators were able to practice intercropping and intraseasonal crop rotation, practices essential for food security and supplementary income.

Celeste Cossa's experience inside the cotton regime was different from that of Adelina Penicela in one important respect. A lean and wiry woman, Celeste played a critical role in introducing women in Chibuto to plows in direct defiance of the prevailing taboos. Celeste cultivated cotton from 1940 to 1950. Her first plot of land was one hundred meters square, double the legal requirement set by the Cotton Board for single women. Like many of the other women in the region, Celeste described cotton work as a "*chibalo*" and distinguished between her own fields and those of the state: "The cotton field belonged to the government. In order to be able to work in my own field afterward, I had to be there on time. It was like *chibalo*."[147] As a widow without older children or immediate kin nearby, Celeste was dependent on extrafamilial labor. She remembered brewing maize beer for *tsima* "because, if it rained early before I had finished weeding, I did not want to be beaten." On other occasions Celeste used money her deceased husband had earned in South Africa to purchase imported Portuguese wine, which she offered to her neighbors after they worked her field on Sundays. Celeste also exchanged labor with her neighbors to alleviate production bottlenecks, and, when the demands of cotton and maize were most acute, she was not reluctant to take on such "male" tasks as chopping and clearing large trees.

But Celeste Cossa's most radical departure from prevailing cultural practices was her refusal to respect prohibitions against women's working with oxen and plows. Historically, cattle-related activities such as milking, slaughtering, and building kraals and fences were considered male tasks.[148] Control over cattle herds was a source of power and status, and women were generally prohibited from going near them; it was widely believed that their presence would contaminate the livestock. Because of the labor shortages and production pressures under the cotton regime, Celeste disregarded this taboo.

Celeste was among the first women to use ox-drawn plows in Chibuto. As the eldest daughter of a migrant laborer, responsibility for herding fell on her.

I was the senior daughter. My father worked in South Africa. I became a shepherd. And in the pastures [with other shepherds] I learned how to

---

[146] Amélia Novana and Regina Mate of Manjacaze noted that it was quite common for most women to maintain three different fields—one for cotton, one for manioc, and a third for corn, peanuts, and beans (interview with Celeste Cossa, Amélia Novana, and Regina Mate, Maputo, 31 July 1991).

[147] Interview with Celeste Cossa et al.

[148] See Junod, *Life of a South African Tribe*, vol. 2, 49–50.

work with oxen. One of the first things I had to do was put the yoke on the oxen shoulders. I also got a robe to put over the rear. Then it was necessary to obtain a plow and begin to train the oxen to pull it.[149]

Although Celeste did not indicate how her family acquired the plow, her father probably either purchased it in South Africa or used some of his mining income to acquire it on one of his visits home. Her husband had saved enough from his mine wages to purchase a team of oxen and a plow. So, when cotton arrived, Celeste was better off than most women.

Celeste Cossa's violation of long-held cultural values apparently did not cause an uproar in the community. In her oral testimony she made no mention of a public outcry or personal problems arising from her stance. On the contrary, other women sought her assistance. Celeste provided it at no charge; it is unclear whether she even demanded labor reciprocity.

Under the direction of Celeste and others like her, the number of women in Chibuto using plows increased dramatically.[150] Unlike in Manjacaze, where there was little grazing land and plows were only marginally useful on the sandy soils, in Chibuto there was sufficient water and good land to grow cotton, and the heavy wet clay soils were difficult to turn with a hoe. Plows saved precious time and energy. However, the introduction of ox-drawn plows proved to be a mixed blessing, as we shall see.

Just as most women did not conform to the colonial image of helpless and abandoned wives, so not all men in southern Mozambique were absent migrant laborers; in virtually all rural communities some men preferred to remain at home.[151] One of those was Simão Mangueze Mucambe, born in 1909, who lived near Cambine in Inhambane. Cambine was the center of a major missionary community established by the American Methodist Episcopal Church at the turn of the century. As a young man Simão worked for the American missionary, Ira Gillet, and he spent his adult life inside this tightly knit Christian community.

The missionaries at Cambine not only engaged in an aggressive campaign to convert "raw heathens" to Christianity, but also saw themselves as aiding the government "in the training and uplifting of the native."[152] In their schools, adult education classes, cooperatives, and Christian villages, missionaries worked to instill notions of hard work, frugality, and the need to pay taxes. Their year-end report for 1927 celebrated the fact that "there was not a native Christian who had to be arrested for the nonpayment of taxes."[153] These missionaries also promoted a vigorous agricultural training program. "At Cambine," wrote Ira Gillet, "we had a thousand-acre farm. I was a farmer and I liked it, even though my profession was that of a missionary."[154] As part of the training they introduced plows, ox-driven

---

[149] Interview with Celeste Cossa et al.

[150] Ibid; interviews with Leia Mbazima, Maputo, 27 July 1991; Benjamin Mavunja, Chibuto, 12 February 1979.

[151] Interviews with Gonçalo Chilundo, 8 August 1991; Simão Mangueze Mucambe, Maputo, 12 July 1991.

[152] *Official Report of the South East African Mission Conference of the Episcopal Methodist Mission Conference* 14(1930), 124.

[153] *Official Journal of the South East African Mission Conference of the Methodist Episcopal Conference* 11(1927), 134.

[154] Ira Gillet, "Early Years in Africa," 69.

carts, better quality seeds, new farming techniques, and additional famine coping strategies.[155]

Thus, when the colonial regime introduced cotton, it encountered at Cambine a fairly receptive farming population. Simão was thirty years old at the time.

> I grew cotton from the first year [1938] until it was abolished [1961]. First the *régulo* organized us. There were plots of one, two, or three hectares depending on the size of the group that would work on them. But soon the Portuguese learned that this system did not bring high yields. So, they said that each family must have its own one-hectare field. There was a warehouse where we used to go to pick up the seeds.[156]

He remembered that the work was very hard and that because of the thick stumps, it was not possible to use plows. Simão and his wife sowed the cotton seeds in December with the help of their children. Some years, when the grass was very thick, they had to weed the cotton field five times.[157] To ease the labor burden Simão and his wife worked in collective labor groups, known in Cambine as *maphupe*, and at critical moments in the agricultural cycle they organized work parties. For all their labor, they did not earn enough from the cotton fields to pay their taxes. To do so, they had to sell a portion of their peanut or maize crop to the *cantineiros*. And yet Simão chose not to become a migrant laborer:

> To me it was not worth going to South Africa, because when I worked in my field I had corn, peanuts, and other products that I could exchange for blankets, trousers, and other things that I needed. The man who went to South Africa when he came back, he found his family without food. He would then trade a blanket for maize that I had produced, I could eat and dress without having to go to Joni [Johannesburg], because what he brought back he would sell to me.[158]

Conclusion

Despite the common features of the cotton regime, there were significant differences from one part of the colony to another in the scale of production, the organization of work, and the ways in which cotton affected the daily lives of growers. The most visible difference was that of scale. Throughout the 1940s, the north outstripped the rest of the colony. In the 1949–50 campaign, for example, approximately 60 percent of all the cotton growers in the colony lived in Nampula, Cabo Delgado, and Niassa (see Table 4–1). Together these growers cultivated 175,000 of the 285,000 hectares—60 percent—of cotton land. By contrast peasants in central Mozambique planted 85,000 hectares, those in the south a mere quarter of that amount.[159] As Table 4–4 indicates, average peasant output, and by extension cotton income, followed this broad pattern. Yields per hectare in the north were almost

---

[155] Interview with Simão Mangueze Mucambe.

[156] Ibid.

[157] Ibid.

[158] Ibid.

[159] AIA, JEAC, "Áreas Cultivadas."

TABLE 4-4 Regional Variations in Production, 1949-50 Cotton Campaign[a]

Region	Production	No. producers	Production/producer
South			
Gaza	3,875,478	21,281	185
Inhambane	1,481,337	33,738	45
Total	5,356,815	54,019	99
Central			
Manica e Sofala	12,167,052	56,499	217
Tete	-	-	-
Zambézia	12,485,107	00,169	125
Total	24,652,159	156,668	158
North			
Cabo Delgado	16,212,842	69,245	235
Niassa	8,503,365	41,993	207
Nampula	30,764,580	183,560	168
Total	55,480,787	294,898	189

Source: Based on AIA, JEAC, "Areas Cultivadas, Produção de Algodão-caroço por Produtores e Número de Cultivadores," n.d.

[a] These figures are slightly different from those in Bravo, *A Cultura Algodoeira*.

twice as high as they were in the south. Growers in Cabo Delgado led the way, averaging almost 235 kilograms per producer. At the other extreme, peasants in the southern province of Inhambane produced less than one-fifth that amount.

The disparities between Cabo Delgado and Inhambane illuminate the causes of these variations in production across the colony. Few parts of Mozambique were better suited for cotton than Cabo Delgado.[160] With the exception of the Makonde highlands and a narrow coastal belt, the district's warm temperatures, fertile soils, and moderate rainfall offered an excellent habitat. But the relative success of the cotton regime in Cabo Delgado cannot be reduced simply to ecological factors. Because colonial officials considered Cabo Delgado a "backwater" region not contributing to the metropolitan economy, they targeted it as a major cotton zone. The economic agenda of the two concessionaires, SAGAL and CAM, converged with the agenda of the colonial state. Cotton was their only business, unlike many other concessionary companies. These companies therefore sought to incorporate as many peasants into the regime as possible and to stem the outflow of male workers. To a greater degree than anywhere else in the colony, rural households in Cabo Delgado remained intact and the conjugal work team was the principal unit of production.

---

[160] Conditions were roughly the same in Nampula, and indeed the very best ecological conditions stretched across an area from central Nampula to the Montepuez area of Cabo Delgado. On average, peasant productivity was higher in Cabo Delgado and, after World War II, many more cotton-growing households were deprived of men for an appreciable part of the agricultural year.

Indeed, men were forced to assume a greater role in agricultural production than they had in the past. The relatively low level of male out-migration meant that acute labor shortages tended to be short-term and not a central feature of the cotton regime. Households experiencing labor shortages could organize work exchanges with matrilineal relatives who lived in the same village. Bride-service further helped to alleviate immediate production problems.

Inhambane was the opposite of Cabo Delgado in almost every respect. Erratic rainfall and drought recurred with devastating regularity. To complicate matters, the colonial state had long defined the region as a labor reserve for the South African mines. Although there were colonial officials who argued that the outflow of African men stifled rural development, theirs was a minority voice. Portugal derived too handsome a profit to alter this practice. More than 35 percent of the "active" male population labored in the South African mines at any point in time during the 1940s.[161] A smaller but still significant number worked in the colonial capital, Lourenço Marques. Aware of these ecological and demographic constraints, the owners of Sul de Save Cotton invested most of their resources in their adjacent Gaza holding and made this the preferred cotton zone. For their part, whenever they could, overburdened women in Inhambane limited the size of their cotton plots in order to minimize labor output. The average grower in the 1948–49 campaign planted slightly more than half that of her counterpart in the north.[162] Unlike the wives of absent plantation workers in central Mozambique, these women could not count on their husbands and sons returning sometime during the cotton season. Moreover, migrants' wives could not rely on their own kin who, in the patrilineal south, did not usually reside in nearby communities. And unlike their female neighbors in Gaza, women in Inhambane did not have the option of farming with plows, since there were precious few plows around.

For most growers cotton remained "the mother of poverty." This was particularly true for women who, as cultivators in their own rights, as guardians of household food security, and as victims of sexual threats, were perpetually on the front line in peasant struggles against the cotton regime. Focusing on these women as victims, however, leaves the story of the cotton regime incomplete. The experiences of Rosa Maria Ernesto, Adelina Penicela, and Celeste Cossa reveal another, previously hidden, dimension of this story, characterized by individual initiatives and flexibility and by creative adaptation to the hostile world of cotton. Their accounts and those of their compatriots across the colony who organized labor exchanges, disregarded prior taboos and gendered notions of work, and bent colonial rules demonstrate that women were the principal architects of coping strategies that in both small and large ways made life more bearable within the cotton regime (see Chapter 9).

---

[161] First, *Black Gold*, 112.

[162] A total of 33,928 growers planted 12,348 hectares, or .36 of a hectare per peasant. AIA, JEAC, "Áreas Cultivadas"; Bravo, *Cultura Algodoeira*, 130.

5

Peasants at Work: Marketing and Ginning

For the hundreds of thousands of Mozambican women and men trapped inside the cotton regime, the work of cotton did not end when they picked the last boll from the field. Because the cotton companies made no provisions for transporting the crop to market, this burden fell entirely on the conscripted cotton growers. Many rural Mozambicans also toiled in the primitive ginning factories under difficult and unhealthy conditions. The concessionary companies secured their labor needs, whether for transporting or for ginning the fiber, through a combination of market incentives and coercion. For most factory workers of the cotton regime, the uncertainties were many and the benefits few. This chapter explores the experiences of rural Mozambicans at the cotton markets and in the factories. Because much of the material on factory conditions is based on oral evidence and is not corroborated by written material, it is difficult to ascertain the frequency of industrial diseases and accidents and other critical issues that figure prominently in individual oral accounts.

In many respects the organization of the marketing system and ginning mills offers a classic example of merchant capital at work.[1] Like their counterparts throughout colonial Africa, the concessionaires organized the circulation of commodities, in this case cotton. Some of the worst abuses cannot be attributed simply to the logic of merchant capital; they also reflect the specific nature of the Portuguese concessionary companies, which did not have sufficient capital to do the job they set out to do and therefore had to squeeze the peasants. Supported by state-imposed marketing arrangements and monopolistic practices, they profited in the short run by plundering the Mozambican countryside.

Marketing

The central objective of the cotton regime in Mozambique was to bring as many peasants and as much land as possible into the system at minimal expense. This

---

[1] For a discussion of merchant capital, see Geoffrey Kay, *Development and Underdevelopment: A Marxist Analysis* (New York, 1975).

cost-minimizing philosophy spilled over into marketing. As a result, there was substantial delay in setting up an efficient commercial network to handle the high-
volume bulk trade in cotton. Instead, the state transferred the risks and costs of
transporting cotton to the rural markets onto the growers. Even before peasants
had harvested the first cotton boll, they had to clear the paths and repair the washed-
out bridges that linked their communities to the cotton markets. "The lack of funds
in the state budget to maintain the transportation system," acknowledged a former
colonial official, "necessitated that the cost be born by indigenous laborers with
some assistance from the concessionary companies."[2] Company agents also com-
mandeered local labor to rebuild the markets.

After the harvest was completed, the concessionaires transformed cotton growers into conscripted porters. "On market days and even on the days immediately
before," noted one colonial official, "the roads were crowded with men, women
and children transporting cotton on their heads in a variety of makeshift sacks."[3] A
Portuguese journalist traveling through the north in 1945 described this scene in
more vivid detail:

> Along the bush roads that have hardened the soles of the Blacks, hun-
> dreds of men, women and children walk carrying *cangarras* [makeshift
> sacks] of cotton on their heads. They are coming from their fields to-
> ward the main road and from there they will continue marching single
> file, many nude, under the hot sun, to the market. The Ford wagon in
> which we are traveling to Porto Amélia often has to slow to a crawl
> and we are forced to blow our horn because the road is so crowded
> with Africans on their way to Rio Monapo [the market place].[4]

Only in the south, where the number of cotton growers was relatively small and
where ox-drawn carts were available for taking cotton to market, were producers
freed from this back-breaking task.[5]

The colonial cotton marketing system was characterized by rigid time restrictions and strict deadlines for bringing cotton to market. The time restrictions were
caused primarily by the companies' insufficient manpower.[6] Because markets were
kept open for only a few days during the harvest season, producers were under great
pressure to bring their crop to the designated location by the specified date. To do so
required all of their household labor and sometimes the addition of casual workers.
If they failed to bring their crop to market on time, their cotton cards would not be
signed by colonial officials. This was tantamount to breaking the law, and offenders
were punished accordingly. To compound the pressure on the growers, the predeter-
mined market dates did not always make sense in terms of the local production
process. Sometimes markets were scheduled too early, coinciding with the final round
of cotton picking. In other cases, dates scheduled too late meant the crop remained in
peasants' villages without proper storage and often became soiled.[7]

---

2   Bravo, *Cultura Algodoeira*, 119.

3   Ibid.

4   *Notícias*, 8 August 1945.

5   Interviews with Makwati Simba et al., Chibuto, 13 February 1979; Leonarda Fátima Madime,
Chidenguele, 20 November 1979.

6   Typically the markets were opened at two different intervals during the harvest period.

7   Cotton officials came to realize this problem and reorganized scheduling so that regional markets
would be open a few days per month for two or more successive months.

As part of their cost-minimizing strategy, the cotton companies initially decided not to provide burlap sacks, which would have allowed peasants to transport their crop safely and efficiently. Growers had to carry the crop on their heads in a variety of makeshift bundles. Some used large bamboo baskets or wrapped their cotton in bamboo mattings. Others transported the crop in cages made of millet stalks or trays made of fine interwoven fibers from the trunks of trees. Still others bound the cotton in rags, but the crop often fell out and got dirty.[8] Without proper packaging, the cotton was liable to spoil from rain, from the dust on the roads, and from sweat. Because they knew that dirty fiber had very little value at the market, many growers did not even stop to pick up the strands that fell. Enough cotton was strewn along the roadside to support a group of "scavengers" who survived by "collecting the cotton which had fallen on the ground and bringing it for weighing after the last sales were completed."[9] In the late 1940s, the concessionary companies finally began to distribute some gunny sacks.

The limited number of markets meant that cotton growers had to haul their loads long distances. Both women and men recalled carrying the heavy sacks, which often weighed thirty to fifty kilograms, for two or three days on poorly cleared paths and bush roads.[10] Contemporary government reports confirmed the paucity of accessible markets.[11] In some regions, peasant growers had to travel thirty kilometers or more.[12] One Portuguese critic reported that it was common "for collection points to be located four days from the cotton fields."[13] Manuel Baptista, a former hunter, remembered encountering growers "carrying fifty kilogram sacks on their head. Women carried their babies as well. Sometimes they had to walk nearly seventy-five kilometers."[14] Not until 1946 did the Cotton Board finally order the companies to establish local markets "so that sellers will not have to travel distances longer than fifteen kilometers."[15] This was still quite a distance to walk carrying such a heavy load.

If the growers were lucky en route, they would be able to arrange shelter and foodstuffs such as porridge, chicken, or manioc from villages adjacent to the bush roads. More often, however, they slept in groups of as many as forty or fifty people along the side of the road, surviving on the manioc they carried with them.[16] During the night they had to guard against wild animals or thieves (often including *sipais*). And shortly after they arrived at the market, many had to retrace their steps to fetch the remainder of their crop. Some made two or three trips each season.[17]

8   Interviews with Sajene Kwalima et al., Morrumbala, 30 July 1976 (Head Collection); Arridhi Mahanda et al., Balama, 23 July 1979; Adelina Cedo and Andre Marques da Pinha, Montepuez, 21 July 1979; AIA, JEAC, "Conf. 1941: Rel. Esp. Sobre Mercados," António de Freitas Silva, Reg. Ag., n.d.

9   AIA, JEAC, "Rel. An. 1945," João Contreiras, Insp. dos SAU, May 1945.

10   Interview with Valente Yota, Macia, 19 February 1979.

11   AIA, JEAC, "Dossiers Diversos 1939–1941," António Mira Mendes to Chefe de Fisc., 29 July 1941; AIA, JEAC, 605/8 Vasco de Sousa e Fonseca e Lebre, Reg. Ag., 12 August 1946; AIA, JEAC, 601/8, "Relatório," João Ferreira da Silva, Admin. do Mogincual, 1 November 1946.

12   AIA, JEAC, 601/8, "Relatório," João Pereira da Silva, Admin. do Mogincual, 1 November 1946.

13   João Gaspar Faria, "Produção Algodoeira," *Searra Nova* 1083(1948), 2.

14   Interview with Manuel Baptista, Nampula, 9 July 1991.

15   AHM, FGG, Processo (1926–1948), Pasta A/6, Cx. 40, JEAC, Del. de Moçambique, SFFE, "Reajustamento das Bases para a Campanha Anual na Prov. do Niassa."

16   Interviews with Manuel Baptista; Joaquim Carajola, Nampula, 9 July 1991.

17   AIA, JEAC, 605/8, Vasco de Sousa de Fonseca a Lebre, Reg. Ag., 12 August 1946.

PHOTO 5   Colonial cotton market. Courtesy of Arquivo Histórico de Moçambique. Rebelo Júnior, photographer.

"If you only had two sacks to sell," recalled an elder from Macomia, "when the *sipais* saw you at the market they would arrest you and send you off to the plantation because you did not fill your quota."[18] Illness was no excuse; when people were too frail to make this journey, they had to employ others to transport their cotton. Cotton officials ignored these arrangements; there was little they could do. One senior inspector conceded as much in 1945:

> I have verified that not all the sellers actually produce the cotton. As a result of illness or other difficulties, growers hire one or more workers, depending on the size of the load, to go to the market and sell the cotton. In a sea of thousands of growers it is extremely difficult for the handful of officials, primarily white, to discover this deceit.[19]

---

[18] Group interview, Macomia, 30 July 1979.

[19] AIA, JEAC, "Rel. An. 1945," João Contreiras, Insp. dos SAU, May 1945.

Because approximately two-thirds of the weight of raw cotton was seed, which the concessionary companies neither processed nor paid for, the burden of transporting was even greater than it appeared. Only in the late 1940s did the companies begin to process the seeds and, under pressure from the Cotton Board, pass on a small portion of the additional income to the growers[20] (see Chapter 6).

The cotton markets were little more than temporary collection points in the villages of influential chiefs, at local administrative posts, and adjacent to major roads. Often they were simply open-air fairs, with a table, a set of chairs, and a scale, where company agents and government representatives consummated their transactions (see photo). According to one state official, the cotton warehouses were huts "constructed of bamboo and covered with grass and matting on the ground . . . incapable of protecting the cotton."[21] Despite the presence of hundreds and sometimes thousands of peasants gathered at these fairs, there were neither sanitary facilities nor shelters to protect them from inclement weather. In some cases a tent covered the actual area where the sales took place, but this created an additional set of health problems. The administrator of Memba, a major cotton center, reported:

> The market is simply a location covered with a "parrot" under which there is a scale and a payment table. The dirt floor is not even covered with reeds or bamboo. Each day thousands of Africans pass through this enclosure bringing with them a vast quantity of cotton. As they trample through, the thick dust particles from the floor and from the cotton make it difficult to breathe. It becomes suffocating. Your nose and respiratory tract get irritated and congested, making it hard to conduct business.[22]

Colonial authorities permitted villagers from the immediate area to hawk dried meat and fish, pounded manioc, ears of corn, and fruit on the perimeter of the cotton fair grounds.[23] European and Asian merchants also set up temporary stalls several days before the cotton market formally opened, and they remained there for a few days after the fair had closed.[24] Government officials believed that the presence of the itinerant traders, who sold everything from cloth to wine and from cooking oil to soap, would be an added incentive to cotton growers. For the traders, the markets provided an opportunity to get easy access to the hard-earned cotton income of the growers.

Consumer goods were not the only inducement offered to growers. During the early 1940s, several companies distributed free salt to attract producers. CNA employed this strategy at its markets in Manica e Sofala.[25] Other companies, aided by local Portuguese officials, organized festivities to celebrate the benefits of cotton and awarded prizes to the most productive cultivators and their chiefs. On one occasion in 1947, the governor general of Mozambique appeared before thousands of southern producers and extolled the virtues of hard work; he then led the peasants in singing the Portuguese national anthem. According to a reporter, it was "a

[20] Quintanilha, "The Problem of Cotton Production," 49.

[21] AIA, JEAC, Conf. 1941, "Rel. Esp. Sobre Mercados," António de Freitas Silva, Reg. Ag., n.d.

[22] AIA, JEAC, 601/8, "Rel.," Nicolau João de Melo, Admin. da Circ. de Memba, 13 November 1946.

[23] Bravo, *Cultura Algodoeira*, 119.

[24] AIA, JEAC, "Montepuez 1944," Carta do Aj. da Del. to CP da JEAC in Montepuez.

[25] AHM, Cx. 39, ISANI, "Relatório da . . . Sofala, 1943–44," Abel de Souza Moutinho, Insp. Admin., 12 May 1944.

PHOTO 6 Growers receiving payment at colonial market. Courtesy of Arquivo Histórico de Moçambique. Rebelo Júnior, photographer.

moment of great enthusiasm and joy."[26] A former administrator also remembered "that the markets had a festive atmosphere."[27] Nunes Faria Madé, a former cotton grower, offered a very different recollection: "We waited sometimes for a week before we were able to sell our cotton. During the period, we did everything we could including organizing dances, so that they would think we were happy."[28] Because the markets were tightly regulated public spaces, Madé and the other cotton growers relied on such subterfuge to discourage official supervision and to reduce the likelihood of arbitary punishments.

For their part, company officials and their police maximized their control over market events by herding growers together by chieftaincy. Each chieftaincy was assigned a specific place where members were to remain seated until they were told to get in line. The lines themselves were long, and standing in the hot sun was physically draining.

Transactions were delayed because state functionaries who supervised the fairs sometimes "failed to arrive on the designated date."[29] One Cotton Board official

---

[26] *Notícias,* 23 June 1948.

[27] Bravo, *Cultura Algodoeira,* 119.

[28] Interview with Nunes Faria Madé, Paulo Madeira, and Caetano Maio, Nicoadala/Namacurra, 19 July 1991.

[29] AIA, JEAC, Conf. 1941, "Rel. Esp. Sobre Mercados," António de Freitas Silva, Reg. Ag., n.d.

working in the south warned that this tardiness was causing serious problems. "It is of maximum importance that the markets begin on time because the delays are having a demoralizing effect on the Africans who are losing immense amounts of valuable time for reasons which are not of their making."[30] Delays were often longer in the north, where the concessionaires had to organize markets over vast areas. According to one Cotton Board inspector, "Peasants are forced to sit on the ground for two or three days and sometimes longer because there was only a single scale or because a company functionary had to travel fifty to eighty kilometers from another market."[31] Only after the growers' cotton was classified and weighed and their production and income recorded in the official registry and on their cotton cards did growers receive their payment:

> Two employees of Sul do Save Cotton stood astride the two scales, verifying the weight and writing it on a check stub which they handed to the grower who then moved on to the Cotton Board officials, who determined if the employees had properly classified the fiber. The grower then took the stub to another company employee who calculated the value in *escudos* according to the table of fixed prices and recorded the amount. The grower then received that sum from the company paymaster. The final transaction was verified by the administrator and the Cotton Board inspector.[32]

For the growers, eager to return home to their fields, this long, bureaucratic process was frustrating.

In principle, the state took precautions to prevent serious market abuses by company agents. By law, the local administrator or one of his subordinates was required to oversee all market transactions. Regional Cotton Board inspectors were assigned to the trading sites as well, because of concerns that local officials were in company pay.[33] Some vigorously enforced the regulations; others quite close to the companies were suspect.

These safeguards notwithstanding, market irregularities and abuses were widespread. Company buyers, often in concert with government officials, developed a variety of techniques to bilk the peasants. In some cases they used the excuse of currency shortages to impose a barter system.[34] CAM representatives at the big cotton fair in Montepuez practiced this subterfuge regularly. Instead of paying the prescribed rate, they substituted salt, hoes, cigarettes, and other commodities.[35] Apart from the strong probability that these trade goods were overvalued, neither salt

---

[30]   AIA, JEAC, "Notas Recebidas," Palma Galião to CD da JEAC.

[31]   AHM, Governo Geral, Colónia de Moçambique, "Rel. duma Insp. Feita na Prov. do Niassa (1938–1940)," Insp. Pinto Correia, vol. 1, pasta 109, 92.

[32]   AIA, JEAC, 601/8, "Rel.," Admin. Substituto da Circ. dos Muchopes, Alexandrino Graça, 23 September 1946.

[33]   AIA, JEAC, "Rel. Acerca Duma Viagem às Provs. do Niassa e Zambézia de 6 de Junho a 18 de Julho de 1946," J. Fonseca George, Eng. Ag., September 1946; AIA, JEAC, "Zona Algodoeira dos Muchopes," J. Fonseca George, Eng. Ag., September 1947.

[34]   AIA, JEAC, Conf. 1941, "Rel. Esp. Sobre Mercado," António de Freitas Silva, Reg. Ag., n.d.; AIA, JEAC, 605/8 (1946), "Posto Técnico Algodoeiro de Montepuez Rel. Anual Ref. ao Ano de 1945," Vasco de Sousa de Fonseca Lebre, Reg. Ag.

[35]   AIA, JEAC, 605/8, "Posto Técnico Algodoeiro de Montepuez Rel. Anual Ref. Ao Ano de 1945," Vasco de Sousa da Fonseca Lebre, Reg. Ag.

nor hoes could be used to pay taxes nor to meet other household needs in an increasingly monetized colonial economy. Company buyers also used their discretionary authority to downgrade the quality of peasants' cotton. Since lower-grade fiber did not command a price anywhere near first-quality cotton, this strategy offered the companies an easy way to maximize profits.[36] In 1946 the maximum price paid in northern Mozambique for first-quality cotton was 1.4 *escudos* per kilogram. By comparison, the "lowest grade" cotton fetched a price of only 1.05 *escudos* per kilogram—a difference of about 30 percent.[37] The sellers had no legal recourse. The cotton regime remained outside the colonial legal system, for all intents and purposes.

Peasants were similarly without legal recourse when company officials manipulated the cotton scales. An administrator in the south described how easy this was to do:

> Tampering with the scales is simple and reducing the weight by a kilogram or a fraction of one is difficult to detect. Nothing seems out of the ordinary since the company agent will simply mark the weight on the check stub and hand it over to the seller who is unaware that his cotton has been discounted by one kilogram.[38]

If we believe the reports of Cotton Board field agents, this practice occurred quite regularly across the colony.[39] Although it is impossible to calculate the magnitude of this type of fraud, Sena Sugar representatives acknowledged that their 1938 crop included more than 10,000 kilograms for which there was no record of payment.[40] A government official supervising the Zambézia market of Ile in 1946 reported that CAM had somehow acquired over 2,000 kilograms more than they had actually purchased.[41]

This pattern of deception was not lost on the cotton growers, even if they were unable to read the scales or to calculate the value of each category of cotton. But growers could not question too loudly for fear of retribution. Makwati Simba from Gaza stressed this point. "The *sipais* stood on either side of the scale. The sacks weighed much more than it registered but if you complained, they beat you. If you continued to complain they beat you more."[42] Perhaps Vicente Taulegues of Metocheria in the far north summed it up best:

> When we arrived at the market, they had their scales there. They thought that since we could not read or write and that we did not know anything about bookkeeping they could make up whatever numbers they wanted.

---

[36]   AIA, JEAC, Conf. 1947, Gastão de Mello Furtado to Adj. da Del., 20 June 1947.

[37]   Between 1939 and 1946 there were three grades of cotton. From 1946 to 1951 there were only two classifications (Bravo, *Cultura Algodoeira*, 179).

[38]   AIA, JEAC, 601/8, "Rel.," Alexandrino Graça, Admin. Substituto da Circ. dos Muchopes, 23 September 1946.

[39]   AIA, JEAC, Conf. 1941, "Rel. Esp. Sobre Mercados," António de Freitas Silva, Reg. Ag., n.d.; AIA, JEAC, 601/8, "Rel.," António Marques, O Encarregado da Circ. do Ile, 30 January 1946; AIA, JEAC, Conf. 1947, Gastão de Mello Furtado to Adj. da Del., 20 June 1947.

[40]   AIA, JEAC, 7/48, SSE, Gerência do Sena Sugar Limited to Gov. da Prov. da Zambézia, 28 August 1939.

[41]   AIA, JEAC, 601/8, "Rel.," António Marques, Encarregado do Circ. do Ile, 30 January 1946.

[42]   Interview with Makwati Simba et al.

They told us that our cotton weighed "so much" and that we therefore were entitled to "so much.". . . We always received little money, but we could not complain because there were police hiding nearby and, if they heard you, they would jump out and beat you.[43]

This show of force did not prevent bolder peasants from initiating counterploys. Village members sometimes adulterated the fiber by placing pebbles or pumpkin particles in the center of the cotton sacks in order to increase their weight. Despite the punishment company officials meted out, the regime was unable to suppress this practice completely.[44] Subterfuge at the market place, as in the cotton fields, was an important weapon in the arsenal of the weak (see Chapter 10).

What local cotton growers could not know was that manipulating prices and quality standards was part of a colonywide policy promoted by the companies and supported by many local administrators—even though Board inspectors and Native Affairs authorities tried to thwart these abusive practices. The objectives were simple: handsome profits for the companies and an adequate supply of cheap high quality cotton for the metropolitan textile industry.

Suppressing prices paid to the growers was the most obvious way to achieve the first objective, although officials were slow to realize that it compromised the second. With strong representation on the Cotton Board, the concessionary companies and their textile allies from the outset lobbied to drive down official producer prices. Concessionaires argued that the high cost of machinery, seeds, petroleum, and sacks, exacerbated by the onset of World War II, cut into their profit margins and jeopardized their cotton operations.[45] They contended, quite correctly, that internal transportation costs were also higher in Mozambique than in neighboring colonies. The long distances from rural markets to the ginning mills and from the mills to the coastal ports drove up the cost of transport.[46] So did delays and accidents on the poorly maintained dirt roads and the fact that most concessionaires lacked sufficient transport to haul all the cotton from the markets to the mills and therefore had to pay independent haulers hefty rates.[47] Metropolitan textile firms also complained about prices, but not too loudly, since they were enjoying a huge increase in sales and were primarily concerned about the quality of the fiber.[48] If these arguments were not sufficiently compelling, company officials trotted out the old shibboleth that excessively high cotton prices "result in the native having too much money with the consequent disinclination to do any work."[49]

---

[43] Interview with Vicente Henrique Taulegues and Mário da Cruz Soares, Metocheria, 17 January 1979.

[44] Interviews with Makwati Simta et al.; Romeu Mataquenha, Tirani Ntuka, and Mussa Vaquina, Montepuez, 19 July 1979; Manuel Sitói et al., Guijá, 16 February 1979; group interview, CV Luís Carlos Prestes, Gaza, 2 February 1979.

[45] AIA, JEAC, "Papéis Diversos: Despachos," J. Anachoreta, CSD, 12 June 1940.

[46] From the cotton fair at Mogincual, for example, to João Ferreira dos Santos' ginning mill was 210 kilometers. After the cotton was cleaned it had to be transported another 159 kilometers to the port at Lumbo (AIA, JEAC, João Ferreira dos Santos, "Provisão Para a Campanha Algodoeira de 1940," 4 June 1940).

[47] Only CAM and the Búzi Company had a sufficient number of trucks to collect the cotton at the rural markets. AIA, JEAC, "Prov. de Manica e Sofala," João Contreiras, Insp. dos SAU, May 1945.

[48] Pitcher, *Politics in the Portuguese Empire*, 124–26.

[49] SSE, File 98/44, General Manager, 25 April 1944.

TABLE 5–1 Income from Select Peasant Crops, 1940 and 1950 (in *escudos*)

Crop	Yield/ha (kg)	Price/kg*		Income/ha	
		1940	1950	1940	1950
Cotton	450	$97	1$80	436$	810$
Peanuts	550	$80	2$07	440$	1,138$
Beans	800	$52	1$18	416$	1,358$
Corn	1,000	$40	1$00	400$	1,000$
Rice	1,500	$70	$92	1,050$	1,380$

Source: AIA, JEAC, "Reajustmento dos preços do Algodão aos Restantes Produtos da Agricultura Indígenas." J. Fonseca George, Engenheiro Agrónomo, March 1951.
Note: *actual price before inflation

Not surprisingly, the concessionary companies and their allies prevailed. The Board agreed to reduce prices. The 1938 price to growers for first-quality fiber was about 15 percent less than in the preceding year.[50] Prices across the colony remained unchanged between 1938 and 1941.[51] The following year, when the Board announced a modest price increase of less than a penny per kilogram, company officials complained that they would suffer irreversible damage.[52] Their lobbying again paid off. Over the course of the following three years, cotton prices were rolled back. Between 1942 and 1946 the average price decreased from less than 1$25 *escudos* to 1$18 *escudos* per kilogram. Anne Pitcher has demonstrated that from 1939 to 1946 real producer prices declined by almost 40 percent and that it was not until 1951 that the real price surpassed the 1939 level. In 1945 the price paid for one kilogram of ginned Mozambican cotton in Lisbon was more than nine times what the growers themselves received.[53] Even though it took approximately three kilograms of raw cotton to produce one kilogram of clean fiber and transportation costs were high, the price differential secured a handsome profit for the concessionaires and provided the textile industry with cheap raw fiber.

The extremely modest price increase that peasants received, coupled with the high risks and low yields, underscored the vulnerability of cotton growers. Portuguese critics of the cotton regime calculated that in 1945 the staple yielded the lowest per-hectare income of any cash crop, including rice, which was also a forced crop.[54] Cotton Board officials in the early 1950s made a similar assessment (see Table 5–1).[55]

---

[50]   AIA, JEAC, "Rel. da Insp. de JEAC 1940," João Contreiras, Adj. da Del. de JEAC to Pres. da JEAC

[51]   See Bravo, *Cultura Algodoeira*, 178–83.

[52]   AIA, JEAC, "Companhia da Zambézia," João Ferreira dos Santos, Telegram from Concessionaires in Niassa to JEAC, 6 October 1942.

[53]   Pitcher, *Politics in the Portuguese Empire*, 291; Mánuel Guerreiro Beatriz, "A Classificação e os Preços em Moçambique de 1930 a 1962," *Gazeta do Algodão* 14 (1962), 363; AIA, JEAC, "Prop. Moç.: Elementos Para o Século," Gastão de Mello Furtado, 15 June 1954. 1$25 is the common way of writing 1.25 *escudos*.

[54]   João Gaspar Faria, "Produção Algodeira," *Searra Nova* 1083(May 1948), 2.

[55]   AIA, JEAC, "Papéis Diversos: Despachos," J. Anachoreta, CSD do Sul do Save, 12 June 1940.

The Board's decision to impose a three-tiered pricing system in 1938 to replace the previous two-tiered system provided the concessionary companies with an opportunity to squeeze peasants still further. Since company buying agents were unilaterally responsible for classifying the fiber into one of three categories, peasants were helpless if their crop was designated as second or third quality. "It is common knowledge," wrote one administrator, "that there are great differences in the criteria used to classify [cotton], despite the fact that the standards are posted in all the administrative districts where there are markets."[56] As previously noted, the price differences were substantial as were price variations for the same cotton categories across the colony. The highest price paid for first-quality cotton in 1939 was 1$10 *escudos* per kilogram; the lowest price for the poorest quality was only half that amount. Seven years later the gap had widened. Prime quality cotton earned a return of as much as 1$40 *escudos* per kilogram, while third-class fiber yielded returns as low as sixty-five *escudos* per kilogram in "backwater" regions such as Maniamba.[57] Given the short-term profit-maximizing agenda of the concessionary companies, it is hardly surprising that from 1938 to 1947 the proportion of marketed cotton designated as third quality jumped from 14 percent to over 20 percent; in some areas it reached almost 30 percent.[58] While soil erosion may have contributed to a decline in overall cotton quality or classifiers may have gotten better at their job, neither factor explains why the percentage of premium fiber remained unchanged during this period. A more likely explanation is that concessionary officials simply downgraded to third quality a portion of the cotton that in previous years they would have defined as second-class fiber. The observation of a leading Portuguese expert, N. S. Bravo, that some concessionary personnel "buy first-quality cotton at second-quality prices" certainly supports such a conclusion.[59]

By 1947, the Cotton Board appears to have realized that manipulating the classification system alienated most growers and was counterproductive in the long run. It abandoned the three-tiered pricing system as part of its broader effort to promote an incentive-based cotton marketing system (see Chapter 6).[60] The concessionary companies mounted a concerted campaign to reverse this policy; when they failed to do so, they tried to subvert the policy on the ground. Some firms, such as Monteiro & Giro and SAN, refused to purchase soiled cotton at what they considered to be inappropriately high prices.[61] Other companies retained a de facto third category or subtly discouraged peasants from bringing impure fiber to the

---

[56]   Bravo, *Cultura Algodoeira*, 181.

[57]   Prices for the same quality cotton varied within the colony. As a rule the Cotton Board set higher prices in the south where it was trying to compete with the mines for labor, and in regions whose economies were already highly monetized. Peasants living in frontier areas received appreciably less. see Bravo, *Cultura Algodoeira*, 178.

[58]   AIA, JEAC, Rel. da Insp. de JEAC, "Esboço Estatístico Ref. a 1941," vol. 6, João Contreiras, n.d.; AIA, JEAC, Gastão de Mello Furtado, Adj. da Del. to Sub–Del. da JEAC, 19 June 1947; José Gaspar Faria, "Producão Algodeira."

[59]   Bravo, *Cultura Algodoeira*, 181.

[60]   In 1945, the JEAC altered the three-grade classification for ginned cotton to six grades, reflecting textile companies' concerns about the uneven quality of the fiber. Carlos Bastos and Ribeiro E.K. de Queiroz, *O Algodão: Da Colheita à Industrialização* (Porto, 1947).

[61]   AIA, JEAC, Conf. 1947, Eugénio Ferreira de Almeida to Del. da JEAC, 7 August 1947; AIA, JEAC, Conf. 1947, José da Cunha Dias Mendes to CD de JEAC, 11 August 1947.

TABLE 5–2 Annual Tax Obligations and Cotton Income by Region, 1943–1950

Period	Region[a]	Tax Obligation (in *escudos*)[b]	Approx. income per producer in *escudos*
1943–47	South	200–500 (adult males); 100 (adult females)	65 (1943)
	Center	75–90 (adult males, except Beira) 25–35 (adult females, except Beira)	50 (1943)
	North	50–90 (adult males) 25–50 (adult females)	130 (1943)
1947–57[c]	South	240 (adult males; females exempt)	550 (1950)[d]
	Center	110–120 (adult males outside Beira;	140 (1950) females exempt)
	North	70–120 (adult males; females exempt)	100 (1950)

Sources: BOM; RTE, Estatística Agrícola (1943–1950); Bravo, *A Cultura Algodoeira*, 135–39; AIA, JEAC, "Areas Cultivadas, Produção de Algodão–Caroço por Hectare e Número de Cultivadores Totais por Concelhos e Circumscriçoes."

[a]Within each of the three regions tax obligations varied somewhat.
[b]There was a surcharge of between 10 and 15 percent for late payment of taxes.
[c]This rate remained in effect until 1957.
[d]The sharp increase in income was a result of the state's decision to permit two-thirds of the 1943 growers, who were living in marginal lands, to withdraw from the system.

market.[62] In response, many growers refused to pick late-blooming cotton, which was normally of lower quality. Others destroyed part of their crop rather than spending additional time and labor transporting it to market.[63] Still others found alternative local markets for their cotton or, where possible, smuggled it across the border.[64] These strategies to circumvent the market are discussed at length in Chapter 10; here it is sufficient to note that these covert acts of defiance put some pressure on colonial authorities to reform the cotton regime.

While there were variations in peasants' cotton income from one region to another, average producer income was better in 1950 than it had been in several of the preceding years. However, cotton income remained pitifully low despite the Board's pricing reforms (see Chapter 6). Real income derived from the fiber barely kept up with inflation, and in most years it actually declined. In 1950, the 536,000 growers in the colony earned 101,000 *contos*, or slightly under 188 *escudos*, each (approximately U.S $7).[65] For all the fanfare in Lisbon about market reforms, little

---

[62]   Ibid.; AIA, JEAC, A. Felgeiras e Sousa, Sub–Del. de JEAC, Posto de Nampula to CD da JEAC.
[63]   AIA, JEAC, Conf. 1947, Eugénio Ferreira de Almeida to Del. da JEAC, 7 August 1947.
[64]   AIA, JEAC, A. Felqueira e Sousa, Sub–Del. de JEAC, Posto de Nampula to CD da JEAC, 25 June 1947.
[65]   Bravo, *Cultura Algodoeira*, 81; AIA, JEAC, "Areas Cultivadas."

had really changed. To be sure, cotton prices had risen at a faster rate than most cash crops, but a government study completed in 1951 found that cotton was still the least remunerative cash crop and that its real value was actually less than it had been in 1939.[66]

More to the point, 188 *escudos* did not buy a great deal after taxes. Indeed, in some regions of northern and central Mozambique, cotton income per producer did not even cover the cost of taxes typically paid by adult males (see Table 5–2).[67] And even where it did, tax fees still represented a significant drain on household income and made it difficult for most peasants to purchase basic consumer goods. A 1951 list of consumer prices for popular commodities in central Mozambique illustrates the peasants' plight. A blanket cost between fifty and eighty *escudos*, a long-sleeved sweater was thirty *escudos*, and cloth cost between fifteen and twenty *escudos* per meter.[68] Peasants whose cotton cultivation caused them to end the harvest with insufficient food supplies also paid hefty prices to restock their reserves. Twenty kilograms of corn or sorghum cost between thirty-six and forty *escudos*, and the price for beans or peanuts was double that amount.[69] For a family of five, twenty kilograms of corn or sorghum typically lasted about ten days. Since peanuts and beans were not the mainstay of rural diets, they could be made to last for an appreciably longer period. Pigs or goats purchased for special occasions cost from thirty to fifty *escudos*, and chickens went for up to ten *escudos* each.[70]

Many growers used cotton money to pay off debts they had accrued during the year by purchasing food, cloth, agricultural implements, and cheap alcohol on credit.[71] *Cantineiros* insisted that such debts be repaid immediately after peasants returned from the cotton market. In the world of frontier justice failure to do so often carried dire consequences. Growers from the south stressed this point: "It was common to borrow a 100$00 *escudos* from the *cantineiros* but only receive to 50$00 *escudos* worth of goods. And if we did not repay it on time, the *cantineiros* came looking for us with their guns. So we had to flee."[72] By the time most peasants returned home in August from the cotton market, they had very little to show for their year's labor.

Working in the Cotton Gins

Not all Africans involved in the labor of cotton worked in the fields. Many were employed in ginning mills and warehouses, where they cleaned and bailed the cotton lint and prepared it for export. SAGAL, for example, employed 3,000 work-

---

[66] Bravo, *Cultura Algodoeira*, 183.

[67] The only exception was the Makonde highlands where the tax rate was seventy *escudos*.

[68] AIA, JEAC, Conf. 1957–59, Henrique Nogueira Soute e Silva, Admin. de Espungabera, 21 December 1956.

[69] AIA, JEAC, Conf. 1957–1959, José Guilherme de Almeida, Reg. Ag. de BTT, 4 January 1957.

[70] Ibid.

[71] AIA, JEAC, "Prov. de Manica e Sofala," João Contreiras, Insp. dos SAU, May 1945; AIA, JEAC, 9191 "Inquérito Económico Agrícola Cultura Algodoeira," Francisco Neves Ferrão, Ag. Fisc., n.d.

[72] Group interview, CV Magul, Bilene, 20 February 1979.

TABLE 5–3 Salaries of African Workers at CAM Mill, Namapa, 1947

Job Description	No. of Employees	Salary in escudos (25 working days)
Overseer	4	150
Senior machine operator	2	195
Assistant machine operator	1	130
Press operator	12	143
Assistant press operator	6	104
Cotton gin worker	6	91
Assistant cotton gin worker	3	78
Chupador worker	3	78
Porter	12	78
Bale sewer	4	78
Burlap maker	2	78
Water carrier	4	78
Loader	30	78
Servant and maintenance worker	154	78

Source: Based on AIA, JEAC, "Confidencial 1947," António Mira Mendes, SD JEAC, Beira, to CD da JEAC, 20 December 1947.

ers at its huge plant and storage facilities in Montepuez.[73] CAM hired more than 1,100 workers for its mills in Meconta, Mogovolas, and Nampula.[74] By contrast, CNA employed 70 and 110 workers at its small mills in Magude and Sone, respectively.[75]

Prevailing race, class, and gender systems shaped hiring practices in the cotton factories. European men held the small number of supervisory positions. Asian and mulatto men filled most intermediary positions, particularly as office staff. African men comprised the bulk of the factory labor force. Included in their ranks were skilled laborers and workers who performed menial tasks, full-time employees and seasonal workers, those who came voluntarily and those who were conscripted. Most factories also recruited a handful of children. There is no evidence that women were ever hired for factory work, which is not surprising given the state-concessionary company view that women's role within the cotton regime was to remain in the fields.

The majority of factory workers volunteered, in a manner of speaking: they chose the factories over the cotton fields and the world of *chibalo* labor. Only a handful of Asians, mulattos, and Africans who managed to get some education were in a position to make this choice. André Marques de Pinha spent his adult life at the SAGAL plant. He worked in the warehouse and subsequently moved into a low-level clerk's position.[76] Factory salaries, he explained, were considerably higher

[73] Arquivo de SAGAL, "Corresp. com as Autoridades Admins.," Admin. de SAGAL to Admin. da Circ. de Montepuez, 28 January 1959.

[74] AHM, SR, Cx. 77, ISANI, "Rel. Insp. Ord. ao Dist. do Niassa," Estevão e Sousa, n.d.

[75] AHM, Cx. 40, ISANI, "Relatório . . . do Distrito da Beira, 1946," João Mesquita, 5 May 1947; AHM, Cx. 45, Indígenas, "Rel. Ord. à Circ. de Chemba," George Christovão de Sousa Franklin, 2 October 1959.

[76] Interview with Adelina Cedo and Andre Marques da Pinha, Montepuez, 21 July 1979.

than wages paid on European plantations, settler farms, or state public work projects. For Faquir Abadre, a machinist, the mill offered real if limited economic opportunities. He earned about 150 *escudos* per month, which in most plants was near the top of the salary scale for skilled African labor (see Table 5–3). His income was sufficient to meet his tax obligations, to purchase food and clothing, and occasionally to hire casual labor to assist his wife in the cotton fields.[77] Saide Julião was also among the fortunate few. His father was a *sipai* and enrolled his son in a local Muslim school. There Saide learned artisanal skills as well as some rudimentary Portuguese. When SAGAL opened its Montepuez factory in 1937, Saide was hired as a mason's apprentice working under a Portuguese named Silvestre.[78] Within a few years his salary increased from 40 to 120 *escudos* per month.

These men were the exceptions. Most Africans working in the mills were employed as menial laborers. They worked as porters, loaders, pressers, waste gatherers, sweepers, and in a variety of other labor-intensive jobs without which the factories could not operate. Although the salary structure varied slightly from one factory to another, in the late 1940s most people in these jobs were earning from two to four *escudos* per day (roughly U.S. $0.08 to $0.16). Wages at the Mopeia mills were probably toward the lower end of the scale; there the lowest-paid African employees received an average of fifty *escudos* (U.S. $2) per month in 1947.[79] This amount was less than a third of what the machine operators earned, but it was still about twenty *escudos* per month more than the wages of press-ganged plantation laborers. By contrast, the minimal monthly wage at CAM's mills was between seventy and eighty *escudos* (U.S. $2.80 to $3.20).[80] Since most African cotton factory employees worked for six or seven months of the year, they typically earned more than double the income of their male counterparts who were forced to grow cotton.[81]

The concessionary companies augmented their work force with conscripts and children. Whenever the harvest was unexpectedly high, *chibalo* workers were used to alleviate production backlogs at the ginning mills and warehouses. Company officials contracted these workers through the local administrators and their network of cooperating chiefs. Conscripts unloaded the trucks and wagons that brought the raw cotton from the market to the gins and then baled, packed, and loaded the lint onto trucks or trains. They also performed a variety of other tasks, ranging from fetching wood to general maintenance.[82] Children worked as waste gatherers and sweepers, collecting bits of cotton that had been left scattered on the factory floor.[83] *Chibalo* workers and children were at the bottom of the wage scale, earning as little as one *escudo* per day as late as 1947.[84]

---

[77] Interview with Faquir Abadre, Montepuez, 23 July 1979.

[78] Interview with Saide Julião, Montepuez, 23 July 1979.

[79] AIA, JEAC, Conf. 1947, 20 November 1947.

[80] Ibid.

[81] Interview with Adelino Cedo and Andre Marques da Pinha; confirmed in interview with Paulo Roque, Nampula, 27 May 1987.

[82] Interviews with Ramissa Promose, Montepuez, 23 July 1979; Adelino Cedo and Andre Marques da Pinha.

[83] Interview with Adelino Cedo and Andre Marques da Pinha.

[84] AIA, JEAC, Conf. 1947, 20 November 1947.

PHOTO 7 Working in a ginning mill. Courtesy of Arquivo Histórico de Moçambique. Rebelo Júnior, photographer.

Just as the composition of the labor force varied, so did the work schedule of factory employees. Unskilled laborers typically began their day at six in the morning and worked until the late afternoon.[85] During peak periods most factories organized two twelve-hour shifts. Machine operators and mechanics normally labored eight or nine hours per day all year round.[86] Most Africans, on the other hand, worked on a seasonal basis; they were called up in June, shortly after growers had picked their first crop, and they stayed until December when the plants closed down. Most of the skilled workers at the Montepuez plant spent a substantial portion of their adult lives at the factory. By contrast, low-paid unskilled laborers remained there for a much shorter period, after which they would return to work in the countryside.[87]

Unskilled workers were organized into gangs under the close supervision of African and European overseers. Each brigade was assigned a set of daily tasks. Factory police harassed and beat workers suspected of shirking their responsibilities.[88] The labor regime in the factory could be as brutal as it was in the fields.

---

[85] AHM, SR, Cx. 77, ISANI, "Rel. da Insp. Ord. ao Dist. de Nampula," Hortêncio Estevão de Sousa, Insp., 1948; interview with Adelino Cedo and Andre Marques da Pinha.

[86] Interviews with Saide Julião; Adelino Cedo and Andre Marques da Pinha.

[87] AHM, Cx. 39, ISANI, "Relatório . . . Manica e Sofala, 1946," João Mesquita, 5 May 1947; interviews with Adelino Cedo and Andre Marques da Pinha; Saide Julião; Ramissa Promosse.

[88] Interview with Adelino Cedo and Andre Marques da Pinha.

Within such close quarters, factory workers had even less autonomy than their rural counterparts, and fewer means of protest. Strikes, slowdowns, and sabotage were not tolerated, and if workers even tried to present their grievances to upper-level management, they faced harsh retribution. In this matter skilled laborers were treated no differently; "cheeky" Africans, no matter their function, had to be kept in their place. Saide Julião, a stone mason, remembered the reaction when he and his coworkers tried to meet with a management team visiting the plant:

> No one was allowed to speak with the people who came from Pemba. We could not explain our situation. We were not even allowed to enter the offices. Rachide and I were beaten. The carpenter, bricklayers, and iron workers all went with us to complain. The overseer scoffed at us. "You want to complain to the white bosses," they mocked. Then they beat us again and docked a week of our pay.[89]

"Agitators" were often sent to work as penal laborers.[90]

Difficult working conditions in the mills were not due solely to strict labor discipline. As long as the cotton industry could depend on a large enough labor pool, there was no reason to spend money to improve the working conditions or daily lives of factory laborers. The mills and warehouses were poorly ventilated, hot, and without appropriate lighting. Most serious was the large amount of floating lint, dust, and dirt, especially in the picking and carding rooms. The thick, polluted air made breathing difficult and caused serious respiratory problems. According to Saide Julião, working conditions were terrible, even in the more modern plants with better ventilation. "The dust, especially from the second- and third-quality cotton, was terrible. It was difficult to breathe. Many people became ill and spit up blood."[91] Another employee at the mill recalled that "as a result of the dust many workers suffered from tuberculosis. There were no medical facilities at the factory. Those who were seriously ill were sent to the district hospital."[92]

The Cotton Board had warned as early as 1939 that the dust particles posed a serious health hazard and that ventilation in the mills had to be improved, threatening to revoke the license of any company that failed to comply.[93] Yet few companies followed these directives, and no punitive actions seem to have been taken.

For workers seriously hurt in industrial accidents, the lack of proper medical facilities at or near the workplace often sealed their fate. Retired employees told of colleagues who died in bizarre accidents and workers who lost fingers or hands or had limbs mangled in the cotton gins and bailers.[94] Faquir Abadre described the plight of a fellow worker at the SAGAL factory in Mahate:

> He had his arm entangled in the cotton gin. He was sent to the hospital where he remained for three months. His hand was *rachada* [split] and permanently damaged. Subsequently the company fired him and sent him

---

[89] Ibid.

[90] AHM, SR, Cx. 77, ISANI, "Rel. Insp. Ord. ao Nampula," Hortêncio Estevão de Sousa, Insp., 1948.

[91] Interview with Saide Julião.

[92] Interview with Ramissa Promose.

[93] AIA, JEAC, CAM, 13 February 1939, CD de JEAC to Societé Coloniale Luso–Luxembourgoise, 30 September 1939.

[94] Interviews with Ramissa Promose; Faquir Abadre; Saide Julião.

home. There were other cases like this and no one treated them as if it were a big deal.[95]

Even these serious accidents did not motivate the industry to improve safety standards or to upgrade medical facilities. After all, the preponderance of victims were "*pretos*" (blacks). A local official complained in 1948: "[CAM] does not provide any medical assistance to the sick. Only a few days ago the management began to draw up a list of medicines that would be necessary for the small first aid station that it will establish to offer aid to the native."[96]

Inadequate factory rations exacerbated the medical problems. Across the colony cotton companies ignored, manipulated, or defied state regulations that workers receive specified minimum amounts of meat, fish, vegetables, and grains. In some locations, such as the large CAM factory at Nampula or the SAGAL mill at Montepuez, employees did not receive rations at all. Instead they got a small allowance from which they were expected to arrange their own food. They either drew on household reserves, if their family lived nearby and had adequate food stores, or they purchased food from the local population or the *cantineiro*.[97] Many employees supplemented their diets by cultivating, in the evenings and on Sundays, small gardens adjacent to their sleeping quarters.[98] Other mills provided rations that were inadequate in both quantity and quality. A state inspector visiting CAM's Meconta factory discovered that the diet consisted almost entirely of ground manioc and peanuts "in such advanced state of decay that they had lost all their nutritional value."[99] Meat, fish, and vegetables were completely absent from the workers' diets. The situation was only marginally better at CNA's Sone factory. And when the SAGAL management finally agreed to provide foodstuffs to workers at Montepuez in 1944, it gave them only porridge with a bit of sugar twice a day.[100]

The companies were equally reluctant to provide adequate accommodations for mill workers. CAM's large factory in Mogovolas, which employed more than 1,200 workers, for example, had no housing facilities whatsoever. Most Africans commuted daily from their homes, sometimes traveling two to three hours in each direction;[101] migrant laborers from the surrounding regions had to make their own arrangements. Despite the uncertainties, many viewed the factories as less threatening than the cotton fields. Where the companies did build compounds, conditions were appalling. A government inspector discovered that the compound at the Sone mill lacked latrines, running water, and cooking facilities, and that the walls and floors of the living quarters were filthy.[102] Conditions were no better at Meconta, where hundreds of workers were crammed into twenty makeshift huts.

[95]   Interview with Faquir Abadre.

[96]   AHM, SR, Cx. 77, ISANI, "Rel. da Insp. Ord, ao Mogovolas," Hortêncio Estevão de Sousa, 1948.

[97]   AHM, SR, Cx. 77, ISANI, "Rel. Insp. Ord, ao Nampula," Hortêncio Estevão de Sousa, Insp., 1948.

[98]   Interview with Adelino Cedo and Andre Marques da Pinha.

[99]   AHM, SR, Cx. 77, ISANI, "Rel. da Insp. Ord. ao Meconta," Hortêncio Estevão de Sousa, 1948.

[100]   Interview with Saide Julião.

[101]   AHM, SR, Cx. 77, ISANI, "Rel. da Insp. Ord. ao Mogovolas," Hortêncio Estevão de Sousa, 1948; AHM, SR, Cx. 77, ISANI, "Rel. da Insp. Ord. ao Meconta," Hortêncio Estevão de Sousa, 1948.

[102]   AHM, Cx. 45, ISANI, "Rel. Ord. a Circ. de Chemba, 1959," António George Cristóvão de Sousa Franklin, 2 October 1959.

Each worker was allocated four square meters—hardly enough to stretch out his tired body.[103] Unsanitary conditions, leaking thatched roofs, and damp earthen floors probably contributed to a number of diseases including tuberculosis, dysentery, and pneumonia.

The industry's minimization of expenditures extended to the factory production process.[104] The lack of transport meant that cotton often arrived late, disrupting production schedules. At other times the fiber arrived unexpectedly when there was no room in the warehouses, so it was left unprotected in piles outside.[105] Additionally, most companies relied on inefficient and out-of-date saw gins, pressers, and bailers.[106] As late as 1957 a cotton technician discovered African workers still trampling cotton by foot rather than using pressing equipment.[107] The CAM factory at Mualama and the SAGAL plant at Montepuez were the most noteworthy exceptions.

In every respect, the companies' cost-minimizing policies were shortsighted and ultimately disastrous. Inefficient techniques and secondhand equipment kept production costs low, but they also ensured low productivity and an inferior product. The outdated machinery in the factories required a great deal of slow and dangerous hand labor to keep it operating. As a result, output per mill per hour was less than half that of more modern factories in neighboring Nyasaland and Southern Rhodesia, where British textile interests intervened more directly than did their Portuguese counterparts in Mozambique. And even when the fiber was cleaned, sorted, and ready for packing, reliance on antiquated pressers meant that ginned lint was rarely condensed into maximum-density bales. Less dense bales generated higher transportation costs, thus further reducing the profit margin. At a time when concessionaires were complaining that transport costs were jeopardizing profit margins, modernizing factory equipment would obviously have been a prudent strategy. Instead, the cotton industry continued to pursue "backward principals and practices of entrepreneurship" designed to minimize costs rather than to maximize output.[108]

Supported by state-regulated market arrangements and monopolistic practices, the concessionaires profited in the short run by plundering the Mozambican countryside. But pumping out wealth through unequal exchange could not, in the long run, yield sufficient amounts of high-quality cotton to meet the needs of either the textile industry or a state anxious to reduce imports of foreign fiber. Cotton Board officials concluded that undercapitalization, cost minimization, and incompetence would strangle the system. The only alternative was to reform the cotton regime and "rationalize" production, a policy the Board gradually initiated in the aftermath of World War II.

---

[103]   AHM, SR, Cx. 77, ISANI, "Rel. da Insp. Ord. ao Meconta," Hortêncio Estevão de Sousa, 1948.

[104]   At a certain point this cost–minimizing strategy becomes self–defeating and profits will drop. But there is little evidence that this issue was discussed in a serious way.

[105]   AIA, JEAC, 605/8, Posto 1946, Luís Salema, Ag. Fisc., "Rel. do Serviço," October 1946.

[106]   Fortuna, "Threading Through," 246–47.

[107]   Ibid.

[108]   Ibid.

6

Reforming the System: Rationalizing the Labor Process

By the late 1940s the contradictions in the cotton regime had become obvious. The increases in cotton output only exacerbated the regime's chronic problems. Food shortages, social unrest, peasant flight, and environmental degradation were the most obvious indicators of the magnitude of the crisis in rural Mozambique. Lisbon's commitment to promoting cotton collided with growers' increasing antipathy toward the staple (see Chapter 10). For all the regime's pressure on the rural population, colonial cotton output failed to keep pace with metropolitan needs. In 1949 cotton exports from Mozambique and Angola satisfied only 79 percent of metropolitan needs, down from 96 percent in 1946.[1] Colonial authorities were not unaware of the adverse impact of their policy. Many came to realize how tightly they were squeezing the peasants. A growing number of voices insisted that the cotton scheme in the colonies needed to be revamped. The only question was how to go about reforming the system.

This issue provoked an intense debate. While some colonial state officials advocated expanding cotton production at all costs, others thought intensification through brute force a serious mistake and argued that the neglect of food crops was counterproductive. Still others favored a policy of "guiding the peasants" by using a combination of moral and material incentives. Proponents of a more rational system of production gained support from colonial planners, local extension officers, labor inspectors, and agronomists who argued that the cotton regime in Mozambique was archaic and inefficient. Textile interests in Lisbon, angry about the poor quality of Mozambican cotton, also sought reform.[2] While not always acting in unison, these different fractions of capital exercised a great deal of influence on the Cotton Board and state officials. Although the interests of Lisbon and the

---

[1]   AIA, JEAC, "Prop. de Moç.," 720/0–6-34.

[2]   See, for example, Bastos and de Queiroz, *O Algodão*.

textile and concessionary interests were closely intertwined, colonial policy on issues as critical as market reform and control over Mozambican land and labor did
not always mirror the concerns of concessionary. The latter opposed the reforms,
which they considered to be costly and highly problematic.

The new cotton policy began to take shape immediately after World War II,
but many of its critical components—such as planned cotton communities, cooperatives, and price reforms—were not enacted until the 1950s. This time lag and
the uneven implementation of the reforms meant there was no watershed or defining moment marking a radical transformation in the cotton regime. Changes were
incremental and uneven. The sweeping reforms of 1946 embodied in Decree 35.844[3]
marked the beginning of the Cotton Board's decade-long effort to transform the
regime by harnessing the most "energetic" male labor to the best cotton lands. This
legislation specifically called for the elimination of inappropriate regions from the
cotton regime and the establishment of "free zones" where peasants could grow
the staple voluntarily. Through a combination of social engineering, scientific farming, and nutritional science, the Cotton Board believed it could increase productivity, ease hunger, reverse ecological degradation, and ensure rural social order, and
in the process transform peasants into "modern" cotton farmers.

Lisbon was hardly unique in its efforts to rationalize cotton production. A decade earlier most other colonial regimes had begun to introduce the principles and
rhetoric of scientific farming. Agricultural departments in the British, French, and
Belgian colonies experimented with soil conservation schemes, seed breeding, pest
control, and crop rotation.[4] These initiatives were part of a broader policy shift
from coercion to incentives. Most colonial powers concluded that prewar agricultural regimes had reached the limits of their possible expansion.[5] Only the Portuguese tried to rationalize production by combining elements of scientific farming
with new material incentives and the continued reliance on coercion. This contradictory policy ultimately failed.

Voices for Reform

It was not an accident that calls for reforming the cotton regime in Portugal began
in earnest following the end of World War II. Anne Pitcher has argued convinc-
ingly that changes in the international environment as well as in Portugal's own
domestic and colonial priorities drove colonial policymakers to reform the cotton
regime.[6] At an ideological level, she notes that the defeat of the Axis powers forced
the Salazar government to retreat from its corporate-fascist rhetoric and rigid to-

---

[3]   Decree 35.844 was published in *BOM*, 1, 45 (9 November 1946), 459.

[4]   See Isaacman and Roberts, *Cotton, Colonialism, and Social History,*

[5]   This new agricultural policy was not limited to cotton. Soil conservation and scientific farming be-
came the hallmark of most rural development schemes in the 1930s and 1940s. See, for example, Paul
Richards, *Indigenous Agricultural Revolution: Ecology and Food Production in West Africa* (London, 1985);
William Beinart, "Introduction: The Politics of Colonial Conservation," *JSAS* 15(1989), 145–62; William
Allen, *The African Husbandman* (New York, 1965).

[6]   Pitcher, *Politics in the Portuguese Empire*, 97–178; M. Anne Pitcher, "From Coercion to Incentive," in
Isaacman and Roberts, *Cotton, Colonialism, and Social History.* Although I date the impact of the reforms
somewhat later than Pitcher, her writing on this subject has informed my work.

talitarianism. At home, Salazar's pronouncements became less authoritarian and increasingly stressed the language and principles of neoclassical economic theory. Modernization, rationalization, and productivity, notions borrowed from the postwar discourse of the Allies, became the order of the day.[7] For Portugal's colonies this new stance meant talk about labor reform and modernizing agriculture and industry.[8]

Economic considerations also prompted a revision of the state's development strategy, both at home and in the colonies. During the war years Portugal had enjoyed a rare balance-of-payments surplus.[9] By 1947, however, this positive trend had been reversed, and the Salazar regime once again turned to the colonies to alleviate the problem. Replacing imports purchased on the international market with those produced in the colonies was one way to offset the balance-of-payments deficit.

In most respects, the agenda of colonial planners meshed with that of the metropolitan textile interests.[10] After the war, the Salazar regime focused on modernizing the metropolitan industrial sector, particularly textile manufacturers, which were the country's major exporters. The state promoted the structural reorganization of the industry by, for example, allowing larger firms to acquire modern automatic looms to replace outdated mechanical ones.[11] The textile industry was positioned to expand exports appreciably, but to do so required an increased supply of cheap high-quality cotton. Industry officials, concerned that the erratic output and uneven quality of Mozambican and Angolan fiber would stifle the expansion of the textile industry, demanded that colonial cotton production be revamped.

Although production in the colonies had increased substantially, it remained erratic. Between 1943 and 1947, for example, Mozambican exports varied annually by as much as 30 percent. Moreover, even in peak years metropolitan demand outstripped colonial production. As a result, Portuguese textile factories had to purchase more cotton on the open market. In 1946 the industry bought 1.8 million kilograms from foreign sources. By 1949, this figure had skyrocketed to almost eight million kilograms.[12]

To make matters worse, the gap between the price paid for colonial cotton and the price paid on the international market kept widening. World market prices were about 15 percent more expensive than Mozambican fiber in 1940; by 1949, the spread was nearly 200 percent. Against the backdrop of a looming crisis, the influential *Journal do Comércio de Lisboa* in 1949 called on the government to promote cotton self-sufficiency:

The fact that cotton production was very weak during the past campaign, relative to metropolitan industrial needs, required us to purchase foreign

---

[7] M. Anne Pitcher, personal communication, 7 February 1994.

[8] Marcelo Caetano, *Relações das Colónias de Angola e Moçambique com os Territórios Estrangeiros Visinhos* (Lisbon, 1946), 72. Cited also in Bender, *Angola Under the Portuguese*, 349.

[9] This surplus was generated by wage remittances from immigrants, shipping fees, and tourism among other sources. Fernando Rosas, *Portugal Entre a Paz e a Guerra* (Lisbon, 1990), 153–34; Pitcher, "From Coercion to Incentive."

[10] Textile interests were concerned primarily about issues of price and quality, not about balance-of-payments problems, which were a major consideration for state authorities.

[11] Pitcher, *Politics in the Portuguese Empire*, 158–65.

[12] AIA, JEAC, "Prop. Moç.," 720/0-6-34.

cotton on a scale that placed an enormous burden on our balance of payments and an unnecessary tax on our nation as a whole. . . . It is necessary
to stimulate production in the colonies not only to meet current industrial
needs but . . . to compete in new world markets.[13]

The irregular quality of colonial cotton compounded the problems facing the
textile companies. Industry representatives complained that the fibers were uneven
in length, dirty, full of seeds, and badly ginned. In a newspaper article boldly entitled "White Gold Coming from Our Colonies," the writer expressed the industry's
concern that the haphazard quality of Mozambican cotton was undermining
Portugal's competitive position in the international textiles market.[14] In 1946 alone,
the textile industry lodged ninety-six formal complaints with the Portuguese government about the poor quality of cotton imported from the colonies.[15]

Industry spokesmen attributed the inferior quality of African-grown cotton to
the inefficient system of production. They complained about the "primitive" methods Africans used to cultivate cotton, the poor choice of land, and the lack of appropriate labor control. They also lambasted the concessionary companies for failing to invest in mechanized agricultural equipment and ginning equipment and
for relying on an outmoded system of marketing and transportation.[16] The cotton
regime was archaic, these critics insisted, and had to be changed.

Demands for change from the metropole meshed with criticism from colonial
officials. While agreeing about the need for new technology, this group also contended that cotton yields could be improved if the state relied on moral and material incentives instead of on brute force. Many promoted a paternalist agenda and
sought to control the most rapacious practices of the concessionary companies.[17]
While paternalism never became a guiding ethos for the cotton regime, it offered
Portuguese officials a language to justify the cotton scheme not only to themselves
but to the African peasants they sought to control. Authorities in Mozambique echoed the belief that the introduction of new technologies, new market opportunities, and new cultural values could transform the lives of peasant cotton growers
even without eliminating coercion.[18]

For some local administrators, the paternalistic notion of "helping the natives"
to better themselves was more than romantic myth or political fabrication. A number of these officials took Portugal's "civilizing mission" seriously and were ap-
palled by the abuses committed by the cotton companies.[19] They also recognized
that forced cotton cultivation precipitated substantial social unrest, which made

---

13 *Journal do Comércio de Lisboa*, 19 September 1949.

14 *Diário de Lisboa*, 20 November 1941.

15 Pitcher, "From Coercion to Incentive," 15.

16 Carlos Bastos, *Comércio e Indústria Textil em Portugal* (Porto, 1950), 154; Pitcher, "From Coercion to
Incentive."

17 Research on a variety of economic and social institutions from plantations to industrial workplaces
suggests that paternalism and coercion were noe mutually exclusive; they were often integrally connected
parts of a larger strategy of social control. For a discussion of the paternalist ingredients in the Mozambican
cotton regime, see Allen Isaacman, "Coercion, Paternalism and the Labor Process: The Mozambican Cotton Regime 1938–1961,"*JSAS* 18, 3(1992), 487–526.

18 AIA, JEAC, "Prop. de Moç.," A. Felgueiras e Sousa, 24 May 1950.

19 Vail and White, *Capitalism and Colonialism*, 299.

their own lives more difficult. Some local officials opted to protect their African "wards."[20] In 1947 one official hoped he could

> persuade people that the *chefe de posto* is not *"o branco"* who collects taxes, but *"o amigo"* who helps them in their afflictions, resolving their little problems, rendering them justice with regard to friends or enemies, giving them counsel in their manner of living and also in the way they cultivate their land.[21]

Toward this end, some officials eased their enforcement of all aspects of the cotton regime.[22] In some instances, local administrators actually intervened to limit the power of the concessionary companies. In one highly publicized case in 1947, officials of the Búzi Company were furious at a local administrator who characterized cotton production as a form of slavery and exempted a number of pregnant and ill women from the system.[23] Those administrators who protested loudly or who made visible compromises were the exception, but in the postwar period they constituted an important voice for reform.

Native Affairs inspectors, charged with protecting the health and well-being of the colonized population, generally took their mandate seriously. Their reports, based on firsthand observations from all over the colony, constituted a powerful indictment of the cotton regime. After listening to northern peasants present a litany of cotton-related complaints, one inspector warned: "We cannot, indeed, we must not allow the overseers, whether working for the cotton or rice companies, to pursue policies that are in their own interests."[24] Another inspector traveling through the south questioned the wisdom of a system that forced peasants to grow cotton in unsuitable highland regions and prohibited them from cultivating peanuts in fertile lowland areas.[25] Despite their criticisms, most inspectors concluded that cotton offered greater hope for progress in Mozambique and would be less disruptive than alternative proposals.[26]

Within the state apparatus, men in closest proximity to the cotton fields—Cotton Board inspectors, agronomists, soil scientists, technicians, and extension officers and, particularly, the employees of CICA—were the most vigorous proponents of reform.[27] The exasperation of one Cotton Board official when he discovered that company overseers had destroyed eighteen fields of maize and designated them as cotton plots[28] was typical of their reactions. So was the outrage of another who objected "to the extraordi-

---

20   This term is derived from Marvin Harris, *Portugal's African Wards* (New York, 1960).

21   Quoted in Vail and White, *Capitalism and Colonialism*, 299.

22   Interview with Faria Lobo, Nampula, 26 May 1987.

23   AIA, JEAC, Conf. 1947, Dir. da Comp. de Búzi to Del. da JEAC, 7 December 1947.

24   AHM, SR, Cx. 89, ISANI, "Relatório . . . de Mecufi, Realizada no Ano de 1950/1951," António Policarpo de Sousa, Insp. Admin., 1951.

25   AHM, SR, Cx. 20, "Insp. ao Conc. de Gaza e Circs. do Bilene, Manhiça e Magude, 1953," António Policarpo de Sousa Santos, Insp. Conc. de Gaza.

26   AHM, SR, Cx. 20, "Rel. Insp. Ord. à Intend. de Gaza," João Villas Boas Carbeiro de Moura, Insp. Admin., 1953.

27   This material, which was formerly housed in the Cotton Board archives, has now been integrated into the Arquivo Histórico de Moçambique. At the present, only a small fraction of the documents are available, with the remainder in the process of being reorganized and catalogued.

28   AIA, JEAC, "Papéis Diversos," Vivaldo Guerreiro to CSD da JEAC, 18 August 1941.

nary profits a handful of cotton companies make by exploiting the producers."[29] Yet despite their frustrations, they envisioned the possibility of a healthy and prosperous peasantry increasing cotton output through incentives rather than coercion. The words of Professor Quintanilha, the first director of CICA, were more than a self-serving rationalization: "We wanted to make the cultivation of cotton profitable enough so that peasants would cultivate it voluntarily."[30]

To ease the burden on peasants, agricultural technicians working for the Cotton Board advocated a number of concrete reforms. They argued that peasants living on inappropriate lands should be exempt from cotton production, that a system of crop rotation should be introduced to conserve the soil and increase productivity, and that prices should be increased so that peasants would grow the staple voluntarily.[31] CICA's scientific staff also opposed concessionary company efforts to impose a second cotton season, contending that such a policy would yield only marginal returns and would increase the possibility of plant diseases by preventing peasants from burning the cotton stalks. An additional planting, they further argued, would divert badly needed labor away from food production.[32] For these "experts" a reorganization of the cotton regime was the key to rural development and social progress in colonial Mozambique.

To underscore this premise, they pointed to the success of CNA, which was considered to be the model concessionary cotton company. CNA had introduced a limited system of voluntary cotton cultivation in Manica e Sofala in 1942. Men who agreed to grow the crop received the designation *agricultor do algodão* and were exempted from *chibalo* labor. They were also required to cultivate one hectare of food crops plus an additional half-hectare of food for each wife. CNA overseers carefully selected fertile lands, delivered the cotton seeds well before the first rains, established a rational production calendar, and built cotton markets no more than five kilometers apart. If colonial reports are to be believed, they also kept coercion to a minimum, using the threat of *chibalo* rather than the whip to "encourage" cooperation with the new arrangements.[33]

Both cotton and food production surged within CNA's territory.[34] Cotton output rose well above the national average, and in some areas yields doubled within a year.[35] Average peasant production in Chemba for the 1942–43 campaign was 402 kilograms, while in Gorongosa it approached 600 kilograms.[36]

Reforms on the Ground: Creating New Rural Men

In response to these calls for change, the Cotton Board introduced a number of reforms in the postwar period.[37] Many were borrowed from the practices of CNA. In

---

[29] AIA, JEAC, "Rel. An. de 1945," João Contreiras, Insp. dos SAU, May 1945.

[30] Interview with A. Quintanilha, Maputo, 12 March 1979.

[31] AIA, JEAC, "Papéis Diversos," J. Anachoreta, CSD, 12 June 1950.

[32] AIA, JEAC, "Rel. Técnico," Fonseca George, Chefe de Secção Fomento, Lourenço Marques, 10 April 1947.

[33] Company officials reminded *agricultores* that if they failed to meet their cotton obligations they would lose their legal exemption from *chibalo*. AIA, JEAC, "Rel. Técnico," Fonseca George, Eng. Ag., 1945.

[34] AIA, JEAC, "Prov. de Manica e Sofala," João Contreiras, May 1945.

[35] Ibid.; AIA, JEAC, 601/8, "Rel.," Felipe Luís James, Sec. da Admin. de Manica, 31 January 1946.

[36] AIA, JEAC, "Prov. de Manica e Sofala," João Contreiras, May 1945.

[37] AIA, JEAC, "Papéis Diversos," J. Anachoreta, CSD, 12 June 1940.

Price in Escudos at 1961 Prices

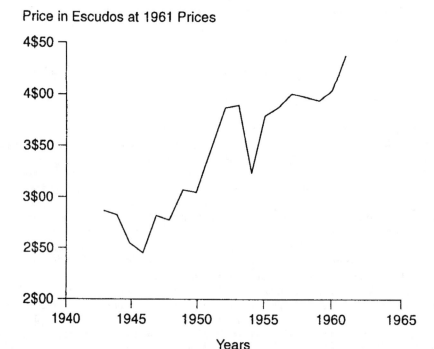

GRAPH 6-1. Average Real Price Paid per Kilogram of Cotton in Northern Mozambique, 1943–1961

Sources: Bravo, *A Cultura Algodoeira*, 135; RTE, *Recenseamento Agrícola* (Lourenço Marques), 1940–1941; RTE, *Estatística Agrícola* (Lourenço Marques), 1941–1960; Direcção Provinçal dos Serviço de Estatística Geral, *Estatística Agrícola* (Lourenço Marques, 1960–1964); AIA, JEAC, Exportação de Algodão Colonial, "Produtos por Distrito," 1951.

the 1940s CNA had developed a network of localized markets connected by motorized vehicles. Company officials located these markets near the principal production centers and within five kilometers of each other. As a result, cotton growers did not have to spend so much time and energy transporting their cotton crop.[38]

The state mandated similar market reforms throughout the colony in 1946. Decree 35.444 required concessionary companies to locate fairs within fifteen kilometers of the cotton fields. The sites had to be approved by the local administrator, the governor of the province and, ultimately, the Cotton Board. The most remote areas were expected to upgrade market facilities and to announce the dates when each market would be open well before the first cotton harvest. To protect the rights of growers, this legislation also required local administrators to oversee all market transactions.[39]

---

[38]   AIA, JEAC, "Prov. de Manica e Sofala," João Contreiras, May, 1945.

[39]   *BOM*, 1, 45, 9 November 1946, 462.

Tons (Thousands)

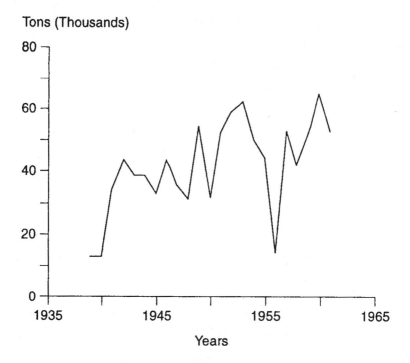

GRAPH 6–2. Cotton Production in Northern Mozambique

Source: Based on Bravo, *A Cultura Algodeira,* 136–38.

Little by little, most of these reforms were implemented, despite considerable opposition from concessionaires. By the early 1950s the cotton companies had constructed a network of rural markets throughout the countryside, and the state undertook a massive program of road building. While the new roads eased the burden of porterage in the short term, recruiting labor to build and maintain these roads and providing rations to road workers exacerbated local food and labor supply problems. Of course, the rural communities were expected to shoulder these costs. Nevertheless, by the end of the 1950s most peasants could make the journey to the cotton market within a day and with only minor inconveniences.

The most significant market reform imposed by the Cotton Board was price liberalization. Until the late 1940s the state had essentially frozen producer prices and in some years had actually reduced them.[40] In 1948 the Board set the price for first-quality cotton at 1$51 *escudos* per kilogram, a modest increase from the war period, but less than half the price paid to peasants in nearby Nyasaland.[41] The real amount paid to growers more than doubled over the next decade to 3$21 *escudos*

---

[40] Bravo, *Cultura Algodoeira,* 184; AIA, JEAC, "Papéis Diversos Despacho," J. Anachoreta, CSD do Sul do Save, 12 July 1940.

[41] I am grateful to Elias Mandala for this information.

Income in Escudos at 1961 Prices

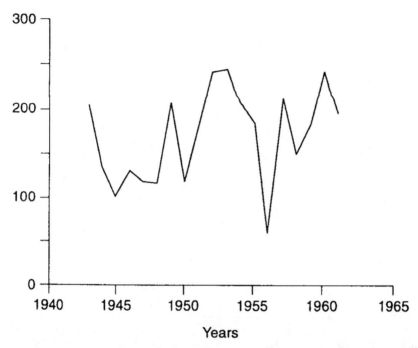

Graph 6–3. Real Cotton Income per Producer, Northern Mozambique, 1943–1961

Sources: Bravo, *A Cultura Algodoeira*, 135; RTE, *Recenseamento Agrícola* (Lourenço Marques), 1940–1941; RTE, *Estatística Agrícola* (Lourenço Marques), 1941–1960; Direcção Provinçal dos Serviço de Estatística Geral, *Estatística Agrícola* (Lourenço Marques), 1960–1964); AIA, JEAC, Exportação de Algodão Colonial, "Produtos por Distrito," 1951.

per kilogram of raw cotton (see Graph 6–1).[42] During this same period, the price concessionaires received for their ginned cotton in Lisbon increased at a somewhat slower rate. Nevertheless, at no time during the 1950s did cotton producers ever receive more than 17 percent of the export price.[43]

These relative improvements stimulated a sharp increase in peasant output. Production in the north, the colony's principal cotton zone, increased from slightly more than 30,000 tons in 1950 to more than 65,000 tons one decade later (see Graph 6–2). This jump is all the more significant since it occurred without any major technological innovations and actually coincided with a modest reduction in the amount

---

[42]   Pitcher, "From Coercion to Incentives."

[43]   Even allowing for the fact that it took approximately three kilograms of raw cotton to produce one kilogram of ginned fiber, the 17 percent figure clearly demonstrates the limited benefits in relationship to the risks that growers incurred. AIA, JEAC, "Prop. de Moç.," 720/0–6–34, 15 June 1954; AIA, JEAC, "Copiador Geral de Notas–Conf., 1958–1959," Gastão de Melo Furtado to Dir. dos SNI; AIA, JEAC, "Diversos, Mapas, Estatísticos e Elementos Informativos," n.d.; Pitcher, "From Coercion to Incentive."

of land peasants devoted to cotton. Even allowing for annual variations in output, this figure represented nearly a 150 percent increase in productivity. A similar pattern occurred throughout the rest of the colony.

Higher prices and increased productivity meant increased cotton incomes in the 1950s. For northern growers real earnings more than doubled (see Graph 6–3), although income fluctuated widely from year to year and plummeted in the aftermath of the 1956 hurricane.[44] In a few of the more fertile regions, such as Mocuba and Morrumbala in central Mozambique, producers were earning from 1,200 to 1,700 *escudos* per year (between U.S. $40 and $55), several times what they had earned a decade earlier.[45] Abdul Satar, a merchant who lived in Morrumbala in the Zambézia district during this period, described a noticeable change in peasant attitudes toward the staple:

> Cotton was obligatory. And in the beginning no one liked it. But much later growers began to prefer cotton to other crops because it yielded a higher income. There were individuals I knew who sold their crop for 12,000 *escudos* [U.S. $420] and more. In those days it was a lot of money.[46]

For northern Mozambique as a whole, the percentage of agricultural income peasants derived from cotton jumped from approximately 30 to 60 percent during the 1950s.[47]

The Cotton Board's most ambitious piece of social engineering was its 1948 plan to transform the most "productive" peasants into authentic cotton farmers committed to sustainable and progressive agricultural development. This project sought to divide the rural population into two gendered categories, *agricultores do algodão* and *cultivadores do algodão*.[48] The former were to be eighteen- to fifty-five-year-old men who agreed to cultivate one hectare of cotton plus an additional half-hectare for each wife beyond their first spouse.[49] They were also expected to plant food plots the same size as their cotton fields. *Agricultores* were eligible for technical assistance from the state, production bonuses, and relocation into planned cotton communities (*concentrações de algodão*). Most important, in accordance with a 1949 decree, these men were shielded from *chibalo* and theoretically could not be conscripted to work on European plantations.[50] For male producers who preferred this "peasant option" to working as unpaid or poorly paid migrant laborers, *agricultor* status held an obvious attraction. Wives of *agricultores* who met the state requirement were subsumed under this legal category.

---

44   Bravo, *Cultural Algodoeira*, 195.

45   Ibid.

46   Interview with Abdul Satar, Quelimane, 19 July 1991.

47   RTE, *Recenseamento Agrícola* (Lourenço Marques), 1940–1941; RTE, *Estatística Agrícola* (Lourenço Marques), 1941–1960; Direcçao Provincial dos Serviços de Estatística Geral, *Estatística Agrícola* (Lourenço Marques), 1960–1964. In part this dramatic shift can be explained in response to the price stimulus. But if cotton was a dynamic peasant crop, cultivation of other crops was fairly stagnant.

48   The project was first proposed in 1944 legislation (Dip. Leg. No. 919, 5 August 1944). In 1948 the plan was fleshed out in AIA, JEAC, "Bases Para a Campanha Algodoeira" and approved by the governor general of Mozambique. Bravo, *Cultura Algodoeira*, 117.

49   In the Niassa province the governor refined the category of *agricultor*. All men between the ages of eighteen and thirty had to cultivate somewhat less. Bravo, *Cultura Algodoeira*, 117.

50   Legislation cited in AIA, JEAC, 84 (1958–59), Gastão de Mello de Furtado to CSD de JEAC, 9 February 1960.

TABLE 6–1 Number of *Agricultores* and *Cultivadores* by Company, 1960–1961

Company	Agricultores	Cultivadores
Algodoeira do Sul do Save	11,660	44,706
Companhia Nacional Algodoeira	20,628	15,859
Companhia do Búzi	3,604	7,472
Companhia da Zambézia	3,932	18,970
Sociedade Algodoeira de Tete	5,618	4,303
Lopes & Irmão	10,968	11,078
Monteiro & Giro	4,620	1,037
Sena Sugar Estates	—	14,893
Companhia Algodões de Moçambique	94,798	80,814
João Ferreira dos Santos	17,924	12,244
Sociedade Agrícola Algodoeira	32,616	1,681
Sociedade Algodoeira do Niassa	18,145	22,622
Total	224,573	285,679

Source: AIA, JEAC, "Semente Distribuida, Area Semeada, Agricultores e Cultivadores por Zonas Algodoeiras, Campanha de 1960/61."

The majority of women, however, were not offered this choice. Along with older men with physical handicaps and those considered less motivated, they were lumped together as *cultivadores de algodão*. *Cultivadores* were required to cultivate a half-hectare each of cotton and food crops. To ensure that the two legal categories were not obscured, state officials issued white cotton books to *cultivadores* and red cotton books to *agricultores*.[51] In colonial ideology, *cultivadores de algodão* were "subsistence producers," "shifting agriculturalists," "recalcitrant nomads," "vagrants," and "vagabonds"—social categories synonymous in Portuguese minds with economic stagnation and social unrest.

Many men seized the *agricultor* option as a way to make their lives within the cotton regime more bearable. By 1961, the final year of the regime, slightly more than 40 percent of the registered cotton growers had qualified as *agricultores*.[52] Substantial variations in this percentage among regions reflected differences in local ecological conditions and political economies, in the range of choices available to a particular set of growers, and in the practices of specific concessionary company employees (see Table 6–1). In the labor-exporting areas of the south, less than 20 percent of the eligible men opted for this status; in the northern cotton zones of Niassa, Nampula, and Cabo Delgado, by contrast, this figure ranged from 45 to 60 percent (see Table 6–2).[53]

Since *agricultores* enjoyed distinctly better working conditions along with more technical support and fewer risks of crop failure, this bifurcation of rural commu-

---

[51] AIA, JEAC, 660/55 (1952), António Mendes, 8 March 1949.

[52] The first wife of each *agricultor* was not counted under either category; she was considered her husband's "helper." I am grateful to Anne Pitcher for clarifying this point. See AIA, JEAC, "Sementes Distribuidas, Área Semeada, Agricultores e Cultivadores por Zonas Algodoeiras, Campanha de 1960/61."

[53] For the 1958–59 cotton campaign the figures were, Inhambane 18.7 percent, Gaza 19.9 percent, Niassa 45 percent, Nampula 61 percent, and Cabo Delgado 63.3 percent. AIA, JEAC, Gastão de Melo Furtado to Gov. de Niassa, 24 February 1959.

TABLE 6-2 Percentage of *Agricultores* by District*

District	Percentage	District	Percentage
Zambézia	18.0	Niassa	45.0
Inhambane	18.8	Manica e Sofala	50.1
Gaza	19.9	Nampula	61.1
Tete	21.5	Cabo Delgado	63.3

Source: AIA, JEAC, Gastão de Mello Furtado to Gov. de Niassa, 24 February 1959.

Note: *Wives of *agricultores* were included in this category.

nities should, in theory, have had a far-reaching impact on the labor process. In practice, however, the distinction between *agricultores* and *cultivadores* was not always as significant as the legislation would suggest. "The criteria," lamented one official, "are never rigorously fulfilled [and] it is rare to find any Africans who cultivate the entire recommended area."[54] Moreover, for all its attention to reform, the cotton regime continued to rest on force. *Agricultores* were not immune from beatings. Production bonuses were minuscule (see below), and state technical assistance was also quite limited. Even the guarantee that *agricultores* would not be press-ganged for plantation or *chibalo* labor was often violated.[55] The post-World War II resurgence of the capitalist agricultural sector in the north, particularly sisal production, and the expansion of the state program to build all-weather roads required able-bodied men, regardless of their legal cotton status.

To strengthen the reform agenda, advocates of change promoted construction of a network of planned cotton communities closely resembling the *paysannats* program in the Belgian Congo. The proposal, first envisioned in the 1946 legislation, called for relocating hundreds of dispersed rural households, giving them parcels of fertile land and technical support, and introducing European notions of crop rotation. It was obvious from the outset, however, that improving the lives of peasant producers was not the plan's first concern. Rather, this policy was a logical extension of earlier efforts to control peasant labor allocation more effectively by aggregating scattered cotton fields into easily supervised blocs. Enthusiastic supporters of the program insisted that such a development strategy would increase cotton production, guarantee food security, and reduce problems of soil erosion, but not once did Cotton Board officials consider building on local systems of knowledge or on indigenous agricultural practices and techniques such as intercropping. In 1948 the state established the first cotton communities.

Colonial authorities initially targeted *agricultores* and their families for membership in these new communities. Single women, widows, and unproductive male *cultivadores* were not given the option of joining. In areas where state officials found it difficult to stimulate *agricultor* interest in the *concentrações*, however, they often pressured large numbers of *cultivadores* into joining. Whatever the initial composition of the communities, colonial authorities were committed to expanding the eco-

---

54 Bravo, *Cultura Algodoeira*, 117.

55 AIA, JEAC, "Papéis Diversos," A. Figueira e Sousa to Gov. de Niassa, 21 February 1952; AIA, JEAC, "Conf. 1957–1959," Júlio Bossa, 14 September 1959.

nomic and social distinction between those who settled in the *concentrações* and those who remained outside.

Concentrações offered much greater economic possibilities to cotton growers, at least in theory, than the existing cotton scheme. Each household was to receive between five and seven hectares of land, almost half of which would be allowed to lie fallow at any one time. On the remainder of their land, peasants each year would cultivate one hectare of cotton, one hectare of corn or sorghum and other food crops, and one hectare of manioc. Mixed cropping held out a number of advantages, including insurance against crop failures, reduced labor demands, improved disease control, and more efficient use of physical resources by crops with different needs and characteristics. State agronomists also planned to introduce a system of furrowing and ridging in order to minimize soil erosion. In some coastal areas there were also plans for members to plant one hectare of cashews or similar tree crops. In tsetse-free zones in the south, cattle keeping would be combined with agriculture.

State officials predicted that the *concentrações* would transform the countryside. In 1951, a Native Affairs inspector working in northern Mozambique described the imagined benefits of planned communities this way:

> We must convince them that the *concentrações* provide the best defense against fevers, sleeping sickness, and other epidemics. Because growers will be concentrated in a common place it will make it easier for the Government to provide agricultural and veterinary assistance, medical aid and moral, spiritual and educational support.[56]

Four years later, at a gathering of local administrators, Dr. Álvaro Henrique de Gouveia e Melo, governor of Zambézia, stressed that the *concentrações* were a central feature of Portugal's larger civilizing mission:

> The objective is to establish permanent communities of natives in the most fertile regions, where we can indicate to them what are the most profitable crops, assist them technically, uplift them morally and enable them to profit from the rational use of the land. In short, it is our intention to wrench them from their customary routines, which have been so prejudicial to them, to the land they occupy, and to the economy of the district.[57]

Toward this end, government blueprints called for the construction of a school, a health clinic, and a church in each community. Planners believed that out of these communities would emerge a whole new class of commodity producers tied to the Portuguese material and cultural world.[58]

For the state, this latest effort to restructure production was highly attractive. State officials believed that scientific farming would alleviate food crises, reduce soil erosion, and convince peasants to "abandon their natural nomadism" and their hostility toward cotton.[59] They also hoped that prosperous communities would stem

---

[56]   AHM, SR, Cx. 89, ISANI, "Relatório . . . de Mecúfi, Realizada no Ano de 1950/1951," António Policarpo de Sousa, Insp. Admin., 1951.

[57]   Gov. do Dist. da Zambézia, Acta da Conf. dos Admins. (Quelimane, 1956), 28.

[58]   J. Fonseca George, "Concentrações Algodoeiras," *Sociedade de Estudos da Colónia de Moçambique* (1946), 9.

[59]   AIA, JEAC, "Rel. Técnico," Fonseca George, Chefe de Secção de Fomento, 10 April 1947.

the rural exodus from the colony. This concern was particularly acute in southern Mozambique, where many local officials complained that "African men who migrate to the South African mines generally return home at the end of eighteen months impoverished, contaminated with venereal disease, to find their family in disarray, their cattle lost and their land abandoned."[60] Just as cotton in the north was defined as the agent for progressive social change, in the south it was perceived as one way to cure the social ills caused by male migration.

At first glance, the *concentrações* also appeared to provide many advantages to Mozambican cotton growers, particularly to "progressive farmers" with an entrepreneurial bent.[61] A system of crop rotation that incorporated food crops offered to peasant producers the possibility of alleviating production bottlenecks and hunger. Indeed, a 1950 government study completed in Nampula calculated that a typical family of four living on a *concentração* and cultivating 1.8 hectares of food in addition to cotton would produce more than 2,000 kilograms of foodstuffs. Even assuming that the daily intake figure was one kilogram per person, which was quite high, the average household, the report concluded, would still have a 500-kilogram food surplus.[62] Such a surplus could be held in reserve, exchanged for labor, sold, or distributed as gifts. (This optimistic scenario did not take into account families of five or more, for whom there would be little or no food reserve.) Locating peasant plots in one concentrated block adjacent to their homes would also enable household members to spend more time in their fields, since they would not have to travel from one site to another. Access to tractors, better seeds, and the opportunity to grow other cash crops were all supposed to increase household income still more. Crop rotation and ridging would reduce soil degradation and erosion. Most important, peasants who registered were legally exempt from contract labor.[63]

Predictably, however, the rural population assumed the social cost of this experiment as well as the risks of production they had always borne. Government planners selected sites without reference to historical residence patterns. Families were often divided when elderly men and women deemed "unproductive" were left behind.[64] Officials had even less appreciation for the fact that entire communities would be disconnected from their ancestors' spirits, whom they considered the spiritual protectors of their lands. When chiefs and village elders complained that moving to *concentrações* would alienate the ancestors who were the guardians of fertility, colonial officials simply dismissed their concerns as the "prognosis of witches and other superstitious people."[65] Ironically, this cavalier attitude undercut

---

[60]   AHM, Cx. 21, "Rel. da Insp. Ord. à Intend. de Gaza," António Policarpo de Sousa Santos, 1955.

[61]   To the best of my knowledge there is no extant documentation on the social composition of peasants who voluntarily joined *concentrações*.

[62]   AIA, JEAC, "Brigada de Mogovolas," Álvaro Martins da Silva, Eng. Ag., 29 September 1951. By comparison, the putative daily intake in Northern Rhodesia was estimated at between 0.38 and 0.48 kilograms per person. See Henrietta Moore and Megan Vaughan, *Cutting Down Trees: Gender, Nutrition, and Agricultural Change in the Northern Province of Zambia, 1890–1990* (Portsmouth, 1994), Ch. 3. The Portuguese figure did not calculate the amount of flour actually produced from a kilogram of corn or from other grains. One kilogram of corn typically yields about two-thirds of a kilogram of flour, which would still be greater than the Northern Rhodesia figure.

[63]   Interview with Faria Lobo, 9 July 1991.

[64]   Habermeier, "Algodão," 38.

[65]   Bravo, *Cultura Algodoeira*, 114–45.

the authority of some of the chiefs on whom the colonial regime depended. Those chiefs, who were themselves the descendants of the original "owners" of the land, had inherited immense ritual authority over the well-being of their entire territory and people, authority trooted in the ritual power of the ancestors. Relocating to new regions robbed them of this spiritual authority. Cotton Board and company officials conceded there were real costs to relocating, but argued that the benefits of the concentraçoes outweighed their disadvantages.[66] When peasants had second thoughts or refused to move, they were pressured or coerced.[67] An elder in the north recalled the hardships he and his neighbors experienced:

> We received an order to abandon our lands and our villages, and open up a new area where we would cultivate cotton in concentrações. Each family had to clear the bush and cut the trees in the prescribed areas. Those who refused were sent to the sisal plantations. Others disappeared. They were sent to São Tomé [to work on the cocoa plantations]. Only the old, widows and the ill remained. When a man died or was weakened by illness or old age, a son or a nephew had to take his place.[68]

Senior government officials acknowledged this problem and warned subordinates against using excessive force to establish concentrações.[69] Some reported that coercion was counterproductive. The administrator of Mocuba attributed the success of the concentrações in his region to his decision to eschew such coercive practices. He stressed careful planning, consultation, and patience:

> From the outset our objective was to move Africans living in the infertile regions to fertile areas. To achieve this objective we met with the local population and discussed in great detail the advantages that they would derive from making this move. They paid a great deal of attention. But on the designated day, only a small percentage of the population appeared at the site of the new concentração. However, the concessionaire did not lose interest and undertook a number of projects [to make the location attractive] most notably opening up a twelve-kilometer dirt road. Little by little, the Africans began to recognize the advantage of relocating and today there is an appreciable number who live in the concentrações where cotton and food crops are cultivated side by side with good results.[70]

Despite this kind of testimonial, coercion continued.

Once resettled, many growers found that they often had to work longer and harder than before in a much more controlled environment. The concessionaires had merely transposed the working methods of the 1940s into the cotton communities of the 1950s. In so doing, they also tightened their grip on cotton growers. The bevy of company overseers, chiefs, and sipais patrolling this confined space further reduced the partial autonomy of most peasants living inside the concentraçoes. One cotton official frankly noted that "within the concentrações we had more or less

---

[66]   Interview with Faria Lobo, 9 June 1991.

[67]   Ibid.; AHM, SR, Cx. 89, ISANI, "Relatório . . . de Mecúfi, Realizada no Ano de 1950/51," António Policarpo de Sousa, Insp. Admin..

[68]   Quoted in Habermeier, "Algodão," 39.

[69]   Dist. da Zambézia, Acta da Conf. dos Admins., 29.

[70]   Ibid.

TABLE 6–3 Number of Cotton Growers in *Concentraçoes*

Number of Familes

Concession	District	Settled	To Be Settled	Area	Total
CAM	Zambézia	11,176	3,380	5	55,880
SAGAL	Cabo Delgado	2,866	690	7	20,062
JFS	Zambézia	–	–	–	–
CNA	Manica e Sofala	291	320	7	2,037
CZ	Tete	–	–	–	–
LI	Zambézia	1,251	930	7	8,764
MG	Zambézia	2,139	1,459	5	10,669
SAN	Niassa	1,266	460	5	6,330
CCB	Manica e Sofala	1	–	na	na
ASS	Inhambane	2,137	2,320	5	10,685
	Total	30,943	16,899	1	65,220

Source: Fortuna, "Threading Through," 336.

perfect control over the work of each peasant every day. We could never have exercised such power when their cotton fields were dispersed."[71]

Despite the exhortations and efforts of state and Cotton Board officials, by the end of the 1950s the planned communities had failed to transform rural production on any appreciable scale or to create many "authentic" cotton farmers. For their part, several of the concessionaires, particularly those in central Mozambique already committed to plantation production, showed little interest in this project. Neither Sena Sugar nor the Zambezi Company bothered to organize a single cotton community within their holdings, while the Búzi Company had only one (see Table 6–3). Other firms remained lukewarm. Of all the concessionaires, only CAM vigorously pursued the *concentração* strategy. And even firms that showed interest were met by the skepticism of many local administrators.[72] Their ambivalence is clearly apparent in the report of one official who confronted the task of moving hundreds of households in Zambézia:

> The *concentrações* offered a number of advantages to the producers and certainly facilitated supervision of cotton production. But as a result of the intense opposition from most growers they also created many inconveniences and an enormous amount of work for the administrators and indigenous authorities.[73]

In 1958, after more than a decade of official hyperbole, the government acknowledged that only 30,000 families had been integrated into the *concentrações*.[74] This figure represented less than 15 percent of all cotton growers and a tiny fraction of the rural population at large.[75] Moreover, fully half of the integrated grow-

---

71 Interview with Faria Lobo, 9 July 1991.

72 See, for example, Dist. da Zambézia, Acta da Conf. dos Admins., 30–31.

73 Bravo, *Cultura Algodoeira*, 114–15.

74 Cited in Fortuna, "Threading Through," 273.

75 According to official government reports, the 11,000 households coincided with about 55,000 people. The population of the three northern provinces in 1950 was slightly more than two million.

ers resided in Zambézia and were part of CAM's concession (see Table 6–3). Even in Zambézia, the governor acknowledged in 1958 that few communities had lived up to state expectations because they were located haphazardly. In a particularly damning assessment, he concluded that "the cotton *concentrações* are absolutely reprehensible and have to be abolished and reorganized."[76] That the governor felt compelled to remind local administrators to limit the construction of *concentrações* to well-watered fertile land where cotton growers would still have time to grow food suggests the extent to which the resettlement guidelines had been disregarded.[77] Confidential government reports from the far north of the colony to the southern district of Gaza also reveal a pattern in which officials, under pressure from their superiors, organized *concentrações* in inappropriate locations.[78]

Some planned community complexes were successful, however. Muianga, a 1,900-hectare *concentração* in the fertile lands of the Limpopo Valley selected by Cotton Board inspectors in 1947, was a case in point. Its residential area and fields were located less than three kilometers from the river and the cotton market, and a large food market was nearby. Some 378 *agricultores* and their families had re-settled at Muianga by 1949. Each household received at least five hectares of land; a few received as many as ten. The villagers brought with them 420 plows and 590 oxen to drive the plows and to transport water barrels on carts from the Limpopo River to the fields and homesteads of the members. Ox-drawn plows also made it easier to till the heavy clay soils of the Limpopo Valley. By 1953 Muianga was prospering. Its 378 families sold 445,916 kilograms of cotton, an average of more than 1,000 kilograms per family. They also produced a substan-tial amount of corn and beans. By the 1955–56 campaign, there were 413 families living and working at Muianga.[79]

But Muianga was the exception. Most *concentrações* lacked machinery and "prac-tically all the work was done by hand, with hoes and knives."[80] Only a few of the larger communities had tractors. Water shortages occurred throughout the 1950s. In 1960 the director of CICA noted the need for many more artesian wells. "Once a regular all-year supply of drinking water is assured, difficulties in the transference of population to areas with better soils will be much easier to remove."[81] Although agronomists insisted that cotton output would increase substantially if pesticides were used, peasants never received any.[82] And in direct contravention to the origi-nal concept of the *concentrações*, fields were occasionally located several kilometers from the growers' residences. As a result, many peasants became disillusioned. Some were allowed to drop out of these communities, while others fled.[83] The ad-ministrator of Mogincual noted with disgust in 1958:

---

[76]   Dist. da Zambézia, Acta da Conf. dos Admins., 28.

[77]   Ibid., 29–30.

[78]   AIA, JEAC, "Rel. do Chefe dos Serviços Técnicos Distritais," Armando Antunes de Almeida, Septem-ber 1957; AIA, JEAC, "Planos de Trabalhos, Cabo Delgado 1958," 3 March 1958; AIA, JEAC, "Conf. 1957–1959," Armando Antunes de Almeida, 3 July 1959.

[79]   AIA, JEAC, AT, 929/3, "Concentração da Muianga."

[80]   Ibid.

[81]   Quintanilha, "Report," 17.

[82]   Interview with Faria Lobo, July 1991.

[83]   AIA, JEAC, "Conf. 1957–59," Elias Gonçalves Valente, Eng. Ag. to Sub-Del. da JEAC, 3 March 1958.

Two hundred and forty-four Africans had abandoned the cotton *concentração*, where rarely anyone had even cleared two hectares and where no one had even bothered to build a hut. These peasants worked with a complete lack of interest, and the income they earned was insufficient to destroy their old habits and predilections.[84]

The Cotton Board established a rural welfare and improvement fund linked to the policy of planned cotton communities. The Fundo do Algodão (Cotton Fund) came primarily from a tax levied on peasant cotton production, although concessionary companies and Portuguese importers contributed as well.[85] The state earmarked the money primarily for growers residing on the *concentrações de algodão* and as a reward for loyalist chiefs. By the late 1950s the Cotton Fund had allocated approximately one million dollars to rural communities.[86] The funds were used to build wells and storage bins, to purchase water pumps and agricultural equipment, and to provide rural health care and schools—thereby relieving the colonial state of this expense. By 1957 fully 50 percent of all funds were being used to construct seventy-six health posts and seventeen maternity stations scattered throughout the colony.[87] Minuscule amounts trickled down to peasants living outside the planned communities.[88] The Cotton Fund thus became a vehicle to redistribute fairly sizeable amounts of money from the least to the most advantaged segments of rural society.

Portugal's effort to encourage African farmers to organize autonomous cotton cooperatives in the 1950s was even less successful than its attempt to establish planned cotton communities. Like much of the colonial cotton policy, these efforts were modeled on the Belgian experiment in the Congo begun in 1947. Eight years later Decree 40.405 made Mozambican cotton producers eligible to be part of the Portuguese cooperative scheme. What was unique in this new legislation was the right of Africans to organize "autonomous" ventures. According to the decree's proponents, these "cooperative agricultural societies represent a new vehicle of civilization and a useful method of incorporating the Africans into the productive activity of the region."[89]

The most significant feature of the 1955 legislation was the state's willingness to leave the organization of the production process firmly in the hands of the members of the cooperatives. Those cotton growers who organized cooperatives would be free from the most abusive and degrading aspects of the cotton regime. No longer would company overseers and African police be on their backs. No longer would they have to fear *chibalo* labor. No longer would somebody else organize the alloca-

[84]　AIA, JEAC, "Conf. 1957–1959," Admin. do Mogincual, 6 January 1958.

[85]　The concessionary companies initially paid twenty *escudos* per ton and the textile interests were also charged a tax on a percentage of imports. Both fees were appreciably smaller than the deduction that growers were forced to pay (see Decree 40.405, Department of State, 00859, "Annual Economic Report Province of Mozambique—1951," Donald Lamm, American Consul in Lourenço Marques, 13 March 1952).

[86]　AIA, JEAC, "Diversos, Mapas, Estatísticas e Elementos Informativos," Fundo do Algodão Receitas, n.d.

[87]　AHM, FGG, Cota 489, "Assistência Sanitária e Social às Populações das Regiões Algodoeiras Propostas nos Termos dos Decretos 34.671 e 35.844 ate 31 de Dezembro 1957."

[88]　Ibid.; AIA, JEAC, AT 929/3/0, "Fundo do Algodão, 1952," Comissão Administrativa do Fundo do Algodão, Acta no. 6, 29 October 1952; AIA, JEAC, 660, 55 (1952), n.d.

[89]　*BOM*, 51/55, "Decreto 40.405," 24 November 1955.

tion of labor in ways that prejudiced household food security. The legislation also permitted cooperatives to control the cotton marketing and production process, although there was little likelihood that a peasant-based organization could accumulate sufficient capital to gin or market the lint. Otherwise, the local concessionary company retained first claim to the raw cotton. A three-person secretariat, advised by a functionary of the state Cotton Board, would oversee each cooperative.

As with most of Lisbon's reforms, the 1955 legislation had neither an immediate nor a far-reaching impact in Mozambique. The concessionaires adamantly opposed this initiative, predicting a sharp reduction in output if peasants were allowed to organize cooperatives and were no longer forced to cultivate cotton. Many local administrators, especially in the north, also feared that cooperatives would become hotbeds of nationalist agitation and social unrest as they had in neighboring Tanganyika.[90] A conference of administrators in Zambézia warned that "without much more preparatory work it would be premature to organize cooperatives."[91]

Given this opposition, it is hardly surprising that few peasant-based cooperatives were established. Within the first two years after the legislation was passed, not a single cotton cooperative had been registered. In 1957 a dozen Makonde peasants led by Lázaro Kavandame formed the Mozambique African Voluntary Cotton Society in the northern district of Cabo Delgado. Membership skyrocketed to almost 1,500 within four years (see Chapter 9). At about the same time the governor of Inhambane formally opened the Zavala cooperatives.[92] Encouraged by state officials, who offered substantial material incentives, and with the support of a number of prosperous chiefs, membership increased to more than 1,300 by 1959. Although there were obvious differences between these two cooperatives (see Chapter 9), they seem to have been the only cotton-based associations organized in response to the state's 1955 initiative.

State officials intervened in the production process in two other significant ways. Beginning in the early 1950s they not only encouraged but in some areas actually forced the expanded cultivation of manioc with an eye toward reducing food deficits[93] (see Chapter 7). In doing so they effectively reversed prior policies that precluded the integration of household production with export production.[94]

A more significant state intervention was permitting peasants who lived in inappropriate regions to cease cultivating cotton. The 1946 decree called for the "elimination of unsuitable regions."[95] This policy encountered stiff opposition from the concessionary companies, who fought to expand the spatial boundaries of the cotton regime.[96] Nevertheless, the Cotton Board, armed with compelling data of rural impoverishment and hunger and fearing social unrest, moved to restrict new concessions and to remove inappropriate areas. In 1947, the Board began to eliminate the most unsuitable

---

[90]   See Lionel Cliffe, "Nationalism and the Reaction to Enforced Agricultural Change in Tanganyika During the Colonial Period," and John Saul, "The Role of the Cooperative Movement," in *Socialism in Tanzania*, ed. Lionel Cliffe and John Saul (Dar es Salaam, 1973).

[91]   Dist. da Zambézia, Acta da Conf. dos Admins., 26.

[92]   Adam, "Cooperativização Agrícola," 62. The cooperatives had been operating in embryonic form since 1955.

[93]   AIA, JEAC, "Conf. 1957–1959," Vasco de Sousa Fonseca Lebre, Reg. Ag., 10 March 1958.

[94]   Ibid.

[95]   *BOM*, 1, 45, 9 November 1946, 461.

[96]   For an elaboration of the role of the Cotton Board, see *BOM* 1, 45, "Decreto 35.844," 9 November 1948.

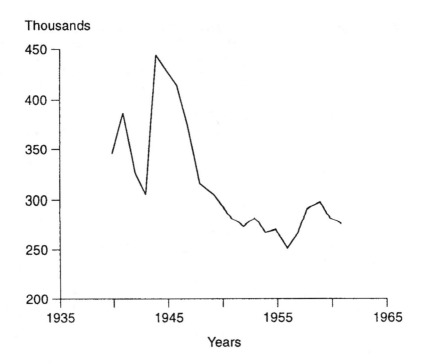

GRAPH 6–4. Numbers of Producers in Forced Cotton Regime in Northern Mozambique, 1939–1961

Source: Based on Bravo, *A Cultura Algodoeira,* 135, 139.

lands and to bar concessionary companies from expanding into marginal areas.[97] Throughout the rest of the decade this policy was implemented in fits and starts, with company officials often bribing state authorities in an effort to blunt the reforms.[98] Nevertheless, from 1947 to 1952 more than 120,000 growers, primarily from the north, were freed from the cotton regime (see Graph 6–4).[99]

With the completion of the first comprehensive study of climatic conditions, soil types, and plant diseases in 1953, the Cotton Board intensified its land-withdrawal policy. According to U.S. Embassy officials, between 1954 and 1955 alone approximately 50,000 additional hectares of marginal land were taken out of the cotton system.[100] Over the remainder of the decade the lands available for cotton production continued to shrink, although not without resistance from the concessionaires. They even managed to open up new areas in marginal zones, particularly in Tete and Inhambane. The

---

[97]　Decree 35.844 called for the establishment of cotton zones and elimination of unsuitable lands Bravo, *Cultura Algodoeira,* 141.

[98]　Interview with A. Quintanilha.

[99]　Bravo, *Cultura Algodoeira,.* 81.

[100]　This figure must be treated with caution since it is based on the assumption that there were 822,000 acres (approximately 332,700 hectares) in production in 1954 compared with 711,000 acres (approximately

struggle between local Cotton Board officials and the concessionary companies was still going on as late as 1960. In that year, for example, Sul do Save Cotton was forced to give up its holdings in the Serra do Bilene after state agronomists demonstrated that the cold climate and poor soils were not conducive to cotton production. After twenty years of cotton devastation, 1,005 peasants were finally freed from this burden.[101] Across the colony, thousands of peasant growers were released from the tyranny of the cotton regime. In 1944 there had been approximately 791,000 peasants trapped within the system. This figure had decreased to 510,000 by 1961, with the sharpest decline coming in the rainy zones of Zambézia.

State efforts to rationalize cotton production extended to the industrial sector. Until the end of World War II Mozambique was one of the few cotton-producing regions in the world that did not process cotton seeds into oil. Instead, the ginning mills simply discarded the seeds.[102] Under pressure from the Cotton Board, the concessionaires gradually relented. In 1947 they processed 798 tons of oil and other industrial by-products from cotton seeds. Four years later this figure was almost 10,000 tons.[103] By the end of the 1960s cottonseed oil and other by-products generated more than 100,000 *contos* ($3.3 million), roughly one-quarter the total value of cotton exports from Mozambique.[104]

Efforts to develop a local textile industry were less successful. Despite its neomercantile strategy, Lisbon allowed a limited number of textile plants to be built in the colony. Colonial planners hoped that these factories would stimulate peasant production by making highly prized cotton cloth available at a more affordable price.[105] Local textile production began in Mozambique in 1951, in the Manica province. By 1960 there was one large textile mill and four smaller ones. Together they utilized less than 2,000 of the 46,000 tons of ginned Mozambican cotton.[106] The large mill, owned by the Sociedade Algodoeira do Fomento Colonial, was located in Vila Pery and produced fairly specialized commodities such as table cloths, white cotton cloth, calico, and canvas, none of which was geared to the large African market.

The Reforms Reevaluated

At first glance, it appears that the efforts to rationalize the cotton regime produced some impressive results. The sharp fluctuations in the number of hectares under cotton cultivation disappeared, and production increased substantially. So did pro-

---

287,700 hectares) one year later. Both these figures are somewhat higher than Portuguese estimates, which in 1950 had about 630,000 acres (254,960 hectares) in use. Since new areas were being incorporated into the cotton regime, especially in the Tete province, it is possible that total area under cultivation increased even as marginal lands were dropped out. Department of State, "Economic Review, 1955," R. Smith Thompson, American Counsel General, 6 March 1956.

[101] AHM, CE, SEAV 9, 116 (a.b.), Gov. do Dist. de Gaza, "Rel. do Gov. 1955–1960," Gov. Oscar Freire de Vasconcelos Ruas, 1960.

[102] Interview with A. Quintanilha.

[103] AIA, JEAC, "Prop. de Moç.: Elementos Para O Século," Gastão de Melo Furtado, 15 June 1954.

[104] Bravo, *Cultura Algodoeira*, 86.

[105] Interview with A. Quintanilha; *Notícias*, 13 June 1945; *Lourenço Marques Guardian*, 13 June 1945; Bravo, *Cultura Algodoeira*, 81–84.

[106] Bravo, *Cultura Algodoeira*, 82–83.

ductivity and peasant income. And for the hundreds of thousands of growers who were released from the scheme, the reforms obviously had far-reaching implications. Cotton production had also risen in the "free zones," where peasants were encouraged but not forced to grow cotton.[107] As for those growers who remained inside the system, by 1960 more than 40 percent gained the theoretical advantages associated with *agricultor* status.[108] It seemed as if Lisbon had taken a first step toward bifurcating cotton producers along gender (and to an extent class) lines and had begun the process of creating "authentic" cotton farmers.

Juxtaposed against these successes were a number of chronic problems, some of which actually became more acute in the 1950s. The metropolitan textile industry continued to complain about the poor quality of Mozambican fiber.[109] Problems of soil exhaustion increased. For all its experiments with seed breeding, crop burning, and pesticides, CICA had still been unable to contain jassid and bacteriosis, which continued to devastate cotton.[110] Crop losses in excess of 60 percent were reported as late as the 1960s.[111]

Nor did the reforms alleviate rural opposition (see Chapter 10). For most peasants, cotton and coercion still went hand in hand. So did cotton and poverty. Metropolitan interest groups adamantly opposed large price increases, and falling cotton prices on the international market reinforced their position. For all the market reforms, in 1958 producers earned an average of only 520 *escudos* (U.S. $18) for a year's labor, and taxes consumed a good portion of the cotton income.[112] This figure represented less than two-thirds what Tanganyikan, Kenyan, Southern Rhodesian, and Congolese growers earned.[113] And many growers still carried their crop to market in makeshift sacks, confronted problems of rigged scales, and faced price-gouging by European and Asian *cantineiros* whose shops surrounded cotton markets.[114]

For all the modernizing rhetoric of the state, the cotton regime still rested on force,. This fact—obvious to every cotton grower after years of experience within the system—made it nearly impossible to promote African "commodity producers." Even when cotton production was, in fact, more profitable than other economic activities, it held no appeal for most Mozambican peasants.

The coercive nature of the cotton regime and the state's policy of expropriating the most fertile peasant lands for European settlers reinforced peasant skepticism in the south, especially after the colonial state embarked on the multimil-

---

[107] AIA, JEAC, 84 (1957–59), Elias Gonçalves Valente to CD da JEAC, 23 October 1957.

[108] Colonial reports estimate that there were 240,000 *agricultores* and 280,000 *cultivadores*.

[109] Pitcher, "From Coercion to Incentive," passim.

[110] Quintanilha, "Report," 10–13.

[111] A. Antunes de Almeida, "Losses Caused by Insects to the Cotton Crop in Mozambique," *Agronomia Moçambicana* 1(1967), 127–32.

[112] AIA, JEAC, 84 (1958–1959), Gastão de Melo Furtado to Gov. do Distr. da Zambézia.

[113] The prices paid to producers for first–quality cotton (in *escudos*) were Tanganyika 4$70, Kenya 4$13, Congo 4$60, and Rhodesia (Northern and Southern), 6$40. The price disparities were not as great for second–quality cotton (AIA, JEAC, "Copiador Geral de Notas–Conf., 1958–1959," Gastão de Melo Furtado to Dir. dos SNI). In 1958 male taxpayers typically had to pay between 100 and 330 *escudos* (roughly U.S. $3.50 and $11), depending on the region in which they lived.

[114] AIA, JEAC, "Rel. do Chefe dos Serviços Técnicos Distritais," Armando Antunes de Almeida, September 1957; AIA, JEAC, "Conf. 1957–1959," João Belo, Prác. Ag. de JEAC, 13 February 1957.

lion dollar Limpopo dam and irrigation scheme in 1952. More than 9,500 immigrants from Portugal were resettled in the Limpopo Valley. Many of them cultivated cotton with substantial state aid.[115] Given this situation, it is hardly surprising that less than 20 percent of the "economically active" male population in this region opted to be *agricultores de algodão* and that the number of men working in the gold mines actually increased by 15 percent during the life of the cotton regime.[116]

The situation was somewhat different in central Mozambique, but the outcome was similar. There, the critical role of the plantation sector meant that creating a class of "progressive" male farmers was not only not a high colonial priority but it was actively discouraged by powerful agricultural interests. The copra plantation in Quelimane and the tea estates at Gurué required an abundant supply of male labor. The needs of cotton were clearly subordinate. And in the Sena Sugar concession and to a lesser degree on the Búzi Company and Zambezi Company holdings, men were prohibited from cultivating cotton or for that matter any other crop. Their task was to work in the sugar fields. Only women and children were permitted to cultivate cotton.

In the north, increased capitalist penetration from the 1940s on undercut efforts to maximize the number of *agricultores*. Increased labor demands on peasants from other sectors left fewer available to become prosperous cotton farmers. The post–World War II period witnessed the expansion of tobacco plantations, an increased number of settler farms, the growth of a timber industry, and an intensive state campaign to build all-weather roads, bridges, and railroad lines.[117] But as previously noted, it was the resurgence of the moribund northern sisal industry that removed thousands of men from cotton production.[118]

Although "progressive" northern cotton farmers were theoretically exempt from conscription, in reality they were not. CAM officials complained bitterly that in one part of Nampula more than two hundred men wanted to cultivate cotton as *agricultores* but were intimidated by the local administrator, who intended to send them off as contract laborers once they had cleared the lands for their wives. A Cotton Board official who subsequently interviewed the men confirmed that "they preferred to work on their land and grow cotton voluntarily, but . . . the administrator would not let them."[119] Romeu Mataquenha of Montepuez told a similar account:

> The *sipais* passed through our fields and noted who was behind schedule. They informed the chief, who drew up a list of lazy people in response to the orders of the administrators. Those on the list were bound and sent to

---

[115] Department of State, "Annual Economic Report—Mozambique 1952," Donald Lamm, American Consul, 27 January 1953.

[116] In 1939 there were 88,499 Mozambicans employed in the gold mines; by 1961, this figure had jumped to 100,200. First, *Black Gold*, 32–33.

[117] AHM, SR, Cx. 95, ISANI, "Rel. da Insp. Ord. do Dist. de Nampula da Prov. do Niassa," Hortêncio Estevão de Sousa, 1949.

[118] Fernandes, "Alguns Aspectos," 138; Álvaro Navarro Soeiro and Francisco Manuel Fernandes, "O Sisal de Moçambique," *Assembleia Técnica da Associação dos Produtores de Sisal da Prov. de Moçambique,* vol. 13 (Braga, 1961), 59.

[119] AIA, JEAC, "Conf. 1944–1946," Fernando Rebelo da Costa Abure to CD da JEAC, 27 November 1945.

the administrator's office and from there were forced to work for six months on the Sena Sugar or Nangororo [sisal plantations].[120]

This collusion between poorly paid administrators and plantation interests was a fact of life. For many officials these extralegal payments were the only compensation for their difficult life in the interior. According to Arturo Dias, a Portuguese settler who had lived in the interior for many years, "when I came to Mozambique 75 percent of the government officials scattered throughout the bush were honest and upright. Now I find that 75 percent are not completely honest; they get rich in one assignment in the bush."[121]

But it was not only avaricious local administrators who disregarded the labor codes. The governor of Niassa declared in 1951 that any man, including *agricultores*, who failed to produce 400 kilograms of cotton would be sent to work on the European estates.[122] Eight years later the governors of Nampula and Niassa required *agricultores* to sell a minimum of 750 *escudos* worth of cotton in order to retain their exemption from contract labor.[123] A Cotton Board agronomist estimated that between one-half and three-quarters of the *agricultores* could not possibly satisfy this requirement.[124] To no avail, Native Affairs inspectors and local Cotton Board representatives protested that this policy undercut efforts to create a class of "authentic" male farmers.

These new labor demands in northern Mozambique dramatically increased peasant flight. By 1948 almost 28,000 Makonde from Cabo Delgado had relocated to southern Tanganyika; the number of Makua immigrants from northern Mozambique had increased dramatically as well.[125] Ironically, many of the Mozambicans migrated to work on Tanganyikan sisal plantations whose conditions of employment they considered far superior to those on the sisal estates in Mozambique.

One of the most obvious outcomes of increased labor recruitment and increased flight was the progressive feminization of cotton production in many parts of the north. Throughout the ensuing decade, more and more cotton zones were affected. In 1957, an agronomist traveling through Cabo Delgado observed "that cotton is cultivated only by women, elders, and the handicapped."[126] A senior cotton official writing the next year complained that throughout the north "the contract labor system robbed households of male labor just when planting was begun."[127] The recruitment of a large number of men from November to May undercut the Cotton Board's strategy of recasting men as the principal cotton producers.

---

[120] Interview with Romeu Mataquenha, Tirani Ntuka, and Mussa Vaquina, Montepuez, 19 July 1979.

[121] Department of State, "Native Labor in the District of Manica e Sofala," William Taft III, American Consul General, 3 July 1958.

[122] AIA, JEAC, "Papéis Diversos," A. Figueira e Sousa to Gov. de Niassa, 21 February 1952.

[123] AIA, JEAC, "Conf. 1957–1959," Júlio Bossa, 14 September 1959.

[124] AIA, JEAC, "Conf. 1957–1959," Armando Antunes de Almeida, Eng. Ag., 29 September 1959.

[125] Alpers, "'To Seek a Better Life,'" 375; Rui Pereira, "Antropologia Aplicada na Política Colonial Portuguesa do Estado Novo," *Revista Internacional de Estudos Africanos* 4/5(1986), 227–28; Dias, *Os Macondes*, 115.

[126] AIA, JEAC, Del. de Moçambique, BT de Moç., "Rel. An. Ref. ao Ano de 1957 (Campanha Algodoeira de 1956–57)," Manuel de Oliveira Barros, Reg. Ag. de 2ª classe, 4 January 1958.

[127] AIA, JEAC, "Conf. 1957–1959," Gastão de Mello Furtado to Pres. da JEAC, 1 September 1959.

If the Board failed to create "new men," it also failed to win over the hearts and minds of most peasants who remained inside the system. Force was not only the most important and persistent characteristic of the cotton scheme, but of rural colonial labor policy in general. The shadow of *chibalo* was a powerful incentive to grow cotton no matter how distasteful it was.

Finally, thirty years of cotton had exacerbated a number of chronic agro-ecological problems. Intensive cotton production robbed soils of nutrients throughout the colony, exacerbating the food crises (see Chapter 7). Throughout colonial Africa, extension officers had introduced different types of conservation practices to control the loss of soils through erosion. Their heavy-handed technical solutions, ranging from discouraging cultivation on steep slopes to tie ridging and reforestation, yielded at best mixed results.[128] What was unique about the Mozambican situation was the absence of any concerted conservation effort whatsoever. In 1951 one agricultural engineer lamented that the colony did not have the resources to reverse environmental degradation, "nor at the moment is it possible to improvise on a sufficient scale to have a major impact."[129] Six years later other agronomists complained that the Búzi Company "had not even made an attempt to protect the grass cover, the most elementary anti-erosion strategy."[130] Many of the cotton communities, purportedly organized around principals of scientific farming, similarly failed to introduce this simple technique to protect valuable topsoil.[131] CAM, the largest cotton concessionaire, finally implemented a soil conservation program at the end of the decade, but by then the damage was already done.[132]

The degradation of the land not only decreased cotton yields, but left peasants more vulnerable to what colonial officials referred to as "the calamities of nature." What they failed to understand or acknowledge was the degree to which "natural catastrophes" were man-made. Thus, for example, the decline in cotton production from 103,000 tons in 1954 to 86,000 one year later was not caused exclusively by flooding.[133] In the absence of an adequate drainage system, heavy rains became massive floods destroying crops and carrying off topsoil. Given Mozambique's erratic rainfall patterns and badly eroded soils, it is not surprising that this problem continued to affect rural production during the remainder of the decade.[134]

Conclusion

When the Cotton Board set out to reform the cotton regime in the late 1940s, its goals were to increase production and individual productivity, to ease problems of

---

[128] Prentice, Cotton, 266; Feierman, *Peasant Intellectuals*; Chipungu, *The State, Technology and Peasant Differentiation*; Anne Mager, "The People Get Fenced: Gender Rehabilitation and African Nationalism in the Ciskei and Border Region, 1945–1955," *JSAS* 18(1992), 761–82.

[129] AIA, JEAC, "Papéis Diversos," Francisco Feio, Eng. da JEAC, 21 September 1952.

[130] AIA, JEAC, 901, "Planos de Trabalho 1958, Comp. de Búzi," António José Carvalho Pereira, 10 March 1959.

[131] AIA, JEAC, "Rel. do Chefe dos Serviços Técnicos Distritais," Armando Antunes de Almeida, September 1957.

[132] Ibid.

[133] Department of State, "Economic Review," R. Smith Simpson, American Consul General, 6 March 1956.

[134] AIA, JEAC, BT, "Rel. da Campanha Algodoeira 1956," Manuel de Oliveira Barros, Reg. Ag., 23 April 1957.

hunger and environmental degradation, and to transform peasants into enthusiastic cotton farmers. Despite the introduction of modest reforms, in 1961 the cotton regime suffered from the same problems that had plagued it fifteen years earlier. These were clearly spelled out to the president of the Cotton Board in a 1961 report marked "secret and urgent" from a senior field inspector. To make the system work properly, the inspector called for a more careful selection of cotton lands, the distribution of sacks, an improvement in the quality of *capatazes*, and higher prices paid to growers.[135] Conspicuously absent from his recommendations was any reference to abolishing coercion. As long as the cotton regime rested on force—whether to ensure that *cultivadores* labored in the cotton fields according to the Board's calendar or to compel *agricultores* to relocate into planned communities—no amount of reformist legislation, well intentioned acts by local administrators, or economic incentives to growers would convince Africans to plant cotton voluntarily. That the reforms failed to reduce food insecurity hardened peasant opposition. By 1961 there was growing sentiment in Lisbon that the forced cotton regime was anachronistic and that it was useless to try to "fix" it.

---

[135] AIA, JEAC, Corr. Exp. 1961, "Insp. Superior de Admin. Ultramarina," Mário Costa to Pres. da JEAC, 10 March 1961.

7

Cotton and
Food Insecurity

*At harvest time the natives miscalculate their food requirements; they
sell too much of their produce and consequently suffer from hunger.*

José da Cunha Dias Mendes,
cotton inspector, December 31, 1940

*Hunger periodically rages throughout much of the colony. It is caused
primarily by the decline in the cultivation of food crops which results
from the siphoning off of enormous amounts of labor to cultivate cotton.*

João Contreiras, Cotton Board inspector to
president of the Cotton Board, May 1945

João Contreiras was right. Contrary to the assertion of his colleague, food shortages and malnutrition among rural Mozambicans were not self-induced. The cotton regime precipitated an unprecedented colonywide subsistence crisis punctu-
ated by periodic local famines. Mozambican peasants underwrote the Portuguese
textile industry with their labor and were forced to sacrifice their own food security. The burden on women's time was particularly acute. If the intensity, duration,
and scale of the food crisis during the cotton regime were unprecedented, malnutrition was not unique to the era of forced commodity production. Seasonal food
shortages and longer-term famines antedated both the cotton scheme and the colonial period. Food shortages certainly recurred with disturbing frequency in southern Mozambique. On this point elders from the Gaza district were in agreement:
"Famines are not only a problem today, they were a problem long ago in the time
of our ancestors. When there was no rain there was no sorghum or corn. When it
rained a lot our granaries were full for two or three years.[1]

During the early colonial period, both Mozambican and European observers
vividly recounted the devastating effects of rural subsistence crises. Famines in the

---

[1]   Group interview, CV Samora Machel, Chibuto, 15 September 1979.

south, often descriptively named in the ways of storytellers to keep a memory of a world gone awry, are documented for 1897, 1903, 1912–13, 1917–18, 1922, 1931 and 1937.[2] *"Fome de gafanhoto"* (the famine of the locusts), for example, recalls the hunger and destitution brought by a swarm of locusts that destroyed all of the corn fields and food supplies.[3] For other parts of the colony, the record of precotton food crises is far less complete than it is for the south. Nevertheless, there is evidence of periodic famines throughout the nineteenth century from the Zambézi Valley in central Mozambique to the northern reaches of the colony.[4] Although contemporary observers have tended to attribute these subsistence crises to natural disasters, particularly drought and pestilence, devastation of the Mozambican countryside brought about by the slave trade, the Mfecane, and Chikunda and Yao raiding all disrupted local food economies.[5]

Just as famines were not simply "natural" events in precolonial Mozambique, so twentieth-century famines cannot be understood in isolation from the transforming influences of colonial capitalism.[6] The introduction of wage labor, the shift to cash crop production, and colonial marketing policies all affected rural food security in the Portuguese colony. Nor can historical analysis of subsistence crises ignore the processes of rural differentiation and increasingly unequal access to scarce resources that characterized the Mozambican peasantry during the colonial period.

To stress the social basis of famine in colonial Mozambique is not to diminish the significance of environmental factors in determining rural food security. The uncertain and relatively short rainy season was the critical geographical variable affecting food supplies throughout most of Mozambique. There is evidence that the south in particular suffered regularly from droughts of varying intensity and duration.[7] But fragile and infertile soils, intense heat, and unseasonable cold spells imposed constraints on agricultural production in many parts of the colony, and pests, plant diseases, floods, and cyclones occasionally devastated the food econo-

---

[2]   Interview with Simone Sitói, Guijá, 16 February 1979; group interview, CV Samora Machel, Chibuto, 15 September 1979; interview with Makausse Muhate by Gerhard Liesegang, Manjacaze, 15 July 1980, AHM T/Tno.GZ009; Keys, "Report of the Inhambane and Limpopo District," 69–70; SMA, Box 6/70D, "Report of the Ricola Station 1931–32," M. Schaller, n.d.; Sherilynn Young, "Women in Transition: Southern Mozambique 1975–76: Reflections on Colonialism, Aspirations for Independence" (paper delivered at the Conference on the History of Women, College of St. Catherine, St. Paul, MN, 21 October 1977).

[3]   Interview with Makausse Muhate.

[4]   See, for example, M. D. D. Newitt, "Drought in Mozambique, 1823–1831," *JSAS* 15, 1(1988), 15–35.

[5]   Ibid.; Alpers, *Ivory and Slaves*; Isaacman, *Mozambique: The Africanization of a European Institution*; Mandala, *Work and Control*. If the record for the precotton period remains fragmentary, it nevertheless supports recent scholarship that has rescued the debate on the food crisis from resting on a set of naturalist paradigms that had dominated the literature (see Sara Berry, "The Food Crisis and Agrarian Change in Africa," *ASR* 27, 2[1984]:59–112).

[6]   The impact of colonial capitalism on food security in Africa has been the subject of intense debate. See, for example, Robert Bates, *Markets and States in Tropical Africa: The Political Basis of Agricultural Policies* (Berkeley, 1988); Berry, "The Food Crisis"; Deborah Bryceson, *Food Insecurity and the Social Division of Labour in Tanzania, 1919–1985* (New York, 1990); Keith Hart, *The Political Economy of West African Agriculture* (Cambridge, 1982); Megan Vaughan, *The Story of an African Famine* (Cambridge, 1987).

[7]   Sherilyn Young is engaged in pioneering research attempting to quantify the causes and periodicity of droughts in southern Mozambique. See Sherilyn Young, "Climate in Southern Mozambique: Identifying and Quantifying the Extent of and Periodicity of Twentieth–Century Drought," paper presented at African Studies Association meeting, Toronto, November 4, 1994.

mies of particular areas. The periodic flooding of the Zambézi, Shire, Punguè, and Limpopo Rivers that washed away peasants' crops is a case in point.[8]

The elders were right: without rain there would be no corn or sorghum. But however much irregular rainfall was a source of apprehension and insecurity in the countryside, adequate precipitation alone could not guarantee food security for all. Famines had as much to do with the command over scarce resources as they had to do with the environment. In the case of the cotton regime, this was even more true.

The Portuguese cotton scheme was predicated on the ability of the colonial regime to divert household resources, particularly labor, away from the food economy and into commodity production. This was a political decision. It was about power and the politics of production. The more the state-concessionaire alliance succeeded in appropriating peasant labor, thus jeopardizing peasants' strategies to avoid famine, the more growers became vulnerable to hunger. In addition, because textile interests controlled the terms of exchange and because the state imposed an oppressive tax system, Mozambican peasants had little disposable income with which to purchase the food they could no longer grow. Moreover, European and Asian merchants in the countryside kept food prices high, particularly when food was scarce. The results were predictable. Food shortages and local famines occurred with regularity throughout the life of the cotton regime.

This said, the seasonal dimensions of rural impoverishment need to be stressed. The wet season preceding the harvest was when cotton growers, particularly the poorest producers, were most vulnerable, when a number of adverse factors often impinged simultaneously. Food was often in short supply and the previous year's grain had already been consumed. Food prices tended to be high. Agricultural work was at its most intense. Overburdened women had little time for cooking and family hygiene. Illness was widespread, with newborns the most vulnerable. Scholars working in areas as diverse as Nigeria and the Indian subcontinent found that "this time of year is marked by loss of body weight, low birth weights, high neonatal mortality, malnutrition and indebtedness. It is the hungry season and the sick season. It is the time of the year when poor people are at their poorest and vulnerable to becoming poorer."[9] The cotton regime simply exacerbated this tendency.

Cotton left many people hungry, but some cotton growers and their families were much more vulnerable than others. David Arnold's broad formulation of the politics of food could be describing the Mozambican reality during the cotton regime:

> Historically food was one of the sinews of power. Its importance was felt at all levels of society, both by those who suffered directly for want of basic sustenance and those whose authority and security and profit were threatened as the indirect consequence of death and much starvation. Food was and continues to be power in a most basic, tangible and inseparable form.[10]

---

[8]   AIA, JEAC, AT 9352, Boletins de Informação, Companhia da Zambézia, 1946/47; AIA, JEAC, 86 (1958), José da Cunha Dias Mendes to Chefe da Del. de JEAC, 10 March 1958.

[9]   Robert Chambers, Richard Longhurst, and Arnold Pacey, eds., *Seasonal Dimensions to Rural Poverty* (London, 1981), xv.

[10]   David Arnold, *Famine: Social Crisis and Historical Change* (Oxford, 1988), 3.

Peasant producers took advantage of their limited autonomy to try to minimize their vulnerability (see Chapter 9). They adapted to the demands of the cotton regime by drawing on local knowledge, cultural resources, and historical practices. But because their autonomy was only partial, growers could not circumvent the cotton scheme entirely. They could neither migrate in times of famine, nor be absent from their fields for a few days to beg or borrow food from relatives. The principal way to increase the ratio of labor they allocated to food versus cotton was to work longer and harder.

State officials gradually began to realize the devastating implications of their cotton policies. By the 1950s the Cotton Board had developed the broad outlines of a famine relief program as part of the state's broader campaign to rationalize the cotton regime. But the famine policy was filled with ambiguities and contradictions. Officials stressed the need for a food-first strategy, but insisted that it be cotton-centered and that it not jeopardize cotton output. Cotton, after all, was Portugal's "white gold." But to ensure its continued production, growers needed to be healthy enough to continue working in their cotton fields. This nutritional component was for the most part ignored, and many Mozambican peasants were pushed against the margins of subsistence.

Cotton, the Labor Bottleneck, and the Politics of Food Security

The demands of cotton created a serious labor problem for most peasant households. Peasants experienced this bottleneck both in quantitative and qualitative terms.[11] According to the literature on agricultural production, any month in which labor requirements are greater than 15 percent of the total annual output is considered a "bottleneck."[12] It is a period when excessive labor demands are collapsed into a relatively short period. By this criterion, there were two periods of acute labor pressure in the cotton zones throughout most of Mozambique. The first was the month between late November and late December when peasants were pressed to plant cotton in addition to sowing their major food crops (sorghum, corn, peanuts, and beans). The second and more acute labor crisis occurred during January and February, when growers had to reseed, thin, and weed cotton while also cleaning their gardens. Weeds strangled cotton, but they also threatened food output.

Table 7–1 is a composite work calendar derived from the recollections of former cotton growers in the northern area of Nampula, from cotton officials, and from recent ethnographic accounts and household surveys.[13] It graphically depicts the extent to which cotton production conflicted with the cultivation of basic foodstuffs. The data make clear why in Nampula and elsewhere most peasant families found it impossible to sustain the precotton food cropping system. Although these

---

[11] See Tom Bassett, "Breaking Up the Bottlenecks in Food–Crop and Cotton Cultivation in Northern Côte d'Ivoire," *Africa* 58(1988), 147–73.

[12] Ibid.; Paul Richards, "Ecological Change."

[13] Interview with Faria Lobo, Nampula, 26 May 1987; interview with Paulo Roque, Nampula, 27 May 1987; interview with Paulo Zucula, Minneapolis, 15 August 1989; CEA, *Transformação da Agricultura Familiar*, 22–23.

TABLE 7-1 Labor Input per Crop and per Month in a Typical Peasant Household in Nampula

Task	Oct	Nov	Dec	Jan	Feb	Mar	Apr	May	Jun	Jul	Aug	Sep	Total
Cotton													
Land preparation	10	10	10	–	–	–	–	–	–	–	–	–	30
Planting/thinning	–	–	5	5	–	–	–	–	–	–	–	–	10
First weeding	–	–	8	8	4	–	–	–	–	–	–	–	20
Second weeding	–	–	–	–	20	–	–	–	–	–	–	–	20
Third weeding	–	–	–	–	–	20	–	–	–	–	–	–	20
Harvesting	–	–	–	–	–	–	–	15	15	–	–	–	30
Packing	–	–	–	–	–	–	–	–	–	5	–	–	5
Destroying stalks	–	–	–	–	–	–	–	–	–	8	4	–	12
Subtotal	10	10	23	13	24	20	0	15	15	12	4	0	147
Maize													
Land preparation	15	15	–	–	–	–	–	–	–	–	–	–	30
Planting	–	6	4	–	–	–	–	–	–	–	–	–	10
Two weedings	–	–	15	15	10	–	–	–	–	–	–	–	40
Harvesting	–	–	–	–	–	–	8	8	–	–	–	–	16
Subtotal	15	21	19	15	10	0	8	8	0	0	0	0	96
Sorghum													
Land preparation	15	15	–	–	–	–	–	–	–	–	–	–	30
Planting	–	–	6	6	–	–	–	–	–	–	–	–	12
Two weedings	–	–	–	20	10	10	–	–	–	–	–	–	40
Harvesting	–	–	–	–	–	–	4	6	6	–	–	–	16
Burning Stalks	–	–	–	–	–	–	–	–	–	2	–	–	2
Subtotal	15	15	6	26	10	10	4	6	6	2	0	0	100

TABLE 7-1 Labor Input per Crop and per Month in a Typical Peasant Household in Nampula (cont.)

Task	Oct	Nov	Dec	Jan	Feb	Mar	Apr	May	Jun	Jul	Aug	Sep	Total
Manioc													
Land preparation	-	-	20	10	10	-	-	-	-	-	-	-	40
Harvesting	-	-	-	-	-	-	-	-	-	15	15	-	30
Replant/process	-	-	-	-	-	-	-	-	-	-	15	30	45
Subtotal	0	0	20	10	10	0	0	0	0	15	30	30	115
Dry beans													
Land preparation	-	10	10	10	-	-	-	-	-	-	-	-	30
Planting	-	-	-	-	10	-	-	-	-	-	-	-	10
Weeding	-	-	-	-	15	10	-	-	-	-	-	-	20
Harvesting	-	-	-	-	-	-	10	10	-	-	-	-	20
Subtotal	0	10	10	10	25	10	10	10	0	0	0	0	85
Total person-days	40	56	78	74	79	40	22	39	21	30	34	30	

figures are estimates, they do indicate the pressures on peasant households, particularly during the months of December, January, and February. To meet basic household consumption requirements and to satisfy colonial demands required between seventy and eighty labor days per month. Assuming that peasants typically worked twenty-five days per month, it would take three people working full-time to satisfy this monthly demand. This calculation is based on the further assumption that climatic conditions permitted them to work all of these days. But the torrential downpours typical of January and February often prevented peasants from working their crops for much of this period. As a result, households had to marshal additional labor in concentrated periods of time to fill the gap. When this additional labor factor is added into the equation, the number of workers actually required was significantly higher than the initial calculation.[14] For labor-starved households, this burden could be unmanageable.

Even working longer hours and drawing on extrafamilial labor, most households found it physically impossible to sustain the food production system established prior to the cotton regime. In the face of colonial oppression, peasants had little choice but to divert badly needed labor from food to cotton. Cotton growers throughout the colony faced this dilemma. Not only was there less time for major crops such as sorghum and beans, but women often had less opportunity to collect plants and grubs, and men did not hunt and fish as they had in the past. Although colonial agronomists tended to discount these activities, they provided valuable sources of vitamins, minerals, and proteins.[15] Everywhere the consequences were devastating.

Labor bottlenecks also carried emotional and mental costs. Because the most acute labor crunch in January and February coincided with seasonal food shortages, growers often went to their fields hungry or malnourished when they faced the most demanding tasks. According to Manuel Sitói, "It was a time when we were forced to eat grass, roots, and tubers."[16] It was also a time of anguish for many parents who watched helplessly while young babies died from malnutrition and hunger-related diseases.[17] Murinvona Mpemo of Gilé was visibly moved as she told her own personal tragedy:

> It was terrible. We had to work cotton and as a result could not keep up our gardens. This caused the hunger. Many babies died in the months of January, February, and March. Most were very young. I had ten children. Three died and seven survived. They all died during the hunger period.[18]

Other state policies exacerbated the food crises. During the first decade of the regime colonial authorities regularly increased the minimum size of peasant cotton plots, thereby diverting more and more labor from the food economy. Even after one hectare became the standard plot size, administrators and aggressive overseers pressured peasants to grow more (see Chapter 3). The Cotton Board's decision that

---

[14]   I am grateful to Paulo Zucula of the Mozambican Ministry of Agriculture for this information.

[15]   The nutritional value of luminous and wild plants, grubs, and small game is an important subject that requires careful scholarly attention (personal communication from Jan Vansina, August 14, 1994).

[16]   Interview with Manuel Sitói et al., Guijá, 16 February 1979.

[17]   Interview with Rosa Maria Ernesto, Nampula, 11 July 1991; interview with Murinvona Mpemo, Nampula/Gilé, 9 July 1991.

[18]   Interview with Murinvona Mpemo.

cotton must be grown in separate fields made it even more difficult for households to meet their food requirements. There was no compelling reason, scientific or social, why cotton could not be intercropped with foodstuffs. To the contrary, cultivating mixed fields helped to maintain soil humidity, initially increased soil nutrients, and reduced erosion. The Portuguese, however, considered it an impediment to cotton cultivation in Mozambique. If intercropping had been legalized, it would have been far more difficult to oversee the daily work practices of growers and to divert their labor from the food economy.

The interrelationship of food and land figured profoundly at a cultural level as well. Across the colony, ancestor worship was a vital part of the agricultural cycle.[19] Peasants invoked the spirits of the dead to guarantee the fertility of the land and the well-being of their families. In many areas growers conducted religious ceremonies to propitiate the ancestors before they planted. The most elaborate of these ceremonies took place during the harvest. Villagers gathered for three to four days of dancing, eating, socializing, and prayer. The cotton regime challenged these time-honored practices. The most immediate threat came from Portuguese *capatazes*, who often viewed these "obscurantist activities" as a waste of precious time at critical junctures in the agricultural cycle. Bishop Machado, who as a child helped his mother in the Inhambane cotton fields, recounted the conflict over the first fruits ceremony:

> Cotton had a substantial impact on our cultural life because peasants had to cultivate it all the time, there was not sufficient time to organize the important ceremonies [*timhamba*] to give thanks to our ancestors, which took three or four days. The people in our village were afraid that if the *capataz* found them at home evoking the spirits they would be beaten, but if they did not they would anger the deceased. Often we had to postpone the *timhamba* until after we harvested the cotton or we had to shorten ceremonies from four days to only one. But we always did it.[20]

In other regions peasants were permitted to propitiate the ancestors in the early mornings and late evenings and when they had fulfilled their cotton obligations.[21]

Even when the *capatazes* did not intervene, it could still be difficult to prepare an appropriate offering, particularly in times of scarcity. But no matter how little food there was, growers found a way. "Even if we only had a bit of sorghum, we would pound it together with the husks and make our offerings," stressed Celeste Cossa.[22] If there was no food at all, peasants would hunt for game and collect roots and tubers to give thanks to the ancestors.[23] Muiluta Razão from Netia in Nampula

---

[19]   Interview with Daniel Rekula by Arlindo Chilundo, Netia, 30 September 1993; interview with Muiluta Razão by Arlindo Chilundo, Netia, 30 September 1993; interview with Celeste Cossa, Amélia Novana, and Regina Mate, Maputo, 31 July 1991; interview with Bishop João Somane Machado, Maputo, 23 July 1993; Martinez, *O Povo Macua,* 54–56; Manuel Gama Amaral, *O Povo Yao* (Lisbon, 1990), 383–86; Dias, *Os Macondes,* 116–17; Junod, *Life of a South African Tribe,* vol. 1, 394–400; Feliciano, "Antropologia Económica," 197.

[20]   Interview with Bishop Machado.

[21]   Interview with Daniel Rekula; interview with Muiluta Razão.

[22]   Interview with Celeste Cossa et al.

[23]   Interview with Bishop Machado; interview with Gonçalo Mazungane Chilundo, Maputo, 20 July 1993; interview with Mateus Katupha, Maputo, 25 July 1993.

stressed that "when we didn't have any maize or sorghum . . . we used *uti* [a fruit from a small tree]. . . . We gathered it in the forest. Then we cooked it and made it into flour."[24] Cotton-induced food shortages intensified pressure on rural communities to meet their spiritual obligations, but all rose to the occasion since the consequences of failing to propitiate the ancestors would be devastating. "If we did not give thanks the ancestors would get angry and our situation would become even worse."[25]

At times the colonial assault on food production was even more direct. One way to divert peasants' labor from food crops was to destroy those crops altogether. Throughout the 1940s company overseers and some state officials employed this tactic on a regular basis. At a 1948 meeting in the Nampula district with the Native Affairs inspector, twenty-two peasants and chiefs from throughout the area angrily denounced "the African *capatazes* who destroyed their gardens so that they would have to cultivate cotton and rice."[26] In nearby Imala, a peasant named Ernesto Utiana complained to the same inspector that "*capataz* Musa had pulled out all of his manioc and ordered him to grow cotton in its place."[27] In the far south, an overly ambitious Cotton Board official "forced women to destroy corn that was already growing and required them to plant cotton." When questioned by his superiors, the official denied the specific accusations but affirmed that it was his "responsibility to prevent Africans from planting food crops on land reserved for cotton."[28]

The most intense struggles were waged over peanuts, which were an important foodstuff in many parts of the colony as well as a significant cash crop. Unlike cotton, peanuts grew near the surface of the soil and did not require deep cultivation. Instead of depleting the soil of valuable nutrients, peanuts (like other legumes) improved the soil where they were grown because of their nitrogen-fixing qualities. Peanuts also required much less weeding than cotton and could be picked in one harvest rather than several. Thus, peanuts were not nearly as demanding a crop as cotton; on average they required about fifty labor-days per hectare. Moreover, peanuts could easily be intercropped with food crops. They were an important part of peasants' diets, but they also yielded a much larger cash revenue per hectare than cotton—almost twice as much in the 1940s. In all but the most humid areas, peanuts were the commodity of choice for peasant producers. Alberto Momola of Nampula was adamant: "If we had a choice we preferred to plant peanuts. We received more for it than for corn, manioc, or cotton. "[29] So was Adelina Penicela of Gaza:

> Peanuts were our most important crop. We could not give up peanuts. In the old days we used peanuts, not imported cooking oil. You could eat peanuts with any kind of food: pumpkin leaves, manioc leaves, and chicken as well. I also earned more money from selling peanuts. But very often I just exchanged peanuts for clothing.[30]

---

[24] Interview with Muiluta Razão.

[25] Interview with Celeste Cossa et al.

[26] AHM, SR, Cx. 77, ISANI, "Relatório da . . . Nampula," Hortêncio Estevão de Sousa, Insp., 1948.

[27] AHM, SR, Cx.77, ISANI, "Relatório da . . . Imala," Hortêncio Estevão de Sousa, 1948.

[28] AIA, JEAC, "Papéis Diversos 1941," J. Anachoreta Chefe da Sub–Del. do Sul do Save to Pres. de Del. de JEAC, 11 September 1941.

[29] Interview with Alberto Momola et al., Nampula, 27 May 1987.

[30] Interview with Adelina Penicela, Maputo, 3 July 1986.

For all these reasons, state and company officials had to intervene to prevent cotton growers from diverting their labor to peanuts. In some areas they simply destroyed peanut fields.

The only region where destroying food crops does not seem to have been reported was in the plantation zones of central Mozambique. There, concessionaires had less interest in cotton than in food they needed to feed migrant laborers working on their estates. Companies acquired this produce through a combination of incentives and coercion.[31] "Our problems increased," one peasant living in the Sena Sugar concession of Mopeia insisted, "since we had to produce more for sale and as a result there was much more hunger."[32]

It is clear that the diversion of labor to cotton had a far-reaching impact on food security. Reports from the cotton zones stressed the inverse relation between cotton and food production. As early as 1941, *Notícias*, a leading Mozambican newspaper, warned:

> The expansion of cotton production . . . and of other forced cultures have had a prejudicial effect on corn and peanuts which are indispensable to the Africans' diet and no less profitable to the producers than cotton. It is excellent, even magnificent that cotton production has increased . . . but it does not make sense for the colonial economy that this expansion should come at the expense of corn.[33]

In a confidential report to the president of the Cotton Board six years later, a senior agronomist concluded that "it is becoming increasingly more appropriate to attribute food shortages to cotton."[34] The situation had not improved by 1950, when the bishop of Beira expressed outrage that in one of his parishes "which had been a rich granary producing an abundance of food . . . the introduction of cotton had left the people living in the region suffering from hunger."[35] Former producers in Imala in the Nampula district remember how the tyranny of the cotton regime, combined with a particularly bad cold spell one year, left them without food. "Many people died. Some days more than twenty, thirty, or even forty. Everyone was afraid."[36]

Unfortunately, there are no aggregate production statistics for colonial Mozambique to provide an accurate measure of the impact of cotton on the food economy. In their absence, marketing statistics are the next best indicator. Obviously there is no exact correlation between what peasants produced and what they chose to market. But in the context of the cotton regime, sales figures do provide a rough indication of agricultural production trends.

---

[31] AIA, JEAC, 9352 AT, "Boletim de Informação, 1946–47, Sena Sugar Estates"; interview with Luís Alberto et al., Mopeia, 1–2 August 1976 (Head Collection).

[32] Interview with Luís Alberto et al.

[33] *Notícias*, 19 July 1941.

[34] AIA, JEAC, Copiador Geral de Notas 4 Trimestre 1947, Gastão de Mello Furtado to Pres. da JEAC, 11 December 1947.

[35] AIA, EA, "Ordem Anticomunista," Sebastião Soares de Resende, n.d. The passage quoted in the government report is derived from Resende's colonial critique entitled *Ordem Anticomunista* (Lourenço Marques, 1950).

[36] Group interview, Imala State Farm, 4 May 1979.

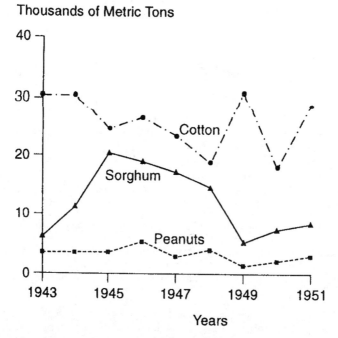

Graph 7–1. Marketed Production of Selected Crops in Nampula, 1943–1951

Sources: Bravo, *A Cultura Algodoeira*, 81; RTE, *Recenseamento Agrícola* (Lourenço Marques), 1940–1941; RTE, *Estatística Agrícola* (Lourenço Marques), 1941–1960; Direcção Provinçal dos Serviço de Estatística Geral, *Estatística Agrícola* (Lourenço Marques, 1941–1951).

Sales of every basic food crop but manioc and corn declined between 1946, when the cotton regime was firmly in place, and 1951,[37] the year of the reforms (see Table 7–2). Increased marketing of manioc was probably the result of the state policy, begun in the late 1940s, to force peasants both to increase manioc production and to sell the yield as part of the famine relief program. The marginal increase in sales of corn probably reflects a decision by many peasant households to cultivate more corn and less sorghum in order to reduce competition with cotton, even though corn was less drought-resistant than sorghum (see below). It is not entirely clear, however, why if food supplies were tight, growers were willing to sell more corn. Tax pressure and the need for basic consumer goods are the most likely explanations. Alternatively, the small increment may have come from the fields of more prosperous growers (see Chapter 8), for whom food shortages were not a problem, or from households entirely outside the cotton regime. Sales of peanuts, beans, sorghum, *mafurra*, and *mexoeria* all fell precipitously. Only in the case of rice, also produced within a coercive system, was the decrease relatively small. This decline in marketed food crop was most pronounced in the

---

[37] In 1951 climatic conditions in parts of the north were particularly bad, and therefore the decline was more acute in that year than in preceeding years.

TABLE 7-2   Marketed Food Crops, 1946 and 1951 (tons)

Crop	1946	1951	Crop	1946	1951
Peanuts (shelled)	29,159	10,932	Mafurra	5,211	1,635
Rice (unprocessed)	14,565	12,866	Sorghum	16,688	30,725
Beans (assorted)	9,524	3,826	Mexoeira	3,648	1,564
Sesame seeds	2,208	1,559	Maize	26,102	31,000

Source: AIA, JEAC, "Propaganda Moçambique: Elementos Para a Século," Gastão de Mello Furtado, 15 June 1954.

Nampula district, the center of the cotton regime. Sales of sorghum declined from almost 19,000 tons to slightly more than 8,000 tons, and peanuts from 5,300 tons to less than 3,000 (see Graph 7–1). During the same period, cotton sales in Nampula increased modestly, although there were substantial variations from year to year. The sharp declines in the marketing of food crops, including corn and manioc,[38] coupled with the increases in cotton sales suggest the labor decisions peasants were being forced to make.

Local marketing statistics for the same period often reveal even greater disparities between cotton sales and sales of food crops. In the northern circumscription of Macomia, the sale of peanuts declined steeply from 277 tons to 95 tons; so did sorghum. The sale of cotton, by contrast, jumped by 400 percent (see Appendix C). In the circumscription of Nampula, peanut sales dropped from 2,000 tons to 700 tons, sorghum from 990 to 220 tons; cotton sales, by contrast, increased by 200 tons (see Appendix D). In the fertile Zambézian circumscription of Morrumbala, peanut and sorghum sales plummeted, while cotton sales increased fourfold (see Appendix E). A number of environmental and demographic conditions helped determine food output, but cotton was always a factor.

Perhaps the best documented and most tragic testimony to the devastating effects of cotton on rural food security comes from the circumscription of Mogovolas in Nampula district. In the late 1940s, the colonial state and cotton interests unleashed a vigorous campaign against the peasant food economy, destroying peanut and corn fields, forcing peasants to grow their food crops on cotton-eroded soils, and allocating the best terrain for cotton cultivation. In the words of one local official, "the richest lands have been dedicated to cotton and the poorest to cereals and other food crops."[39] While state intervention kept cotton production in Mogovolas fairly stable throughout the 1940s, marketing statistics for food crops suggest that food production dropped sharply. Sales of sorghum fell from 143 tons in 1946 to 2 tons in 1949 and a mere ton in 1950. Peanut sales declined by approximately 300 percent. Even manioc was in short supply at local markets (see Appendix F). State power had left peasants extremely vulnerable, so much so that in 1951, a particu-

---

[38]   The marketing of manioc declined from 5,975 tons to 5,259 tons, and corn plummeted from 2,688 tons to 1,027 tons. RTE, *Estatística Agrícola 1946–1951.*

[39]   AHM, FGG, Tabela 5, Cota 489, Álvaro Martins da Silva, Chefe de Brigada, 11 October 1951.

larly bad year, several thousand peasants in Mogovolas are reported to have died from starvation.[40]

The colonial attack on food crops had a second important consequence for rural food security. Since peasants had to privilege cotton production, they also had less capacity to grow other cash crops such as sesame or sunflowers.[41] As a result, they lost disposable income that might have been used to purchase the food-stuffs they were unable to produce themselves.

Because Mozambican peasants were forced to sell their cotton under conditions over which they had little control, they not only assumed all the risks of production but derived few of the benefits. Artificially depressed prices meant that only the most productive cotton growers or those households with off-farm income could afford to purchase foodstuffs to supplement the reduced quantity they were able to produce themselves. Food crises thus must be situated in a larger struggle over who sets the terms of commercial exchange and questions of entitlement—the totality of moral, political, and economic rights that individuals and households commanded to gain access to food resources.[42]

Perhaps most important of all, the imposition of cotton was ecologically questionable in many parts of Mozambique and placed severe long-term strains on local systems of food production. Soil erosion almost always accompanied cotton cultivation, exacerbating the loss of rich top soil and depleting the soil's nutrients. Land degradation was not a natural by-product of cotton agriculture but a consequence of cotton grown within a particular labor regime and political economy.

Lisbon's insistence in the early 1940s on incorporating as much land as possible into the cotton scheme was the primary reason for the rampant deforestation and soil erosion. One opponent of the Portuguese land management system in Mozambique observed in 1948 that

> the main activity of the Africans is the destruction of forests and shrubs in order to create the necessary area to grow cotton—a task that requires a great deal of labor and results in the thoughtless burning and devastation of rich vegetation. Because the Africans are not permitted to use the same land for a second cotton season, once they harvest the crop, they are forced to open up new areas creating new devastation. In this way hundreds of thousands of hectares of forest are destroyed annually to promote cotton, and the soil is devoured by erosion and ultimately becomes infertile.[43]

A state botanist exploring forestry conditions in Zambézia one decade later complained about the destructive effects of cotton cultivation on the region's once rich vegetation:

> The trees are chopped and then burned; cotton is grown here for one year only; the next year they grow maize, *mapira*, and manioc. Each year they have to clear different lands for cotton. In the process all the

---

[40]   Armando Castro, *O Sistema Colonial Português em África* (Lisbon, 1978), 284–88.

[41]   The one cash crop that did increase dramatically was cashews, grown primarily in the coastal regions.

[42]   The notion of entitlement is derived from Amartya Sen's pioneering work, *Poverty and Famines: An Essay on Entitlement* (Oxford, 1981).

[43]   Faria, "Produção Algodoeira," 2.

trees are being destroyed, and the trees are more valuable than the cotton being produced here. Forests are being destroyed from Milange to Quelimane, from Derre to Mocuba in Lugela, Alto Molócuè, Alto Ligonha, Meconta and Namialo. All that is left are weeds.[44]

A colleague reported that in Derre alone 10,000 hectares of forest reserve had already been lost by 1955 because of the cotton regime.[45] Apart from depleting the soil's nutrients, deforestation had at least two other adverse effects on rural food security. It deprived rural communities of a variety of wild fruits that played an important part in their diet, especially in times of crop shortages,[46] and it meant that in many areas women had to travel further to collect firewood, leaving them less time to plant, process, and prepare food for their households.

But deforestation and the destruction of vegetation that could have prevented soil runoffs were not the only causes of erosion. In some areas, particularly in the south where there was an increasing shortage of well-watered land, peasants were expected to cultivate cotton on the same plot for three or more years in a row.[47] While this policy limited the extent of deforestation, it meant that after a few years cotton quickly depleted the soil's nutrients. Growers then either had to cultivate some of their food crops on these exhausted lands or else allow them to lie fallow for several years, a luxury that became increasingly difficult in the face of European settlement and land appropriation. Agronomists observed a similar pattern of soil exhaustion in parts of the north as well.[48]

Land exhaustion accompanied labor exhaustion; but the cotton scheme persevered in its own involuted way. In the final analysis, environmental protection and soil management were even lower priorities than food production for the state-concessionary alliance. The small number of extension officers and the slow pace at which anti-erosion programs were implemented reflected Lisbon's priorities. But the growing food crisis throughout the colony, highlighted by the Mogovolas famine, finally forced the state to act.

The State Famine Relief Program

Whether as a consequence of the explicit assault on food production, of willful neglect, or of disinterest, Lisbon perpetuated hunger in rural Mozambique throughout the first decade of the cotton regime, despite the efforts of a small number of administrators to point out the counterproductive nature of this stance. "I believe that the cultivation of corn, sorghum and manioc is as important as cotton production," wrote the administrator of Maganja da Costa in 1945, "for without food, no

[44] AIA, JEAC, 929/5, "Rel. da Viagem da Zambézia e Tete Para Estudos das Possibilidades Florestais, 1957," J. Garde Cardoso.

[45] AIA, JEAC, 929/5, Henrique Vieira Pinto, "Rel. do Eng. Silvicultor H. Vieira Pinto, Sobre uma Diligência na Reserva Florestal do Derre," 8 May 1955.

[46] See, for example, Junod, *Life of a South African Tribe*, vol. 2, 15–18.

[47] AIA, JEAC, "Zona Algodoeira dos Muchopes," J. Fonseca George, Eng. Ag., 5 September 1947; AIA, JEAC, "Zona Algodoeira Homoíne," João Dias de Deus, Reg. Ag., October 1947.

[48] AIA, JEAC, 605/8, João M. Estevão de Souza, 8 October 1946; AIA, JEAC, "Brigada de Mogovolas," Álvares Martins et al. to Del. da JEAC, 25 September 1951.

one can work."[49] Warnings and paternalistic rhetoric aside, colonial planners never gave serious consideration to provisioning the countryside in times of dearth. When the state did import extra foodstuffs, impoverished cotton growers rarely had sufficient funds to buy them.[50] Some of the larger concessionary companies distributed imported food at fixed prices. And, in 1941, Sena Sugar imported hundreds of tons of grain from Angola to ease drought conditions.[51]

The colonial state's famine relief program developed slowly during the 1950s as a component of the Cotton Board's policy of rationalizing cotton production and reforming the cotton regime (see Chapter 6). For example, included among the criteria for becoming an *agricultor do algodão* was the requirement that farmers plant food gardens the same size as their cotton fields. Similarly, the planned communities, or *concentrações*, were predicated on a crop rotation system that incorporated food crops in order to alleviate production bottlenecks and famine. Agricultural cooperatives gave peasants even more latitude with respect to food production and greater control over the allocation of household labor. At least part of the rationale behind allowing peasants to stop producing cotton in unsuitable areas was to ensure food security. Even the price reforms at the cotton markets increased the capacity of cotton growers to purchase more food with their earnings.

The most salient feature of the famine relief program was that it remained cotton-centered. The colonial notion of "food first" did not mean that cotton was to become second priority. The manioc campaign launched in the 1950s offers a perfect example. It was no accident that the colonial state decided to promote a food crop that was an ideal complement to cotton. Manioc could be grown on marginal lands, was drought-resistant, and did not have to be fully ripe to be edible. More important, manioc required relatively little labor beyond the initial clearing and mounding of the land, and because it was harvested after cotton, its cultivation did not create a labor bottleneck.

Ironically, the state's manioc campaign, like the cotton regime, was often forced, and peasants were not permitted to consume all the manioc they produced. Across the colony peasants were told that they had to cultivate a specified amount of manioc, varying from region to region. In the aftermath of the 1951 famine in Mogovolas, the administrator there wrote:

> The production of [manioc] cannot be allowed to diminish, because it has become such a critical part of their diet. Every year, in the month of April, we will proceed with a "manioc campaign" in which every African will be obligated to prepare a *machamba* of manioc. This is the month when they are not occupied with other work and when the rains are well suited for this initiative.[52]

Faria Lobo, a cotton official who supervised production in nearby Nampula, acknowledged that "not only did we force them to grow manioc, but to cultivate

---

[49]   AIA, JEAC, 601/8, "Relatório," Pedro João Francisco Lopes, Admin. da Circ. de Maganja da Costa, 30 December 1945.

[50]   Keys, "Report of the Inhambane and Limpopo District," 69–70.

[51]   SSE, File 44, "Final Cotton Report 1941," 30 November 1942.

[52]   AHM, PM, Gov. do Niassa, Circ. de Mogovolas, "Relatório da Circ. Admin. de Mogovolas, Ano de 1953," Manuel Maria Souto e Silva, Admin., 26 February 1954.

plots that were sufficiently large to guarantee subsistence."[53] In Zambézia the governor imposed a similar policy in 1951. And to the south in Inharrime, peasants were required to plant manioc fields at least 150 meters by 100 meters. Senior officials acknowledged in a confidential 1958 memorandum that they were still exploring new methods "to pressure peasants to intensify the cultivation of manioc."[54]

In Chibuto where the white soils proved unsuitable for cotton, peasants were told to plant manioc instead. Leia Mbazima remembered that after cotton was abolished, "we were forced to spend three days a week working in our manioc plantations and the remainder of the week we could work in our food gardens."[55] The state also organized a number of manioc plantations, recruiting labor from the ranks of the rural poor. Impoverished women, teenagers, and elderly men made up the bulk of the work force. They received food and a small wage. Labor discipline on the manioc plantations was backed by the threat of force and by the common knowledge that if workers did not work, they would not receive food in times of shortages.[56]

The state required peasants in most parts of the colony to grow manioc in addition to cotton. Justa Joaquim of Namacurra in central Mozambique remembered how "we had to find time to plant manioc to feed ourselves and to sell some for cloth."[57] Aide Matupera of Macomia recalled that the "administrator distributed manioc stalks and anyone who did not plant them was sent to jail."[58] According to his neighbor Xibuca Minga,

> Manioc became a forced crop along with cotton. This increased our suffering. How was a person supposed to cultivate two large fields at the same time? And we could only keep a part of the manioc. We had to give another part to the administrator and we used a third part to buy cloth.[59]

Xibuca Minga's story highlights the contradictory character of the manioc campaign. Although the program was allegedly initiated to alleviate rural hunger, it did not necessarily permit growers to keep what they produced. In some areas where peasants no longer had to grow cotton, local authorities occasionally confiscated the entire manioc crop. Leia Mbazima remembered that "the administrator distributed manioc stalks, which we were forced to plant. The results were very positive. Only we did not ever know what happened to the manioc."[60] State officials sold much of this manioc to peasants in cotton zones where food supplies were dangerously low: "[The administrator] arranged the manioc. . . . He went and got it and brought it to us so that we would not starve and would be able to work

---

53 Interview with Faria Lobo. 26 May 1987.

54 Distrito da Zambézia, Acto da Conf. dos Admins.; AIA, JEAC, "Confidência 1957–1959," Vasco de Sousa da Fonseca Lebre, Reg. Ag. to Chefe da Del. da JEAC, 10 March 1958.

55 Interview with Leia Mbazima, Maputo, 27 July 1991.

56 AIA, JEAC, Álvaro Martins da Silva, Eng. Ag., 22 October 1951.

57 Interview with Justa Joaquim, Nicoadala/Mocuba, 17 July 1991.

58 Interview with Aide Matupera, Xibuca Minga, et al., Macomia, 27 July 1979.

59 Ibid.

60 Interview with Leia Mbazima.

in the cotton fields."[61] In other instances the manioc was sent to European estates to ensure that migrant laborers had sufficient rations.[62] The fact that many local and provincial administrators ordered peasants to sell a substantial portion of their manioc harvest suggests that their overarching concern was probably not feeding individual households, but minimizing food deficits at the regional and provincial levels.

In addition to the manioc campaign, there were several more modest efforts to alleviate hunger in the countryside. In 1950, Cotton Board officials proposed that *agricultores de algodão* be pressured to grow food crops on a large-enough scale to feed their less productive neighbors. If *agricultores* refused, they would forfeit their privileged legal status and their exemption from forced labor.[63] The planned cotton communities, organized around Portuguese notions of crop rotation and scientific farming, were also designed to tackle the problem of scarcity in the countryside. Nevertheless, there is evidence of famine in areas where *concentrações* were supposed to ensure food security. Montepuez in the Cabo Delgado district and Eráti, Murrupula, and Lutuli in the district of Moçambique all experienced serious shortages during the the 1950s. The food situation was not much better in the *concentrações* of Cabo Delgado.[64]

Concerned about the continuing food crisis, a senior cotton official urged the president of the Cotton Board and the governor general of the colony to order concessionaires to give the highest priority to food production in the planting cycle. In a confidential 1959 report to the Board president, Gastão de Mello Furtado echoed the concerns that the administrator of Maganja had raised fifteen years earlier: "It is absolutely necessary that cotton producers have a full stomach in order to work." Furtado proposed distributing corn seeds, which peasants would be obliged to pay back at the corn harvest. Such radical state intervention was necessary, he contended, because "a majority of the population is malnourished."[65]

Conclusion: Cotton, Malnutrition, and Disease

Food insecurity and hunger were integral features of the cotton regime. Colonial practices and policies had abrogated much of the control that peasants had historically exercised over their food economy. Hardly a year passed during the cotton era in which food problems were not reported in one cotton zone or another. Portuguese documents tended to make only brief references to rural subsistence crises, often alluding to them in vague terms such as *"fome,"* which can mean either "hunger" or "famine," or using even the more obscure notion of *"deficiências."* Both terms hide more than they reveal. Moreover, famine and malnutrition are not necessarily the same. Debilitating malnutrition that affects the working capacity of

---

[61]   Interview with Pruan Hassan.

[62]   AIA, JEAC, "Conf. 1957–1959," Vasco de Sousa Fonseca Lebre, Reg. Ag., 10 March 1958.

[63]   AIA, JEAC, "Propaganda Moçambique," António Mira Mendes to G. M. Furtado, 12 June 1950.

[64]   AIA, JEAC, "Conf. 19571959," Gastão de Mello Furtado, 20 August 1959; AIA, JEAC, Del. de Moç., BT de Moçambique, "Rel. An. Ref. ao Ano de 1957 (Campanha Algodoeira de 1956–1957)," Manuel de Oliveira Barros, Reg. Ag., 4 January 1958.

[65]   AIA, JEAC, "Conf. 1957–1959," Gastão de Mello Furtado to Pres. de JEAC, 1 September 1959.

growers, their resistance to disease, and their fertility can occur without famine. Whereas famines attracted the attention of colonial agronomists and local administrators, they generally ignored the causes of nutritional imbalances in rural diets. As a result it is often difficult to tell from these documents the magnitude or rhythm of rural food crises during the cotton regime. The tendency of Portuguese commentators to presume that "seasonal famines" were natural events in Mozambique and that African diets were inherently deficient colors most colonial accounts of food and disease. In a 1954 special issue of a leading Mozambican journal, *Sociedade de Estudos de Moçambique*, which explored the causes of rural poverty, Manuel Simões Alberto, a prominent Portuguese scholar, proclaimed: "Rural Mozambicans, left to themselves, living in their traditional tribal life, guided by their traditional ancestral customs, eat poorly and waste enormous amounts of grains making beer, which has a prejudicial effect on their health and morality."[66] Alberto's observation tells us more about the assumptions of Portuguese nutritional scientists than about the reality on the ground in Mozambique. Drawing on a wide array of contemporary colonial sources, two foreign experts in the field of nutrition reached a similar conclusion, placing the responsibility for a host of diseases on "traditional" imbalances in local diets.[67] For their part, former growers described all but the most serious crises in very general terms.

Notwithstanding these lacunae in the data, there is no doubt that the forced cultivation of cotton left peasants more vulnerable to famine. The cotton regime eroded a number of agronomic strategies that peasants had historically employed to guarantee food security. Intercropping and mixed cropping were prohibited. Many peasants found it difficult to maintain a combination of upland and valley fields. Most were forced to reduce the range of food crops they grew. Previously peasants had been very conscious of hedging their risks by planting an array of food crops in case environmental conditions caused a shortage of the main staple. Their shift to less drought-resistant labor-saving crops during the cotton era, most notably corn, increased the risks of famine still further. Colonial practices not only undermined existing famine avoidance strategies, but restricted the freedom of peasants to make new adaptations.

It is thus hardly surprising that famines occurred with disturbing regularity, particularly in the north—the principal cotton zone.[68] Famines were reported in at least seven of the twenty-three years of the cotton regime.[69] Despite colo-

---

[66] Manuel Simões Alberto, "O Problema da Alimentação Entre as Populações Rurais Nativas de Moçambique," *Sociedade de Estudos de Moçambique* 24(1954), 119.

[67] May and McLellan draw this conclusion from a variety of colonial sources that they read and incorporate uncritically. In sharp contrast to the "backward Africans," they characterize the Portuguese plan for development as "imaginative, realistic and humane." *The Ecology of Malnutrition*, 277. For a broad review of the colonial discourse on famine and disease see Carlos Santos Reis, *A Nutrição no Ultramar Português*, 187–218 passim, but particularly 211.

[68] Extant documentation for the preceding period suggests that famines occurred more frequently in southern Mozambique; if this is correct, the shift provides us with important insights into the etiology of famines in colonial Mozambique.

[69] There is extant documentation of famines in 1938, 1942, 1950, 1951, 1956, 1957, and 1959. Key, "Reports on the Inhambane and Limpopo District," 69; Fortuna, "Threading Through," 240–41; AIA, JEAC, 1949, "Rotações e Afolhamentos," A. Fegueiras e Sousa to Chefe da Del. da JEAC, 28 March 1950; AIA, JEAC, Gastão de Mello Furtado to Gov. Ger., "Brigada de Mogovolas 1951," 15 August 1951; Castro, *O Sistema Colonial*, 277; Capela, *Escravatura*, 20.

nial famine relief programs, there are indications of widescale hunger as late as 1958. On February 16, 1958, the bishop of Beira made the following entry in his diary:

> I received M., the *chefe de posto* of Ancuase who informed me about horrible things taking place in Niassa. The Administrator G. through his cotton policy has caused many Africans to die from hunger. An employee of the cotton company wrote a report in which he noted that there was no justification for him to remain there since there were so few Africans and those who had survived were close to death.[70]

The evidence that cotton exacerbated food shortages, especially during the preharvest period, is even more compelling. Cotton officials, native inspectors, and local administrators across the colony openly acknowledged this fact. J. Anachoreta, a senior Cotton Board official responsible for overseeing production in the south, concluded in 1941 that "more than fifty percent of the growers could not cultivate cotton without prejudice to their food crops."[71] The story was the same in Chinde a decade later.[72] Even after all the reforms were implemented, colonial medical authorities found that many cotton growers were still malnourished.[73]

Food shortages were most acute during the preharvest period, which occurred during the rainy season. The connections between malnutrition and rural work were especially clear in female-headed households, where women had to cultivate their gardens, care for children, gather firewood, fetch water, assist the sick and the elderly, and perform all of their other chores in addition to producing cotton. The multiple demands on these women's time made it difficult for them to provide adequate food. Their dilemma was compounded during the peak labor periods, which came at a time when food supplies were nearly exhausted and the new year's food had not yet ripened. Elders recalled that it was during this period that women and children suffered the most.[74] Murinvona Mpemo's grief in the aftermath of her babies' starvation highlights the fact that famines are as much about feelings, vulnerability, and despair as they are about caloric intake.

It is difficult to know precisely the nutritional status of most rural Mozambicans under the cotton regime, since few dietary surveys were undertaken during the colonial period. Those studies that exist confirm that food intake in the countryside was neither adequate nor well balanced.[75] Two American scholars came to the same conclusion: "Unfortunately, as far as can be determined, these basic require-

---

[70] Quoted in Capela, *Escravatura*, 20.

[71] AIA, JEAC, "Papéis Diversos 1941," J. Anachoreta to Chefe da Sub–Del. do Sul do Save to Del. da JEAC, 11 September 1941.

[72] AIA, JEAC, 660, 55 (1), A. Dias de Meneses, Dir. da Admin. Civil da Zambézia to CP da JEAC, 18 January 1952.

[73] Alberto, "Problema de Alimentação," 113–26; Carlos Manuel dos Santos Reis, "Alimentação da Mãe Indígena e Aleitamento," *Anais do Instituto de Medicina Tropical* 10(1953), 1345–437; Silva, "Problema Alimentar," 691–712; Carlos Manuel dos Santos Reis, "Aspectos da Alimentação Indígena em Mocímboa da Praia" (unpublished manuscript summarized in Reis, *A Nutrição*, 208).

[74] For a broader theoretical and comparative discussion of the seasonal famines and their nutritional implications, see Feierman, "Struggles for Control," 100–103.

[75] Alberto, "Problema da Alimentação," 113–26; Silva, "Problema Alimentar"; Reis, "Aspectos da Alimentação Indígena."

ments are not being met in most Mozambique diets. Only the paid laborers, whose diet is prescribed by law, and the armed forces have a satisfactory regime." [76]

In her recent book, Penvenne demonstrates that, in fact, few contract laborers actually received the legally prescribed food rations.[77] If European dietary surveys were vague and not terribly informative, the oral record is anything but ambiguous. Africans inside the cotton regime remember with great clarity going to bed hungry, and barely surviving on roots and tubers during parts of the year. Moreover, weanlings and young children do not thrive if they do not eat a number of times during the day. If mothers are in the fields and can only cook a large evening meal, the nutritional intake is barely sufficient.

The health consequences of inadequate rural diets have not been sufficiently explored to warrant definitive conclusions about the epidemiology of malnutrition, but conversations with women who cultivated cotton in Mozambique and comparative evidence from other parts of Africa suggest the potentially devastating consequences of low nutritional levels combined with harsh climatic conditions.[78] Heavy rains in particular left rural communities reeling. Women with whom I spoke stressed that babies and young children were most vulnerable. Rosa Maria Ernesto of Nampula recalled that during the rainy season "many children died from hunger and anemia and others were left so frail that the measles killed them."[79] Other women reported that diarrhea was a principal cause of infant death. Portuguese researchers frequently observed kwashiorkor among young children. They also found birth weights to be particularly low, increasing the probability that newborns would not survive and that the weights and heights of older children would be well below those of their counterparts elsewhere in Africa.[80] A detailed 1953 study of the diet of rural women and its impact on breastfeeding "confirmed that the native mother's diet, even when it has sufficient calories for lactation, is defective if one consider the demanding work that the native women have to accomplish."[81] This researcher found that mother's milk was deficient in quantity and nutritional value, leaving newborns and young children frail and subject to a wide variety of medical problems.[82]

Why some groups were affected and other groups escaped largely unscathed is ultimately linked to questions of power and control over scarce resources. The Portuguese had the power to impose a new labor regime that deprived rural households of scarce resources and undermined food security. To do so they had to rely on and to provide support for African chiefs, *sepais*, and *capatazes*. They and their families all enjoyed much greater food security than did peasants working the land.

---

[76]   May and McLellan, *Ecology of Malnutrition*, 264.

[77]   Penvenne, *African Workers and Colonial Racism* .

[78]   Interview with Murinvona Mpemo; interview with Rosa Maria Ernesto; interview with Leia Mbazima; interview with Catarina Jossias Simbine and Nely Simbine, Maputo, 8 August 1991; group interview, CV Paulo Samuel Kankhomba, Massingire, 7 February 1979; Feierman, "Struggles for Control," 99–101; Susan Schofield, "Seasonal Factors Affecting Nutrition in Different Age Groups and Especially Preschool Children," *Journal of Development Studies* 11, 1(1974), 22–40.

[79]   Interview with Rosa Maria Ernesto.

[80]   May and McLellan, *Ecology of Malnutrition*, 273–75.

[81]   Reis, "Alimentação da Mãe Indigena," 1433.

[82]   Ibid.

A relatively small number of men and women also benefited from their colonial connections and from systems of patronage. Among cotton growers, those with the greatest access to extra-household labor or off-farm income were less vulnerable than their poorer counterparts. Female-headed households without wage remittances from men tended to be especially vulnerable, as did debtor households trapped in a cycle of impoverishment. In 1938 a missionary in the south described the desperate plight of most rural households:

> Famine conditions exist in most parts of [Gaza and Inhambane]. At a recent meeting in the Bileni country, thieves came at mid-day, attempting to steal the visitor's clothing. The pastor told us of natives who are so desperate for food, that they had killed others, and sold their clothing for food. Many huts are broken into and robbed. . . . The food shortage began six months ago and naturally, has grown more acute as the months passed. Food supplies have been imported by the shipload for those who have money to buy it, but at exorbitant prices. But what of the thousands who live a hand to mouth existence?[83]

There is also some evidence that gender hierarchies shaped access to food within many rural households. When men were present, they and their older sons often ate first and best, their wives and little children last and least.[84] One Portuguese researcher concluded that "diet often depends on age; children, especially those being breast-fed, are the most vulnerable."[85] During periods of scarcity, such shortages could mean the difference between life and death. The opportunity for men to find employment on plantations and in mines also gave them a greater chance to escape hunger.[86] However meager their diets, European owners of plantations and mines recognized that their workers required a minimal level of nourishment. In the final analysis, access to food at the household, communal, or regional level was inextricably linked to growing disparities in power and wealth that were part of the larger process of rural differentiation.

---

[83] Keys, "Report of the Inhambane and Limpopo District," 69.

[84] Interview with Gonçalo Mazungane Chilundo, Zavala, 1 August 1993; AHM, S.E.A.V., 7, 298, Jorge, "Notas sobre os Hábitos Alimentares dos Indígenas do Ribáuè," February 1960.

[85] Silva, "Problema Alimentar," 706.

[86] For an analysis of the relationship between gender, wage employment structures, and famine in colonial Malawi, see Vaughan, Story of an African Famine.

8

Cotton and Rural Differentiation

It was not by chance that most rural households trapped inside the cotton regime were impoverished. The state had restructured the labor process so that the risks of production fell entirely on them. It was the cotton growers who ultimately suffered from unpredictable rains and uncontrolled plant diseases and pests, who lost control of what they produced where and when, who were forced to sell cotton at artificially depressed prices.

National and regional income statistics reveal the precarious position of the majority of rural producers. Although real income from cotton doubled between 1943 and 1951 (see Table 8–1) and increased steadily thereafter, the average returns for growers were still minuscule. Per capita cotton income in 1957 was a little over 350 *escudos* (less than U.S. $13),[1] of which taxes consumed approximately one-third (see Table 5–2). One Portuguese official calculated that when this cotton income was divided among all household members, it came to between 30 and 120 *escudos* (U.S. $1 to $4) per person, depending on the region.[2] It was not surprising, therefore, that virtually every elder stressed that cotton was "the mother of poverty." Their sense of perpetual crisis is captured by a female character in Luis Polanah's novella:

> Cotton is a thankless crop. . . . If it's a bad year and we lose all the cotton, does someone pay us for the work we did? If, in the bargain, we have the misfortune of not getting anything from our own field, what will we eat during the year? How will we clothe our children? Where can we go for help? And on top of all that they say we don't want to work.[3]

The wail implicit in this passage was heard throughout Mozambique. Yet some cotton producers managed to prosper despite these impediments. A few entrepreneurs diversified into other arenas, and a small number managed to eke out a liv-

---

[1]   This figure was for peasants in northern and central Mozambique, who constituted the overwhelming majority of growers. Bravo, *Cultura Algodoeira*, 135.

[2]   AIA, JEAC, 84 (1958–1959), Gastão de Melo Furtado to Gov. do Dist. da Zambézia.

[3]   Luis Polanah, *The Saga of a Cotton Capulana*, trans. Tamara L. Bender, ed. Allen Isaacman (Madison, 1981), 31.

TABLE 8–1 Index of Total Real Cotton Income by Region, 1943–1961
(1943 = base 100)

Year	South	Central	North	Colony
1943	100	100	100	100
1944	79	116	98	103
1945	90	86	69	76
1946	108	61	89	81
1947	245	170	91	123
1948	207	141	75	102
1949	235	147	159	159
1950	201	127	83	103
1951	350	253	180	211
1952	579	181	237	237
1953	1,002	361	252	323
1954	840	306	155	235
1955	808	213	175	219
1956	1,206	276	51	178
1957	857	331	224	289
1958	882	281	171	240
1959	1,154	519	216	356
1960	1,169	460	277	378
1961	940	421	240	337

Sources: RTE, *Recenseamento Agrícola* (1940–1941); Direcção Provinçal dos Serviços de
Estatística Geral, *Estatística Agrícola* (1960–1964); RTE, *Censo da População em 1940*
(1942); RTE, *Recenseamento Geral da População em 1950*, vol. 3: *População Não
Civilisada* (1953–1955); Direcção Provinçal dos Serviços de Estatística, *Recenseamento
Geral da População na Província de Moçambique, 1960* (1960).

ing through their advantageous position in the colonial order, through hard work,
or through access to extrafamilial labor.

How individual growers fared under the cotton regime depended on regional
ecological and economic conditions, access to technology, the composition of their
households. Peasants cultivating cotton in the well-watered fertile regions of
Morrumbala or Mocuba had a better chance of prospering than their counterparts
in the cooler highland areas of Niassa or in the drier regions of Inhambane. Similarly, most growers living adjacent to the major rivers benefited from rich alluvial
soils, except in times of flooding. In Búzi, where more than half the cotton lands
were river-fed, yields were great enough that a number of growers could purchase
tractors.[4] But growers located on the margins of the flood-prone Zambézi River
lost their crops with alarming regularity. Cotton growers in the tsetse-free south
and in smaller pockets in the north were able to use ox-drawn plows, although
plowing turned out to be a mixed blessing. However, most producers in
Mozambique were not able to use this technology. For example, there were 443,000
head of cattle in Gaza and 67,000 in Inhambane in 1956. The number of cattle in

---

[4]   AIA, JEAC, 901, "Planos de Trabalho 1958, Companhia de Búzi," António José Carvalho Pereira, 10
March 1958.

Nampula in the same year was less than 8,800, and in Cabo Delgado it was only 553.[5]

Regional opportunities for households to supplement cotton earnings through off-farm income varied substantially. Migrant laborers from southern Mozambique earned appreciably more working in the South African gold mines than their central and northern counterparts earned working on settler farms or European plantations. Similarly, both urban and agricultural salaries in the south were appreciably higher than elsewhere in the colony. Farm workers in the Gaza province in 1944, for example, earned one hundred *escudos* per month; in Inhambane they earned between fifty and seventy. By comparison, in the Zambézia, Niassa, Nampula, and Cabo Delgado districts, plantation wages of thirty to forty *escudos* were the norm.[6] This differential wage structure continued throughout the entire period of the cotton regime. Prices for cotton also varied by region. They were highest in the highly monetized areas of the south and lowest in the far north. However, regional wage variations were partially offset by higher tax rates in the south. Peasants in the Gaza province paid four times as much in taxes in 1943, for instance, as peasants in Niassa (see Table 5–2).[7] Cotton growers living closer to markets and to major transportation arteries enjoyed an obvious advantage, but they were also subject to greater control by state and company officials. Proximity to missionary stations could also be decisive, particularly in southern Mozambique where evangelizing, the imposition of a Protestant work ethic, and plowing often went hand in hand.

The demographic composition of individual households affected their capacity to cope with the labor demands of the cotton regime. Households with a large pool of healthy and productive workers were in a better position. The labor configuration of a household depended on the ages of household members and the percentage of adults who were absent. Adelina Penicela and many of her neighbors in Manjacaze, whose husbands were laboring in the South African mines and whose older children were working on European farms or attending school, faced very different problems from those of Rosa Maria Ernesto of Nampula, whose husband and children toiled alongside her in the fields.

Finally, growers' experiences of cotton varied according to when they entered the cotton scheme. Households enmeshed in the system from the outset suffered under all of the flawed colonial policies as well as from the unbridled avarice of concessionary companies, rural merchants, and textile interests. As a result of reforms, peasants brought into the regime during the 1950s received higher prices for their cotton. These new growers came from the ranks of teenagers who had to register in the cotton scheme when they turned eighteen and from households living in frontier areas such as Tete.

---

[5]   Morgado Reis, "Main Food Areas and Nutritional Diseases in Mozambique," in *Comunicações Portuguesas Ao III Congresso da Associação Científica dos Países do Oceano Índico* (Lisbon, 1958), 2.

[6]   AHM, SR, Cx. 99, ISANI, "Relatórios . . . do Niassa, 1ª parte, 1943," Carlos Henriques Jones da Oliveira, 1943; AHM, SR, Cx. 62, ISANI, "Relatórios . . . Zambézia e Respectivos PAs, 1944," José Franco Rodrigues, n.d.; AHM, SR, Cx. 30, ISANI, "Relatórios . . . de Inhambane, 1944," Raul Cândido dos Reis, n.d.

[7]   The tax was two hundred *escudos* in Gaza and fifty *escudos* in Niassa. In most of central and northern Mozambique it was between seventy-five and ninety *escudos*. *BOM*, Series 1, no. 25, José Bettencourt, Gov. Ger., 27 June 1947).

While there were, theoretically, a number of routes out of poverty, all ultimately depended either on securing extra-household labor or on supplementing
cotton revenue with off-farm income, generally from migrant labor.[8] The latter
option required that the value of the wages gained by a migrant's family be
greater than the value of his labor at home. This was not always the case, particularly in the major cotton zones of northern and central Mozambique, where
most migrant laborers were press-ganged to work on European plantations and
farms or on government projects at depressed wages. Under such conditions few
conscripts were able to assist their families in any meaningful way. However,
there was a handful of skilled labor and factory jobs at the cotton gins and mills
at which men could earn relatively high incomes; so could a small number of
African teachers, truck drivers, rural nurses, tailors, and itinerant traders. Some
of these wage workers invested in the cotton economy. But the largest infusion of
indigenous capital into the countryside came from migrant laborers who worked
in the mines of South Africa.

Many households pursued both strategies, but only the loyalist chiefs (*régulos*)
and the *machambeiros* of southern Mozambique prospered. Together they probably
constituted less than 1 percent of all cotton growers.

Chiefs and Cotton Accumulation

No Africans profited more from the cotton regime than chiefs loyal to the colonial
state. Few chiefs gave unwavering allegiance to the Portuguese. Rather, they acted
out of self-interest to protect their position within their communities. If they did
not carry out Portuguese directives, they could be removed or replaced. Sometimes chiefs tried to protect their closest subjects, and on occasion they spoke out
against the most abusive features of the system. A few even covertly defied the
cotton regime. Most *régulos*, however, did not see a contradiction between their
public posture as guardians of their communities and their appropriation of their
subjects' labor. After all, chiefly power, no matter how contested, had its privileges—a notion that clearly antedated the colonial period.

Since the exploitation of peasant labor enabled chiefs to fulfill their twin obligations as labor supervisors and as model farmers, colonial officials not only
sanctioned but enforced this practice. As early as 1939, colonial officials noted
the number of "large cotton fields belonging to the indigenous authorities but
worked by their subjects."[9] An elder from the southern area of Chibuto bitterly
recalled that "every Sunday Chief Cossa sent his *madodas* [assistants] to bring all
the people to work his land. If they refused, many were sent to the administrators where they were beaten and imprisoned."[10] A *mestizo* trader in Morrumbala
described the behavior of the chiefs in that region of Zambézia: "Sometimes [the
chiefs] paid for the labor but most often did not. They simply threatened the villagers and ordered them to work the land. At the end of the harvest they earned

[8]   Gavin Kitching, in *Class and Economic Change in Kenya* (New Haven, 1980), has demonstrated how
rural stratification in colonial Kenya was often a product of differentiation in urban salaries.

[9]   AIA, JEAC, "Notas Recebidas," Palma Galião to Chefe da Del. da JEAC, 12 May 1939.

[10]   Interview with Benjamin Mavunja, Chibuto, 12 February 1979.

eight or nine *contos* [U.S. $240–$270].[11] A peasant from the north offered a slightly different version:

> The chiefs never worked in the cotton fields. Instead they requested assistance from the local administrator who sent *sipais* to collect people to work on [the chiefs'] land. They cleared, seeded, and weeded it. This way the chiefs could collect twenty or thirty sacks of cotton. They earned much more than anyone else.[12]

Cotton producers from every region of the colony related similar accounts of being forced to work without pay on the chief's lands. What varied in these accounts was the form and the amount of peasant labor extracted. Some had to work every Sunday—their only free time during the cotton season.[13] Others labored for several days before they were permitted to return home.[14] Many were apprehended at critical junctures in the agricultural cycle, precisely when their own fields required the most care. The size of the chief's holdings, the number of his immediate family members who worked in the cotton fields, and the pool of potential laborers living within his domain determined the demands he placed on the local population.

Many chiefs augmented their work force with penal laborers. As representatives of the Portuguese regime and as guardians of traditional law, *régulos* litigated an array of cases ranging from petty theft and drunkenness to tax fraud and adultery. Those convicted, often the most destitute and powerless, regularly ended up working the chief's land. So did those who could not pay their taxes. Manuel Sitói explained:

> Here in Guijá, Régulo Mbike had a large field. Throughout the season our wives went periodically to plant, weed, and collect cotton. Those of us who were unable to pay our taxes had to spend the entire season working his land as well. At the end of the year we did not receive anything.[15]

Pruan Hassan and his compatriots in the northern circumscription of Montepeuz recounted a similar story.[16]

Impoverished widows and wives of migrant laborers who had not received their husbands' remittances were particularly vulnerable. They had little recourse when the chief demanded their services. Saivina Manhiça, from Mocuba in Zambézia, recalled: "Women, particularly elderly women, worked the chiefs' fields. . . . We were grabbed early in the morning by the *sipais* while we were working in our fields and ordered to go."[17] The son of Chief Niquaria, a prosperous northern

---

[11]   Interview with Manuel Pinto, Quelimane, 19 July 1991.

[12]   Interview with Amasse Nuitha, CV Nawana, Montepuez, 20 July 1979.

[13]   Interviews with Marcelina Joaquim, Juliana Lias, and Hirondiena Tonia, Mueda, 25 April 1979; Benjamin Mavunja; Romeu Mataquenha, Tirani Ntuka, and Nussa Vaquina, Montepuez, 19 July 1979; Rafael Naxtaro et al., Alto Molócuè, 16–17 July 1976 (Head Collection).

[14]   Interviews with Makwati Simba et al., Chibuto, 13 February 1979; Samora Machel et al., 27 February 1979; Monica Shapina and Beatriz Anestina, Lichinga, 15 August 1980; group interview, CV Magul, Bilene, 20 February 1979.

[15]   Interview with Manuel Sitói et al., Guijá, 16 February 1979.

[16]   Interview with Pruan Hassan et al., 20 July 1979.

[17]   Interview with Saivina Manhiça, Nicoadala/Namacurra, 17 July 1991.

cotton producer, described how his father profited from this exploitative relationship: "[He] had eight hectares of cotton worked entirely by convicted criminals
and widows who were unable to pay their taxes. In return for their labor they
received some porridge at noon and cooked manioc in the evening."[18] Poorer women
in southern Mozambique were the most vulnerable, both because of the higher tax
structure and the failure of many miners to send home sufficient wage remittances.

Sometimes if chiefs required additional workers, they tapped into the pool of
the young and the elderly, who were not even registered in the cotton scheme. In
1953 Régulo Guvera of Bilene had more than five hundred peasants working in his
fields during peak labor periods. Most were young boys, none of whom were paid;
Guvera's neighbor Chief Uabada employed eighty young peasants under similar
conditions.[19] During times of hunger many régulos expanded this work force by
offering food to prospective laborers.[20]

From this broad set of peasant narratives emerges a picture of a one-sided
relationship far removed from any notions of reciprocity. The relationship between
chiefs and their subjects, which was remarkably constant over time and space, shared
four common characteristics. First, few peasants managed to remain outside the
grasp of the indigenous authorities. Second, the chiefs' fields were notably larger
than those of their subjects'. Third, peasants were expected to give these royal fields
the highest priority, particularly when time-sensitive tasks needed to be accom-
plished. And finally, no matter how much time peasants spent on their chief's land,
they were still required to maintain their own plots at an acceptable level. That
peasants accused of shirking their own cotton responsibilities were often forced to
work an extra stint in the chief's fields was one of the great ironies of the cotton
regime. "Even if we missed only a day," an elderly woman remembered angrily,
"we were taken to the chief's kraal where we had to work for a month."[21] These
abuses generated a great deal of hostility toward the régulos and were a source of
deep divisions within many communities (see Chapter 10).

Access to conscripted labor was just one of the benefits offered to the chiefs to
secure their collaboration. Favored chiefs were the principal recipients of state aid.
Extension officers provided chiefs with high-quality seeds and used their plots to
demonstrate principles of scientific farming. Régulos also received imported hoes,
shovels, and other basic implements, which they sometimes redistributed to subordinate headmen as part of an informal system of patronage.[22]

Initially much of this technical assistance had little more than symbolic value,
a situation that changed with the establishment of the concentrações. For the first
time the state provided plows, oxen, seeders, graders, and even some tractors.[23]

---

[18]   Interview with Eugénio Niquaria, Montepuez, 24 July 1979.

[19]   AHM, SR, Cx. 20, "Relatórios . . . Magude, 1953," António Policarpo de Sousa Santos, Insp. Conc. de
Gaza.

[20]   Interview with Benjamin Mavunja; Daima Magaga Mbela, Kndaba Nchamada Otinga, and Mangane
Nkula Nquenia, Macomia, 30 July 1979.

[21]   Group interview, CV Luís Carlos Prestes, Gaza, 2 February 1979.

[22]   Notícias, 15 December 1941; interview with Gabriel Mucave, Guijá, 20 February 1979.

[23]   AIA, JEAC, "Rel. Técnico," Fonseca George, Chefe de Secção de Fomento, Lourenço Marques, 10 April
1947; AIA, JEAC, "Reajustamento das Zonas Algodoeiras de Moçambique," 1953; Faria Lobo, Nampula,
26 May 1987.

Since the implementation of these planned rural communities depended on the support of the *régulos*, it is hardly surprising that chiefs received the best lands and greatest access to whatever technical support and machinery were available. One senior agronomist argued that such a strategy was necessary "so that other peasants can see with their own eyes the wonderful results achieved by these new methods."[24]

Some loyalist chiefs received grants from the Cotton Fund, whose coffers were filled primarily through a tax levied on peasant production.[25] While most of the money went to expand rural health services, the state also purchased water pumps, storage bins, and expensive agricultural equipment that the *régulos* controlled.[26] Sometimes the chiefs were the direct beneficiaries of Cotton Board largess. In the northern circumscription of Mecúfi, for example, the state paid for the construction of houses—complete with wind-driven mills—for Chiefs Mexilo and Megama. Each house cost the equivalent of more than U.S. $1,000[27]—an amount roughly equivalent to the annual cotton income of fifty producers living in their domain.

The chiefs also profited from preferential treatment at cotton markets. State and company officials found a number of ways to circumvent official price ceilings when they were buying cotton from *régulos*. Sometimes they automatically designated the chiefs' cotton as premium class. In other instances, chiefs received the higher, unofficial rate normally reserved for the small number of European growers who planted cotton, among other cash crops, on their estates.[28]

It was clear to everyone present that state and company officials were acting in collusion with the chiefs. Former growers from Namapa stated frankly that they were aware of the situation but could do nothing about it: "Our chiefs had the largest fields and the price they received was not the same price as ours. Even when their cotton was weighed at the same location, at the same market, at the same hour as ours, they, like the Portuguese, received much more."[29] These subsidies frequently came at the expense of the chiefs' subjects. Romeu Mataquenha recalled:

> When we arrived at the market the chief would meet with the overseers to discuss how much cotton we brought. When the Europeans placed our cotton on the scale it always registered less than fifty kilograms [the normal weight of a sack filled with cotton]. We subsequently learned that the chief received payment for the kilogram or two that they had discounted from each of us.[30]

Sometimes officials made no effort to hide this chicanery; it was just the way things were done. "When we received payment for our cotton," recalled one producer,

---

24 AIA, JEAC, "Rel. Técnico," Fonseca George; confirmed in interview with Faria Lobo, 26 May 1987.

25 AIA, JEAC, "Diversos, Mapas, Estatísticas e Elementos Informativos, Fundo do Algodão Receitas," n.d.

26 Ibid.; AIA, JEAC, AT, 929/3/0, Fundo do Algodão, 1952, Comissão Admin. do Fundo do Algodão, Acta no. 6, 29 October 1952; AIA, JEAC, 660, 55 (1952), n.d.

27 AHM, SR, Cx. 92, "Relatório . . . de Cabo Delgado," Amadeu Pacheco de Amorim, 13 February 1962.

28 The story of European production of cotton generally falls outside the scope of this study, but the production of settler estates was inconsequential.

29 Interview with Nanjaia Taibo et al., Namapa, 2 May 1979.

30 Interview with Romeu Mataquenha et al.

"we were told by the European functionary that we had to give our chief ten *escudos* for each sack of cotton we brought."[31] Since most chiefs in the cotton zones had a minimum of five hundred growers living within their domain, and a few had several times more, such ploys could yield substantial dividends.[32]

The chiefs benefited in many ways from promoting cotton in their communities. Not only did they receive a portion of what their subjects earned, but they were also given production bonuses. In 1941 a senior economic officer on the Cotton Board "proposed that prizes be awarded to those authorities who did a particularly good job promoting cotton."[33] The Board adopted this recommendation and allocated money to build houses for "chiefs who each year not only demonstrate the greatest interest in the crop but also whose subordinates voluntarily cultivate the largest areas and produce the highest percentage of premium cotton."[34] A number of companies followed suit. Some offered bicycles, radios, and clothing as well as agricultural implements. Others companies made payments in cash.[35] Many chiefs redistributed some of this largess to their principal headmen, who helped them enforce the cotton regime.[36]

These practices continued throughout the life of the cotton regime. As late as 1960 SAGAL "distributed khaki shirts and pants to the chiefs and village headmen . . . who distinguished themselves in the cultivation of cotton."[37] However, by this time loyalists had come to expect annual bonuses, and when they did not receive them, they showed their displeasure. Some bold individuals refused to continue supervising production.[38] Others surreptitiously worked for labor recruiters who scoured the countryside in search of workers for the plantations and European farms and even for the cocoa estates of São Tomé.[39]

In general, chiefs in the south seem to have prospered more than their counterparts to the north. Access to ox-drawn plows and higher prices for cotton, plus a bigger rake-off of taxes and "gifts" from returning miners, provided greater possibilities of capital accumulation. By contrast, in the poorer and less populated areas to the north, bonuses and taxes paid to chiefs were smaller; for example, the payments chiefs received from taxes averaged only 1,200 *escudos* per year in the

[31] Interview with Benjamin Mavunja. A similar arrangement was reported in a group interview with former growers at CV Samora Machel (Chibuto, 15 September 1979).

[32] AHM, SR, Cx.77, ISANI, "Relatório . . . de Nampula," Hortêncio Estevão de Sousa, Insp. Admin., 1948.

[33] AIA, JEAC, "Informação no. 83/141," João da Silva Contreira to Chefe da Del., 26 March 1941.

[34] AIA, JEAC, "Dossiers Diversos 1939–1941," J. Furstena, Chefe da Del., 12 September 1941.

[35] See, for example, AHM, SR, Cx. 20, "Relatório. . . Magude 1953," António Policarpo de Sousa Santos, Insp., Conc. de Gaza.

[36] *Notícias*, 15 December 1941.

[37] AHM, SR, Cx. 91, ISANI, "Relatório . . . Macomia," Amadeu Pacheco de Amorim, 19 May 1961.

[38] AIA, JEAC, "Conf. 1957–1959," A. Costa Mesquite, 22 February 1958; AHM, SR, Cx. 20, "Insp. ao Conc. de Gaza e Circ. do Bilene, Manhiça e Magude, 1953," António Policarpo de Sousa Santos, Insp., Conc. de Gaza.

[39] This practice antedated the cotton regime. Moreover, many chiefs were already recruiting labor, while simultaneously supervising the cotton regime. AHM, SR, ISANI, "Relatório . . . Nampula," Hortêncio Estevão, Insp., 1948; AHM, CE, SEAV, 1, 10, "Rel. do Gov. do Dist. do Niassa Ref. ao Ano de 1956," Augusto Vaz Spencer, Gov. do Dist.; AHM, SR, Cx. 95, ISANI, "Corresp . . . Niassa, 1ª parte, 1943," Carlos Henriques Jones da Silveira, 1943.

1940s, a mere fraction of what chiefs in the southern provinces obtained.[40] Many chiefs in Cabo Delgado, Nampula, and Zambézia complained they could not even afford to purchase a proper hat and uniform, important symbols of power in the new colonial order. A Native Affairs inspector concurred and urged "that they be given coats, hats, boots and clothing to enhance their status."[41]

But disparities among chiefs were far less significant than the gap between chiefs and their peasant subjects. By the 1950s this gap was increasingly reflected in lifestyle and in access to the material and cultural world of Portuguese colonizers. A Native Affairs officer in 1951 lauded Chief Megama of Mecúfi "for the way he learned to live like any European, purchasing a truck, teaching his children to speak Portuguese, . . . carrying himself with the appropriate comportment and dressing meticulously."[42] Further south, the governor of Gaza marveled that "the really important chiefs lived in a manner which was quite civilized. They owned good homes, art and automobiles."[43] In Inhambane, prosperous chiefs had built homes with running water, electricity, and indoor plumbing.[44] Others wore Portuguese uniforms, complete with insignias and medals, lived in European-style homes, flew the Portuguese flag, learned Portuguese, sent their children to missionary schools, and acquired as many other trappings of European culture as they could. Typical of the shift in worldview was the attitude of one *régulo* in Mueda who complained bitterly that the missionary schools "teach our children the doctrine in Makua . . . while [we] wanted them to read and write Portuguese and to learn bookkeeping."[45] The son of Chief Niquaria of Montepuez boasted that "we lived in a stone house and owned two motorcycles, while the rest of the population lived in huts and only had bicycles."[46] Chiefs, of course, were not the only Africans interested in acquiring such symbols of modernity; they just had more opportunities to do so.

A few chiefs also adopted Portuguese strategies of accumulation by investing in areas of the economy previously closed to Africans. Some took advantage of less restrictive commercial laws enacted in the 1950s to open up shops in the rural areas. In 1951 Régulo Megama, who had been honored by the state for his loyalty and "civilized" demeanor, was among the first Africans allowed to open up a small shop in northern Mozambique.[47] Although Portuguese and Asian merchants concerned about local competition viewed such entrepreneurial ini-

---

[40] AHM, SR, Cx. 96, ISANI, "Relatório . . . Niassa," Part 2, Capitão Henriques Jones da Silveira, Insp. Admin., 1944.

[41] AHM, SR, Cx. 62, ISANI, "Informação . . . Mulevala," Júlio Augusto Pires, Insp. Admin., 1948.

[42] AHM, SR, Cx. 89, ISANI, "Relatório . . . Mecúfi," António Policarpo de Sousa, Insp. Admin., 1951.

[43] AHM, CE, Cx. SEAV, 9, 116 (a,b), Gov. do Dist. de Gaza, "Rel. do Gov. 1955–1960," Gov. Óscar Freira de Vasconcellos Ruas, 1960.

[44] Prov. de Moçambique, *Relatório da Administração da Circ. de Zavala—Sobre as Cooperativas da Sua Area* (Lourenço Marques, 1958), 15–18.

[45] AHM, Cx. 92, "Relatório . . . dos Macondes, 1951–1961," Amadeu Pacheco de Amorim, 27 February 1962.

[46] Interview with Eugénio Niquaria.

[47] AHM, SR, Cx. 89, ISANI, "Relatório . . . Mecúfi," António Policarpo de Sousa, Insp. Admin., 1951. Chief Megama covertly supported FRELIMO during the liberation struggle. Like a number of other chiefs and African merchants, he straddled in order to maximize his opportunities (personal communication, Arlindo Chilundo, 21 April 1994).

tiatives with alarm, they were unable to block them. By the end of the decade loyalist chiefs were receiving commercial licenses with some frequency. In the Makonde highlands, four chiefs long engaged in clandestine sales of soap, cigarettes, and cooking oil felt confident enough of the outcome to request formal trading licenses.[48]

Other chiefs invested hundreds of dollars in African cooperatives, which the state placed under their control.[49] Cooperatives, especially in the south, catered to "modern farmers" who employed seasonal laborers. To secure capital and to prevent poorer, less "civilized" peasants from becoming members, the founders often maintained rigorous entrance requirements, including stiff membership fees. In Zavala, for example, applicants had to be formally nominated by two members and had to demonstrate prior success in commercial agriculture. The combined assets of the six Zavala cooperatives included seventeen Ferguson tractors with attached plows, weeders, and seeders; 1,030 ox-drawn plows; and substantial capital reserves kept in the bank.[50] The chiefs, who were among the most affluent members, lived in large houses with electricity, plumbing, running water, and the other amenities of a European home.

A number of well-placed village headmen and rapacious *sipais* used their monopoly of power in much the same way the chiefs did. They forced peasants to labor in their cotton fields and extorted payments from the local population. They also had access to the best land and available technology. Many received gifts and bonuses from the concessionaires and sold their crops at favorable market prices.[51] The headmen often benefited from the largess of the chiefs; in this way they also accumulated capital, although on a smaller scale. In the southern region of Bilene at least four senior village headmen owned ten cattle or more, two plows, and multiple fields.[52] To the north, in Mecúfi, one particularly prosperous headman saved enough to open a shop.[53]

African overseers in the pay of the concessionary companies also fared well. Although they earned appreciably less than their European counterparts, indigenous *capatazes* thrived under the cotton regime. Consider Paulo Roque, an overseer working in Nampula province. Paulo was hired by the Mozambique Company in the early 1950s to supervise laborers working in the ginning mill. His initial salary was 150 *escudos* per month, almost twice the wage of a typical laborer under his command. During the next four years Roque's salary doubled. Company officials were so pleased with his efforts that they promoted him to field overseer in 1955. His salary jumped to 500 *escudos* per month. "In the first year," he recalled, "I had to travel by *machilla*, but then the Company gave me a bicycle and afterwards

[48] AHM, SR, Cx. 92, ISANI, "Relatório . . . dos Macondes," Amadeu Pacheco de Amorim, 27 February 1962.

[49] For a history of these cooperatives, see Adam, "Cooperativação Agrícola."

[50] Prov. de Moç., *Relatório da Administração*, 15–18.

[51] See, for example, AIA, JEAC, "Registo de Chefe dos Serviços Técnicos Distritais," Armando Antunes de Almeida, September 1957; AHM, SR, Cx. 91, ISANI, "Relatório . . . Macomia," Amadeu Pacheco de Amorim, 19 May 1961.

[52] AHM, SR, Cx. 20, ISANI, "Relatório . . . Magude," António Policarpo de Sousa Santos, Insp. do Conc. de Gaza.

[53] AHM, SR, Cx. 89, ISANI, "Relatório . . . Mecúfi," António Policarpo de Sousa, Insp. Admin., 1951.

a motorcycle."[54] By 1960 Roque was earning 1,000 *escudos* per month (approximately U.S. $40). In that year the average grower in Nampula earned less than 450 *escudos* (about U.S. $15) for an entire season of work.[55] Roque's situation was not unique. African overseers across the colony received between 800 and 1,000 *escudos* monthly, and their assistants about half that amount.[56]

Machambeiros and Other Entrepreneurs: The Prosperous Few

Unlike the loyalist chiefs, African commercial farmers (*machambeiros*) did not derive their privileged position from political power and ties direct to the colonial regime, although they often benefited from the labor of poorer members of their community. The term *machambeiros*, "owners of large fields," was not a legal category, but an informal, loosely defined social category of prosperous farmers primarily living in southern Mozambique's fertile Limpopo Valley. As a result, it is hard to get a sense of their exact numbers and how fluid membership in this category was. Indeed, elders often distinguish between the small number of "great" and the more numerous "lesser" *machambeiros*. Almost all grew cotton as well as a variety of other cash crops. Most had accumulated capital by working in relatively high paying jobs in the South African mines, then reinvested a portion of their income in the rural economy. Others received agricultural training and support at Protestant missionary stations.[57] Miriam Paulo of Manjacaze explained that

> the great *machambeiros* had large fields with many cattle and many people. They began to appear in the 1930s. . . . I remember Calidji of Panga, Nguilazi, and the famous *machambeiro* Leão. . . . They initially earned their money by working in the South African mines. Some also inherited wealth from their fathers who had worked in the mines as well. Afterwards they began to prosper from farming.[58]

Merely working in the mines and having access to alluvial lands, however, was no guarantee of achieving the comfortable lifestyle enjoyed by the *machambeiros*. While the average Mozambican miner earned a salary several times higher than what he could earn from agriculture back home, it was still a paltry sum, with many expenses to pay.[59] Miners in South Africa received about 240 *escudos* per month in 1942, for example, totaling 3,600 *escudos* for a typical eighteen-month stint.[60] Even

---

[54] AHM, SR, Cx. 20, ISANI, "Relatório . . . Magude, 1953," António Policarpo de Sousa Santos, Insp. Conc. de Gaza.

[55] Bravo, *Cultura Algodoeira*, 164.

[56] AIA, JEAC, "Corr. Expedidas," Henrique Nobre Guerreiro, to Dir. dos Serviços Técnicos da JEAC, 18 March 1961.

[57] Interview with Ira Gillet, Milwaukee, Oregon, 18 August 1981. Mr. Gillet was a missionary at Cambine station in Inhambane from 1915 to 1959.

[58] Interview with Miriam Paulo, Maputo, 16 May 1987.

[59] Roesch estimates that in 1936 miners earned six times as much as the average household from agriculture ("Socialism and Rural Development," 59).

[60] Interview with Gonçalo Mazungane Chilundo, Maputo, 8–9 August 1991; AHM, SR, Cx. 21, ISANI, "Relatório . . . Muchopes," Francisco de Melo e Costa, Insp. Admin., 30 January 1942.

before miners received their first wages, however, they owed the mining company approximately 480 *escudos* for their passports, identification cards, mine passes, transportation, and clothing. This sum was deducted from their salaries. The trip home was also costly. Portuguese officials estimated it at well over 100 *escudos* for transport, food, and lodging. Returning miners were also expected to offer their chiefs a small "gift," normally 80 *escudos* per tour of duty, and pay a municipal and transportation tax.[61] Because of these expenses, Gonçalo Chilundo, from Zavala, stressed that "a number of men decided it was not worth all the hardships to earn so little and chose to remain at home."[62] This was not the prevailing view, however.

Basic mining salaries had more than doubled by 1955, but even with bonuses they were still less than 560 *escudos* per month. Portuguese officials noted that many miners returned home with little or no disposable income; between 1951 and 1954 the average Mozambican miner brought home less than 1,500 *escudos* (U.S. $52).[63] Adelina Penicela, the wife of a miner, contended that the reality was often worse: "Most men who came back had used their savings on some clothing and utensils. If they brought 300 or 400 *escudos* with them that was a lot."[64]

Mozambicans employed as senior *ndunas*, or "boss boys," in the mines earned as much as four times the usual salary in the early 1940s.[65] While this wage gap narrowed over the next two decades, *ndunas* continued to be paid appreciably more than the workers they supervised. Other Mozambicans in skilled mining positions such as electricians, drivers, and nurses fared even better; some were able to send home the equivalent of U.S. $100 or more and brought home with them a still larger sum.[66] The vast majority of *machambeiros* came from these two groups of relatively privileged miners.

While most migrants used their meager savings to help their families, *machambeiros* invested a portion of their earnings in cattle, plows, carts, and imported hoes to expand the productive capacity of their households. This process of accumulation was long and difficult. In the 1950s it cost between 1,000 and 1,500 *escudos* to buy a single ox, and about 500 *escudos* to buy a plow.[67] One study suggests that it often took these peasant-migrants between ten and fifteen years before their economic position was sufficiently secure for them to sever their ties to the mines. Nevertheless, their life histories stand in sharp contrast to poorly paid migrant laborers who spent up to 70 percent of their active working lives on the mines in a desperate effort to make ends meet.[68]

---

[61]   AHM, SR, Cx. 21, ISANI, "Relatório . . . Muchopes," Francisco de Melo e Castro, Insp. Admin., 1941.

[62]   Interview with Gonçalo Mazngane Chilundo.

[63]   AHM, Cx. 21, "Rel. da Insp. Ord. A Intend. de Gaza," António Policarpo de Sousa Santos, 1955; AHM, SR, Cx. 20, "Rel. da Insp. Ord. à Intend. de Gaza," João Villas Boas Carbeiro de Moura, Insp. Admin., 1953. See A. Rita–Ferreira, *O Movimento Migratório de Trabalhadores entre Moçambique e a África do Sul* (Lisbon, 1963), 79–80.

[64]   Interview with Adelina Penicela, Maputo, 3 July 1986.

[65]   AHM, Cx. 21, ISANI, "Relatório . . . Muchopes," Francisco de Melo e Costa, Insp. Admin., 30 January 1942.

[66]   First, *Black Gold*, 86–95.

[67]   Interviews with Gonçalo Mazungane Chilundo; Bishop João Somane Machado, Maputo, 10 May 1987; Benjamin Mavunja.

[68]   First, *Black Gold*, 138.

The wages brought home by the *machambeiros* enabled many of them to expand the size of their households by marrying a second or a third wife and by having more children. Additional family labor eased the production bottleneck and allowed them to expand their fields. Since bridewealth payments rose from between 1,500 and 2,000 *escudos* in the early 1950s to approximately 5,000 *escudos* by the end of the decade, multiple marriages were not an option available to most returning miners.[69]

Most *machambeiros* expanded their work force beyond their families. They recruited part-time agricultural laborers who sold their labor power for either a small wage or for food. Sixty *escudos* (approximately U.S. $2) for a month's labor was considered high in the early 1950s.[70] Several elders in Magude described how they "walked great distances to find a *machambeiro* who would hire us just in exchange for food."[71] *Machambeiros* also drew upon a pool of day laborers, primarily women and children, during peak work periods. In Inhambane this practice was known as *chigwadza*. Bishop Machado described how *machambeiros*

> gave us one escudo for each row of cotton that we weeded. A line was one meter wide and one hundred meters long. If there was not too much grass I could finish the task in less than a day. When I was done I received the *escudo*. I bought a pencil or a notebook with the money. At the time I was nine.[72]

The combination of substantial amounts of labor, ox-drawn plows, and river-fed lands, particularly in the Limpopo Valley, made *machambeiros* some of the most prosperous cotton producers in the colony. In good years they could earn several hundred dollars from the sale of lint, plus a substantial return from wheat, peanuts, and beans, which they generally sold to local *cantineiros* or to less fortunate members of their own community:

> The *machambeiros* produced a great deal of food and cereals; there were others in the region who were unable to produce anything. They had no alternative but to go to the *machambeiros'* home and purchase food from them. With this money the *machambeiros* bought more oxen and plows and arranged to have people come and work for them.[73]

In a world of poverty, these entrepreneurs clearly enjoyed a relatively privileged position. Some *machambeiros* accumulated additional capital by renting out their oxen and plows to poorer neighbors.[74] Celeste Cossa, who taught a number of other women the art of plowing, remembered how expensive it was to rent this equipment. "At that time [the 1950s] they paid twenty-five *escudos* for just one hour and fifty *escudos* for two hours."[75] More enterprising

[69]   Interview with Gonçalo Mazungane Chilundo; AHM, CE, Cx. SEAV, 9, 116 (a,b), Gov. do Dist. de Gaza, "Rel. do Gov. 1955–1960," Gov. Oscar Freire de Vasconcellos Ruas, 1960.

[70]   Interview with Miriam Paulo.

[71]   Group interview, CV Magude, Macia, 28 February 1979.

[72]   Interview with Bishop João Somane Machado.

[73]   Interview with Miriam Paulo.

[74]   Interviews with Minosse Sitói et al., Gaza, 2 February 1979; Valente Yota, Macia, 10 February 1979; Miriam Paulo; Bishop João Somane Machado.

[75]   Interview with Celeste Cossa, Amélia Novana, and Regina Mate, Maputo, 31 July 1991.

machambeiros rented out young boys as well to drive their plows. They charged a fixed fee based on the size of the plot. The rate, which had been one *escudo* per meter in the 1940s, rose over the next decade by 250 percent.[76] The lack of motorized vehicles to haul peasant cotton to the regional markets provided many *machambeiros* with the opportunity to rent out their ox-driven carts for additional fees.[77] Renting plows also provided an opportunity for a number of southerners like Maphoissane of Zavala, who did not initially labor in the mines. A relatively well-off miner arranged with Maphoissane to take care of his large herd of oxen and his plows while he worked in South Africa. In exchange Maphoissane was to clear and till the cotton fields and gardens that belonged to the miner's wife. Maphoissane then sold his services to other households who needed their fields plowed.[78]

A number of *machambeiros* also invested in agricultural cooperatives. These ventures, backed by government loans, combined modern technology with cheap African labor.[79] Members voluntarily cultivated cotton as well as other crops and were therefore escaped the abuses associated with the cotton regime. By 1958 there were approximately 1,800 Africans who belonged to agricultural cooperatives in southern Mozambique.[80] Other *machambeiros* diversified into trade and craft production in order to accumulate additional capital.

During this period the *machambeiros* became a self-defined and widely recognized social group who were acutely aware of their own success. Jossias Zungueni of Bilene described to me how he left mine work after a number of years in order to concentrate on agriculture. He used his savings from the mines to purchase a plow and grew cotton, maize, and beans. After several years, he had saved enough money from the sale of these commodities to purchase a cart and additional oxen and to expand his fields. For Jossias, "cotton was a good thing, even if the Portuguese did not pay us enough."[81]

Many *machambeiros* lived in comfortable homes with running water and electricity. They, even more than the chiefs, internalized the accumulation strategies of the Portuguese. A number entered the colonial cultural world as well. They converted to Christianity, sent their children to missionary schools, and internalized the Protestant work ethic. Some even formally became *civilisados*, or "civilized" Africans, a privileged legal and cultural category that, in 1954, was replaced by the less objectionable term *assimilados*. *Assimilados* were exempt from forced labor and African taxation, had freedom of movement, and theoretically had the right to participate fully in the life of colonial society.[82] "It was a way of seeking a less degrading life for our children"[83] and strategically equipping them for success in the colonial order. In Chibuto and Muchopes, two cen-

---

[76] Interview with Bishop João Somane Machado.

[77] Interview with Miriam Paulo.

[78] Interview with Gonçalo Mazungane Chilundo.

[79] Prov. de Moç., *Relatório da Administração da Circunscrição de Zavala—Sobre As Cooperativas da Sua Área* (Lourenço Marques, 1958).

[80] Rita–Ferreira, *O Movimento Migratório*, 170–73.

[81] Interview with Jossias Zungueni, Bilene, 19 February 1979.

[82] M. D. D. Newitt, *Portugal in Africa: The Last Hundred Years* (London, 1981).

[83] Interview with Raul Honwana, Maputo, 1 June 1987.

ters of *machambeiro* life in the Gaza district, sixty-four Africans had attained this privileged status by 1955.[84]

It is inaccurate, however, to treat the *machambeiros* simply as aspiring capitalist farmers co-opted by the colonial regime. While they were relatively privileged, their position remained fairly precarious. And when state policies challenged their hard-won privileges, many *machambeiros* vigorously defended them, pushing for reforms in the cotton markets and organizing the most effective boycotts. They also protested when the state attempted to settle Europeans on their historic lands and when missionaries tried to force their children to grow cotton (see Chapter 10).

For all the ambiguities of their social position, *machambeiros* held a special place in the popular culture of southern Mozambique. Most peasants admired their success in the face of adversity. Everyone knew the name of the most prominent *machambeiros* in their region. Just as Miriam Paulo spoke with pride about the great *machambeiros* of Manjacaze, so elders in Chibuto boasted about the number of plows and the size of the herds belonging to Zacarias Cossa and Zacarias Macamo.[85] Their compatriots in nearby Guijá remember vividly the market boycotts that *machambeiros* organized, and in Zavala and Morrumbene the entrepreneurial skills of the *machambeiros* are legendary.[86]

By the end of the cotton regime there were probably only a few thousand *machambeiro* families in southern Mozambique.[87] Their numbers and economic clout might have continued to expand had it not been for the influx of Portuguese farmers in the 1950s into the Limpopo Valley. The idea of the Colonato de Limpopo (Limpopo Settlement Scheme) dated back to the 1920s and was revived in the 1950s as part of Lisbon's broader strategy of relocating 75,000 Portuguese families to Africa.[88] At the outset, approximately 2,000 African households were forced off their historic land,[89] including a number of *machambeiros* and their families. Many did not receive the promised compensation, nor were they allowed to resettle in other irrigated areas or to use pastures fenced off for European cattle.[90] The Colonato scheme also blocked their access to badly needed water. Peasants, rich and poor alike, for whom water was the key to survival, found this situation intolerable: "The Africans are very angry. They were not only left without sufficient terrain to cultivate their normal crops, but they can no longer get to the Limpopo River."[91] A

---

[84] J. Montalvão Marques, *Esboço Para Uma Monografia Agrícola do Posto–Sede dos Muchopes e dos Alguns Regulados do Chibuto* (Lisbon, 1958), 56.

[85] Interview with Benjamin Mavunja.

[86] Interviews with Simone Sitói, Guijá, 16 February 1979; Bishop João Somane Machado; Gonçalo Mazungane Chilundo; Simão Mangueze Mucambe, Maputo, 12 July 1991.

[87] Because *machambeiro* was a social but not a legal category, their numbers do not appear in any government statistics. In 1970, after an intense colonial campaign, there were 6,996 farmers who cultivated between ten and twenty hectares. This represented less than 0.4 percent of the total number of growers. Direcção Geral de Comércio Externo, *Moçambique Economic Survey* (Lourenço Marques, 1975), 25.

[88] For an excellent discussion of the *colonato* program, see Bender, *Angola Under the Portuguese.*

[89] Kenneth Hermele, *Land Struggles and Social Differentiation in Southern Mozambique: A Case Study of Chokwe, Limpopo, 1950–1987* (Uppsala, 1988), 38.

[90] Ibid., 39–41.

[91] AHM, SR, Cx. 26, ISANI, "Relatório . . . Guijá," 12 March 1957, António Policarpo de Sousa Santos, Insp. Admin..

similar process of land alienation took place in Inhambane, though on a somewhat smaller scale. Bishop Machado described it as follows:

> Portuguese settlers came and took the best lands close to the river in Morrumbene near places like Pagola and Matengela. They organized rice and sugar plantations and those who had the land were ordered to work for them for twenty-five *escudos* a month. If anyone refused they were forced off the land. In addition they had to grow cotton.[92]

Few *machambeiros* would have been able to sever their ties to the mines without the resourcefulness and hard work of their wives. After all it was the "women left behind" who challenged the prevailing cattle taboos,[93] and it was those same women who learned to plow, to clear the fields, to recruit laborers, to negotiate with unscrupulous merchants, and to manage the family budget. The wives of *machambeiros* became commercial farmers in their own right.

A number of poorer women in the south, receiving little financial support from their absent husbands, found a measure of prosperity by adopting new farming methods. Women living adjacent to the Cambine mission station in Inhambane abandoned the practice of shifting agriculture and adopted a system of fixed cultivation. By adding local fertilizers (humus), aerating the soils, and carefully rotating their crops, they were able to prosper. Cotton and food production jumped dramatically. In the 1951–52 cotton campaign the average female grower in Inhambane earned nearly 3,500 *escudos* (approximately U.S. $120) from cotton, plus a smaller amount from their surplus food crops.[94] At about the same time, a number of women in Gaza began to experiment with wheat production in response to new market demands precipitated by the influx of European immigrants. By adding wheat to their mix of crops, women could triple their incomes. In 1951 the average producer earned more than 1,100 *escudos* (approximately U.S. $40) from wheat as compared to 435 *escudos* (U.S. $15) from cotton and slightly less from rice.[95] By 1954 average income derived from the sale of wheat had jumped to 2,600 *escudos* (almost U.S. $90). Industrious women with access to fertile lands, plows, and sufficient labor earned even more. A Native Affairs inspector reported that it was not uncommon "to encounter women who earned five or six *contos* from farming."[96] Between 1951 and 1954 the number of peasants, primarily female, growing wheat jumped from 95 to 1,160.[97]

Outside the highly monetized world of southern Mozambique, there were considerably fewer opportunities for men or women to profit from the cotton-based economy. To be sure, there were small pockets of prosperity, such as in the Chemba–Gorongoza–Dombe region of Manica. There, a combination of favorable ecological conditions and a far-sighted CNA concessionary company policy of encouraging

---

[92]   Interview with Bishop João Somane Machado.

[93]   For an interesting comparison see Schmidt, *Peasants, Traders, and Wives.*

[94]   Fuller, "An Ethnohistoric Study," 151–55.

[95]   AHM, SR, Cx. 20, "Rel. da Insp. Ord. à Intend. De Gaza," João Villas Boas Carbeiro de Moura, Insp. Admin., 1953.

[96]   Ibid.

[97]   AHM, SR, Cx. 20, ISANI, "Relatório . . . Magude," António Policarpo de Sousa Santos, 19 November 1954.

peasants to produce cash crops as well as cotton stimulated local production. By 1945 several cotton growers were reported to have earned nearly 3,000 *escudos* (over U.S. $120) from cotton, and an equal sum from the sale of maize. They lived "in well constructed homes made from local material, with beautiful verandas, splendid roofs and mosquito nets covering their windows," prompting a Portuguese observer to claim that "those peasants who had a large family and enough children preferred cotton to all other activities."[98] Jaime, a peasant from Chemba, worked his fields with his wives and many of their twenty-four children. In 1943 Jaime's family sold 250 sacks of cotton and 1,070 bags of corn, earning over 25,000 *escudos* (approximately U.S. $1,000).[99] Abdul Satar Mohammed Hussene, a *mestizo* merchant who settled in the well-watered Morrumbala circumscription of Zambézia in the late 1940s, recalled that there were also a small number of fairly prosperous cotton growers with whom he traded.[100]

One cotton advocate estimated that 1 percent of all northern growers earned 2,900 *escudos* (approximately U.S. $100) per year, considered "a small fortune for the Africans."[101] His calculations were probably overly optimistic, for nowhere in the rest of the colony did a group of small capitalist farmers emerge equivalent to the southern Mozambican *machambeiros*. A senior Cotton Board official's observation that Gaza "was the only province where one frequently meets the *machambeiros*, Africans who own hundreds of head of cattle and cultivate a few dozen hectares of land," was as true in 1960 as it had been twenty years earlier.[102]

However, a small number of northerners either benefited from the cotton regime or manipulated it to their advantage, including a handful of highly paid cotton factory workers and truckers who transported the ginned cotton. Manuel Baptista, one of the first Africans to qualify as a trucker, earned almost $15 a month in the early 1940s, more than most growers received in a year.[103]

A few African merchants, teachers, and prosperous migrant laborers in the north diversified into cotton production and other agricultural activities.[104] They hired a combination of local labor and seasonal workers to cultivate their lands. In the Makonde region of the north, returning migrants from the sisal plantations in Tanganyika used their savings to purchase fertile lands, which were becoming increasingly scarce.[105] In an area with no tradition of private property, the commodification of land became an important marker of rural differentiation. Others profited by smuggling cotton into neighboring colonies where prices were considerably higher.[106]

---

[98]   AHM, SR, Cx. 39, ISANI, "Relatório . . . Manica e Sofala, 1946," João Mesquita, 5 May 1947.

[99]   AHM, SR, Cx. 39, ISANI, "Relatório . . . Sofala," Abel de Souza Moutinho, Insp. Admin., 12 May 1944.

[100]   Interview with Abdul Satar Mohammed Hussene, Quelimane, 19 July 1991.

[101]   AIA, JEAC, "Prop. de Moç.," A. Fegueiras de Sousa, 24 May 1954.

[102]   AIA, JEAC, "Rel. An. 1939–1941: Actividades de Sub–Del. do Sul do Save em 1940," João Contreiras, n.d.

[103]   Interview with Manuel Baptista, Nampula, 9 July 1991.

[104]   Interview with João Cornélio Mandande, Mueda, 30 July 1979; Dias, *Os Macondes*, 114.

[105]   Dias, *Os Macondes*, 112–14.

[106]   Interviews with Saide Julião, Montepuez, 23 July 1979; Ramissa Promose, Montepuez, 23 July 1979; Faquir Abadre, Montepuez, 23 July 1979; AHM, SR, Cx. 63, ISANI, "Relatório . . . Namacurra," Júlio Augusto Pires, 27 October 1949.

Few traders were as successful as Abdul Satar Mohammed Hussene. A *mestizo* of Afro-Indian descent, Hussene's first venture was fairly modest: "I brought dried fish in Mutarara and sold it inland at Ile," he recalled, "and gave the profits to my wife to purchase more fish."[107] He also traversed the countryside in search of peanuts, corn, and beans, which he resold in the inland towns at handsome profits. With the help of senior government officials Hussene secured a bank loan in 1942 and opened up a shop at Derre. Business boomed. Within a few years he was able to purchase a truck, build a second shop, and organize a large cotton plantation complete with a tractor. He recruited laborers without much difficulty and within a few years production began to flourish; by the early 1960s he was producing 160 tons of cotton.[108]

Lázaro Kavandame's path to becoming a cotton entrepreneur was quite different. Like many peasants from the Makonde highlands, Lázaro had migrated to Tanganyika, where he worked as a labor recruiter for sisal planters in the Morogoro and Linde regions. He returned home in middle of the 1950s and with the capital he had accumulated opened up a small shop as well as a banana field and cotton field. Shortly thereafter, Kavandame advocated the formation of an African cotton-marketing cooperative, similar to the prosperous peasant-based associations he had seen in Tanganyika. He worked closely with a small number of Makonde teachers, catechists, and traders whose privileged economic positions had shielded them from the abuses of the cotton regime. The Protestant missionaries at Imbubu supported the idea and aided Kavandame, who was elected president of the Mozambique African Voluntary Cotton Society (see Chapter 9).

From the outset the cooperative prospered. Kavandame hired unemployed laborers to plant his crop. In 1958 they produced 150 sacks of cotton, which yielded approximately $700.[109] Most members of the cooperative, drawing only on household labor, produced less than ten sacks, suggesting that Kavandame had employed a fairly sizeable work force.[110] With his profits Kavandame acquired additional land beyond the four hectares allocated to each member of the cotton cooperative, expanded his shop at Mtchi, and opened a second store at Imbo. In 1959 the colonial officials sent Kavandame to a school at Mariri, ostensibly so that he could master Portuguese and communicate more effectively with colonial officials. However, a number of cooperative members insisted that this was simply a ploy to keep Kavandame under surveillance and to curtail his nationalist activities. All agree there were few Africans in the 1950s as powerful or as prosperous as Lázaro Kavandame.[111]

The World of the *Agricultores* Revisited

Although some *machambeiros* originally came from the ranks of the *agricultores* and retained this legal status, the world of the *agricultores* was fundamentally different

---

[107] Interview with Abdul Satar Mohammed Hussene.

[108] Ibid.

[109] Ibid.; interview with Tanga Karinga de Tangadica et al., CV Imbo, Mueda, 31 July 1979.

[110] Ibid.; interview with Cocote Zimu et al., Montepuez, 23 July 1979.

[111] Ibid.; interviews with João Cornélio Mandande, Mueda, 1 August 1979; Jonas Nakutepa et al., Mueda, 31 July 1979; Tanga Karinga de Tangadica et al.. See also Yussuf Adam and Anna Maria Gentile, "O Movimento dos Liguilanilu no Planalto de Mueda 1952–1962," *Estudos Moçambicanos* 4(1983), 41–75.

from that of either the chiefs or the *machambeiros*. Their position within the colonial order differed from these local elites in three significant ways: their focus was not so much on accumulation as on avoiding colonial abuses, their legal status was much more tenuous, and they could not pass this status to their heirs. As a result there is no evidence that *agricultores* constituted even a vaguely defined social group or that they acted in a self-conscious manner that distinguished them from the majority of cotton producers. Whereas the colonial-constructed categories *machambeiro* and *régulo* conformed with local notions of how people fared under the cotton regime, most growers did not recognize *agricultores* as a distinct social category.

The overriding concern of the *agricultores* was to avoid the worst abuses of the regime rather than to accumulate wealth. Under law, those growers who became *agricultores* were freed from contract labor, increasing the likelihood that their households would be able to survive within the cotton regime. But their protected legal status was contingent on continuing to meet production requirements, which in turn depended on factors beyond their control: rainfall, temperature, plant diseases, or illness within the family could strip them of their position and return them to the ranks of the more vulnerable *cultivadores*. Chiefs and *machambeiros* were far more secure. They had access to local labor and capital reserves. Finally, most *agricultores* had no guarantee that their hard-earned legal status would be inherited by their male heirs. Male offspring had to meet the same requirements as their predecessors, and in some cases even more stringent conditions were imposed. And female relatives, by law, were barred from holding this position under any circumstances. By comparison, the male heirs (whether sons or nephews) of most loyalist chiefs and *machambeiros* inherited their wealth, status, and power, guaranteeing them a privileged position within their local communities.

If *agricultores* inhabited a world apart from the *machambeiros* and the chiefs, it was still a world that held out far more possibilities for survival than did that of the *cultivadores*. Higher productivity meant that they normally had a sufficient surplus to organize work parties. On occasion, they might even hire casual laborers. Neither was an option for most *cultivadores*. *Agricultores'* red cotton cards ensured that they were usually protected from the exactions of labor recruiters. They were also probably treated somewhat better on a day-to-day basis than the *cultivadores*, upon whom most state and company officials looked with contempt. Finally, many *agricultores* received some technical assistance, which generally was out of the reach of the *cultivadores*. The *agricultores* were, after all, Portugal's "modern" African farmers-in-the-making, a vital feature of Lisbon's "civilizing mission."

By 1960 they numbered more than 224,000 peasants had opted to be *agricultores*, approximately 40 percent of all registered cotton growers.[112] This group contained a much higher percentage of actual growers, since their senior wives were automatically subsumed within, but not counted under, this category.

Apart from the legally mandated exclusion of women, the most striking feature of the *agricultor* category was that it varied substantially from one region to another. There were sharp distinctions within provinces as well (see Table 6–3). These variations can be explained largely in terms of the preexisting political econo-

---

[112] AIA, JEAC, "Sementes Distribuidas, Área Semeada, Agricultores e Cultivadores por Zonas Algodoeiras, Campanha de 1960/61." In the 1960–61 campaign there were approximately 285,000 registered *cultivadores*.

mies onto which the cotton regime was imposed. In sharp contrast to the northern provinces, where most households initially remained intact, the survey found that "the districts of Inhambane and Gaza provide the major contingent of workers for South Africa [and in] the District of Zambézia, despite its large population, the major part of the labor force work on the sugar, tea, and copra plantations."[113] Added to these migratory patterns, the gendered colonial definition of work and the underlying assumptions about the appropriate domestic role of women as their husbands' helpers largely determined the size of the *agricultor* category.

While the colonial literature drew a sharp distinction between the two groups of cotton growers, the benefits that the *agricultores* actually enjoyed must not be overstated. The assessment of a Native Affairs inspector that "the condition of almost all the *agricultores* in Bilene is quite precarious"[114] held true for the rest of the colony as well. Even the legal guarantee that *agricultores* would not be press-ganged to work on European plantations or public works projects was not always honored. Although there appears to be no documentation indicating how many former *agricultores* were conscripted, complaints from senior Cotton Board Officials suggest that it happened with some regularity.[115] "The progress brought about by cotton," lamented a senior Board employee in 1959, "is jeopardized by the forced recruitment of *agricultores* who fail to produce 750 *escudos* of cotton."[116]

Conclusion

Although women and men, chiefs and commoners, *cultivadores* and *agricultores*, *machambeiros* and migrant laborers were trapped in the same regime, each experienced a different reality. With land generally available, prices mostly fixed, and variations in technology limited, differentiation was ultimately based more on access to labor than on these other factors. For most cotton growers, access to extra-household labor was a necessity for survival; for a few it became a precondition for accumulation. As a rule, the most vulnerable peasant families were female-headed households without access to extrafarm income and with a disproportionate number of nonproductive members. Despite price reforms and some increased opportunities for off-farm employment, this broad pattern was fairly constant throughout the cotton regime. To be sure, the number of *machambeiros* probably increased and the gap between the rural poor widened as a result of the sharp jump in the number of *agricultores*. But the settler influx limited the growth of the *machambeiro* community and the proliferation of *agricultores* could not mask their vulnerable position. From one year to the next *agricultores* could and did lose their relatively privileged legal status. As a result, neither the expansion of the *machambeiro* community nor the *agricultor* boom is likely to have transformed the patterns of differentiation within rural household or communities involved in cotton production. Consider 1960 income statistics from Litundo in northern Mozambique. In Litundo, 403 peasants grew cotton. Most barely earned $30 that year, but the poor-

---

[113] AIA, JEAC, Gastão de Melo Furtado to Gov. de Niassa, 24 February 1959.

[114] AHM, Cx. 21, ISANI, "Insp. a Bilene, 1954," António Policarpo de Sousa Santos.

[115] Ibid.

[116] AIA, JEAC, Gastão de Melo Furtado to Gov. de Niassa, 24 February 1959.

est earned $6 or less. "All were women and elders."[117] At the other end of the spectrum, chiefs and *machambeiros* used their political and economic clout to expand the work force they commanded and to diversify their investments. They prospered precisely because they were never entirely dependent on cotton.

The devastating, if uneven, impact of the cotton regime had far-reaching consequences throughout rural Mozambique. On the one hand, it forced peasant growers to develop a repertoire of coping strategies to survive. On the other, it accentuated hostility toward the colonial regime and intensified rivalries and divisions at the community and domestic levels.

---

[117] Bravo, *Cultura Algodoeira*, 197.

9

Coping With the Demands of Cotton

The imposition of the colonial cotton regime left most African growers increasingly vulnerable. Nevertheless, peasants were not helpless victims of colonial exploitation; they could not always be made to do what the Portuguese government and foreign capitalists demanded. Mozambican peasants enjoyed more latitude than other types of unfree labor such as slaves and press-ganged workers.[1] The limits of state power and the peasants' partial autonomy gave men and women within the cotton scheme some space to circumvent the most excessive labor demands. Some peasants managed to intercrop foodstuffs in their cotton fields, to plant less than the required area in cotton, and to avoid performing some of the mandated tasks of cotton cultivation. I explore these insurgent strategies more fully in Chapter 10. Given the potential for reprisals, however, such acts of defiance involved enormous risk. There were less dangerous ways to alleviate labor bottlenecks and food shortages and to make life more bearable.

For the purpose of this analysis, what distinguishes coping from resisting is intent. Growers devised coping strategies to minimize the adverse effects of the cotton regime and to help them and their families survive. These acts, however, often had the unintended consequence of shoring up the system. Resistance, on the other hand, involved a struggle over power and the appropriation of scarce resources. The resisters' intent was not only to improve their daily lives but to undercut the claims of the colonial regime and the textile interests.

The strategies on which cotton growers relied were built on cultural and historical practices that antedated the colonial regime and often varied from region to region. This story is almost exclusively a recollection of the past. The growers and their descendants spoke freely about the lengths they went to ensure that their families survived the burden of cotton. By contrast, few colonial authorities recognized the individual resiliency, strength, and imaginative adaptations necessary to persevere.

---

[1] For an important discussion of the space available to different types of unfree labor, see Peter Kolchin, *Unfree Labor: American Slavery and Russian Serfdom* (Cambridge, MA, 1987).

Coping with Labor Demands

The least complicated coping strategy was for growers simply to extend their work day. This method of self-exploitation was particularly common during periods when labor-intensive tasks, such as weeding and harvesting, had to be completed quickly. Peasants lengthened their work week by beginning their days earlier, working later, and laboring on Sundays, a day when they normally rested. Romeu Mataquenha's description of the peak labor period from December through February powerfully underscores this point: "There were times when I didn't sleep. Instead I spent the entire night working the gardens around my house. If I didn't, there would be no food to eat."[2] Benjamin Mavunja, who grew cotton in Chibuto, struck the same chord: "I began early in the morning, returned home during the hottest part of the day, and went back in the afternoon. There was very little time to work in our gardens. So many evenings, especially after the rains, I cultivated my *machamba* under the light of the moon."[3] Growers had little choice but to drive themselves in this manner. But there were physical limits to their endurance, and men and especially women all had other tasks besides cotton cultivation to perform—gathering wood and water, preparing food, and working on the chief's fields.

Throughout Mozambique, overworked parents increasingly relied on the labor of their children and their elderly relatives, both of whom were nominally exempt from the cotton regime.[4] Fátima Spaneke, a widow in the Nampula district, had five children. By the time they reached school age her two boys and three girls were all working in the family food gardens and the cotton fields.[5] Fátima insisted that she "would never have been able to maintain her fields without the aid of her five children, none of whom were old enough to be registered."[6] Her neighbor Alberto Momola concurred: "By the time my sons and daughters were ten years old they were working cotton. They did it all. Seeding, weeding, cleaning, and harvesting."[7] Caetano Maio, born in Zambézia, first planted cotton when he was eight years old. "My father died here in Mocuba. Afterwards, my mother took us to Uile. When we arrived there she had to grow cotton and I helped her."[8] Manuel Pinto stressed that throughout Zambézia, children "worked side by side with their parents" until cotton officials determined that "they were strong enough to plant their own field."[9]

Margarita Pera of Murrupula remembered that from the time she was very young she had to help her parents in the cotton fields: "I helped to seed and was

---

[2] Interview with Romeu Mataquenha, Tirani Ntuka, and Mussa Vaquina, Montepuez, 19 July 1979.

[3] Interview with Benjamin Mavunja, Chibuto, 12 February 1979.

[4] Interviews with Alberto Momola et al., Nampula, 27 May 1987; Muariri Tocola and Licúrio Makalawila, Pemba, 30 May 1987; Fátima Spaneke et al., Nampula, 28 May 1979; Fátima Konkonko, Pemba, 30 May 1987; Paulo Roque, Nampula, 27 May 1987; Faria Lobo, Nampula, 26 May 1987.

[5] Interview with Fátima Spaneke et al.

[6] Ibid. See also AIA, JEAC, "Brigada de Mogovolas," José Soares, Chefe de Repartição, 11 September 1951.

[7] Interview with Alberto Momola et al.

[8] Interview with Nunes Faria Madé, Paulo Madeira, and Caetano Maio, Nicoadala/Namacurra, 19 July 1991.

[9] Interview with Manuel Pinto, Quelimane, 19 July 1991.

even involved in the three weedings. I also picked the cotton. The only thing that I
. . . did not do was separate the fiber into the different qualities. Only our parents
knew how to determine which was first quality, second quality, and third."[10] By
the time Margarita was a teenager, she had already worked for several years in her
parents' field and had become quite skilled. Under pressure from her parents, she
opened up her own cotton plots and gave most of the income to her parents. The
proceeds meant that they did not have to work quite as hard, for they had extra
money to meet their tax requirements and to purchase food. Justa Joaquim, who
resided in Namacurra, told a somewhat different story:

> I was a young girl, perhaps twelve years old, when I was ordered to
> plant half a hectare of cotton. Many other girls my age had to grow
> cotton as well. We worked in adjacent fields and helped each other clear
> the trees and prepare the soils. . . . After I finished the harvest and
> brought my crop to market, I returned home and assisted my parents.
> Their cotton fields were always behind schedule.[11]

In other households, where labor pressures were not quite so acute, children
went to school once the work in the fields had been completed. Many parents had
no other option than to rely on their young ones as part-time laborers, lest they
feel the wrath of the overseers. Nunes Faria Madé of Zambézia remembered the
first time he labored in his parents' fields in 1946:

> When I returned from school [for Christmas holidays] my parents told
> me that I had to help them in the cotton field. . . . First we cut the trees
> and dried the branches, then we burned the bush. Afterwards we pre-
> pared the land and when the first rain came, I planted the seeds.[12]

Cristina Manhique, an only child, labored with her mother in the Gaza district
while her father worked in South Africa: "I went with my mother every day to our
fields. I even helped her chop trees. We did all the tasks together so that we could
finish early. Then, in the afternoon, I went to school."[13] For those children who
resided at missionary schools, where working in the fields was part of their Christian education, vacations were a time to return to the family cotton plots and food
gardens.[14]

To ease the labor bottleneck, women and older girls took on tasks that colonial
officials and their own male relatives often presumed they were biologically incapable of doing. Particularly in labor-exporting zones, women like Cristina and her
mother hewed trees and cleared heavy stumps. Liassa Lohaninteve's husband was
periodically forced to work on the Guruè tea plantation or as a *chibalo* laborer for
the state. When he was gone, Liassa had "to fulfil the government's orders and
clear the field [myself]." Because the plot was small, she managed to do it "little by
little."[15] In 1945, one Portuguese critic noted that "we must develop a rational system of crop rotation to free women from the violent and inappropriate task of chop-

---

10   Interview with Margarita Pera, Nampula/Murrupula, 12 July 1991.
11   Interview with Justa Joaquim, Nicoadala/Mocuba, 17 July 1991.
12   Interview with Nunes Faria Madé et al.
13   Interview with Cristina Manhique and Esmeralda Candjelo, Maputo, 6 August 1991.
14   Interview with Catarina Jossias Simbine and Nely Simbine, Maputo, 8 August 1991.
15   Interview with Armando Nicula et al., Nampula/Gilé, 8 July 1991.

ping heavy trees."[16] Miriam Paulo, who lived in the Gaza district, described this added burden in personal terms:

> My husband was away most of the time. I only had an axe and a hoe. My oldest children helped. Cutting down large trees and moving heavy stumps was very hard work. I also had to take care of my baby whom I tied to a nearby tree. When she cried, I gave her my breast. But I could never stop working.[17]

In the most radical departure from old work patterns, thousands of women in the south disregarded long-held taboos prohibiting them from working with cattle and began to use ox-drawn plows. Celeste Cossa recalled teaching other women how to farm with plows.[18] Other women received instructions from male relatives and neighbors. According to Essineta Mavaungo,

> We [women] learned to use oxen after we saw how much easier it could make our work. After we felled the large trees we used the oxen to remove heavy stumps. Then we attached plows to the oxen and cleared our cotton fields. . . . With our husbands [in the mines] we had to learn to work with oxen and plows to make our life more bearable. We learned from some men in our villages. We did not have to pay them anything.[19]

The gradual shift from hoe cultivation to plow agriculture was the most significant technical adaptation to the labor crises of the cotton scheme. Plowing reduced the amount of time needed to clear the land and to prepare seed beds and facilitated production on the heavy clay soils, which were difficult to work with hoes.

The adoption of plows turned out to be a mixed blessing, however. The heavy work of clearing and tilling the field, preparing the seed bed, and turning the heavy clay soil were made easier by this technology, but sowing, weeding, picking, and sorting were not affected. In fact, the temptation to use plows to enlarge the amount of land under cultivation came squarely up against the need for additional labor to cultivate the added land. To compound this dilemma, state officials and concessionary employees regarded the mere presence of plows in the region as reason enough to increase the size of cotton plots.[20] Finally, cotton exhausted local soils quickly, and plowing exacerbated processes of soil erosion, making it necessary for new fields to be cleared every year or two. While the prevalence of tsetse flies and the generally high price of oxen prevented plow-based farming from being exported to most parts of the colony, the overworked women of the south contended that plows offered one immediate advantage: they "made our life easier."[21]

To ease labor pressures, many growers used the same plots of land for as long as they could, although they recognized that by doing so they were exhausting the soil and causing cotton yields to decline. Fátima Konkonko, from the northern cir-

---

[16] AIA, JEAC, "Rel. An.," João Contreiras, Inspector dos SAU, May 1945.

[17] Interview with Miriam Paulo, Maputo, 16 May 1987.

[18] Interview with Celeste Cossa, 31 July 1991.

[19] Interview with Essineta Mavaungo, Maputo, 6 August 1991.

[20] Interviews with Valente Yota, Macia, 19 February 1979; Manuel Sitói et al., Guijá, 16 February 1979; Benjamin Mavunja; Manuel Manguesse, António Jamessea, and Colano Cuamba, CV Chichingere, Homoíne, 5 August 1980.

[21] Interview with Miriam Paulo.

cumscription of Pemba, stressed that overworked widows and single women in particular "tried to work lands that had been cultivated the previous year."[22] State and company officials, on the other hand, insisted that rural communities clear new cotton fields every two or three years. Some demanded that field clearing be done annually, before farmers cleared new lands for food crops. The fact that peasants were reluctant to clear new cotton fields but eager to open up new plots for food crops suggests that the underlying struggle was not merely about the size of peasants' workloads.

In areas of the matrilineal north, particularly the Nampula district, the bride's mother and domestic group also began to require sons-in-law to labor in their cotton fields as part of their historic bride-service responsibility.[23] Several elders in Nampula insisted that it was common practice for "young men who moved into their wife's village to work in their mother-in-law's field, in addition to cultivating their own cotton field."[24] Murinvona Mpemo from Gilé in Zambézia stressed that such arrangements occurred frequently; others acknowledged that this occurred most often when overworked households needed additional labor or when the son-in-law was not yet registered in the cotton regime.[25]

Drawing on deeply held cultural values and historical practices that emphasized a reciprocal work ethic, cotton growers across the colony organized labor exchanges to ease some of their labor requirements. Paul Richards and others have argued that group labor is a particularly efficient way to cope with tasks that need to be completed rapidly or are tedious or daunting to individual workers.[26] Collective labor expedited tree chopping, bush burning, harvesting, and particularly weeding under the cotton regime. Some producers availed themselves of kinship networks during times of intense labor stress. But as Maria Fijamo acknowledged, overworked kin were not always in a position to help:

> Even if you were ill, you had to grow cotton. And you could not rely on members of your lineage to aid you because they had their own obligations. The only alternative for parents was to keep your children home from school. And even with everyone working, if the *capataz* determined that your cotton field was dirty, he would beat you in public in front of all the people.[27]

Others relied on immediate neighbors, or turned to some combination of friends and family to help with the arduous work of cotton cultivation. These strategies reflected a widespread belief that shared labor was the only way to ensure individual survival. Fátima Konkonko, who came from Pemba, underscored this point:

---

22   Interview with Fátima Konkonko.

23   Geffray and Pedersen, *Transformação da Organização*, 28.

24   Interview with Alberto Momola et al. Faria Lobo, who spent a number of years overseeing cotton, noted this in one of his interviews as well.

25   Interviews with Murinvona Mpemo, Nampula/Gilé, 9 July 1991; Paulo José Manuel, José Pacial, and Manuel Paquelque, Nampula, 10 July 1991.

26   M. P. Moore, "Cooperative Labour in Peasant Agriculture," *Journal of Peasant Studies* 2(1975), 270–91; Paul Richards, "Ecological Change," 1–72.

27   Interview with Maria Fijamo.

There were times when I could not possibly have finished alone. Others were in a similar situation. We agreed to work together weeding one field after another. Sometimes, if we were still behind schedule, the *sipais* would force others who had already finished their fields to help us.[28]

So did Adelina Penicela, a cotton grower from Manjacaze: "You could never cultivate a cotton field alone. There had to be ten, twenty, or even thirty people working. The next day we moved on to another field and so on. . . . If we did it differently we would have fallen behind and the *sipais* would have beaten us."[29] These work groups were often governed by rules covering the allocation of spare labor time, and there were sanctions against defaulters.[30] Growers repeatedly stressed that if their neighbors did not meet their obligations, they could not count on assistance in subsequent years. The demands of cotton made for long memories.

Because most rural families lacked the income necessary to pay for nonfamily labor, they depended instead on these kinds of work-sharing arrangements. Female-headed households not receiving wage remittances from absent males relied particularly heavily on shared labor. According to peasants in Nampula, "Widows and wives of conscripted laborers often worked together. They spent two days working on one field, two days on another, and so on until all the plots were done. They had no other choices; better-off married couples could arrange work parties in their fields."[31] Typically, the organizers of such parties would invite anywhere from ten to fifty neighbors, friends, and relatives to labor for the day in exchange for copious quantities of traditional beer and food, as well as the opportunity to sing, dance, and gossip. Muariri Tocola and Licúrio Makalawila distinguished between beer parties and more substantial work gatherings in northern Mozambique where food was served as well:

> Here in the Pemba region we had two types of work parties. The first we called *ipopwete*. We would prepare beer for all those who aided us with our cotton. Other times we would plan a big feast. We would kill some chickens and goats and brew beer. We would invite all our neighbors. They helped us and then we had a big party. We called this celebration *nkumi*.[32]

In central and southern Mozambique, single women with surplus grain or access to their husband's off-farm income were sometimes also able to organize labor parties. Joaquim Nsaio described one:

> I used some of the money my husband brought back from his job at Sena Sugar to purchase sugar from the local merchants . . . to ferment the grain to make *oteka*. While the alcohol was fermenting I prepared food, chicken, and other drinks. I then invited my neighbors and friends to clean my fields. After they returned, they ate, drank, and danced. No one paid even a half a cent.[33]

---

28 Interview with Fátima Konkonko.

29 Interview with Adelina Penicela, Maputo, 3 July 1986.

30 Ibid.; interview with Miriam Paulo.

31 Interview with Fátima Spaneke et al.

32 Interview with Muariri Tocola and Licúrio Makalawila.

33 Interview with Joaquim Nsaio et al., Morrumbala, 16 July 1991.

Miriam Paulo of the Gaza district stressed that the exchange of food for labor was only one dimension of a complex relationship. At the core was the notion that the community's survival was at stake:

> The basis of *tsima* is always the same. A person prepares beer [*uputso*] and food and invites [his or her] neighbors to help fell the trees or collect the cotton. At the end of the day all the neighbors return to the person's home and consume the food and drink. But they did not assist simply out of desire for food, but out of a sense of mutual responsibility. If a person is invited to *tsima* and fails to participate, then in the future when that person organizes *tsima*, people will be reluctant to participate because that person was not sociable and did not want to live in society.[34]

New social and economic relations also arose out of the quest to ease labor demands. The widespread hiring of casual laborers in southern Mozambique was a case in point. Such arrangements provided employment for the most destitute. The food and income they earned helped poorer households alleviate short-term production pressure. Most of these agreements were temporary, ad hoc measures undertaken to complete a specified task. During periods of food scarcity, it was particularly common for impoverished peasants to sell several days of their own labor or that of their children for food, salt, or other necessities. A group of former cotton growers from Macia in the south remembered that on empty stomachs they "walked all the way to Ilha Mariana where the land was humid and worked there a while in exchange for manioc." Over time such hit-and-miss practices gave way to seasonal hiring of a more permanent type in the south. Women often replaced their absent husbands' labor by hiring young men who were also skilled plowmen.[35] Sometimes the husbands themselves made these arrangements before leaving for the mines.[36] More prosperous cotton growers in the Nampula and Cabo Delgado districts also began to employ casual laborers by the late 1940s.[37] Peasants sometimes hired daily or weekly laborers to thin and weed their cotton fields in exchange for a small amount of sorghum or manioc. This transaction was known as *olimela*. Paulo Roque distinguished this arrangement from the much less frequent practice in which a handful of prosperous growers employed seasonal workers and paid them in cash.[38]

Households needed to have either disposable income or an appreciable surplus of grain and meat before they could organize work parties or employ casual laborers. Thus access to certain coping mechanisms could itself be a marker of rural differentiation. Whereas participating in labor exchanges was an option available to most rural producers, organizing work parties and employing casual laborers were not.

In a coping strategy without precedence, several thousand cotton growers in the late 1950s joined state-sanctioned agricultural cooperatives, which freed them

---

[34]   Interview with Miriam Paulo.

[35]   Interview with Gonçalo Mazungane Chilundo, Maputo, 8–9 August 1991; group interview, CV Magude, Macia, 28 February 1978.

[36]   Interview with Gonçalo Chilundo; Catarina Bendane and Esina Johane Mulhue, CV Mulanguene, Guijá, 17 February 1979.

[37]   Interviews with Faria Lobo, 26 May 1991; Murinvona Mpemo; Fátima Konkonko.

[38]   Interview with Paulo Roque. Faria Lobo reported a similar set of arrangements.

from the most taxing labor demands of the cotton regime and gave them control over their own work schedule. Lazaro Kavandame, president of the Mozambique African Voluntary Cotton Society, stressed to skeptical peasants that by joining the organization, they "would be able to work without fear of the *capataz* and the *chicote*, and that they would not only be able to grow cotton but food to end the hunger."[39] The leadership also promised to raise the price members received for cotton, arguing somewhat simplistically that the reason SAGAL "paid so little was because it had to use money to pay the *capatazes*, but we won't have to pay *capatazes* and there will be more money for us."[40] In fact, Kavandame did negotiate a 40 percent increase in the price SAGAL paid for first-quality cotton, which enhanced the cooperative's standing in the countryside, as did his vaguely camouflaged nationalist appeals.[41] Cotton growers in the southern cooperatives prospered even more.

Finally, a relatively small number of African women entered long-term sexual relationships with European or African foremen at least in part in order to escape the abuses of the cotton regime. Because the colonial state never sanctioned these relationships, it is difficult to learn from archival records how frequently they occurred. Interviews with elderly women and former officials suggest that they were fairly common.[42] Many of the oral accounts indicate that these relationships between African women and Portuguese men were characterized by sexual violence and victimization; for at least some women, however, and perhaps for their families, cohabitation with an employee of the colonial state could alleviate the pressures of the cotton regime. Maria Sindique noted the relatively safe position of these women, who "were never mistreated by the *sipais* or the chiefs."[43] Indeed, according to Celeste Cossa, "Africans living with European *capatazes* did not have to grow cotton. . . . In addition they ate well, dressed well, and lived a good life."[44] While it is difficult to know from the limited sources available what motives women might have had for entering such relationships, it is at least clear that their neighbors did not simply dismiss them as the passive victims of sexual exploitation. The dynamics of these controversial relationships are powerfully illustrated in a scene from Luis Polanah's underground novel, *The Saga of a Cotton Capulana*. A Portuguese foreman brings a young woman for whom he has paid seventy dollars— apparently offered as bridewealth—to the small house he has constructed for her. He awkwardly explains:

> I built this for you, for us to live together. The fields are large and you can plant cotton, manioc, sweet potato, beans or whatever else you like and as much as you like. I had a small well built for you on that side; the machine on top is moved by the wind and draws as much water as

[39]　Raimundo Pachinuapa, "Dados Históricos dum Movimento National Para Libertação Nacional," unpublished MS, 1988.

[40]　Ibid.

[41]　Interview with João Cornélio Mandande.

[42]　Interviews with Armando Cardoso, Nampula, 10 July 1991; Joaquim Nsaio; Maria Sindique et al., Nocoadala/Morrumbala, 18 July 1991; Celeste Cossa, Amélia Novana, and Regina Mate, Maputo, 31 July 1991.

[43]　Interview with Maria Sindique et al., July 31, 1991.

[44]　Interview with Celeste Cossa et al.

you want. I'll hire a boy to help you in the field. I want you to work but I don't want you to kill yourself like the other women.[45]

The existence of such liaisons, as well as the recurring evidence of sexual abuse described in an earlier chapter, reveals the complex and varied ways in which control over sexuality paralleled and at times became intertwined with control over production within the Mozambican cotton regime.

Coping with the Food Crises

Faced with the menace of hunger and starvation, Mozambican peasants also attempted to anticipate and to counteract food crises. The repertoire of strategies growers had at their disposal to cope with food insecurity, however, was quite restricted. In other African contexts, such tactics have included restricting childbirth, eating less at each meal, expanding food sources, or figuring out ways to supplement family food supplies. There is no evidence that cotton producers in Mozambique chose the first option. The scarcity of reliable and detailed records makes it difficult to determine whether rural birthrates declined or the length of time between children changed during the cotton era. One somewhat effective check means of spacing births is an extended period of lactation, during which sexual intercourse was taboo, but there is no evidence that lactation periods were lengthened. Such a reproductive strategy would have been risky for labor-starved communities with high rates of infant mortality and out-migration. And even if children were born further apart, it could be explained by the fact that women who were malnourished and overworked were not conceiving and carrying babies to term. Indeed, several former growers reported that women suffered miscarriages from the backbreaking work of cotton.[46]

The evidence that food consumption decreased during the preharvest months is clearer. However, it is unclear whether cotton growers consciously adjusted their consumption patterns to guard against expected food shortages or whether they were forced to reduce their food intake because of a decline in provisions. This is an important distinction since it gets at the issue of intent.

It was quite common for peasants to seek new sources of food by planting higher-yielding or lower-risk crops, such as manioc, sweet potatoes, pigeon peas, and corn. The dramatic expansion of manioc production, which began well before the state campaign in the 1950s, illustrates what was probably the easiest and most widespread strategy for meeting household food requirements. Drought-resistant manioc offered a number of advantages.[47] Peasants grew "sweet" and "bitter" varieties of manioc (both easily intercropped with maize, sorghum, beans, and peanuts), since they could be harvested last and stored easily and did not compete for labor with any other staples. "Manioc was our most important food crop because it took no work; corn had to be cared for,"

---

[45] Polanah, *The Saga of a Cotton Capulana*, 36.

[46] Interviews with Rosa Maria Ernesto; Maria Fijamo, Quelimane, 19 July 1991; Catarina Bendane and Esina Johane Mulhue, CV Mulanguene, Guijá, 19 February 1979.

[47] For the classic work on manioc, see William O. Jones, *Manioc in Africa* (Stanford, 1959).

was a common refrain.[48] Most important, manioc can be eaten green or ripe, is high in caloric value, and is very filling. Its leaves are also edible; peasants cooked them with coconuts and peanuts to make a popular dish commonly known as *matapa*. By 1961 the growers in northern Mozambique alone were producing more than 1.6 million tons of manioc.[49]

For Mozambicans trapped in the cotton regime, manioc became a critical food source in periods of crisis. Manioc assumed increasing importance in the south in the 1940s after the introduction of the "sweet" variety, which was nontoxic and required less processing than the "bitter" kind. Benjamin Mavunja from Chibuto in the south recalled that he and his family had little time to grow food, so they "depended on the Serra (Xinavane) where the manioc grew."[50] A 1941 newspaper account noted that "the *indígenas* of Gaza have already demonstrated increasing interest in manioc, a crop less vulnerable to climatic inconsistencies."[51] In the central region of Gilé, Liassa Lohaninté remembered that once cotton was imposed, "mealie" made from pounded manioc with beans on top became the cornerstone of rural diets.[52] Elders from the far north described a similar phenomenon: "Before cotton, sorghum was most common. Afterwards we grew a lot of manioc, a little corn, and a bit of sorghum."[53]

Throughout Mozambique, cotton precipitated a manioc revolution. To be sure, manioc had been grown in many areas as a famine crop on a limited scale throughout the twentieth century and probably before. But after the introduction of cotton, manioc became the principal food staple in most parts of the colony. It is estimated that by the end of the cotton regime, manioc constituted 60 to 80 percent of the food intake in the northern cotton zones, replacing sorghum as the mainstay of peasants' diet.[54]

But the shift to manioc had a number of drawbacks as well. Although "bitter" manioc, the more common variety, had high caloric value, its protein and vitamin components were low and largely lost through the intensive processing required to remove its hydrocyanic acid. Moreover, when the amount of time needed to eliminate manioc's toxicity is factored into labor-input calculations, manioc involves roughly the same amount of labor time as sorghum and no longer appears to be a "labor-saving" food crop.[55] The manioc revolution often shifted part of the labor burden from the field to the compound, thus increasing the time and labor demands on women who were responsible for food preparation.

On a smaller scale, peasants attempted to improve food security by growing more sweet potatoes. Sweet potatoes offer many of the same advantages as man-

---

[48] Interview with Marcelina Joaquim, Juliana Lias, and Hirondiena Tonia, Mueda, 25 April 1979. This was not quite the case. Manioc did normally require one weeding but not the extensive care associated with other food crops. Interviews with Paulo Roque; Leonarda Fátima Madime, Chidenguele, 20 November 1979.

[49] Salvador, "Contribuição para o Estudo," 136.

[50] Interview with Benjamin Mavunja.

[51] *Notícias*, 19 July 1941.

[52] Interview with Armando Nicula, Liassa Lohaninteve, and Murinvona Mpemo, Centro Piloto de Deslocados, Nampula/Gilé, 8 July 1991.

[53] Interview with Fátima Konkonko, Pemba, 30 May 1987.

[54] See, for example, Geffray and Pedersen, *Transformação da Organização*, 45.

[55] Richards, "Ecological Change," 30–32.

ioc. They are fast-maturing and fairly low-risk tubers that suit the short growing season of Mozambique. While sweet potatoes require more field labor than manioc, since they must be planted in mounds, the labor ratio, calorie for calorie, is quite similar when manioc's processing time is taken into account.[56] Sweet potatoes require a humid climate, however, so they grow best in riverine areas or in zones with high rainfall. For Mozambican cotton growers, particularly in the moist lowlands surrounding the Limpopo, Punguè, and Zambézi Rivers, sweet potatoes became an important dietary supplement, as they did in the wetter regions of northern and central Mozambique.[57] In times of crisis, this crop was critical.[58] "No one died from hunger; we always had sweet potatoes and pumpkins,"[59] recalled villagers in the Limpopo Valley.

Cotton growers across the colony also planted more pigeon peas. This legume was not terribly demanding and was typically grown adjacent to growers' homes. Pigeon peas can survive under very dry conditions and are rich in proteins; like manioc, they require a considerable amount of female off-field labor, in this case to remove their bitter shells.[60]

The other major adaptation in food cropping was the shift from sorghum to maize, particularly in the central and northern parts of the colony.[61] Sorghum requires more labor than maize, matures more slowly, and is less compatible with cotton. Peasants shifted to maize because they lacked sufficient labor simultaneously to weed cotton and protect the young sorghum from birds. At harvest time, labor-deficient households often had to choose between collecting cotton and gathering sorghum, since both crops matured at the same time. "Because we had to give priority to cotton, sorghum yields declined," said Murinvona Mpemo of Gilé.[62] Most households had little alternative but to reduce the size of sorghum fields to avoid this labor bottleneck.[63] For all these reasons, sorghum gave way to maize. But this shift posed its own problems, since maize was not nearly as drought- or weed-resistant as sorghum and therefore posed a higher risk.

Foraging for roots, tubers, and berries was a particularly common coping strategy for hard-pressed peasant producers. Even in the most fertile areas of Zambézia, cotton growers had to rely on these wild products to close seasonal hunger gaps. According to Nsaio Joaquim of Morrumbala,

> It was the time of the *mangas*—December and January—when there was always hunger. After we weeded the cotton fields and gardens we went into the bush looking for *mangas*. After we had eaten all the *mangas* we gathered other wild fruits. Sometimes we had to dig to pull out

[56]   Ibid., 34.

[57]   Silva, "O Problema Alimentar," 699; AIA, JEAC, AT 9352, Boletim de Informação 1946/47; SSE, n.d.; interview with Nsaio Joaquimo et al., Morrumbala, 16 July 1991.

[58]   Group interviews, CV Samora Machel; CV Magude, Macia, 28 February 1978; interview with Makwati Simba et al., Chibuto, 13 February 1979.

[59]   Group interview, CV Magude.

[60]   Interview with Daniel de Sousa, Maputo, 21 July 1993.

[61]   In southern Mozambique, maize was the dominant grain well before the imposition of the cotton regime.

[62]   Interview with Murinvona Mpemo, Centro Piloto de Deslocados, Nampula/Gilé, 9 July 1991.

[63]   See, for example, Feliciano, "Antropologia Económica dos Thonga," 161.

munjanjes and cook them. They were similar to potatoes but very small potatoes. In this way we survived until the first millet matured.[64]

Peasants throughout the colony used their knowledge of the forest to get them through the harsh preharvest months. One grower from the northern circumscription of Macomia recalled that

we all had to grow cotton and as a result did not have the opportunity to plant enough manioc. . . . So we had no choice but to collect whatever wild fruits we could. We gathered *malido* and *nonge*. Everyone depended on them. Others hunted. No one died, but we suffered a great deal.[65]

Cotton producers became even more dependent on foraging during periods of famine. Faria Lobo, a CAM cotton employee, found peasants living off the forest during the 1950 famine in Murrupula and, six years later, in Eráti and Memba.[66] As late as 1961, Diogo da Câmara Reis, administrator of Mogovolas, reported that "the Makua gathered the most repugnant things such as caterpillars, grasshoppers, white ants, bats, rats and a variety of roots and tubers including some that were highly toxic and produced terrible diarrhea."[67]

The alternative to foraging was purchasing staples, but most peasants lacked the necessary disposable income. One household survey in the early 1960s found that peasants spent between 575 and 875 *escudos* (approximately U.S. $20 to $30) on food, tools, and clothing per year.[68] This figure alone was more than most peasants earned from cotton. To compound matters, the price-gouging and market collusion by merchants meant that soaring prices often accompanied food shortages. According to Paulo Roque, an African *capataz* who worked in Nampula, these inland merchants were the principal beneficiaries of food scarcities: "When there was hunger the *cantineiros* sold food, although they did not have enough for everyone. The price was very high. They always made sure that they profited in these situations."[69]

State officials reported that traders frequently marked up prices by 200 to 300 percent in times of famine.[70] Peasants often found that they had no choice but to purchase food on credit. Some mortgaged a portion of their future crops to repay their debts or to satisfy tax requirements.[71] When they brought in their crops, the traders regularly undervalued them or manipulated the scales. Growers grumbled about these abuses, but had few options. "Once we were told the price we could not refuse. No one opened his mouth."[72] Many peasants remained permanently in debt. Others considered themselves "lucky if we received a little bit of money."[73] The alternative was to exchange badly needed household labor for food. Chico

[64] Interview with Nsaio Joaquim et al.

[65] Group interview, Likanganu, Macomia, 1 May 1979.

[66] Interview with Faria Lobo, 26 May 1987.

[67] Reis, "Macuas de Mogovolas," 162.

[68] Cited in May and McLellan, *The Ecology of Malnutrition*, 266.

[69] Interview with Paulo Roque.

[70] AHM, SR, Cx. 21, ISANI, Província do Sul do Save, "Relatório . . . Muchopes," Francisco de Melo e Costa, Insp. Admin., 30 January 1942; AHM, SR, Cx. 21, ISANI, "Insp. a Bilene, 1954," António Policarpo de Sousa Santos.

[71] Group interview, CV Magul, Bilene, 20 February 1979.

[72] Interview with Vicente Henriques Taulegues and Mário da Cruz Soares, Metocheria, 17 July 1979.

Nhulaialia and Costa Gaio Napire of Namapa remembered that "all the traders in the region had cotton fields and we had no alternative but to work in these fields so that we could get some food."[74] If the cotton growers failed to repay their debts, the *cantineiros* often took the law into their own hands.[75]

The peasants' repertoire of coping strategies was quite restricted. For all the creative adaptations of the growers, the state-concessionary company alliance demanded most of their labor most of the time. Faced with the threat of harsh reprisals, growers devised ways to spread out their labor burden and ease the food crisis. Extending their work day, relying on child labor and bride-service, organizing labor exchanges, disregarding prior taboos and gendered notions of work, and planting manioc and pigeon peas made life somewhat less precarious. Coping enabled most peasants to survive and reproduce, but coping had its limits.

---

[73]   Interview with Margarita Pera, Nampula/Murrupula, 12 July 1991.

[74]   Interview with Chico Nhulialia and Costa Gaio Nampire, Namapa, 2 May 1979.

[75]   Group interview, CV Magul.

10

Cotton,
the Labor Process,
and Rural Protest

Forced cotton cultivation generated considerably more than a mass of impoverished peasants struggling to survive. It also created grumbling, ornery, and defiant growers angry at being locked in a coercive regime in which failure to meet state cotton requirements exposed them to an even more brutal contract labor system. Because the rural population was vulnerable, however, direct confrontation made little sense. Peasants rarely reacted openly or fully against their domination. There were no great peasant revolts or agrarian rebellions in Mozambique during the era of forced cotton production and only a few recorded instances of large-scale strikes and market boycotts. Yet Mozambican cotton growers were hardly quiescent or compliant.

One of the central premises of this study is that the structural position of cotton growers and the prevailing modes of state domination in colonial Mozambique predisposed peasants to engage in hidden forms of resistance.[1] Their covert protests were inextricably linked to practices and power relations embedded in the labor process. Of particular relevance is the degree to which the concessionaires, allied with the state, were able to enforce the mandated obligations and the extent to which growers could circumvent these obligations. In Chapter 3, I describe the disciplinary mechanisms of the Portuguese colonial state that although limited, were sufficient to instill a climate of fear. An ambiguous and fluid situation resulted. Local administrators and company officials demanded a great deal from the peasants but were prepared to accept less. Growers, for their part, challenged the system but continuously monitored their own actions, trying to determine what was feasible and realistic. Their calculations were framed by their daily experiences.

---

[1]   For a broader discussion of hidden forms of resistance, see William Beinart and Colin Bundy, *Hidden Struggles in Rural South Africa: Politics and Popular Movements in the Transkei and Eastern Cape 1890–1930* (Berkeley, 1987); Allen Isaacman, "Peasants and Rural Social Protest in Africa," *African Studies Review* 33(1990), 1–120; Scott, *Weapons of the Weak*.

As Chapters 3 and 4 demonstrate, the imposition and maintenance of the cotton scheme was a protracted process. The authority of a fragile colonial state and of cost-minimizing concessionaires rested essentially on fear and physical intimidation, rather than on effective administration. Because the state-concessionary alliance was thinly and unevenly distributed, neither state nor company officials could constantly oversee the daily labor of thousands of peasants dispersed throughout the countryside. Colonial efforts to demarcate cotton blocs and subsequently to herd cotton growers into *concentrações* were unsuccessful attempts to control the Mozambican peasantry.

Moreover, the nature of the peasant labor process gave cotton growers much greater latitude than rural or urban workers to preserve some autonomy and circumvent some of the controlling mechanisms of the state and the concessionaires. Peasants were not divorced from the means of production; they controlled their own land and, at least to some degree, commanded family labor. Peasants were not subject to the same degree of surveillance and labor control as their worker counterparts; there were always moments when the growers were able to escape supervision. At such times and in such "free spaces"[2] growers took steps to shield critical resources and to minimize colonial exploitation. This partial autonomy, as well as the peasants' recognition of their limited power, helps explain why peasants were prone to engage in hidden forms of resistance rather than in broader social movements. Just as growers were reluctant to become involved in open confrontations, so neither the state nor the concessionary companies were interested in destroying the peasantry. Rather, their objective was to control the peasantry more effectively. For both oppressor and oppressed, jockeying and negotiating to reshape this partial autonomy constituted the principal terrain of struggle.

In the previous chapter, I argue that what differentiated coping from resistance was intent. But in the real world of the Mozambican cotton regime, this analytical distinction did not always hold true. Some forms of resistance may have also inadvertently served as safety valves, perpetuating the system of exploitation. For example, if growers surreptitiously tampered with the cotton sacks they brought to market and defined these acts as "cheating," thus acknowledging some sense of their own wrongdoing, were they not legitimating existing property and class relations? Makonde peasants who joined the African Voluntary Cotton Society and embraced its nationalist agenda while producing more cotton for the colonial regime were engaged in equally ambiguous behavior. And when state officials and company representatives closed their eyes as peasants illegally intercropped, did they not do so, in part, because these acts locked peasants into the status quo? Another possible drawback in defining coping and resistance by the intention of the principal actor is that it ignores the agency of the oppressor, who may define the act differently and who has the power to enforce his definition.[3] These analytical problems notwithstanding, the intent of the growers remains at the center of the analysis.

---

[2]   For a theoretical discussion of the concept of "free social space," see Sara Evans and Harry Boyte, *Free Spaces: The Sources of Democratic Change in America* (New York, 1986).

[3]   Personal communication from James Scott, September 20, 1994.

The labor process provides a strategic entry point into the less visible conflicts within peasant communities and even within rural households. Exploring who actually cultivated the cotton, who assumed the risks of production, and who controlled cotton income challenges assumptions about the moral economy purportedly binding "traditional" African societies. Once families and communities are treated as potential terrains for struggle over power and not necessarily as homogenous or harmonious entities, it becomes possible to explore exploitive and conflictual relationships within them as well as relationships built on consent and cooperation. Many relationships of domination—between chiefs and their subjects, between husbands and wives, between elder and younger generations—antedated but were clearly exacerbated by the cotton regime.

Finally, focusing on how work was organized and resources allocated sheds light on the ways growers thought about domination and power and the ways in which they engaged in a type of mental resistance. At stake was a struggle over meaning. Whose meaning of appropriate behavior, justice, and work would prevail and how it would be determined were at the heart of the matter. That colonial power was mediated through indigenous political institutions and peasants retained their own language, historical memories, and forms of expressive culture reinforced the autonomy derived from the labor process by limiting the degree to which peasants were susceptible to colonial ideology.

Most peasants did not fatalistically accept the existing order or colonial representations of reality. Just as the practice of resistance helped mitigate the daily patterns of material appropriation, so Mozambican cotton growers produced, articulated, and disseminated a repertoire of songs, dances, oral narratives, and gestures that reaffirmed their dignity in the face of public beatings, sexual abuses, and forced deferential behavior. Such "hidden transcripts," in the words of James Scott, answered daily insults to indignity and were the building blocks of a counterideology.[4] This counterideology challenged the racial and cultural arrogance on which the cotton regime was predicated and ultimately challenged the legitimacy of the colonial system itself. Many of the peasant narratives, songs, and proverbs that were at the core of the insurgent culture remain a central part of rural life. They provide the historical material for much of the discussion on peasant dissent.

Hidden or Everyday Forms of Resistance

The ongoing struggle between cotton growers and those who sought to extract scarce resources from them is a critical chapter in the history of the cotton regime in Mozambique. It is a struggle that colonial officials begrudgingly acknowledged when they spoke of the cunning, wily, and disrespectful "natives" who obstructed the cotton scheme.

"Hidden" or "everyday" forms of resistance, concepts derived from American slave and European agrarian historiography, are a way to explore the less visible

---

[4] James C. Scott, *Domination and the Arts of Resistance: Hidden Transcripts* (New Haven, 1990). For an alternative formulation see Timothy Mitchell, "Everyday Metaphors of Power," *Theory and Society* 19, 5(1990), 545–78.

ways in which cotton growers helped make their own histories.[5] Some scholars have argued, however, that the concept of "everyday resistance" can distort or trivialize the notion of resistance, perhaps even render it analytically meaningless.[6] As a description of resistance, the terms *hidden, everyday,* or *routine* are somewhat misleading. Since they are "hidden" only to those powerful individuals whose policies provoked them (and to scholars in search of them), to call these actions hidden is to view them from an elite perspective. This is not surprising: peasants do not usually write their own history, and those who do frequently adopt the perspective of the powerful. But peasants who engaged in such protests disguised or obscured their actions to minimize risk and to maximize control over the resources they most valued. The terms *everyday, day-to-day,* and *routine* are equally imprecise and for the same reasons. Some peasant activities, such as work slowdowns and intercropping, indeed occurred daily; but sabotage, pilfering, and flight clearly did not. *Routine* presupposes that all of these peasant struggles followed a particular trajectory or at least could be reduced to a specific ensemble of actions.

Compounding the problem of semantics is the tendency in the literature to lump together many actions with different intentions and outcomes. Illegal intercropping, feigned illness, sabotage, and flight are quite different forms of opposition, each with divergent intended consequences.

What these hidden or daily protests are presumed to hold in common is that they *were not* rebellions, revolutions, or other broad-based and highly visible social movements—the kinds of acts our scholarly traditions privilege in ways that often distort the historical record. Instead, they were individual, localized forms of opposition. Yet arguments based on negation are often problematic, and distinctions based on scale alone are not always accurate. To the perpetrators of "hidden" or "everyday" forms of resistance, these obscure actions often embodied some notion of collective identity and shared risk and possessed an internal structure and logic, even if that logic is not easily discernible to scholars.[7]

A further consideration for scholars concerning the problem of intent is that peasants' insurgent acts were often clandestine, and many were never recorded. Even if we can document a particular act, it may be extremely difficult to determine the intentions supporting that event. In some cases motivation may be inscribed in the act itself. Such was the case when growers cooked cotton seeds before planting them or when they mixed foreign objects with cotton to increase its market weight. But such relatively unambiguous acts tended to be the exception.

---

[5]   For a discussion of day-to-day resistance, see Raymond Bauer and Alice Bauer, "Day to Day Resistance in Slavery," *Journal of Negro History* 27(1942), 388–419; John Blasingame, *The Slave Community: Plantation Life in the Antebellum South* (New York, 1972); Charles Tilly, "Routine Conflicts and Peasant Rebellions in Seventeenth-Century France," in *Power and Protest in the Countryside,* ed. Robert P. Weller and Scott E. Guggenheim (Durham, 1982). See also Michael Adas, "From Footdragging to Flight: The Evasive History of Peasant Avoidance Strategies in South and South East Asia," *Journal of Peasant Studies* 13, 2(1986), 64–86.

[6]   For a fuller discussion of the strength and limits of this mode of analysis, see Isaacman, "Peasants and Rural Social Protest."

[7]   Adas, "From Footdragging to Flight"; Isaacman et al.,"'Cotton Is the Mother of Poverty"; Scott, *Weapons of the Weak*; Michael Watts, "On Political Diffidence: Non-Revolt, Resistance and Hidden Forms of Political Consciousness in Northern Nigeria, 1900–1945," in *Global Crises and Social Movements,* ed. Edmund Burke (Boulder, 1987).

More often than not, intent may have been intrinsically polyvalent. When growers sneaked off from cotton fields to work in food gardens it may have been a way of simultaneously resisting surplus extraction and feeding an undernourished family. Peasant theft may have been driven by similar concerns. Fleeing or withholding labor were ways of resisting and of making life more bearable. Although multiple motives create a certain analytical ambiguity, in real life people try to kill several birds with one stone all the time.

Despite the problems inherent in the concept of everyday resistance, to ignore the "weapons of the weak" is to ignore the peasants' principal arsenal. Precisely because of the nature of the labor process, there was room for these hidden forms of protest. Such actions rarely made headlines, but they were the most pervasive form of protest in the Mozambican countryside.

Two important qualifications extend and deepen the discussion of hidden forms of resistance. First, although Mozambican peasants repeatedly engaged in these covert acts, clandestine resistance was not a knee-jerk reaction but the result of carefully calculating the potentially serious consequences of defiance. Many peasants remained intimidated, others passively indignant. "How could we resist?" asked two former producers incredulously. "The *sipais* and overseers were always on our backs."[8] Although they were not, it certainly felt that way to many who would not take risks that could lead to harsh reprisals.

Second, the concept of hidden forms of resistance needs to be disaggregated to identify the diverse intentions of the actors as well as the consequences of their actions. The overwhelming majority of these conflicts centered around three critical issues: access to peasant labor, control over peasant production, and the politics of retribution. These social struggles drew on peasants' deeply held values about justice, kinship obligations, and work, values that were embedded in the historical memories and expressive culture that peasants retained and remade as part of their partial autonomy.

The Contest Over Labor

The success of the Portuguese cotton project in Mozambique hinged on control over African labor. As described in Chapters 3 and 4, the state-concessionary alliance introduced a number of coercive policies to increase the amount of labor peasants committed to the cotton regime. They reorganized the rural work day, increased minimum acreage requirements, and expanded the pool of prospective growers. For their part, growers developed strategies to contest each of these initiatives. Stated somewhat differently, control over labor was the central arena of struggle within the cotton regime.

Rural producers withheld their labor in one of three ways: they escaped permanently from the cotton regime, they remained within the system but covertly held back a portion of their labor, or they boycotted the system at strategic moments. Although these tactics are treated as analytically distinct, in reality they were often interconnected. Many growers initially developed mechanisms to circumvent labor obligations but ultimately decided to flee. Others who tried unsuc-

---

8   Interview with Chico Nhulialia and Costa Gaio Nampire, Namapa, 2 May 1979.

cessfully to free themselves from the system subsequently resorted to alternative acts of defiance.

Permanently withholding labor took a variety of forms. To avoid the tyranny of the cotton regime and to regain some measure of control over their lives, thousands of peasants fled to Tanganyika, Nyasaland, and South Africa. This pattern of cross-boundary migration had been a common reaction not only to the harsh Portuguese policies, but also to the better labor and market conditions and lower taxes in the adjacent British colonies even before the imposition of the cotton regime.[9] Forced cultivation simply created an additional reason to flee. Still other peasants managed to convince officials that their lands were unsuitable for cotton production. Whatever concrete form this type of resistance took, withholding labor represented the harshest blow an individual could strike.

Although some scholars contend that equating flight with resistance does "violence to language,"[10] Asiwaju correctly notes that "migration as protest proved far less costly to Africans and had much the same effect on the colonial authorities as . . . more militant forms of protest."[11] Portuguese officials repeatedly stressed the debilitating effects of these clandestine movements in Mozambique. As early as 1940 an official in southern Mozambique complained that peasant flight had become a serious problem: "Africans fleeing the . . . Sul de Save because of cotton is not something new. In 1938 it was reported that many natives abandoned their lands after setting fire to their huts."[12] Six years later, his counterpart in the Niassa district complained that although he had registered 7,447 cotton producers in the administrations of Metangula and Unango, "the actual figure was appreciably smaller since just prior to the planting season many of the peasants fled to Nyasaland."[13] A company field agent in the Mutarara region of Zambézia noted that between 1956 and 1957 some 500 of the 2,200 registered cotton producers had slipped across the border into Nyasaland.[14] And in a confidential 1959 report, a Cotton Board official visiting the north found that "many cotton fields were abandoned, some because the owners fled to the other side [British territories] and others because of contract labor."[15] British authorities in Tanganyika writing in the late 1950s confirmed the increased presence of Mozambican refugees: "In addition to those temporary immigrants who return to their homes, some thousands of Portuguese natives have come in the last few years and settled permanently in Masasi, Tunduru and Songea districts."[16]

---

[9]   Alpers, "'To Seek a Better Life'"; Harries, *Work, Culture, and Identity.*

[10]   Leroy Vail and Landeg White, "Forms of Resistance: Songs and Perceptions of Power in Colonial Mozambique," *American Historical Review* 88, 4(1983), 919.

[11]   A. I. Asiwaju, "Migrations as Revolt: The Example of the Ivory Coast and the Upper Volta Before 1945," *JAH* 17(1976), 577–94.

[12]   AIA, JEAC, "Papéis Diversos: Despacho," J. Anachoreta, Chefe do Sub–del. do Sul do Save, 12 June 1940.

[13]   AIA, JEAC, 601/8, "Relatório," José Cândido Pereira Burugete, Sec. da Admin. de Maniamba, 18 September 1946.

[14]   AIA, JEAC, "Conf. 1957–59," João Belo, Prác. Ag. da JEAC to Sub–del. de JEAC, 13 February 1957.

[15]   AIA, JEAC, "Conf. 1957–1959," João Ferreira, Reg. Ag. to Chefe de JEAC, 24 January 1959.

[16]   Tanzania National Archives (TNA), File 13/63 (Access no. 16), "Mtwara Immigrant Native Labour From P.E.A.," A. E. Kitching to Chief Secretary, Dar es Salaam, 31 March 1957.

The clandestine character of this flight makes it difficult to determine the number of cotton growers who actually escaped. Nor is it always clear what combination of factors precipitated their migration. What is clear is that flight was a regular and recurring phenomenon. As the bishop of Beira noted in 1951: "The exodus of the indigenous population to the neighboring countries is an uncontestable fact and it is provoked exclusively by the rigorous demands of cotton. "[17]

The decision to flee was not easy. There were no guarantees that migrants would have access to land in their new homes, and by fleeing they lost the protection of the ancestor spirits who presided over the lands they had left behind. Moreover, running away could be both arduous and dangerous, for those who remained behind as well as for those who fled.

Among the deterrents to migration, none loomed larger than fear of the unknown—a fear grounded in fact. Peasants often had to walk several hundred kilometers through unfamiliar surroundings, sometimes with children on their backs. The journey held a number of chilling prospects, including lack of food and shelter, attacks from marauding bandits, and the ever-present threat of capture by police patrols. Lofas Nsampa's account highlights the multiple dangers facing African runaways:

> We took food from here [Luabo]. We went on foot. We left our home at night and spent the first night walking. We slept in the bush. Since we did not know the route to [Southern] Rhodesia we had to ask villagers we met on the way. It was far away and we spent a month sleeping in the bush. Many people were killed by lions. When we reached the police station near the border we hid until we were sure that all the police were fast asleep. Then we swam across the river. Those who could not swim had to arrange a canoe.[18]

To minimize these risks, fugitives often formed temporary bands in which they shared knowledge and food and provided mutual protection.[19]

Apart from the physical danger, another strong deterrent to flight was the knowledge that family members left behind would invariably suffer. State and company officials used the threat of retribution to contain flight and to glean information about the whereabouts of runaways. As one woman in Nkanyavane recalled,

> They would come and try to find out where your husband was. And when you said that you did not know . . . they would arrest you and take you to the administration where they made you pull the weeds and sweep around the prison. If you continued to claim that you did not know where your husband was, they would insist that it was not possible. . . . But in fact . . . your husband did not tell you when he deserted. He went because of the suffering, and at the time when he left, he did not know himself where he was going. You would then be arrested and you would return home whenever they decided to release you.[20]

---

[17]   See Resende, *Ordem Anticomunista* , 140–42.

[18]   Interview with Lofas Nsampa et al., Muide Compound, Luabo, 14 November 1976.

[19]   Group interview, CV Likanganu, Macomia, 27 July 1979; interview with Benjamin Jacob, Macomia, 27 July 1979.

[20]   Group interview, Serra Nkanyavane, 17 February 1979.

It was precisely to avoid such reprisals that entire communities fled en masse. Since large-scale migration posed far more serious logistical problems, it occurred less frequently than the flight of individuals or small groups. Yet a number of villages, especially those located near international borders, braved the elements and the unknown to escape the cotton regime. Sitting in front of his home in Macomia in the north, Benjamin Jacob recalled how

> on the prearranged night we brought our knives and clubs in order to protect our wives and children who were carrying food. We moved cautiously in the dark on forest tracks to avoid the *sipais* whom we had been informed were located at Nachidoro. We resolved to fight to the last drop of blood to avoid capture.[21]

After a difficult journey, they arrived at the Rovuma River and crossed safely into Tanganyika. As elders in the Gaza district explained the propensity to flee to South Africa, "There were two problems that caused a person to desert. One was a family dispute. . . . The other was to desert for fear of cotton *chibalo* or other forms of forced labor for the chiefs."[22]

Despite the degree of suffering experienced at the hands of the cotton regime, many peasants were reluctant to separate themselves from their cultural and historical connections. Therefore, instead of migrating to adjacent countries, they fled to inaccessible areas of Mozambique from which they could surreptitiously maintain contact with their families. Generally, this strategy was a short-term solution to an immediate threat created by the anticipated arrival of *sipais*, cotton overseers, or labor recruiters. In 1952 a senior Cotton Board Inspector visiting Ribáuè reported: "The Africans have all fled to the mountains. In the villages you only find the very young, the very old and the wives of the runaways. The men are in hiding and their wives spend days transporting food to these fugitives."[23] These runaways hid in the forests or mountains in makeshift shelters. They survived by supplementing hunting and gathering with the food brought clandestinely by their families. Many ultimately fled to neighboring countries. Others eventually returned to their villages and hoped for the best.[24]

The decision of some fugitives to return contrasts sharply with the tenacity of those runaways who created permanent refugee communities. These fugitive societies bore a striking resemblance to the runaway slave communities of the Americas.[25] Most were situated in rugged mountainous areas or in coastal swamps, where the difficult topography was a natural barrier to Portuguese penetration. The harsh environment severely limited production potential, however, and the refugees had to survive on roots, tubers, perennials, and wild game. Autonomous fugitive communities were reported in the districts of Monapo, Mogincual, Macomia, Balama,

---

[21]   Interview with Benjamin Jacob.

[22]   Group interview, Serra Nkanyavane.

[23]   AIA, JEAC, 660, 55 (1), 1952, Gastão de Melo Furtado, Chefe da Del. to Pres. de JEAC, 22 February 1952.

[24]   Group interviews, CV Luís Carlos Prestes, Gaza, 2 February 1979; CV Magude, Macia, 28 February 1979; CV Nawawane, Montepuez, 20 July 1979; Macomia, 27 July 1979; interview with Benjamin Jacob.

[25]   See Richard Price, *Maroon Societies* (Baltimore, 1979).

Mueda, Montepuez, and Cuamba in northern Mozambique, where colonial state power was weakest.[26]

Consider the history of the fugitive community established on top of Mount Mutuene in the district of Cuamba. The dissidents, under the leadership of a local chief named Namcaoma (whose name in Makua means "rebel"), fled to the Mutuene mountains to avoid labor obligations and taxes. They lived by eating bananas and herding goats. The Mutuene community became a symbol of defiance and a beacon for other runaways. As a result, colonial officials tried in vain to destroy it. Abondio Leveriano Luís recalled:

> Many times the Portuguese soldiers attacked but they were always defeated. The population defended itself by throwing rocks, spears, and other locally made weapons at the invaders. They continued to live there until the last years of the colonial period, independent of the Portuguese, who referred to them as bandits unwilling to be civilized.[27]

A number of other refugee communities were also able to survive both harsh environmental conditions and Portuguese incursions. Elders in Balama recounted with pride the cunning and bravery of those who escaped to the mountains near Meloco:

> They managed to defend themselves by being very clever. As they were on the top of the mountain, when the Portuguese came they allowed them to climb half way before they rolled boulders down on them, killing some. Some of our people hid themselves in caves. When the Portuguese arrived, they placed scrub and wood in the front and set it alight thinking that all those inside would suffocate to death with the smoke—then they left. But as our people were deep inside the cave, the smoke didn't reach them, no one died. So they continued to live there.[28]

Other fugitive communities were probably not so fortunate.

There were less dangerous ways to escape the cotton regime. Some peasants managed to gain their freedom by convincing officials that their lands were inappropriate for cotton and should be dropped from the system. They covertly cooked substantial numbers of the cotton seeds before going through the motions of planting and weeding the crop.[29] Those who engaged in such subterfuge did so with great trepidation. A women in the Luabo region of Zambézia explained that she took great care to avoid detection when "she placed the seeds in a can and toasted them" because she knew that if caught "she would be punished severely."[30] At harvest time growers feigned disbelief when few plants had germinated. Colonial authorities were naturally surprised at the low yields, which they attributed to the poor quality of the soil or to other environmental deficiencies. As a result, many peasants managed to escape from cotton cultivation.

---

26 Interview with Pruan Hassan et al., Montepuez, 20 July 1979; group interview, Macomia, 27 July, 1979; interview with Eugénio Niquaria, Montepuez, 24 July 1979.

27 Interview with Abondio Leveriano Luís, Cuamba, 28 December 1979.

28 Interview with Pruan Hassan et al.

29 Group interview, Serra Nkanyavane, 17 February 1979.

30 Group interview, Muanavine Compound, Luabo, 21 November 1976 (Head Collection).

To be successful, such dissimulation had to be not only hidden but also wide-spread, to create the appearance that the problems were ecological. Sometimes sympathetic chiefs or village headmen organized late-evening meetings where peasants decided to act. Elders in Chidenguele recalled that Régulo Isaias Langa played such a pivotal role:

> He had been called to the administrator's office and beaten because the area under his authority had not produced much cotton. He had also been subject to abuses from the overseers. Because he suffered like the rest of us and recognized that cotton was not profitable, he gathered all the people together and urged them to cook their seeds. They did so and the following year nothing grew. As a result we were allowed to stop cultivating cotton.[31]

Often, however, growers had to take the lead themselves. In nearby Manjacaze, angry women pressured their chiefs to participate:

> Women did not like the work and went to the village chiefs to talk it over. Some of the chiefs did not agree with them and said that [burning the seeds] would just make things worse. But the women argued that something had to be done. So they decided to roast the seeds before planting them. The plants did not grow and the cotton never appeared. The white man could not believe his eyes but we simply told him that the soil was not good enough for the seeds to grow. Then a number of whites came into our area and the village chief was very afraid but he said he knew nothing.[32]

In other cotton zones chiefs and suspected state informers were either excluded from these clandestine meetings or pressured into silence. In a fairly remote part of Mueda, peasants engaged in this subterfuge "without the knowledge of the chiefs, and as a result the local authorities were convinced that the region would never be appropriate for cotton."[33]

Peasants are reported to have engaged in this subversive activity in locations as diverse as Magude, Manjacaze, and Chibuto in the Gaza district, and Montepuez, Pemba, and Mueda in Cabo Delgado.[34] Testimony from former officials confirms that these acts occurred throughout the country.[35] Substantial interregional labor migrations and the fact that distant villages were aware of these acts of defiance raise the possibility that an informal network of communication existed.[36] It is also possible that some local administrators turned a blind eye to these activities. Whatever the case, examples of such chicanery took on heroic proportions, providing the stuff out of which peasants constructed a a culture of insurgency, sometimes embellishing and even fabricating stories of the exploits of reknowned rural

---

[31] Interview with Leonardo Fátima Madime, Chidenguele, 20 November 1979.

[32] Interview with Adelina Penicela, Maputo, 3 July 1986.

[33] Interview with Fátima Konkonko, Pemba, May 30, 1987.

[34] Ibid.; Sherilynn Young, "Changes in Diet and Production in Southern Mozambique, 1855–1960" (paper delivered to British African Studies Association Conference, September 1976), 11–12.

[35] Interviews with Ferreira de Castro, Maputo, 25 September 1978; Manuel Alves Saldanha, Xai Xai, 12 February 1979.

[36] Group interview, CV Likanganu; interview with Benjamin Jacob; AIA, JEAC, 952, "Brigada Técnica de Cabo Delgado," Vasconde Sousa de Fonseca Lebre, 30 September 1949.

"subversives" in the process (see below). At the same time, many who recounted these exploits did so with some concern, mindful that for peasants struggling to survive, dissimulation remains a powerful weapon.

The difficulties in identifying the perpetrators of these practices meant that colonial authorities rarely caught peasants in the act of subverting the cotton regime. Individuals who were caught or turned in by informers, however, suffered harsh reprisals, such as the destruction of their food crops, systematic beatings, and long-term incarceration.[37] Moreover, hard-won exemption from cotton did not necessarily guarantee freedom from forced cultivation, as events in Nkanyavane illustrate. Freed from cotton, peasants there were forced to cultivate and sell rice, an even more labor-intensive crop that yielded lower returns than cotton.[38]

Fleeing and cooking seeds were clearly the most dangerous insurgent measures for cotton growers to pursue. Most elected to express their autonomy by covertly circumventing the state-imposed work schedule. Although European overseers carefully measured and demarcated the amount of land on which each peasant was expected to cultivate cotton, there were too few *capatazes* to ensure that even most of the land was actually cultivated. One Cotton Board official writing about the southern districts in 1941 noted that "the vast majority of the indigenous population is not cultivating the minimum specified area."[39] In the same year the state registered 6,310 peasants in the northern circumscription of Quiterajo, but only 4,100 actually planted a field and the average plot size was under a quarter of an acre.[40] Official provincial statistics from the districts of Zambézia, Nampula, Niassa, and Cabo Delgado reveal that this was not an isolated phenomenon.[41] Seventeen years later an agricultural official reporting to the governor of Tete complained that "most of the cotton fields in the concessionary area of the Cotton Company of Tete are not being cultivated at the minimum required level."[42]

Other peasants began seeding their cotton fields after the designated dates but before the *sipais* arrived, thereby getting to use the initial part of the rainy season to work in their family gardens. The senior agricultural officer in Quelimane noted in 1947 that "the preparation of the cotton fields is way behind schedule in a number of areas."[43] His counterpart to the north in António Enes described an alternative ploy used by peasants to gain time for their own gardens: "The Africans in this part continually fabricate excuses why they have not seeded any cotton yet. This year it is the lack of rain."[44] Reports from cotton company officials and colo-

[37] AIA, JEAC, "Conf. 1957–59," João Belo, Prác. Ag. da JEAC, to Sub–del. de JEAC, 13 February 1957; interviews with Manuel Sitói et al., Guijá, 16 February 1979; Romeu Mataquenha et al., Montepuez, 19 July 1979; Pruan Hassan et al.; Júlio Miambo, Maputo, 14 September 1979; group interview, CV Luís Carlos Prestes.

[38] Group interview, Serra Nkanyavane.

[39] AIA, JEAC, Dossier VZ5 (1940–42), J. Anachoreta, Chefe de Sub–del. do Sul do Save, 23 April 1941.

[40] AIA, JEAC, "Rel. da Insp. de JEAC, 1940," João Contreiras, Adj. da Del. da JEAC, to Pres. de JEAC, 31 January 1941.

[41] Bravo, *A Cultura Algodoeira,* 127.

[42] AIA, JEAC, 2201/8 (1958), Reg. da BT de Tete ao Gov. do Districto de Tete, 20 July 1958.

[43] AIA, JEAC, "Conf. 1947," José da Cunha Dias Mendes, Reg. Ag. ao Chefe do Posto da JEAC, 9 December 1947.

[44] AIA, JEAC, AT, 9352, BI, CAM, 1946/47, Conc. de António Enes, PA do Namaponda, 10 April 1947.

nial authorities in Makonde, Macomia, Marrupa, and Manganja during the second half of the 1940s testify to the regularity with which the rural population planted late.[45] European observers explained this behavior as yet another indication of the uneconomic nature of the Mozambican peasant."You are no doubt familiar with the indolence of the blacks," wrote one local administrator. "They have the habit of waiting to the last moment, which reflects their laziness and bad will, which in this case prejudices cotton production."[46]

There is also ample evidence that growers skipped certain tasks and performed others haphazardly. Colonial officals regularly complained that peasants weeded their cotton plants fewer times and at later dates than the Cotton Board required.[47] That growers often picked as little as twenty or thirty pounds of cotton per day suggests that they did not maximize the harvest.[48] Colonial officials also reported widespread opposition to burning the stalks of cotton plants after the harvest. "As a result of the failure to burn thousands of hectares," one official predicted in 1958, "next year diseases and pests will cause a major disruption in production."[49] While rural cultivators undoubtedly recognized that failure to weed and burn would reduce the quantity and quality of their cotton, they were also keenly aware that the time needed to perform such tasks could be more productively used for growing food and cash crops.

Similar reasoning motivated a number of peasants to leave parts of their cotton crops in the field, although such defiance could prove costly if discovered. Other growers, rather than making repeated journeys to distant markets for insignificant sums of money, scattered the remainder of their cotton crop in the nearby bush or along the roadside.[50] Such anonymous acts were nearly impossible to trace. A confidential Cotton Board report assessing the problems of rural marketing concluded in 1947 that "many peasants refuse to sell the cotton, preferring to burn it and scatter the ashes."[51] One former northern cotton producer recalled:

It took us three days to carry the cotton to the market at Montepuez. Each evening we had to sleep in the forest. And when we arrived at the market the police were waiting for us with new sacks and without even letting us eat, ordered us home to bring more cotton. On the way home my father, exhausted from the journey, told us to bury the empty sacks in the forest. We subsequently burned the remaining cotton which was of secondary quality and scattered it in the forest. Others in our village did the same.[52]

---

[45]   See, for example, AIA, JEAC, 608/8, Mário Guimarães, Ag. Fisc. 31, 1946; AIA, JEAC, AT, 1352, BI, 1946/47; AIA, JEAC, 952, "BT de Cabo Delgado," Vasco Sousa de Fonseca Leone, 30 September 1949.

[46]   AIA, JEAC, "Papéis Diversos," F. Barbosa to Rafael Agapito Guerreiro, 28 October 1939.

[47]   Interview with A. Quintanilha, Maputo, 7 March 1979; AIA, JEAC, "Conf. 1947," José da Cunha Dias Mendes, Reg. Ag. ao Chefe do Posto da JEAC, 9 December 1947; AIA, JEAC, AT, 9352, BI, CAM, 1946/47, Conc. de António Enes, PA do Namaponda, 10 April 1947; AIA, JEAC, 608/8, Mario Guimares, Ag. Fisc., 1946; AIA, JEAC, AT, 1352, BI, 1946/47; AIA, JEAC, 952, "BT de Cabo Delgado," Vasco Sousa de Fonseca Leone, 30 September 1949.

[48]   Interview with Paulo Roque, Nampula, 27 May 1987.

[49]   AIA, JEAC, 1011, J. Montalvão Marques to Gov. do Dist. de Gaza, 19 March 1958.

[50]   AIA, JEAC, AT 9352, BI, CAM 1946/47, 4 BI; AIA, JEAC, AT 9352, BI, CNA, 1946/47.

[51]   AIA, JEAC, "Conf. 1947: Rel. Esp. sobre Mercados," António de Freitas Silva, 1947.

[52]   Interview with Amasse Nuitha, CV Nawana, Montepuez, 20 July 1979.

Similar acts of sabotage were reported in Balama and Porto Amélia in northern Mozambique.[53] Faced with an attack on their long-term security, many peasants fought back in quiet but effective ways. They sold the minimum amount of cotton necessary to avoid punishment.

On rare occasions, producers openly defied the state-concessionary alliance and refused to plant cotton. Labor boycotts were obviously difficult to organize and left participants extremely vulnerable. Nevertheless, colonial officials reported several boycotts shortly after the introduction of the cotton scheme.[54]

The most spectacular labor boycott occurred at Búzi in 1947, when several thousand women organized a strike to protest the demands of the cotton regime. To the disbelief and dismay of the local officials, the women refused to accept the cotton seeds: "Some claimed that they were ill and others had a number of other phony excuses. Still others who had taken the seeds brought them back."[55] Company officials insisted the women were being manipulated by their husbands and that the local administrator was being too lax. The striking women refused to reconsider, adamant that with their men working on nearby sugar plantations they had neither sufficient time nor labor to produce cotton and food. In a token compromise to their militancy, state and company officials offered to exempt pregnant women and mothers of more than four children from cotton production. The others, however, were compelled as before. Most ultimately complied, but the delay and the lack of enthusiasm resulted in a significant break in production.[56]

Such overt challenges to the system were the exception. Most acts of defiance were "hidden," and, for them to succeed, the perpetrators had to remain anonymous. Despite the problems the anonymity of the actors poses for historical reconstruction, the evidence presented in the previous pages suggests that thousands of growers at one time or another engaged in these surreptitious acts. Insurgents drawn from almost all sectors of the rural population surreptitiously contested state and concessionary company claims on their labor. The principal exceptions were chiefs and prosperous farmers, most of whom had a stake in perpetuating the cotton system. After all, it made no sense for farmers who had invested in plows, cattle, or tractors to withhold their labor or to sabotage their crops. Most chiefs had even stronger social, political, and economic incentives not to defy the system.

Although the struggle over labor tended to be generalized, it was not necessarily uniform. Women, who understood the precarious balance between household and commodity production better than any other segment of the population, probably had a greater stake in withholding a portion of their labor than men who were less involved in and benefited more from cotton cultivation. Gender as well as age often determined not only who resisted but the manner in which resistance

---

[53]   AIA, JEAC, 901, "Plano do Trabalho 1958," Júlio Bossa, Sub–del. ao Chefe da Del. de JEAC, 13 May 1958.

[54]   See, for example, AIA, JEAC, J. Anachoreta, Chefe da Sub–delegaçao do Sul do Save to JEAC, 16 December 1939; AIA, JEAC, "Diversos, 1939," José da Cunha Sousa Dias Mendes to Chefe da Del. da JEAC, 13 January 1940; AIA, JEAC, "Copiador Geral de Notas 4° Trimestre 1947," Gastão de Melo Furtado to Director de CICA, 4 October 1947; AIA, JEAC, 601/8, "Rel.," Abel A Teixeira Rebelo, Admin. do Cons. de Nampula, 1946.

[55]   AIA, JEAC, "Conf. 1947," Sub–Del. JEAC, Beira, António Mira Mendes to Chefe da Dele. da JEAC, 20 December 1947.

[56]   Ibid.

was expressed. The labor boycott at Búzi is a case in point. It was probably strategically safer for the women to strike than for men, for however brutally colonial
authorities abused individual women, defiant black men brought out their fury.
Conversely, while there are numerous oral accounts and colonial reports of entire
families fleeing from the cotton regime, the most common phenomenon seems to
have been for men to desert alone. Only in the south, where more off-farm employment possibilities existed (particularly in and around Lourenço Marques), did
women flee without their families in significant numbers. In part, this gendered
response reflects the fact that once free and across international borders, men enjoyed better possibilities of finding work. Moreover, men probably had, or thought
they had, a better chance of surviving the rigors and dangers of clandestine flight.
In southern Mozambique, the social expectation that all "men" migrated at some
time in their lives had deep historical roots and increased their propensity to flee.[57]
On the other hand, with stronger household ties and responsibilities, women were
less mobile. A similar argument holds in the case of elders. When all other things,
such as geographic proximity to the frontier, were equal, the rate of defection from
the colony was probably highest among younger men.

Two contradictory tendencies emerge from an examination of how these
struggles were waged over time. On the one hand, virtually all the broad categories of peasant resistance mentioned above were reported throughout the entire
period of the cotton regime, although it is impossible to determine quantitative
changes from one year to another. On the other hand, certain kinds of resistance
were easier to stamp out. Conspicuously absent from the records of the 1950s are
examples of entire communities openly defying the regime by refusing to accept
cotton obligations or to plant the seeds. Moreover, most of the cooking of cotton
seeds seems to have occurred shortly after the system was imposed. Thus, it appears that as the state and concessionary companies consolidated their power, they
were able to contain or eliminate many of the insurgent activities that explicitly
challenged the regime. Increased surveillance in the 1950s may also have reduced
the number of peasants deserting the cotton regime. As these options to escape or
to reject the cotton system diminished, however, disgruntled peasants placed greater
emphasis on covert tactics aimed at shielding a portion of their labor.

The data also suggest that acts of defiance against forced cotton cultivation
varied markedly by region, in a pattern that may be linked to broader features of
state power and modes of domination. Although the state-concessionary company
alliance lacked the manpower for constant surveillance, growers in the northern
districts of Cabo Delgado and Niassa probably had the greatest opportunities to
resist. Because both districts had long been considered marginal, the state apparatus was weakest there. As the administrator of Mocímboa de Praia in 1946 explained,
"The impact of the concessionary company overseer is minimal since he lives fifty
kilometers from the closest cotton fields and lacks transport, as I do."[58] Throughout
Niassa and Cabo Delgado the skeletal transportation and communications infrastructure undercut social control. As late as 1958 a Cotton Board member noted
that company officials and state appointees in many parts of Cabo Delgado were

---

[57] For a discussion of these historical roots, see Harries, *Work, Culture, and Identity*, 154–60.

[58] AIA, JEAC, João Tavares de Melo, Admin. de Mocímboa de Praia, 22 February 1946.

unable to prevent peasants from abandoning their crops in the field.[59] In addition, both Niassa and Cabo Delgado had vast unpopulated areas, facilitating the establishment of maroon communities and reducing the possibility of detection.

Spatial considerations were important in the struggle over labor in at least three other respects. Regardless of district, cotton producers living at a distance from the main centers of colonial rule and from concessionary company headquarters faced less serious constraints than their counterparts living closer to the seats of power. Peasants living near international borders enjoyed an obvious advantage in terms of flight. Moreover, even within the most controlled environment, peasants could create "free social spaces" where they were able to plan collective action undetected. Evening meetings, family gatherings, work parties, and religious festivals were all potential sites for insurgent thought and action.[60]

The Struggle at the Market and the Politics of Retribution

The contest over labor was the principal terrain of rural conflict, but not the only one. Cotton producers also pursued strategies to minimize surplus extraction and to strike back at the most immediate targets of oppression. There are numerous examples of growers who adulterated the cotton they sold in response to market abuses:[61]

> Sometimes growers filled the bottom half of the sack with low-grade cotton and the top with high-quality fiber. Other times they mixed pebbles with the cotton, generally second quality, and on top of the adulterated cotton they put a small amount of prime cotton. In this way they were able to fill up more sacks and sell them for more money.[62]

Other growers inserted sand, particles of bricks, and pumpkin seeds to increase the weight. They then pounded the cotton, increasing the volume in proportion to the weight and more effectively hiding the foreign objects. In fact, authorities were aware of this method of subterfuge; but despite the severe punishments meted out to peasants who were discovered, neither the colonial regime nor the companies were able to suppress this practice.[63]

Many peasants living in frontier areas smuggled their produce across the border. Portuguese officials were unable to contain the brisk underground economy linking growers in Tete and Zambézia to markets in Southern Rhodesia and Nyasaland. Peasants willing to take the risk of cross-border smuggling in 1958, for instance, received almost a third more for their cotton.[64] This price gap was even

---

[59]   AIA, JEAC, 901, "Planos de Trabalho, 1958," Júlio Bossa, Sub–del. to Chefe de Del. de JEAC, 13 May 1958.

[60]   Interview with Amélia Macuácua, Chibuto, 10 February 1979.

[61]   AHM, SR, Cx. 92, ISANI, "Relatório . . . Cabo Delgado," Amadeu Pacheco de Amorim, 27 February 1962.

[62]   Interview with João Manuel Moreno, Nampula, 28 December 1978; confirmed in interview with Manuel Alves Salvador.

[63]   Group interviews, CV Luís Carlos Prestes; Macomia; interviews with Manuel Alves Saldanha; Manuel Sitói et al.; Makwati Simba et al.; Romeu Mataquenha et al.

[64]   AIA, JEAC, Gastão de Melo Furtado to Gov. Ger., 11 April 1948.

larger before the reforms of the 1950s. A number of peasants in the far north pursued a similar strategy, illegally selling their cotton in Tanganyika. They returned home with cloth and other consumer goods purchased at prices well below those found in the Mozambican countryside. Still other disenchanted growers robbed company warehouses and resold their goods at interior markets.[65]

The threat of punishment no doubt increased the reluctance of growers openly to challenge the way cotton market transactions were structured. From the earliest days of the cotton regime, however, there were moments when threats of reprisal were unable to contain public displays of peasants' rage. Reacting to the 1938 decision to reduce cotton prices, rural producers in João Belo withheld tons of cotton from the market. At a public meeting in Gaza a wealthy *machambeiro* boldly confronted the local administrator. He declared, "'All this business of cotton is a big hoax and I don't know why the senior administrator tells the Africans to cultivate cotton when the Portuguese government does not have the money to pay for it.'"[66] Similarly, after SAGAL introduced a two-tiered pricing system in 1941, growers in Montepeuz "refused to sell [cotton], preferring to burn it or throw it away."[67] Five years later an inspector visiting Mutarara in Zambézia found that growers "claiming to be exploited by the concessionaire . . . are in open revolt, burning or scattering their cotton or simply throwing it in the river rather than bringing it to the market."[68]

Although such boycotts rarely worked, they did call attention to market abuses that colonial officials were belatedly forced to acknowledge. Despite state efforts to rationalize the cotton system, as late as 1958 there were reports of peasants in the far north withholding their cotton after learning that SAGAL was not paying the same price as other concessionary companies.[69] In the same year in the southern region of Guijá, hundreds of peasants held a public meeting to protest the low prices the Sul do Save Cotton Company had offered. At this meeting, organized by such prominent *machambeiros* as Gabriel Mucave, Paulo Chongo, and Simone Sitói, many growers denounced exploitative market practices and resolved "not to sell the cotton until the authorities agreed to raise the prices." A *capataz* named Barboza who was present at the meeting fetched a weapon and attempted to intimidate the protesters. Ultimately, the colonial administrator arrived and, after much heated debate, agreed that in the following year base cotton prices would be increased from three to four *escudos*.[70]

There were other moments when growers lashed out physically at the most immediate structures and symbols of oppression. Like other insurgents acts, the politics of retribution were most often clandestine. Peasants in Macomia told how they ambushed a particularly brutal *sipai* named Vanuma as he was riding his bike along a dirt path, beating him with their hoes and fists. Unfortunately for his as-

[65]   AHM, SR, Cx. 92, "Relatório . . . Cabo Delgado," Amadeu Pacheco de Amorim, 27 February 1962; AIA, JEAC, "Papéis Diversos," C. Pedro Carvalho, Reg. Ag. ao Dir. de CICA, 9 January 1958.

[66]   AIA, JEAC, "Papéis Diversos: Despachos," Chefe do Sub–Del. do Sul do Save, 12 June 1940.

[67]   AIA, JEAC, "Conf. 1941: Rel. Esp. Sobre Mercados," António de Freitas Silva, Reg. Ag., n.d.

[68]   AIA, JEAC, "Prov. de Manica e Sofala," João Contreiras, Insp. dos SAU, May 1945.

[69]   AIA, JEAC, 901, "Planos de Trabalho, 1958," Júlio Bossa, Sub–Del. to Chefe da Del. da JEAC, 13 May 1958.

[70]   Interview with Simone Sitói, Guijá, 16 February 1979.

sailants, Vanuma survived and subsequently identified them.[71] By contrast, in nearby Montepuez such attacks "were initiated by irate individuals and were never anything more organized because we knew that the Portuguese would kill all the perpetrators."[72] Across the colony peasants remembered such isolated incidents against African police who abused women, robbed food, or just pushed them one time too many.[73]

These acts of retribution, as well as the previous examples of smuggling, tampering, and thievery, raise the vexing problem of distinguishing between crime and social protest in agrarian societies, a subject that has stimulated spirited debated among scholars.[74] Viewed from the perspective of most cotton growers, these actions were appropriate behaviors aimed at alleviating suffering, as well as legitimate expressions of dissent. When successfully carried out, such acts of defiance rarely left a paper trail for either contemporary officials or future historians to follow.

The Struggle Over Meaning

Just as hidden forms of protest may have neutralized some of the worst material abuses of the cotton regime, cultural acts produced and performed in rural communities both challenged colonial representations of reality and helped negate the daily insults and humiliations that cotton growers experienced.[75] These symbolic acts were not mere safety valves, substitutes for real resistance: they helped sustain and give meaning to insurgent behavior and represented a tradition of resistance that antedated the cotton scheme (and in many cases the colonial regime itself).

Peasant songs, proverbs, mockery, and dances were the principal uncensored avenues of public dissatisfaction during the colonial period. They were both an alternative to and a negation of the ideology that the state and its allies sought to transmit through an array of dominant cultural institutions and practices, such as the *banjas* and state-organized village meetings and cotton fairs.[76] As such, these cultural expressions were never a "language apart," but were always in political dialogue with the rituals and ceremonies the Portuguese state and their allies used to legitimate the cotton scheme.

---

[71]   Interview with Maulana Samate et al., Balama, 23 July 1979.

[72]   Interview with Pruan Hassan et al.

[73]   Ibid.; interviews with Arridhi Mahanda et al., Balama, 23 July 1979; Eugénio Niquaria; Romeu Mataquenha et al.; Benjamin Mavunja, Chibuto, 12 February 1979.

[74]   For the classic formulation of social banditry, see Eric Hobsbawm, *Bandits* (New York, 1969). For a critique of Hobsbawm's thesis, see Anton Blok, "The Peasant and the Brigand: Social Banditry Reconsidered," *CSSH* 14(1972), 494–503; L. Lewin, "The Oligarchical Limitations of Social Banditry in Brazil: The Case of the 'Good' Thief, António Silvino," *Past and Present* 82(1979), 116–46.

[75]   Symbolic defiance and material forms of resistance possess the same logic, as James Scott (*Domination and the Arts of Resistance*, 183–201) reminds us. They are part of a set of mutually reinforcing practices designed to mitigate or thwart exploitation.

[76]   For a comparison with the cotton regime in Zaire, see Likaka, "Forced Cotton Cultivation." The Portuguese were less adroit than their Belgian counterparts, who developed films, comic books, pamphlets, and plays to convince the subordinated population of the merits of cotton.

In Zambézia men and women had performed songs and parodies mocking labor recruiters and tax recruiters long before the imposition of cotton.[77] The inhumanity of the overseers, the brutality of *chibalo*, and the disruptions of labor migration reverberated through the dances, music, and poetry of dominated groups in southern Mozambique going back to the beginning of the century.[78]

Inside the cotton regime, work songs were the most common expression of rural cultural opposition. Peasants sang them in the fields, along the dirt roads leading to the cotton markets, and in their villages, social spaces usually free from surveillance where growers discovered their shared experiences of oppression and humiliation. Since work songs were sung in local languages and drew on local cultural symbols and metaphors, they were of little interest and often unintelligible to the colonial officials who overheard them. One elder recalled the delight in ridiculing administrators to their face: "They did not have any idea about the meaning. They did not know that we were criticizing them."[79] Loyalist chiefs, African *sipais*, and colonial authorities who understood the local language seem to have disregarded the mocking tone of the songs and discounted their subversive potential.[80] Fátima Konkonko of Pemba recalled:

> As long as the chief found me and the other women working in our cotton they did not stop or pay attention to what we were singing. If he heard afterwards that the wife of so-and-so was grumbling or ridiculing him he might order her to his compound and beat her or might just say "I heard it from afar but it was not worth stopping to deal with it."[81]

At the same time, producers reserved their most explicitly subversive expressions for those locations and moments when they were certain of their privacy.[82]

There was a whole genre of songs ridiculing cotton officials, demystifying their power, and rejecting their paternalistic claims. In performing these songs, both the singers and their audience turned the world of the cotton regime upside down, reversing the existing social order. In their pathbreaking study of the underground culture of Sena Sugar, Leroy Vail and Landeg White describe a typical performance:

> [The song] begins with the women standing in a circle, eyes fixed on the ground, bending forward from the waist and clapping or clacking pieces of wood or shaking tin *machacha* as accompaniment to the lead

---

[77]   See Vail and White, *Capitalism and Colonialism*, 340–66.

[78]   See "A Voz de Mineiro," *Estudos Moçambicanos* 1(1980), 77–90; First, *Black Gold*, 162–66; Penvenne, *African Workers*; Harries, *Work, Culture, and Identity*, 154–60; Junod, *Life of a South African Tribe*, 284.

[79]   Interview with Gonçalo Mazungane Chilundo, Maputo, 8–9 August 1991.

[80]   Otto Roesch reports that in the forced rice–producing zones of the Limpopo Valley, peasants working in the paddies would sing the most insulting songs about overseers, *sipais*, and administrators, even in their presence without retribution. These insults were part of the give–and–take built into the labor process (Otto Roesch, personal communication, 25 January 1994). In much the same vein, Vail and White argue that the labor overseers knew that the growers would work harder having insulted them and therefore just shrugged off the insults. Thus the work songs were a kind of protected speech. Leroy Vail and Landeg White, *Power and the Praise Poem* (Charlottesville, 1991), 221.

[81]   Interview with Fátima Konkonko.

[82]   Interviews with Amélia Macuácua; Pruan Hassan et al.; Romeu Mataquenha et al.

singer and the response. Then, one at a time, they perform solo dances.
. . . After several verses, however, the song breaks off while the drama
is performed, enacting its main theme. This happens most frequently
in songs which satirize particular individuals—a policeman, a cotton
overseer, a *chefe de posto*. The stage is the circle of singers which remains unbroken, and anyone, it seems, can perform, the actors frequently being replaced half-way through by women who feel they can
do better. The audience consists of the remaining women, who scream
with laughter at the caricature of bribery, and beatings and rape.[83]

To the north in Balama, peasants toiling in their fields anticipated the arrival of the
overseers with the following refrain:

> This monkey is stopping here, why?
> He is stopping here because he has nothing else to do.[84]

And in the cotton warehouses of Montepuez, growers mocked the *capataz* by singing behind his back:

> Look, look over there.
> Look at that guy.
> He is stopped over there scratching his penis.[85]

In the growers' repertoire were a number of songs implicitly challenging the
colonial representation of the cotton regime as a benign modernizing institution.
Performers offered a much harsher view that captured the suffering they and their
families experienced. Southern peasants walking to their cotton fields in the early
morning repeatedly chanted the following refrain as if to remind themselves of the
perils that lay ahead:

> You have to flee, men, because the *capataz* is coming.
> Flee men, flee women, the man of cotton is coming.[86]

Their neighbors in Chibuto were no less adamant about the brutal nature of
the system. Marching in long lines to distant markets with fifty-kilogram sacks of
cotton on their heads, they chanted:

> We worked and were paid nothing
> We were forced to work in the fields
> We carried cotton on our head
> We were seized and we cried
> We were beaten in this land
> Lopes beat us.[87]

Many of these work songs stressed that the problem was not the cotton but
the larger colonial order that exploited women and men alike. Women in the Gaza
district lamented the absence of their husbands forced to go to the South African
mines:

---

[83] Vail and White, *Capitalism and Colonialism*, 344.

[84] Interview with Maulana Samate et al.

[85] Interview with Adelina Cedo and Andre Marques da Pinha, Montepuez, 21 July 1979.

[86] Interview with Makwati Simba et al.

[87] Interview with Benjamin Mavunja.

Leader: Hei! you [fellow women], my energy is wasted,
Chorus: My energy is wasted; it is wasted.
Leader: When I build a home,
Chorus: My energy is wasted; it is wasted.
Leader: When I plaster the hut,
Chorus: My energy is wasted; it is wasted.
Leader: When I cultivate the fields,
Chorus: My energy is wasted; it is wasted.
Leader: He has deserted me.
Chorus: My energy is wasted; it is wasted.

At the end of this song a woman who had experienced this pain steps forward and declares, "Your husband has not deserted you [on purpose]. It is the white men who are responsible for this."[88] Although women in Zambézia lived in a different colonial context than their southern counterparts, they were united by their common position within the cotton regime and by the fact that more often than not their husbands were also gone from home. It is therefore not surprising that these women shared the same critique of the social order in which they found themselves:

I cultivate my cotton,
  I suffer, my heart is weeping
Picking, picking up a whole basketful
  I suffer, my heart is weeping
I've taken it to the Boma there
  I suffer, my heart is weeping
They've give me five *escudos*
  I suffer, my heart is weeping
When I reflect on all this
  Oyi-ya-e-e
I suffer, I do
  I suffer my heart is weeping.[89]

Some song performances adopted an even more militant posture. In Inhambane, cotton producers defiantly declared "Hikarate"—"we are fed up":

We are fed up from suffering under the Portuguese
We are being tortured by cotton
We are fed up from suffering under the Portuguese.[90]

This spirit of defiance was fostered in the numerous renditions of heroic acts against the cotton regime that were transmitted in conversation, gossip, rumor, and more formalized oral traditions. Actual acts of resistance were incorporated into the insurgent ideology. The audience for these renditions often extended across regions, ethnic groups, and generations. Numerous elders referred with pride to the men and women who had cooked cotton seeds.[91] They often spoke with admiration for cotton growers far removed from them who had successfully defied the

---

[88]   Quoted in First, *Black Gold*, 164.

[89]   Quoted in Vail and White, *Capitalism and Colonialism*, 352–53.

[90]   Interview with Gonçalo Mazungane Chilundo, 8–9 August 1991.

[91]   Interviews with Manuel Alves Saldanha; Manuel Sitói et al.; Makwati Simba et al.; Romeu Mataquenha et al.; group interviews, Macomia; CV Luís Carlos Prestes.

system. Many former cotton growers remembered hearing about compatriots who had organized maroon communities, tampered with the gunny sacks, or attacked particularly brutal overseers and *sipais*. The children and grandchildren of cotton growers recite stories of these exploits as well. That these insurgent traditions, real or apocryphal, endured as living texts testifies to how deeply they were inscribed in the collective memory.

Sculpture was also an effective medium for depicting the dual themes of misery and ridicule that pervaded popular impressions of the cotton regime. The despair of an anguished female cotton producer, holding her head in her hand, was a common motif of Makonde art. Skeletal figures obviously suffering from hunger or Africans with their hands and legs bound are a variation on this theme. As Edward Alpers has noted, the distorted features of an African *sipai* represent his lack of humanity, and his exposed penis ridicules him just as clearly as the epigrammatic refrain about the overseer in Montepuez or the song of the infamous "Paiva" of Sena Sugar fame.[92] The sculpture carved by Makonde artists, who always remained close to their peasant roots, reflected anger born of hunger.[93]

The creation of an opposition culture was an important political act. By singing, acting, carving, or speaking their own histories, peasants taught one another new ways of thinking about themselves and their world. Defiance of the dominant culture was an act of empowerment and often heightened peasant opposition, which in turn influenced their consciousness. Similarly, successful acts of defiance provided heroic episodes from which peasants could construct an oppositional ideology. There was a profound relationship between dissident thought and dissident action and between the hidden forms of protest and the hidden transcripts of the oppressed.

Internal Dissent:
Conflict Within Cotton-Growing Communities

Peasant opposition to the state-concessionary alliance was one dimension of rural conflict. A less visible and less documented struggle took place within rural communities and households. This struggle, too, was directly linked to the uneven impact of the cotton regime. As discussed in Chapter 8, the cotton regime accentuated competition and division between chiefs and their subjects, between wealthier and poorer peasants, between creditors and debtors, between women and men, and between young and old. These conflicts, which occurred within communities and within households, greatly exacerbated rivalries and tensions that often antedated the era of forced cotton cultivation.

The most pronounced ruptures occurred between chiefs and their subordinate populations. This is hardly surprising, given the contradictory roles chiefs were expected to play. To the state, they were paid functionaries, but to their

---

[92]   Edward Alpers, "The Role of Culture in the Liberation of Mozambique," *Ufahamu* 12(1983), 166; Vail and White, *Capitalism and Colonialism*, 340–43.

[93]   Much of this protest art surfaced after the liberation struggle began in 1962. Iinterviews with Wussa Maliwa, Sene Nampade, and Charles Malaya, Mueda, 31 July 1979; Nanelo Ntuamunu et al., CV Muila, Mueda, 1 August 1979.

subjects they were guardians of community resources and tradition. Both sides sought their services as mediators. Few could do both tasks successfully. Because the colonial state and the cotton interests were spread so thin on the ground, chiefs were called on to play a decisive role in restructuring rural production. And even as their subjects were becoming increasingly impoverished, most chiefs prospered.

Even strong hereditary chiefs co-opted by the colonial administration had little room to negotiate within the strictures of state power. As a result, their ability to command loyalty and to govern by consensus declined. Chiefs had to make judicious calculations about when to enforce cotton policies and when to speak out against them. Each decision carried an obvious cost. However much some may have wished to straddle, most chiefs usually opted to enforce cotton requirements. They understood that collaboration on their part was a fact of colonial life and that there were many obvious benefits they could reap from collaboration.

Regardless of their privileged position or of the enhanced state of their own material lives, chiefslived and worked in an atmosphere both tenuous and ambiguous. The arrogant and capricious behavior of their European superiors, as well as of the local police and state overseers, regularly subjected them to humiliation and reminded them that they too were Africans. Many chiefs were harangued and abused by frustrated administrators and overseers because their subjects had not fulfilled their cotton obligations. Elders in Chibuto in southern Mozambique recalled the shame experienced by Chief Masheleni: "He was beaten with a *palmatória* in public in front of all the people. The *régulo* may not be publicly punished. That is why he killed himself when he heard that the administrator was looking for him again."[94] Others such as Régulo Muico of Balama and Régulo Cuamba of Niassa fled to avoid retribution from angry colonial authorities.[95]

The tenuous and shifting nature of the chiefs' relationship with the colonial regime created similar uncertainty in chiefs' relationships with their subjects. As local government representatives, they had the power to protect their closest followers. Although their patronage and authority were limited, most could determine who was exempt from forced labor, who received the choicest cotton lands, and who benefited from the technical assistance and agricultural implements that the state and companies periodically provided. As state functionaries, chiefs could also raise issues of more general concern to the peasantry. Annual *banjas* with local administrators provided a forum for chiefs to speak out on behalf of their communities. Many complained of price-gouging by local merchants, land thefts by settlers, and abuses by *sipais*. Some even criticized the cotton regime. At one such meeting in Nampula, a state inspector recorded that "*régulos* in Namapa and Naracôa protested vehemently against the company overseers whom they accused of perpetrating all types of extortions."[96] At another gathering in Cabo Delgado, Chief Chava criticized SAGAL, the local cotton concessionary company, and the colonial administration for failing to provide the promised technical assistance.[97] On occasion some chiefs even conspired with their subjects to circumvent state

[94] Group interview, Serra Nkanyavane.

[95] Interviews with Pruan Hassan et al.; Arridhi Mahanda et al.

[96] AHM, SR, Cx. 77, ISANI, "Relatório . . . Eráti, vol. 3," Hortêncio Estevão de Sousa, 1948.

[97] AIA, JEAC, "Conf. 1957–1959," A. Costa Mesquita, 22 February 1958.

cotton requirements. Portuguese officials complained in 1949 that Chief Corvetta of Inquinjir in northern Mozambique was so opposed to the cotton regime that he refused to oversee production.[98] Régulo Muhano of Mogincual was more creative. He informed authorities that once he had received the appropriate medicines from the ancestors to protect his subjects, cotton production would commence.[99] A few chiefs even organized seed-cooking operations.[100] These examples notwithstanding, most chiefs enforced the cotton scheme.

To the extent that chiefs were perceived as the vacillating, untrustworthy executors of an exploitative colonial policy, they often became the focal point of rural discontent. As is true of language in any fluid context, meanings shift over time, and throughout the colony the very meaning of the term *régulo* was transformed during the cotton regime from a title of veneration to one of contempt. "You, Chuquela, you are proud of your position," southern Mozambican peasants mockingly challenged, reminding this *régulo* that "you are only a chief made by the white man."[101] Women in Zambézia also expressed their hatred through song, while begrudgingly acknowledging the *régulo*'s power:

> You can do it, you can do it, you can do it . . .
> You can find the chief and beat him up
> You can do it, but the chief is a powerful man.[102]

Disdain for chiefs similarly permeates Luis Polanah's fictional portrait of daily life in Inhambane during the cotton regime. At one critical meeting where the *régulo* implored his subjects to work harder because "cotton is the wealth of this land," some "peasants sitting in the front row could be heard muttering, 'What insolence, I swear! Does he think he is talking to milk-drinking children?. . . This is all suckling talk.'"[103]

Occasionally this grumbling against the *régulos* erupted into open conflict. The son of Régulo Nequina of Montepeuz recalled that a peasant had beaten Nequina after the latter had raped the peasant's wife in the cotton fields.[104] In the adjacent districts of Imala and Mossuril, the local population rose up against despotic chiefs, while in Gilé they colluded with members of the traditional royal family to poison the state-appointed chief.[105]

Subtle threats and pressure against the *régulos* were often more effective and certainly less risky than overt violence. Although their disguised nature makes it difficult to gauge their regularity, evidence from diverse cotton zones suggests that chiefs were often highly susceptible to certain types of pressure. Witchcraft accusations discouraged several *régulos* in Nampula, Manica, and Sofala from overseeing

---

[98]   AIA, JEAC, 952, "BT de Cabo Delgado," J. Casta Rosa, 13 March 1949.

[99]   AIA, JEAC, 948, "Conf. 1944–46," João Leal Dias de Deus, Chefe de Posto to Dir. dos Serv. da Admin. de Niassa, Nampula, 11 December 1946.

[100] Interviews with Amélia Macuácua; Leonardo Fatima Madime.

[101] Hugh Tracey, *Chopi Musicians* (London, 1948), 68.

[102] Vail and White, "Forms of Resistance," 894.

[103] Polanah, *Saga of a Cotton Capulana*, 62–63.

[104] Interview with Eugénio Niquaria.

[105] José Alberto Gomes de Melo Branquinho, *Prospecção das Forças Tradicionais* (Lourenço Marques, 1959), 197, 202; group interview, Gilé, 7–8 July 1976 (Head Collection).

cotton production.[106] A 1947 confidential memorandum reported that in parts of Sofala, charges of sorcery against several chiefs resulted in a sharp decline in cotton output and that "cotton which had been cultivated was not collected and was allowed to rot on the ground."[107] In villages stretching from Gaza to Cabo Delgado, growers recounted how they pressured chiefs to cook cotton seeds or at least intimidated them sufficiently so that they would not reveal growers' ploy to colonial authorities.[108]

Finally, to the extent that growers engaged in guerrilla activity against the cotton regime, they were also attacking the very basis of the *régulos'* privileged economic position and authority. Many chiefs were removed from power because they could not maintain the appropriate degree of labor discipline and social control over their subjects. Even where indigenous elites in such situations remained in power, their prestige clearly declined. Colonial officials acknowledged that Régulo Camuana of Montepuez had suffered a humiliating defeat in his battle over cotton. "Not only are his subjects' cotton fields in a shameful state, but he has lost so much prestige, that, for all practical purposes, he has ceased to be *régulo*."[109] By 1961 the governor of Gaza had concluded that "the majority of the chiefs lack the capacity to fulfill their responsibilities."[110]

One indication of the chiefs' loss of legitimacy in the eyes of the peasants was the frequency with which alternative leaders stepped forward to challenge the authority of the chiefs. Displaced traditional authorities, headmen who aspired to be chiefs, and religious leaders and elders who had not been tainted by collaboration with the colonial regime often filled this power vacuum. In the words of a popular song heard in the 1940s, "You elders must discuss affairs. The one that the white man appointed was only the son of a commoner."[111] Colonial officials in the north conceded in the 1960s that twenty years after they had deposed Muhahve Tipuite, "he still remains the most powerful man within the chieftaincy."[112] Throughout the cotton period a number of religious leaders in central and northern Mozambique convinced their followers not to relocate to *concentrações* because they would alienate the ancestor spirits.[113] And at a 1957 *banja* in Gaza, several respected *machambeiros*, disgusted with the acquiescence of the *régulos*, took the lead and threatened to organize a cotton boycott if prices were not raised.[114] By the end of the cotton regime, Portuguese officials were reporting a new challenge arising to loyalists from aspiring nationalists.[115]

---

[106]   AIA, JEAC, "Conf. 1947," Dir. da CB to JEAC, 4 December 1947; Branquinho, *Prospecção*, 107.

[107]   AIA, JEAC, "Conf. 1947," Dir. da CB to JEAC, Lourenço Marques, 4 December 1947.

[108]   Interviews with Manuel Sitói et al.; Romeu Mataquenha et al.; Pruan Hassan et al.

[109]   AIA, JEAC, 952, "BT de Cabo Delgado," J. Costa Rosa, 4 April 1949.

[110]   AHM, CE, Cx. SEAV, 9, 116 (a,b), Dist. de Gaza, "Rel. do Gov., 1955–1960," Gov. Óscar Freire de Vasconcelos Ruas, 1960.

[111]   Tracey, *Chopi Musicians*, 43.

[112]   Branquinho, *Prospecção*, 49.

[113]   Ibid., 108–9; Bravo, *Cultura Algodoeira*, 80.

[114]   AIA, JEAC, "Cópia Geral de Notas Conf. 1958–59," Montolvão Marques, Eng. Ag., to Chefe da Del. da JEAC, n.d.

[115]   Branquinho, *Prospecção*.

As a nationalist vision began to sweep through the colony, many rural Mozambicans felt empowered. Gabriel Mucave's autobiographical account illuminates how angry peasants were sometimes unexpectedly thrust into positions of authority, bypassing timid chiefs. Mukave, a prosperous and influential farmer, recalled:

> In 1947 the Padres took our children and made them work on the fields of the church producing cotton. I was the one who started the ball rolling. I decided to consult with the elders of Hlomani. The first idea was to withhold the hoes, to refuse to give our own hoes to the children as the Padres demanded. We approached the chiefs, but they feared the consequence of such actions. This was the beginning of my political activities.[116]

Years later, after an administrator accused Mucave of being a "communist agitator" and threatened to imprison him, Mucave defiantly proclaimed that "there is no room for you Portuguese in Mozambique." The administrator agreed to hear their complaints and to initiate some minor reforms.

Viewed from a slightly different angle, the challenge to the chiefs from the *machambeiros* may have been more than just a struggle between the spokesmen of the oppressed and loyalists. At another level it probably represented a contest between two segments of a developing rural bourgeoisie for control over power and influence in the countryside. The decision of the leaders of the Mozambique African Voluntary Cotton Society to prohibit northern chiefs from joining their organization represents part of a broader struggle over who would lead the peasants. As a result of the economic reforms, a small but growing number of prosperous African farmers and merchants emerged. There are suggestions in the literature that these disparities in wealth were beginning to assume increased social and political significance.[117] To what extent these growing distinctions produced visible conflict remains an open question. My impression is that these tensions existed, simmering well below the surface, but were masked by a shared sense of racial oppression and a growing nationalist sentiment that united most Africans in their opposition to the Portuguese.

The cotton regime also transformed relations between male and female peasants and between generations living within the same household. In a multitude of different and at times contradictory ways, representatives of the colonial state, the concessionary companies, missionaries, and African elders tried to forge a new social order in which chosen men were the principal public actors and women were reduced to a subordinate position within the invisible domestic world. After all, it was official state policy to deny women the possibility of becoming independent *agricultores* and gaining access to critical resources. It was the cotton regime that

---

[116] Interview with Gabriel Mucave, Guijá, 20 February 1979. The broad outlines were subsequently confirmed in the interview with Simone Sitói.

[117] The decision of relatively affluent southern farmers to impose restrictive entrance fees on Africans seeking to join cooperatives is a case in point, as is the competition for land in the fertile Limpopo Valley. And in the northern Mueda highlands in the late 1950s, for the first time, rights of usufruct gave way to private property. Throughout the colony, prosperous Africans employed their impoverished neighbors at salaries well below the wages Europeans paid.

privileged the male-dominated rural household as the basic economic and social unit and reinforced men's power by making payments directly to them whenever possible.

Frustration and marital discord escalated quickly in households at risk, where women were denied control over productive resources but were increasingly expected to assume the burden of managing the rural economy. This tension was reflected in the words of Miriam Paulo:

> We did the work. And at the cotton market we received the money. But our husbands controlled the money. When our husbands were in South Africa we had to guard the money until they returned and then we would present it to them. They could do whatever they wanted with it. If they gave us some money to buy cloth, we would buy cloth. If not, we wouldn't, because it was our husbands who controlled the money.[118]

Elderly women in central and northern Mozambique told a similar story:

> Together with our husbands we carried the cotton to market. Because our husbands were the ones registered, they received the money. When we returned home they showed it to us. The next day we took our children and went to the shop to buy clothing, wine, and a few other things. Our husbands asked us what we needed but it was they who decided what was bought. If we were unhappy, we could complain, but there was nothing we could do.[119]

The lack of control over disposable income often precipitated intense competition within polygamous households. Many of these households, which benefited from labor-sharing arrangements, became a site of struggle between wives competing for access to these resources.[120] Fátima Spaneke and her neighbors in Nampula stressed that it was common "for men to use the cotton income to buy cloth and other goods for their senior wives, and their other wives suffered."[121] In the patrilineal south there is some evidence that struggles over scarce resources pitted daughters-in-law against mothers-in-law; this suggests that intrafemale struggle is an issue that requires greater attention.[122]

Although oral accounts tend to emphasize the dependency and vulnerability of women, the capacity of male household heads to direct and control family labor and other valued resources should not be taken for granted. Fragmentary evidence suggests that many peasant women were able to shield some resources from appropriation by male household heads. The covert strategies women adopted were often similar to those peasants employed against the cotton regime. The "weapons of the weak" could be turned inward.

To protect their meager cotton incomes from grasping husbands, women often hid or withheld a portion of their agricultural earnings. Maria Fijamo, who lived in Zambézia, told the story of a woman in her village whose

---

[118] Interview with Miriam Paulo, Maputo, 16 May 1987.

[119] Interview with Fátima Spaneke et al., Nampula, 28 May 1987.

[120] Interviews with Fátima Konkonko; Murinvona Mpemo, Centro Piloto de Deslocados, Nampula/Gilé, 9 July 1991; Adelina Penicela.

[121] Interviews with Fátima Spaneke et al.; Adelina Penicela.

[122] I am grateful to Jeanne Penvenne for this information.

husband refused to work in the fields or on the plantations with the other men. He just remained in the house and did nothing. The woman worked the cotton fields together with her children. Neighbors helped. After the harvest her husband demanded the money and spent it all. From then on she hid all her products at her parents' home far from his reach. Occasionally when he asked she would say that the only thing she had was a small amount of food that her parents gave her and the children. She told him this for several years all the while continuing this diversion.[123]

Such accounts of dissimulation were not uncommon[124] and at least raise the possibility of an alternative to the plight that many rural women experienced. Tactics such as these were, no doubt, most common in situations where men were away for longer period of time, particularly on mining contracts in South Africa.

Subterfuge was not the only way to shield hard-earned income. Some women willing to challenge prescribed patterns of behavior questioned the presumed preeminence of their spouses. Murinvona Mpemo laughed as she recalled her own domestic struggle, precipitated by her husband's violation of the conjugal contract:

My husband went to the [sugar plantations at Luabo] and I remained and cultivated cotton, which I sold. When he returned we put our money together. But my husband began to spend it all on drink. Then I decided I would withhold my money. I discussed this with my uncle and my family. My husband was furious. But for three years I refused to give him the cotton money because he wanted to spend it on alcohol. After three years he agreed to stop drinking and I agreed to combine our funds once more.[125]

The women in both these oral accounts came from matrilineal societies. The fact that they resided in the same village as their kinsmen made it easier to enlist their support. This was not as easy an option for wives in the patrilineal south, who typically lived in their husbands' communities and whose marriage had been sealed by sizable bridewealth payments.

On the other hand, there is much more evidence of southern women fleeing the intensified pressures within their households. They had several relatively limited options. Women could buy their way out of an unhappy marriage, seek refugee at missionary stations, flee with a lover who might ultimately become a new husband, or clandestinely migrate to the capital city. Rural women liberated from their households often found their new setting as precarious as their old. According to Adelina Penicela,

Many women ran away just like their husbands. They too were tired of suffering. So they decided that the only alternative was to abandon their home and come here to Lourenço Marques. Some worked in the cashew factories. Others rented rooms and turned them into a place where men go to have pleasures.[126]

---

[123] Interview with Maria Fijamo, Quelimane, 19 July 1991.

[124] Interviews with Maria Aguiar and Comalia Niuquanha, Nampula, 11 July 1991; Rosa Maria Ernesto, Nampula, 11 July 1991.

[125] Interview with Murinvoma Mpemo.

[126] Interview with Adelina Penicela.

Fear of the unknown, access to only a few low-paying jobs, and the humiliation often associated with prostitution were not sufficient to deter strong-willed women who were unwilling to tolerate the rural status quo:

> When the men returned home, normally they found that their wives had saved some money. Not that it was easy to save money; it was difficult. But because we did not have to buy food the only things we had to purchase were soap, cooking oil, matches, and kerosene. The men took the money and went to the *cantina*. Some used it to drink rather than to buy goods for the family. When they returned home drunk, they beat their wives. Those women who did not have patience and were unwilling to tolerate such behavior fled to Lourenço Marques. It was not easy to find a job, but many managed to survive.[127]

Often the runaways saved their earnings to repay the bridewealth provided for them and to free themselves and their families from any future obligations.[128] One disgruntled man, however, explained this phenomenon quite differently:

> The home is destroyed. There are many now who have divorced because the women have gone to work to repay the *lobolo* [bridewealth]. These women do not know that a woman is meant to be married and to die with her husband. We, the husband, are those who know how a woman should work.[129]

But whether their quest for freedom was the result of the tyranny of the cotton regime, the excessive demands of their husbands, the emotional strain of a long physical separation, a newfound sense of self-confidence, or some combination of these factors, there is no doubt that many southern women escaped to Lourenço Marques.[130] There is also evidence that a number fled to South Africa in the 1950s, drawn there by higher wages and earning possibilities.[131]

Although there were far fewer opportunities for employment in the towns and port cities to the north, a small number of northern women are reported to have fled to Nampula, Quelimane, Nacala, and Pemba.[132] According to Rosa Ernesto from Nampula, "many women were tired of cotton and tired of being beaten by their husbands in disputes over cotton money and alcohol. They fled to Nacala, Nampula, and other places."[133] Other disenchanted wives preferred to seek refuge with nearby maternal relatives, increasing tensions within rural communities. The flight of women aroused fierce opposition among chiefs, male elders, and state officials, who often acted in unison to contain it. That male elders joined forces with colonial authorities to close off this option suggests the potential female flight had to

---

[127]   Interview with Celeste Cossa, Amélia Novana, and Regina Mate, Maputo, 31 July 1991.

[128]   Interviews with Adelina Penicela; Bishop João Somane Machado, Maputo, 10 May 1987; group interview, CV Paulo Samuel Kankhomba, Massingire, 7 February 1979.

[129]   Quoted in Young, "Women in Transition," 15.

[130]   See Penvenne, *African Workers.*

[131]   Arlindo Chilundo recalls that for "personal reasons" his grandmother, Latina Nhamsue, left Zavala and spent five years in South Africa (personal communication, 12 April 1994).

[132]   Interview with Rosa Maria Ernesto; interview with Paulo José Manuel, José Pacial, and Manuel Paquelque, Nampula, 10 July 1991.

[133]   Interview with Rosa Maria Ernesto.

undermine the rural social order.[134] At such times, race and class differences gave way to a shared notion of gender hierarchies.

The large majority of rural women, who for whatever reasons elected to remain inside the cotton regime, did not give up struggling against the worst aspects of the system. Given the conditions of inequality within which they operated, it seems only natural that women would resist efforts to restructure the labor process in ways that would lengthen their working hours, increase their individual burdens, reduce their access to critical resources, and intensify food shortages. Like other peasants, women's principal weapon was their control over their own labor power. Many of the covert forms of resistance, when viewed from this perspective, can be seen as directed not solely against the cotton regime but also against male elders who controlled the cotton income that women worked so hard to produce.[135]

This type of reactive power, though difficult to document, had important consequences for both the political economy of cotton and for the social reproduction of rural households. It also helped to sustain a spirit of defiance that was captured in some of the songs southern women sang as they worked their fields and as they danced the *makhara*:[136]

> Thinking of cotton and swamp (rice)
> My husband, let us move away, but you refuse
> Thinking of cotton and swamp (rice)
> My husband, let us move, but you refuse[137]

The meaning of this song is clear. It was women who experienced the hardships of forced cultivation, while their husbands were basically content to work in South Africa and return home periodically to collect the cotton money.

Many young men also resisted the efforts of elders to control their labor. In the southern part of the country, young men had the option of migrating to South Africa as well as the possibility of working in Lourenço Marques or on Portuguese estates and farms. Many disaffected teenagers fled clandestinely, although it is not always clear whether they were escaping repressive colonial policies, oppressive household conditions, or some combination of both.[138] For others it was simply the lure of the city. In central and northern Mozambique the situation was more complicated. Because there were appreciably fewer opportunities for wage employment in these regions, labor flight as a means of escape was more problematic.[139]

---

[134] Interview with Maria Fijamo; AHM, Cx. 26, ISANI, "Relatório . . . Guijá," António Policarpo de Sousa Santos, Insp. Admin., 12 March 1957; AHM, Cx. 28, ISANI, "Relatório . . . Muchopes," António Policarpo de Sousa Santos, Insp. Admin., December 1957; AHM, SR, Cx. 20, ISANI, "Relatório . . . Magude, 1953," António Policarpo de Sousa Santos, Insp. Conc. de Gaza, n.d.

[135] Fuller, "An Ethnohistoric Study," 151–52.

[136] *Makhara* is a very popular Chopi dance for both women and men. Participants dance in a circle, while clapping and singing. Often a person enters the middle of the circle to perform, while the others continue dancing.

[137] Interview with Gonçalo Mazungane Chilundo, 8–9 August 1991.

[138] Interview with Simone Sitói; interview with Gonçalo Mazungane Chilundo, 8–9 August 1991.

[139] Urban employment in administrative capitals such as Nampula and Porto Amélia was limited and wages were appreciably lower than in Lourenço Marques. According to Portuguese sources a fairly large number of young men fled from Manica e Sofala district to Rhodesia (AHM, SR, Cx. 39, ISANI, "Relatório . . . Barue, 1951," Adelino Santos Ferrão de Castel Branco, 20 August 1952.

Nevertheless, "a number of teenagers fled rather than obeying their parents," and others "escaped to avoid cotton beatings."[140] Elders agreed that young men were more likely to flee than married women and that teenage boys evaded the cotton regime more frequently than girls. Those who were fortunate found work in town as domestic laborers or gardeners. The remainder often ended up as *chibalo* work-ers,[141] a task even less desirable than growing cotton.

There is also evidence, primarily from Nampula, that in the 1950s young males began to turn the cotton regime to their own advantage. Until then northern matrilineal elders had used the institution of bride-service to secure youth labor for several years at a time, in effect creating unpaid cotton growers out of their future sons-in-law. By the time they had satisfied this labor requirement and mar-ried, most young men were already in their mid-twenties. During the last decade of the cotton regime, an increasing number rebelled against this practice. Instead of providing bride-service, they opened up their own cotton and peanut fields and planted cashew trees.[142] The availability of unused land, increased prices for cotton and other agricultural commodities, and encouragement from state authorities ea-ger to increase the number of cotton producers facilitated this strategy. One former company official stressed that it was the proliferation of planned cotton communi-ties, which teenagers over eighteen years of age could join, that created space for young men to assert their independence:

> Opening up *concentrações* and distributing land and cashew trees to young men encouraged them to relocate independently of their ex-tended families. They were freed from prior obligations and could sup-port themselves and earn a good income.[143]

By reclaiming a measure of control over their own labor, young men were often able to accumulate enough capital to marry while still teenagers and to assert their independence and moral autonomy from elders.[144] Conversely, by cutting their ties with their rural kinship networks, they lost a potential support system in times of crisis. Thus, short-term gains may have posed long-term risks.

The Significance of Peasant Resistance

This chapter portrays cotton growers as political actors enmeshed in a complex and often contradictory array of class, community, and household relationships. They struggled within a brutal regime and sacrificed in a variety of ways to help make their own histories. The boundaries within which they struggled were deter-mined by the degree of relative autonomy they had vis-à-vis the colonial state and the appropriating classes. It was this partial autonomy, unique to peasants and linked to the labor process, that helps explain why cotton growers were prone to engage in subterranean protests rather than in broader social movements. Since

---

[140] Interviews with Rosa Maria Ernesto; Margarita Pera, Nampula/Murrupula, 12 July 1991.

[141] Interview with Armando Cardoso, Nampula, 10 July 1991.

[142] Geffray and Pedersen, *Transformação*, 61–62.

[143] Interview with Faria Lobo, Nampula, 9 July 1991.

[144] Geffray and Pedersen, *Transformação*, 61–67; this process accelerated in the 1960s.

the state and the concessionary companies sought to control rather than destroy the rural population, the principal struggle—in thought as well as action—took place over the continuing definition and redefinition of the peasants' partial autonomy. This struggle was also fought within African households and communities, where the more powerful sought to control for their own benefit the labor of less powerful members.

It is important not to claim too much for these insurgent acts. At best, they produced partial victories that safeguarded or expanded the relative autonomy of the cotton growers but that rarely challenged the colonial-capitalist system of oppression. Some would even argue that these acts, which enabled the peasants to work the system to its maximum, were in effect self-defeating, since they precluded the possibility of dismantling the structures of oppression.[145]

At the same time the very real ways in which these struggles affected the daily lives and working conditions of subject peoples in colonial Mozambique or the impact they had on the cotton regime as a whole must not be minimized. Producers who fled or who successfully cooked their cotton seeds gained freedom from physical abuse and greater control over their economic lives. Similarly, ongoing peasant hostility in marginal cotton lands convinced the Cotton Board of the necessity to exempt these regions from future production.[146] The Portuguese had no alternative in frontier areas such as Niassa, Tete, and Gaza, where widespread rural discontent and desertion forced state officials to declare "free zones" in which cotton production was optional.

Even those growers who could not evade the cotton regime were often able to reduce the level of exploitation through their actions. Illegal intercropping and planting less than the minimum area helped make life more bearable. So did the myriad ways peasants managed to divert labor to food production.

These seemingly inconsequential acts by thousands of Mozambican women and men did narrow the freedom of action of the state and the concessionary companies. Their cumulative effect was to thwart, at least partially, the cotton interests that strove above all to increase the number of bonded peasants and the amount of time they devoted to cotton. Indeed a credible case could be made that state and company officials had to work within the confines of peasant resistance. Abusive policies had to be curtailed somewhat to stop short of provoking too much flight, for without peasant producers there could not be cotton. Even if none of these actions fundamentally altered the cotton system as a whole, they had a direct and significant impact on a large number of growers who carried them out. For families so vulnerable, safeguarding or preserving even one life or making it through just one more season represented a huge personal victory. Even though they did not necessarily have a broad structural impact, these acts ought not be dismissed or trivialized.

Since most acts of resistance were limited in scale and did not explicitly challenge the cotton regime, were they merely futile gestures or did they have systemic importance? Clearly, they failed to paralyze the system, since cotton exports from

---

[145] See, for example, Hobsbawm, "Peasants and Politics," *Journal of Peasant Studies* 1, 1(1973), 3–22; Ann Stoler, "Plantation Politics and Protest on Sumatra's Coast," *Journal of Peasant Studies* 13, 2(1986), 124–43.

[146] Ibid.; interview with A. Quintanilha, 7 March 1979.

Mozambique increased by 700 percent between 1938 and 1961. Nevertheless, peasant opposition was significant.

While it is fruitless to speculate about how much cotton might have been produced had the rural population fully acquiesced to Portuguese demands, there is no doubt that by withholding all or a portion of their labor, peasants substantially reduced total cotton output. The flight of thousands of peasants permanently deprived the cotton regime of critical labor, while the widespread planting of less than the minimum number of hectares further reduced potential output. The tendency of growers to circumvent the state-imposed agricultural schedule also limited total production. Peasants were aware that late planting and minimal and haphazard weeding affected cotton yields and were prepared to assume the consequences of these actions in order to increase the time they could spend in their own gardens. Similar considerations motivated growers who picked cotton rapidly or did not bother to sort it carefully. Others refused to allocate additional labor to burn the plants after the harvest, thereby jeopardizing future production. All of these factors contributed to Mozambique's low yields per hectare, apparently lower than in neighboring colonies,[147] and frustrated the concessionary companies' plans to impose a more stringent production schedule.[148] They also doomed the Salazar regime's goal of self-sufficiency for the Portuguese textile industry. This shortfall in cotton production continued throughout the 1950s, despite the much-heralded reforms. In 1959 the textile industry had to purchase 28 prcent of its cotton abroad at a cost of U.S. $101 million.[149] In short, the vast inefficiencies that were partly caused by unwilling labor were critical in undermining the cotton regime, even though the motivation of most insurgent growers was just to scrape by.

The abolition of the forced cotton concessionary regime in 1961 and the shift to a settler-based plantation system[150] testify to the tenacity and cumulative impact of peasant resistance. They also undercut the proposition that both the colonial state and capital were prepared to tolerate a certain amount of flight, sabotage, and other forms of resistance as a safety valve. In fact, neither state nor company officials could contain localized, clandestine, and highly effective protests that helped convince the powerful textile industry that a new system of production had to be introduced and that the concessionary companies were both cumbersome and unnecessary.

Rural opposition, increasingly militant, had destroyed any illusion that growers could simply be persuaded to cultivate cotton. What distinguished protests of the late 1950s from previous agitation was that they increasingly became embedded in a larger nationalist campaign aimed at expelling Portugal from Mozambique. From Lisbon's perspective, the danger of peasant insurrection was greatest in the cotton zones of northern Mozambique, particularly in Cabo Delgado, although rural dissatisfaction had become more visible throughout the colony. Cotton refugees, who had been living and working in Tanganyika, returned home in the late

---

[147] For comparative statistics during the final years of the system, when output had reached its high point, see Bravo, *Cultura Algodoeira*, 129.

[148] Interview with A. Quintanilha.

[149] Bravo, *Cultura Algodoeira*, 70.

[150] Anne Pitcher ("From Coercion to Incentive") has argued that the shift to settler production actually began in 1958.

1950s and began to sow the seeds of rural discontent. Many had joined the Makonde African National Union (MANU), a newly formed nationalist organization based in Tanganyika that called for an end both to forced labor and to Portuguese rule.[151] In 1961 several thousand northern cotton growers, mobilized by MANU militants, mounted a nonviolent demonstration in the highland Cabo Delgado town of Mueda, where they demanded political independence. Eager to quell nationalist sentiment and to prevent a repetition of such subordination, Portuguese authorities responded with unprecedented brutality—even by colonial standards. Soldiers and police gunned down six hundred unarmed African protesters. For nationalists, the Mueda massacre became living proof that the authoritarian Portuguese regime would never voluntarily renegotiate independence for its African colonies. For Lisbon, increased rural unrest underscored the threat that militant African peasants posed to its colonial order. This spirit of rural insurgency, coupled with growing international criticism of Portugal's forced labor policies, convinced the Salazar regime that it would have to make some highly visible reforms if it had any chance of holding on to its colonial territory. The controversial cotton project had to go.

---

[151] Interviews with João Bonifácio; João Cornélio Mandande. For a general discussion of MANU's nationalist activity see Mondlane, *The Struggle for Mozambique*; Alpers, "'To Seek a Better Life.'"

CONCLUSION

Forced cotton cultivation was not unique to Mozambique. Cotton was not only the premier colonial crop in Africa, it was the premier coerced crop. Although colonial cotton projects shared a number of common features, the Mozambican cotton regime stands out in three important ways.

First was its scale. Fragmentary demographic data suggest that appreciably more peasants were legally required to cultivate cotton in Mozambique than in any other colony, with the possible exception of the Belgian Congo.[1] Extant documentation indicates that in the Central African Republic, for example, the number hovered around 40,000[2] and in Malawi it never exceeded 120,000.[3] By contrast, in 1944 almost 800,000 peasants were formally registered in the Mozambican cotton regime.

The degree and intensity of state intervention also distinguishes the Mozambican scheme from other cotton projects in Africa. Across the continent production and marketing arrangements varied considerably over time, reflecting the changing realities on the ground and the capacity of colonial regimes to enforce their dictates. Virtually all, however, rested on some form of coercion in the field and control in the marketplace. Sometimes this meant forcing growers to work collectively for a limited duration on the "commandant's fields" in the Ivory Coast or on the communal plots in Uganda.[4] In the Sudan the British required tenants to grow cotton as a precondition for access to irrigated land in the Gezira scheme.[5] For their part, French officials in the Sudan imposed a system predicated on voluntary production, but controlled trade in order to stifle the indigenous cotton market and the local textile industry.[6] Rarely, however, was state intervention at the point of production or at the marketplace as total as in Mozambique, where colonial authorities selected the appropriate lands, imposed a daily work schedule, determined how often growers should perform specific tasks, and set the price at the cotton market. But Portuguese colonial authorities did even more than that. They told thousands of cotton growers where to live, when to relocate, what food crops to cultivate, and what values and behavior were necessary to become "modern" farmers.

---

[1] At its highpoint during the early 1930s the cotton regime enmeshed approximately 780,000 peasant households (personal communication with Osumaka Likaka, 20 April 1994).

[2] de Dampierre, "Coton Noire," 128–46.

[3] Personal communication with Elias Mandala, 20 April 1994.

[4] Isaacman and Roberts, *Cotton, Colonialism, and Social History.*

[5] Bernal, *Cultivating Workers.*

[6] Roberts, "The Coercion of Free Markets."

The longevity of Mozambique's forced cotton regime also sets it apart from all the others. Most colonial administrations abandoned the use of force in the 1930s and introduced an incentive-based marketing system. By contrast, Lisbon tenaciously clung to its coercive policies. For all the rhetoric of reform and the changes introduced in the late 1940s and early 1950s, the Mozambican cotton regime rested on force until the day it was abolished.

The combination of these three factors—the long duration of forced cotton cultivation in Mozambique, the extent of state intervention, and the number of growers trapped inside the system—made the devastating effects of cotton more pronounced in the Portuguese colony than anywhere else in Africa. While the roots of Mozambique's rural impoverishment can be found in the precotton colonial policy that deprived communities of thousands of migrant laborers and promoted the production of plantation crops such as sugar, sisal, copra, and tea for export, forced cotton cultivation had a far–reaching impact on the countryside. It further impoverished an already poor country and intensified the distortions in the rural economy that would carry over into the postcolonial period.

Even where it was grown under the most favorable conditions, the technical requirements of cotton made it a demanding and risky crop. The specific structure of the Mozambican cotton regime, predicated on shifting the risks onto the growers, exacerbated the problems African growers would typically have faced. The Cotton Board's decision to restructure the peasant labor process was preeminently political. It was about the politics of production. There was no scientific reason for colonial authorities to assign the most fertile lands to cotton or for cotton to be cultivated in separate fields. The decisions to prohibit intercropping, to destroy peanut plants, and to impose cotton in cool regions made no ecological sense, although they did increase total output for the metropole.

The consequences of these cotton policies were far–reaching, particularly in the north, where most growers resided. Low yields and depressed prices left most households impoverished. With the price reforms of the fifties, income jumped substantially, although at no time did the after–tax income from cotton enable peasants to purchase anything more than a handful of basic consumer goods. That thousands of cotton growers wore rags and had to market one hundred kilograms of raw cotton to be able to purchase a single *capulana* [loincloth] symbolize the degradation built into the system. And because the state forced peasants living within the domain of the concessionaires to privilege cotton over other cash crops, they became excessively dependent on cotton income, no matter how minuscule.

Cotton production also jeopardized food security. Colonial policies and practices eroded a number of strategies growers had employed to feed themselves. Inside the cotton regime, the cultivation of food crops took a back seat to cotton. Peasants could work their gardens only after they had finished laboring in their cotton fields. If their cotton plots fell behind, they had to work longer and harder in them, which left little time to cultivate food. Additionally, the fact that the cotton production cycle coincided with that of sorghum and other critical foodstuffs created a serious labor bottleneck, which state and company officials demanded be broken in favor of cotton. The state's ban on intercropping and the destruction of the gardens of those who failed to comply intensified the food crises.

Twenty–three years of forced cotton also exacerbated a number of serious agro–ecological problems, which further weakened the food economy. The dynamic cotton frontier resulted in rampant deforestation as new lands were continually brought under cultivation. Deforestation deprived vulnerable communities of wild fruits, tubers, and small game and forced women to travel greater distances to collect firewood, thus leaving them less time to cultivate, process, and prepare food. Cotton also robbed the soils of nutrients and, over time, exhausted much of the land's productivity. Because cotton had to be weeded regularly, there was very little grass cover to protect the soil from rains and heavy winds. In many areas soil erosion was an endemic by–product of cotton.

Finally, the cotton regime established a precedent for other micromanaged state interventions into peasant agriculture. The rice concessionary system imposed in 1941 shared many features with the cotton regime. Like the cotton concessionaires, rice companies received monopolies over designated regions. Africans living within these zones were forced to cultivate rice that the companies legally confiscated at fixed prices.[7] Failure to market satisfactory amounts of rice resulted in harsh punishments. In some regions rice overseers were even more notorious than their cotton counterparts. The compulsory manioc scheme and the more limited forced cashew campaign in northern Mozambique were other examples of state intervention at the point of production.[8]

As the previous chapters demonstrate, the highly exploitative relationships and unequal exchange built into the cotton regime disrupted patterns of household production, intensified rural impoverishment, generated widescale hunger, and left the economy more vulnerable to the vagaries of the world market. In these ways, the impact of the Mozambican cotton regime supports the position of underdevelopment theorists and Marxist scholars who stress the devastating effects of commodity production on African communities. The problem with their analysis, however, is that it captures only part of the story. By stressing the distorting structural effects of commodity production, they ultimately reduce all cotton growers to victims of a voracious and all–powerful colonial capitalist regime linked to a hegemonic world economy. In that light, the ways in which growers coped with and struggled against the cotton regime become little more than transitory and futile gestures that had no bearing on the course of history.

This study offers an alternative formulation—one that acknowledges the devastating consequences of the cotton regime but also recognizes that cotton growers were not just passive victims and that the impact of forced commodity production was uneven and varied. It demonstrates how Mozambican growers creatively sought to modify or subvert various aspects of the oppressive regime even though they lacked the power to dismantle it entirely.

The cotton regime impoverished most growers. But it did not impoverish everyone, nor did it impoverish equally. The lives of chiefs, *machambeiros*, African overseers, and factory workers were appreciably different from the lives of *agricultores* and *cultivadores*. *Agricultores* were somewhat better off than *cultivadores*, although their lived experiences were probably not as different as a reading of Portuguese law would suggest.

---

[7]   For a discussion of the rice regimes, see Roesch, "Migrant Labour and Forced Rice Production," 239–70; Vail and White, *Capitalism and Colonialism,*, 318–20.

[8]   For a discussion of compulsory cashew production see AHM, SR, Cx. 76, ISANI, "Relatório . . . Circs. de Moçambiqiue 1936–1937," vol. 1, Capitão Armando Eduardo Pinto Correa, Insp. Admin., 5 April 1938.

The precarious position of most rural producers also cannot mask substantial regional variations in cotton income. Ecological conditions had an obvious impact. Peasants planting cotton in warm, well–watered climates or on rich alluvial soils had a better chance of eking out a living than peasants in areas of erratic rainfall or sandy soils. Opportunities for households to supplement cotton earnings with off–farm income also varied appreciably across the colony. In general, households in the south benefited more from these opportunities than in other parts of the colony. Although there were a number of routes out of poverty, the examples of the chiefs and *machambeiros* and other prosperous growers suggest that the capacity to recruit extra–household labor was critical. Thus, how individual households ultimately fared depended both on regionally specific environmental factors and on how much labor they could mobilize.

Gender and generational hierarchies intensified the uneven impact of the cotton regime. Access to and control over cotton income, across the colony, was gendered both by law and by practice. No matter how productive women were, they could not become independent *agricultores*. Senior wives of *agricultores* acquired that status, but they had no legal claim to their household's cotton revenue. Moreover, at the cotton markets, company authorities typically paid household earnings directly to the men. Even when men were absent and did not work in the cotton fields, they expected their wives to guard the small amount of cotton money until they returned and determined how it was to be used. This arrangement created tensions and abuses, leading a number of women to circumvent this practice and to use the cotton income as they saw fit. Similarly the cotton regime provided little or no reward to teenage boys and girls or elders working in the household's cotton fields.

Throughout this study I have highlighted the array of historical and cultural practices on which peasants drew to alleviate labor bottlenecks, to minimize food insecurity, and to make their lives more bearable. Widespread reliance on beer parties and reciprocal labor agreements are a case in point. Growers also adapted to the new exigencies of the cotton regime. Such was the case when women disregarded the gendered division of labor and began to fell trees or when they defied cultural norms and started to plow. Typically, coping strategies were less dramatic, and involved increasing production of manioc or chick-peas, shifting from sorghum to maize, or simply working longer hours. Even so, coping had its limits. No matter how innovative they were, peasants had to grow cotton, first, last, and always.

The only alternative was to defy the regime. When push came to shove, thousands of growers, if not hundreds of thousands, did so. But, again, the impact of these acts of defiance varied. I have argued that the parameters within which peasants struggled were determined by the relative degree of autonomy they had vis-à-vis the colonial state and the appropriating classes. This partial autonomy helps explain why cotton growers were prone to engage in clandestine forms of protest rather than in broader, more visible social movements. Even within the highly regimented cotton regime there was space for growers who were willing to take risks: they withheld some of their labor, skipped specific tasks, illegally intercropped, engaged in subterfuge, and sneaked off to their food gardens. While it is important not to claim too much for such insurgent acts, they did protect the relative autonomy of the growers in very real ways. The cumulative effect of these seemingly inconsequential acts was to limit production and to expose the inherent fragility of the system. Such acts of defiance helped convince colonial officials in 1961 that forced cotton cultivation was inefficient and anachronistic and that it had to be dismantled. In May 1961 the Salazar regime formally abolished the forced cotton regime. Decree 43.639 prohibited state officials from "intervening to promote the cultivation and marketing of cotton."[9] Through their tenacity, creative adaptations, and defiance, Mozambican peasants had demonstrated that they were more than just history's victims.

The story of cotton in Mozambique does not end with this legislation. Both the colonial regime and the subsequent independent government led by FRELIMO tenaciously implemented policies to sustain cotton production, albeit with quite different objectives. The impact of their respective cotton programs falls outside the scope of this study.[10] However, I should note the most salient changes in the past thirty years of state-managed cotton production and how these changes were a part of the long legacy of cotton.

The radical shift from peasant production to a settler strategy in the post–1961 era represented the culmination of a two-hundred-year debate within the colonial government on the merits of peasant versus settler cotton production. Under the new settler scheme, the state once again intervened vigorously at the point of production, but this time to assist European producers. Colonial authorities appropriated some of the most fertile peasant lands, particularly in Nampula, and redistributed them to white farmers and recent Portuguese immigrants.[11] Many of the African inhabitants remained on the land as tenants and seasonal laborers. The Cotton Institute, which replaced the Board, provided European farmers with low-interest loans and technical assistance and subsidized the use of pesticides and mechanized equipment.[12] To ease labor shortages, particularly at harvest time, many local administrators applied pressure on peasants to work on these cotton enterprises.[13] The Cotton Institute also abolished the state's monopolistic market practices and allowed producers to sell their fiber to the highest bidder.

Offered such inducements, the number of European cotton growers in Mozambique increased dramatically. Whereas only twenty-four settlers chose to plant cotton in 1962, a decade later 872 Europeans planted more than 50,000 hectares.[14] By this time settler production had outstripped the peasant sector, a radical reversal of past trends. Lisbon's effort to change the color of cotton had succeeded. Although total production had declined since the days of the forced cotton regime, in 1974 European farms and plantations produced more than two-thirds of all Mozambican cotton.[15]

---

[9]   BOM 21, 1ª Série, 27 May 1961.

[10]   The promising research of Alice Dinerman on the politics of production and postwar reconstruction in Northern Mozambique and Anne Pitcher's forthcoming study of gender and production in Nampula after 1975 should help fill this gap.

[11]   CEA, A Transformação da Agricultura Familiar," 40–41.

[12]   Instituto do Algodão de Moçambique, Actividades do Instituto de Algodão de Moçambique em 1970 (Lourenço Marques), 220–31.

[13]   Interviews with Bishop João Somane Machado, Maputo, 10 May 1987; Gonçalo Mazungane Chilundo, Maputo, 8–9 August 1991; CEA, Cotton Production, 16.

[14]   Instituto do Algodão de Moçambique, Actividades . . . em 1970 , 65, 95.

[15]   In the 1973–74 campaign, peasant production accounted for only 43,000 tons while settler output was nearly 90,000. Instituto do Algodão de Moçambique, Actividades do Instituto de Algodão de Moçambique de 1974–75 (Machava, 1977), 1–2.

When independence shifted state power to FRELIMO a year later, FRELIMO was theoretically positioned to transform Mozambique's distorted economy. The postindependence state had two options with regard to cotton production. The first was to allow the demise of the cotton industry to continue. After all, the staple was emblematic of colonial rule, and FRELIMO's leaders were acutely aware of the widespread antipathy toward cotton among rural Mozambicans. Throughout the armed struggle, guerrillas fighting in the north targeted concessionary company factories, warehouses, and other holdings. Militants urged growers to refuse to grow cotton, and peasants in the liberated zones were freed from this task. Had the postcolonial state opted to abandon cotton production entirely, the policy would have received wide acclaim. In the minds of thousands of peasants, independence from Portugal meant the end of cotton. But the new Mozambican government tried instead to resurrect the cotton industry.

That FRELIMO continued to promote cotton on state farms and on communal villages, in turn, reflects the narrow economic choices available to the newly independent nation as well as the leadership's miscalculation of how unpopular the crop actually was. Like most third-world countries, but more so, Mozambique's distorted cash-poor economy depended on the export of raw materials like cotton. But whether the postindependent government framed cotton production as part of its socialist agenda or as part of its subsequent free-market structural adjustment initiative,[16] it encountered peasant antipathy. Indeed, critics of the joint cotton ventures that the government first signed in the late 1980s with private investors from Portugal, Great Britain, and South Africa, as well as João Ferreira dos Santos and the Buzi Company, claim that these mixed enterprises resting on peasant production are simply a throwback to the colonial concessionary companies in slightly different garb.

One thing is certain: the story of cotton production in Mozambique is far from over. Forging a development strategy based on industrial crops like cotton that displace labor from food production, damage the ecosystem, and satisfy foreign rather than domestic demands has long–term economic and social consequences. In the minds of most Mozambicans, cotton will always be the mother of poverty.

---

[16] In 1987 the government implemented the IMF–World Bank structural adjustment program known in Mozambique as the PRE (Programa de Rehabilitação Económica).

SOURCES

Interviews

Northern Mozambique

Abadre, Faquir. Montepuez, 23 July 1979.
Afonso, Taele, Jacinto Capembe, Baquile Alguime, and Matise Alguime. Montepuez, 21 July 1979.
Aguiar, Maria, and Comalia Niuquanha. Nampula, 11 July 1991.
Ali, Somali, Muidine Nomae, and Faqui Tuabilho. Mocímboa de Praia, 27 April 1979.
Anjate, Tauria Auputo, Canila Raca, and Arrifa Mussas. Metuge, 6 August 1978.
Baptista, Manuel. Nampula, 9 July 1991.
Bonifácio, Justinho João. Mueda, 2 August 1979.
Carajola, Joaquim. Nampula, 9 July 1991.
Cardoso, Armando. Nampula, 10 July 1991.
Cedo, Adelina, and Andre Marques da Pinha. Montepuez, 21 July 1979.
Cuane, Chamudja. Macomia, 28 July 1979.
da Costa, Bras. Lichinga, 15 August 1980.
da Costa, Jaime José Rodrigues. Quelimane, 15 July 1991.
de Sousa, Daniel. Maputo, 21 July 1993.
Dias, Artúro Augusto. Montepuez, 24 July 1979.
Ernesto, Rosa Maria. Nampula, 11 July 1991.
Ferreira, João. Pemba, 28 April 1979.
Group interview. Balama, 19 July 1979.
Group interview. Base Central, Mueda, 25 April 1979.
Group interview. Communal Village Imbou, Mueda, 31 July 1979.
Group interview. Communal Village Nandimba, Mueda, 3 July 1979.
Group interview. Communal Village Nawawane, Montepuez, 20 July 1979.
Group interview. Likanganu, Macomia, 1 May 1979; 27 July 1979.
Group interview. Macomia, 27 July 1979; 30 July 1979.
Hassan, Pruan, Nemkuela Makorkuru, Masera Tahura, Materi, Nhande Rocha, and Rashide Rocha. Montepuez, 20 July 1979.
Ibraimo, Amade Sique. Chai, 30 July 1979.
Impatata, Bruhane, Umbido Jaweze, and Alfane Mussa. Pemba, 30 May 1987.
Jacob, Benjamin. Macomia, 27 July 1979.
Jeje, José. Nampula, 7 July 1991.
Joaquim, Marcelina, Juliana Lias, and Hirondiena Tonia. Mueda, 25 April 1979.
Julião, Saide. Montepuez, 23 July 1979.
Katupha, Mateus. Maputo, 25 July 1993.
Konkonko, Fátima. Pemba, 30 May 1987.
Lobo, Faria. Nampula, 26 May 1987; 9 June 1991.

Luís, Abondio Leveriano. Cuamba, 28 December 1979.

Macore, Eduardo José. Unango, 19 August 1980.

Mahanda, Aridhi et al. Balama, 23 July 1979.

Mahapiri, Conta, and Marcelino Tetea. Nampula, 27 August 1979.

Mala, Luís Nkayosse, Lafuneti Sufu, Apulaika Nuchuwa, Kassanga Massomwe, Galeja Chuna, and Ndikwona Maduka. Macomia, 27 July 1979.

Maliwa, Wussa, Sene Nampade, and Charles Malaya. Mueda, 31 July 1979.

Mandande, João Cornélio. Mueda, 30 July 1979; Mueda, 1 August 1979.

Manuel, Paulo José, José Pacial, and Manuel Paquelque. Nampula, 10 July 1991.

Mascalane, Saide, Musane Assane, Akime Rajado, and Momade Asane. Maniamba, 16 August 1980.

Mataquenha, Romeu, Tirani Ntuka, and Mussa Vaquina. Montepuez, 19 July 1979.

Matupera, Aide, Xibuca Minga, et al. Macomia, 27 July 1979.

Mavie, Simone Lote. Nhanombe, 2 February 1982. (Ministry of Culture Archives, Maputo.)

Mbela, Daima Magaga, Kndaba Nchamada Otinga, and Mangane Nkula Nquenia. Macomia, 30 July 1979.

Mbundi, Manuel João, Munchenye Likukua, Bustani Miteda, and Maurício. Mueda, 1 August 1979.

Miambo, Júlio. Maputo, 14 September 1979.

Momola, Alberto, João Chakala, Kuteiwa Manke, and Maria Mwezia. Nampula, 27 May 1987.

Moreno, João Manuel. Nampula, 28 December 1978.

Nakutepa, Jonas, Ernesto Lachana, Nkangala Lauka, João Napome, and Gregório José. Mueda, 31 July 1979.

Ncatala, Muarala. Macomia, 28 July 1979.

Nhoco, Mwimbo. Chai, 28 July 1979.

Nhulialia, Chico, and Costa Gaio Nampire. Namapa, 2 May 1979.

Niquaria, Eugénio. Montepuez, 24 July 1979.

Ntuamunu, Nanelo, Chaliamba Victor, Agostinho James, and Muatili Miguel. Communal Village Muila, Mueda, 1 August 1979.

Nuitha, Amasse. Communal Village Nawana, Montepuez, 20 July 1979.

Nzama, Goodwin Alsane. Metangula, 16 August 1980.

Ohiyonga, Arithi. Balama, 25 July 1979.

Pera, Margarita. Nampula/Murrupula, 12 July 1991.

Pinho, Andre Marques de. Montepuez, 23 July 1979.

Promose, Ramissa. Montepuez, 23 July 1979.

Razão, Muiluta. Netia, 30 September 1993. (Interview with Arlindo Chilundo; transcript in possession of author.)

Rekula, Daniel. Netia, 30 September 1993. (Interview with Arlindo Chilundo; transcript in possession of author.)

Roque, Paulo. Nampula, 27 May 1987.

Saide, Abílio Jaime. State Farm Matama, Niassa, 20 August 1980.

Samate, Maulana et al. Balama, 23 July 1979.

Shapina, Monica, and Beatriz Anestina. Lichinga, 15 August 1980.

Spaneke, Fátima, Rotho Malima, Nahlamo Lavala, Amina Lala, and Adelaide Tshakaia. Nampula, 28 May 1987.

Tadeu, Pretinho. Chai, 30 July 1979.

Taibo, Nanjaia, Givela Morove, João Nacuela, Xavier Intala, Chico Nhulialia, and Costa Gaio Nampire. Namapa, 2 May 1979.

Tangadica, Tanga Karinga de, Ernesto Vandaya, Tombo, Jonasse Becar, Camela, Mponda Vale, and Kamanga. Communal Village Imbo, Mueda, 31 July 1979.

Taulegues, Vicente Henrique, and Mário da Cruz Soares. Metocheria, 17 January 1979.

Tiveli, Penguane, and Sando Senda. Lichinga, 7 August 1980.

Tocola, Muariri, and Licúrio Makalawila. Pemba, 30 May 1987.
Vanomba, Zacarias. Muidimbe, 2 August 1979.
Zimu, Cocote, Caciano Salósio, Feliciano João, Iscai Kilama, Zacarias Rafael, and Ambrosio Maguene. Montepuez, 23 July 1979.

Central Mozambique

Many informants from war–torn Zambézia fled to other provinces or to safer zones within Zambézia. In these cases I have listed the site of the interview and then the location of the interviewee's homeland. Several of the interviews listed in this section were collected by Judith Head working with a group of Mozambican interpreters. The transcripts of these interviews are on deposit at the Centro de Estudos Africanos, Universidade Eduardo Mondlane in Maputo. They are designated here as the "Head Collection."

Alberto, Líguene. Nicoadala/Namacurra, 17 July 1991.
Alberto, Luís et al. Mopeia, 1–2 August 1976. (Head Collection.)
António, Augusto. Nicoadala/Morrumbala, 18 July 1991.
Camissa, Tomas. Maputo/Ile, 7 August 1991.
Crespin, Francisco. Quelimane, 19 July 1991.
Fijamo, Maria. Quelimane, 19 July 1991.
Group interview. Gilé, 7–8 July 1976. (Head Collection.)
Group interview. Morrumbala, 30 July 1976.
Group interview. Muanavine Compound, Luabo, 21 November 1976. (Head Collection.)
Group interview. Muide Compound, Luabo, 14 November 1976. (HeadCollection.)
Hussene, Abdul Satar Mohammed. Quelimane, 19 July 1991.
Jafir, Salimo, and Afonso Malema. Quelimane, 19 July 1991.
Joaquim, Justina. Nicoadala/Mocuba, 17 July 1991.
Joaquim, Nsaio, Tambile Mosuvaba, Luisa Jona, and Almeida Sangoo. Morrumbala, 16 July 1991.
Joni, Sabino et al. Gilé, 14–15 July 1976. (Head Collection.)
Kendamale, Sona, and Divarasone Watebo. Nicoadala/Morrumbala, 17 July 1991.
Kwalima, Sajene et al. Morrumbala, 30 July 1976. (Head Collection.)
Madé, Nunes Faria, Paulo Madeira, and Caetano Maio. Nicoadala/Namacurra, 19 July 1991.
Manhiça, Saivina. Nicoadala/Namacurra, 17 July 1991.
Mpemo, Murinvona. Centro Piloto de Deslocados, Nampula/Gilé, 9 July 1991.
Mugonda, Muciere. Nicoadala/Mopeia, 17 July 1991.
Naxtaro, Rafael et al. Alto Molócuè, 16–17 July 1976 (Head Collection).
Nicula, Armando, Liassa Lohaninteve, and Murinvona Mpemo. Centro Piloto de Deslocados, Nampula/Gilé, 8 July 1991.
Nsampa, Lofas et al. Muide Compound, Luabo, 14 November 1976 (Head Collection).
Nuitha, Manuel, and Rodolfo Churupa. Nampula/Gilé, 11 July 1991.
Pinto, Manuel. Quelimane, 19 July 1991.
Rodrigues, Jaime José da Costa. Quelimane, 19 July 1991.
Roldão, Semble, LaFaite Daglasse, Moniz Kapete, and Uassu Subau. Nicoadala/Morrumbala, 16 July 1991.
Sangoma, Fássimo. Nicoadala/Namacurra, 18 July 1991.
Satar, Abdul. Quelimane, 19 July 1991.
Sindique, Maria, Assoengane Mangoela, Hoave Afunuqueira, Massaquia Kanaguenia, Sonanda Rindinho, and Alberto Pais. Nicoadala/Morrumbala, 18 July 1991.

Southern Mozambique

Amati, Sarifa. Xai Xai, 21 August 1977.

Bendane, Catarina, and Esina Johane Mulhue. Communal Village Mulanguene, Guijá, 17 February 1979.

Cambane, Helena Jossias, and Helena Felizmina Chirinda. Maputo, 1 August 1991.

Chilundo, Gonçalo Mazungane. Maputo, 8–9 August 1991; Maputo, 20 July 1993; Zavala, 1 August 1993.

Chissano, Martha. Manjacaze, 15 February 1979.

Cossa, Celeste, Amélia Novana, and Regina Mate. Maputo, 31 July 1991.

Cossa, Celeste, Amélia Novana, and Essineta Namuwiango. Maputo, 26 July 1993.

Cossa, Felipe, Fabião Mate, Sabo Mate, Mecelino Matavale, Tecuasse Freitas, and José. Maputo, 19 July 1993.

de Castro, Ferreira. Maputo, 25 September 1978.

Gillet, Ira. Milwaukee (Oregon), 18 August 1981.

Group interview. Communal Village Luís Carlos Prestes, Gaza, 2 February 1979.

Group interview. Communal Village Magul, Bilene, 20 February 1979.

Group interview. Communal Village Magude, Macia, 28 February 1979.

Group interview. Communal Village Paulo Samuel Kankhomba, Massingire, 7 February 1979.

Group interview. Communal Village Samora Machel, Chibuto, 15 September 1979.

Group interview. Homoíne, 5 August 1980.

Group interview. Imala State Farm, 4 May 1979.

Group interview. Instituto de Algodão, Maputo, 4 August 1993.

Group interview. Serra Nkanyavane, 2 February 1979; 17 February 1979.

Group interview. State Farm de Magul, Bilene, 20 February 1979.

Honwana, Raul. Maputo, 1 June 1987.

Kapucha, Colina. 18 July 1991.

Macamo, Salamão. Guijá, 17 February 1979.

Machado, Bishop João Somane. Maputo, 10 May 1987; Maputo, 23 July 1993.

Machava, Emília. Communal Village Magul, Gaza, 20 February 1979.

Machel, Samora, et al. 27 February 1979.

Macuácua, Amélia. Chibuto, 10 February 1979.

Madime, Leonarda Fátima. Chidenguele, 20 November 1979.

Manguesse, Manuel, António Jamessea, and Colano Cuamba. Communal Village Chichingere, Homoíne, 5 August 1980.

Manhique, Cristina, and Esmeralda Candjelo. Maputo, 6 August 1991.

Mapone, Mutomene, and Maria Mapone. Gaza, 19 February 1979.

Massinga, Rafael. Maputo, 22 July 1993.

Mavaungo, Essineta. Maputo, 6 August 1991.

Mavunja, Benjamin. Chibuto, 12 February 1979.

Mbazima, Leia. Maputo, 27 July 1991.

Meque. Inhambane, 4 August 1980.

Mucambe, Simão Mangueze. Maputo, 12 July 1991.

Muhate, Erasmo. Maputo, 4 August 1993.

Muhate, Makausse. Manjacaze, 15 July 1980. (Interview with Gerhard Liesegang. Arquivo Histórico de Moçambique,T./TnoGZ009.)

Mucave, Gabriel. Guijá, 20 February 1979.

Nstinini, Ernesto. Inhambane, 30 July 1980.

Paulo, Miriam. Maputo, 16 May 1987.

Penicela, Adelina. Maputo, 3 July 1986.

Quintanilha, A. Maputo, 7 March 1979; Maputo, 12 March 1979; Maputo, 12 May 1979.

Saldanha, Manuel Alves. Xai Xai, 12 February 1979.

Sigaugue, Felipe. Chibuto, 15 February 1979.
Simba, Makwati, Xavier Jossene, Mondwai Muene, and Amélia Macuácua. Chibuto, 13 February 1979.
Simbine, Catarina Jossias, and Nely Simbine. Maputo, 8 August 1991.
Sitói, Manuel, Simone Sitói, Marcos Chonga Ezequiell Mabasso, Stefano Felipe, and Sideon Mabunda. Guijá, 16 February 1979.
Sitói, Minosse, Tefasse Mucavele, Tavasse Machave, and Amélia Machave. Gaza, 2 February 1979.
Sitói, Simone. Guijá, 16 February 1979.
Tose, Rafael, and José Finiche. Communal Village Agostinho Neto, 5 August 1980.
Tuno, Eoch, and Armando Pascoal Nhuvane. Communal Village 25 de Setembro, Inhambane, 5 August 1980.
Xerinda, Samuel Alfredo, and Nascio Rodrigues. Maputo, August 4, 1993.
Yota, Valente. Macia, 19 February 1979.
Zucula, Paulo. Minneapolis, 15 August 1989.
Zungueni, Jossias. Bilene, 19 February 1979.

Archives

England

Public Records Office (PRO), London
Foreign Office (FO)
    FO 371/837
    FO 371/81814
    FO 371/8377
Colonial Office (CO)
    CO 691/166
    CO 691/167
    CO 691/174
    CO 691/183
    CO 691/191

Malawi

Malawi National Archives (MNA), Zomba
    NNSP2/1/7
    S1/7B/36
    S1/66A/37
    S1/66B/37
    S1/79A/36

Mozambique

Archive of Sena Sugar Estates Ltd. (SSE), Luabo
    File #44, "Annual Cotton Reports"
    File #133, "Recruiting Quelimane and Angónia, 1930–1939"
Arquivo da Companhia de SAGAL, Montepuez
    "Correspondências com as Autoridades Administrativas, 1959"
Arquivo Histórico de Moçambique (AHM), Maputo

Administração Civil
[CE] Collecção Especial, S.E. A.V., 1, 10; 7,298; 9, 116 (a,b)
[FGG] Fundo Governo Geral, Tabela 4, Cota 294; Tabela 5, Cota 489; Pasta A/6 Cx. 40;
Pasta 109
[GN, CM] Governo do Niassa, Circunscrição de Mogovolas, 1954
[ISANI] Inspecção dos Serviços Administrativos e dos Negócios Indígenas, Cx. 20, Cx.
21, Cx. 26, Cx. 28, Cx. 30, Cx. 39, Cx. 40, Cx. 41, Cx. 45, Cx. 57, Cx. 62, Cx. 63, Cx. 64, Cx.
76, Cx. 77, Cx. 78, Cx. 89, Cx. 91, Cx. 92, Cx. 94, Cx. 95, Cx. 96, Cx. 97
Arquivo de Instituto de Algodão, Junta da Exportação de Algodão Colonial (AIA, JEAC)
This collection has been incorporated into the Arquivo Histórico de Moçambique
[AT] Arquivo Técnico, 1352, 9352
[BT] Brigada Técnica, 1942–1943, 1951, 1952–1953
[CM] Companhia da Zambézia, 1942, 1946
[CAM] Companhia dos Algodões de Moçambique, 1945, 1946–1947
[CNA] Companhia Nacional Algodoeira, 1946–1947
"Confidêncial," 1941, 1944–1946, 1947, 1957–1959
"Dossiers Diversos," 1939–1941, 1940–1942
"Esboço Estatística Referente à 1941"
Files 4/8, 11/69, 84, 86, 952, 601/3,601/8, 605/8, 608/8, 660/55,929/5, 1011, 2201/8
GRANDUCOL Companhia dos Algodões de Moçambique, 1939
"Papéis Diversos," 1939–1941
"Planos de Trabalho," 1958
"Propaganda Moçambique," 1954
"Notas Recebidas," 1939
"Relatório Anuário," 1939–1941
"Relatório das Inspecção de JEAC," 1940–1945, 1940, 1941, 1946, 1947, 1948, 1950, 1954,
1959, 1960–1961
"Relatório Técnico," 1947, 1948, 1952, 1957
"Sociedade Algodoeira de Niassa," 39/181

Portugal

Academia das Ciências de Lisboa
  MS 648 Azul
Biblioteca Pública de Ajuda
  52–x–2–no. 3

Switzerland

Swiss Mission Archives (SMA), Lausanne
  Boite 60/646, 194/1754 B, 697/767 I, 6/70 D

Tanzania

Tanzania National Archives (TNA), Dar es Salaam
  File 13/63

United States

United States National Archives (USNA)
  Collection 705, Reports from U.S. Consulate in Lourenço Marques, 1923–1927

State Department Consular Dispatches for 1950–1963, issued from U.S. Consulate in Lourenço Marques (on deposit at Boston University, FIA/BU).
American Board of Commissioners for Foreign Missions, Harvard University, Cambridge, MA
Letters from Missions, ABC 15.4, Volumes 43, 44, 46.

Periodicals and Newspapers

Boletim Oficial da Colonial de Moçambique [also published as *Boletim Oficial do Governo Geral da Provincia de Moçambique*]
Diário de Lisboa
Journal do Comércio de Lisboa
Lourenço Marques Guardian
Moçambique Documentário Trimestral
Notícias
Agencia de Informação, Information Bulletin
Official Journal of the South East African Mission Conference of the Methodist Episcopal Conference

Books and Articles

Acland, J. D. *East African Crops: An Introduction to the Production of Field and Plantation Crops in Kenya, Tanzania, and Uganda.* London, 1971.
Adam, Yussuf, and Anna Maria Gentile. "O Movimento dos Liguilanilu no Planalto de Mueda 1952–1962." *Estudos Moçambicanos* 4(1983), 41–75.
Adas, Michael. "From Footdragging to Flight: The Evasive History of Peasant Avoidance Strategies in South and South East Asia." *Journal of Peasant Studies* 13, 2(1986), 64–86.
Alberto, Manuel Simões. "O Problema da Alimentação Entre as Populações Rurais Nativas de Moçambique." *Sociedade de Estudos de Moçambique* 24(1954), 113–26.
Allen, William. *The African Husbandman.* New York, 1965.
Alpers, Edward. *Ivory and Slaves in East Central Africa.* London, 1975.
_____. "The Role of Culture in the Liberation of Mozambique." *Ufahamu* 12, 3(1983), 143–90.
_____. "'To Seek a Better Life': The Implications of Migration from Mozambique to Tanganyika for Class Formation and Political Behavior." *Canadian Journal of African Studies* 18, 2(1984), 367–88.
Amaral, Manuel Gama. *O Povo Yao.* Lisbon, 1990.
Arnold, David. *Famine: Social Crisis and Historical Change.* Oxford, 1988.
Asiwaju, A. I. "Migrations as Revolt: The Example of the Ivory Coast and the Upper Volta Before 1945." *Journal of African History* 17(1976), 577–94.
Associação dos Produtores de Sisal de Moçambique. *4° Relatório de Direcçao.* Lumbo, 1951.
Azevedo, Ário Lobo. "Clima, Estudo de Alguns Factores Climáticos." In *Esboço do Reconhecimento Ecológico–Agrícola de Moçambique,* vol. 2. Edited by Junta de Exportação do Algodão. Lourenço Marques, 1955.
Bassett, Thomas. "Breaking Up the Bottlenecks in Food-Crop and Cotton Cultivation in Northern Côte d'Ivoire." *Africa* 58(1988), 147–73.
_____. "The Uncaptured Corvée: Cotton in Côte d' Ivoire, 1912–1946." In *Cotton, Colonialism, and Social History in Sub–Saharan Africa,* ed. Allen Isaacman and Richard Roberts. Portsmouth, 1995.

Bastos, Carlos. *Comércio e Indústria Textil em Portugal*. Porto, 1950.

_____. *Indústria e Arte Textil*. Porto, 1960.

_____. *O Algodão no Comércio e na Indústria Portuguesa*. Porto, 1947.

Bastos, Carlos, and Ribeiro E. K. de Queiroz. *O Algodão: Da Colheita à Industrialização*. Porto, 1947.

Bates, Robert. *Markets and States in Tropical Africa: The Political Basis of Agricultural Policies*. Berkeley, 1988.

Bauer, Raymond, and Alice Bauer. "Day to Day Resistance in Slavery." *Journal of Negro History* 27(1942), 388–419.

Beatriz, Mánuel Guerreiro. "A Classificação e os Preços do Algodão–Caroço em Moçambique de 1930 a 1962." *Gazeta do Algodão* 14(1962).

Beinart, William. "Introduction: The Politics of Colonial Conservation." *Journal of Southern African Studies* 15(1989), 145–62.

Beinart, William, and Colin Bundy. *Hidden Struggles in Rural South Africa: Politics and Popular Movements in the Transkei and Eastern Cape 1890–1930*. Berkeley, 1987.

Bender, Gerald. *Angola Under the Portuguese: Myth and Reality*. Berkeley, 1978.

Bernal, Victoria. *Cultivating Workers: Peasants and Capitalism in a Sudanese Village*. New York, 1991.

_____. "Cotton and Colonial Order in Sudan: A Social History with an Emphasis on the Gezira Scheme." In *Cotton, Colonialism, and Social History in Sub–Saharan Africa*, ed. Allen Isaacman and Richard Roberts. Portsmouth, 1995.

Berry, Sara. "The Food Crisis and Agrarian Change in Africa: A Review Essay." *African Studies Review* 27, 2(1984), 59–112.

_____. *No Condition is Permanent* (Madison, 1993).

Bettencourt, José Tristão de. *Relatório do Governador–Geral de Moçambique, 1940–1942*. 2 vols. Lisbon, 1949.

Blasingame, John. *The Slave Community: Plantation Life in the Antebellum South*. New York, 1972.

Blok, Anton. "The Peasant and the Brigand: Social Banditry Reconsidered." *Comparative Studies in Society and History* 14(1972), 494–503.

Botelho, Sebastião Xavier. *Memória Estatística sobre os Domínios Portugueses na África Oriental*. Lisbon, 1935.

Bowen, Merle L. "Peasant Agriculture in Mozambique: The Case of Chokwe, Gaza Province." *Canadian Journal of African Studies* 23, 3(1989), 355–79.

Bowles, Brian. "Export Crops and Underdevelopment in Tanganyika 1929–1961." *Utafiti* 1(1976), 71–85.

Bozzoli, Belinda, with the assistance of Mmantho Nkotsoe. *Women of Phokeng: Consciousness, Life Strategy, and Migrancy in South Africa, 1900–1983*. Portsmouth, 1991.

Bradford, Helen. *A Taste of Freedom* (New Haven, 1987).

Branquinho, José Alberto Gomes de Melo. *Prospecção das Forças Tradicionais*. Lourenço Marques, 1959.

Braverman, Harry. *Labour and Monopoly Capital: The Degradation of Work in the Twentieth Century*. New York, 1975.

Bravo, Nelson Saraiva. *A Cultura Algodoeira na Economia do Norte de Moçambique*. Lisbon, 1963.

Brett, E. A. *Colonialism and Underdevelopment in East Africa: The Politics of Economic Change*. New York, 1973.

Bryceson, Deborah. *Food Insecurity and the Social Division of Labour in Tanzania, 1919–1985*. New York, 1990.

Buraway, Michael. *The Politics of Production*. London, 1985.

Caetano, Marcelo. *Relações das Colónias de Angola e Moçambique com os Territórios Estrangeiros Visinhos*. Lisbon, 1946.

Cahen, Michel. "O Fundo ISANI do Arquivo Histórico de Moçambique: Uma Fonte Importante da História Social Contemporânea do Colonialismo Português." *Arquivo* 7(1990), 63–82.

Capela, José. *Escravatura: A Empresa de Saque, O Abolicionismo.* Porto, 1974.

Castro, Armando. *A Economia Portuguesa do Século XX 1900–1925.* Lisbon, 1973.

_____. *O Sistema Colonial Português em África.* Lisbon, 1978.

Centro de Estudos Africanos. *Cotton Production in Mozambique: A Survey 1936–1979.* Maputo, 1981.

_____. *Já Não Batem: A Transformação da Producão Algodoeira.* Maputo, 1981.

_____. *Transformação da Agricultura Familiar na Província de Nampula.* Maputo, 1980.

Centro de Investigação Científica Algodoeira. *Esboço do Reconhecimento Ecológico–Agrícola de Moçambique.* Lourenço Marques, 1955.

Chambers, Robert, Richard Longhurst, and Arnold Pacey, eds. *Seasonal Dimensions to Rural Poverty.* London, 1981.

Chang, Jen–Hu. "The Agricultural Potential of the Humid Tropics." *Geographical Review* 58(1968), 333–61.

Chapman, S. J. *The Cotton Industry and Trade.* London, 1905.

Chilundo, Arlindo. "Quando Começou o Comércio das Oleaginosas em Moçambique." *Relação Europa–Africa 3, Quartel do Século 19* (Lisbon, 1988), 511–23.

Chipungu, Samuel. *The State, Technology and Peasant Differentiation in Zambia.* Lusaka, 1988.

Chirwa, Wiseman. "Nyasaland's Labour Sources and the Anguru/Lomwe Immigration 1890–1945." *International Journal of African Historical Studies* 27, 3(1994), 525–50.

Cliffe, Lionel. "Nationalism and the Reaction to Enforced Agricultural Change in Tanganyika During the Colonial Period." In *Socialism in Tanzania,* ed. Lionel Cliffe and John Saul. Dar es Salaam, 1973.

Cohen, Sheila. "A Labour Process to Nowhere?" *New Left Review* 168(1987), 34–50.

Colonia de Moçambique. *Relatório do Chefe dos Serviços de Agricultura 1940–1944.* Lourenço Marques, 1946.

Colonia de Moçambique, Repartição Técnica de Estatística. *Censo da População em 1940.* Lourenço Marques, 1942.

Cooper, Frederick. "Africa and the World Economy." *African Studies Review* 24, 2/3(1981), 1–86.

Correia da Silva, Manuel. "Importância Económica das Principais Culturas e Meios de Transporte na Baixa Zambézia." In *Primeiro Congresso de Agricultura Colonial.* Porto, 1934.

"Court Trial of Mr. Year, The." *South African Missionary Advocate,* 22(1941), 4–5.

Coutinho, J. *A Campanha de Barue em 1902.* Lisbon, 1904.

Cruz, Daniel da. *Em Terras de Gaza.* Porto, 1910.

Dampierre, Eric de. "Coton noir, café blanc: Deux cultures du Haut–Oubangui à la veille de la loi–cadre." *Cahiers d'Etudes Africaines* 2(1960), 128–46.

de Almeida, A. Antunes. "Losses Caused by Insects to the Cotton Crop in Mozambique." *Agronomia Moçambicana* 1(1967), 127–32.

de Amorim, Pedro Massano. *Relatório do Governador 1906–1907.* Lourenço Marques, 1908.

de Carvalho, Mário. "Resultados da Experimentação Algodoeira em Moçambique (1942/ 43 a 1945/6) Análise Estatística e Redacção." *Trabalhos do Centro de Investigação Científica* 2(1951), 372–74.

Dias, A. Jorge. *Os Macondes de Moçambique: Aspectos Históricos e Económicos.* Lisbon, 1964.

_____. *Portuguese Contribution to Cultural Anthropology.* Johannesburg, 1961.

Direcção dos Serviços de Agricultura. *Algodão.* Lourenço Marques, 1934.

_____. *Apensos ao Recenseamento Agrícola de 1929–1930.* Lourenço Marques, 1930.

Direcção Geral de Comércio Externo. *Moçambique Economic Survey.* Lourenço Marques, 1975.

Direcção Provincal dos Serviços de Estatística Geral. *Estatística Agrícola*. Lourenço Marques, 1960–1964.

Distrito da Zambézia. *Acto da Conferência dos Administradores*. Quelimane, 1956.

Duffy, James. *A Question of Slavery*. London, 1967.

Dumett, Raymond. "Obstacles to Government-Assisted Agricultural Development in West Africa: Cotton-Growing Experimentation in Ghana in the Early Twentieth Century." *Agricultural History Review* 23(1975), 156–72.

Evans, Sara M., and Harry C. Boyte. *Free Spaces: The Sources of Democratic Change in America*. New York, 1986.

Faria, João Gaspar. "Produção Algodoeira." *Searra Nova* 1083(1948), 2–4.

Feierman, Steven. *Peasant Intellectuals: Anthropology and History in Tanzania*. Madison, 1990.

_____. "Struggles for Control: The Social Roots of Health and Healing in Modern Africa." *African Studies Review* 28(1985), 86–96.

Finnegan, William. *A Complicated War: The Harrowing of Mozambique*. Berkeley, 1991.

First, Ruth. *Black Gold: The Mozambican Miner, Proletarian and Peasant*. Sussex, 1983.

Fitzgerald, W. W. A. *Travels in British East Africa, Zanzibar and Pemba*. London, 1898.

Fortuna, Carlos. *O Fio da Meada: O Algodão da Moçambique, Portugal e a Economia–Mundo, 1860–960*. Porto, 1993.

FRELIMO. "The Cotton Regime." *Mozambique Revolution* 46(1971), 18–23.

Furnival, J. S. *Netherlands India: A Study of a Plural Economy*. Cambridge, 1939.

Gann, L. H., and Peter Duignan, eds. *Colonialism in Africa, 1870–1960*. 5 vols. Cambridge, 1975.

Geertz, Clifford. *Agricultural Involution: The Processes of Ecological Change in Indonesia*. Berkeley, 1963.

Geffray, Christian, and Mogens Pedersen. *Transformação da Organização e do Sistema Agrário do Campesinato no Distrito do Eráti: Processo de Socialização do Campo e Diferenciação Social*. Maputo, 1985.

Genovese, Eugene. *Roll, Jordan, Roll: The World the Slaves Made*. New York, 1974.

George, J. Fonseca. "Concentrações Algodoeiras." *Sociedade de Estudos da Colónia de Moçambique* (1946).

Gouveia, D. H. Godinho, and Ário Lobo Azevedo. "Os Solos." In *Esboço do Reconhecimento Ecológico–Agrícola de Moçambique*, vol. 2. Edited by Junta de Exportação do Algodão. Lourenço Marques, 1955.

Gregory, S. "Annual, Seasonal and Monthly Rainfall over Moçambique." In *Geographers and the Tropics: Liverpool Essays*, ed. Robert Steel and R. Mansell Prothero. London, 1964.

Grilo, F. Monteiro. *Relatório do Chefe dos Serviços de Agricultura 1940–1944*. Lourenço Marques, 1946.

Guyer, Jane. "Household and Community in African Studies." *African Studies Review* 24, 2/3(1981), 87–137.

Guyer, Jane, and Pauline Peters. "Conceptualizing the Household: Issues of Theory, Method and Application." *Development and Change* 18(1987), 197–214.

Habermeir, Kurt. "Algodão: Das Concentrações à Produção Colectiva." *Estudos Moçambicanos* 2(1981), 37–58.

Hanlon, Joseph. *Mozambique: The Revolution Under Fire*. London, 1984.

Harris, Marvin. *Portugal's African Wards*. New York, 1960.

Harries, Patrick. *Work, Culture, and Identity: Migrant Laborers in Mozambique and South Africa, 1860–1910*. Portsmouth, 1994.

Hart, Keith. *The Political Economy of West African Agriculture*. Cambridge, 1982.

Hermele, Kenneth. *Land Struggles and Social Differentiation in Southern Mozambique: A Case Study of Chokwe, Limpopo, 1950–1987*. Uppsala, 1988.

Herrick, Allison Butler, and others. *Area Handbook for Mozambique.* Washington, 1969.

Hobsbawm, Eric. *Bandits.* New York, 1969.

_____. "Peasants and Politics." *Journal of Peasant Studies* 1, 1(1973), 3–22.

Hogendorn, Jan S. "Economic Initiative and African Cash Farming: Pre–Colonial Origins and Early Colonial Development." In *Colonialism in Africa, 1870–1960: The Economics of Colonialism,* ed. L. H. Gann and Peter Duignan. Cambridge, 1975.

_____. "The Cotton Campaign in Northern Nigeria, 1902–1914: An Example of Public/Private Planning Failure in Agriculture." In *Cotton, Colonialism, and Social History in Sub–Saharan Africa,* ed. Allen Isaacman and Richard Roberts. Portsmouth, 1995.

Honwana, Raul. *The Life History of Raul Honwana: An Inside View of Mozambique from Colonialism to Independence, 1905–1975.* Translated by Tamara L. Bender. Edited and with an introduction by Allen Isaacman. Boulder, 1988.

Hopkins, Anthony. *An Economic History of West Africa.* London, 1973.

Houser, George, and Herb Shore. *Mozambique: Dream the Size of Freedom.* New York, 1975.

Iliffe, John. *The African Poor.* Cambridge, 1987.

_____. "The Organization of the Maji–Maji Rebellion." *Journal of African History* 8(1967), 495–512.

Instituto do Algodão de Moçambique. *Actividades do Instituto do Algodão de Moçambique nos Anos de 1962 a 1967.* Lourenço Marques, 1968.

_____. *Actividades do Instituto de Algodão de Moçambique em 1970.* Lourenço Marques, 1971.

_____. *Actividades do Instituto de Algodão de Moçambique em 1974–75.* Machava, 1977.

_____. *Principal Legislação Referente ao Algodão 1961 a 1967.* Lourenço Marques, n.d.

International Labor Organization. *Portugal in Africa, Report of ILO Commission on the Observance of the Aboliton of Forced Labor Convention, 1957.* London, 1962.

Isaacman, Allen. "Chiefs, Rural Differentiation and Peasant Protest: The Mozambican Forced Cotton Regime 1938–61." *African Economic History* 14(1985), 15–56.

_____. "Coercion, Paternalism and the Labor Process: The Mozambican Cotton Regime 1938–1961." *Journal of Southern African Studies* 18, 3(1992), 487–526.

_____. "The Mozambican Cotton Cooperative: The Creation of a Grassroots Alternative to Forced Commodity Production." *African Studies Review* 25(1981), 5–25.

_____. *Mozambique: The Africanization of a European Institution, The Zambezi Prazos, 1750–1902.* Madison, 1972.

_____. "Peasants and Rural Social Protest in Africa." *African Studies Review* 33(1990), 1–120.

_____. "Social Banditry in Zimbabwe (Rhodesia) and Mozambique, 1894–1907: An Expression of Early Peasant Protest." *Journal of Southern African Studies* 4, 1(1977), 1–30.

_____. *The Tradition of Resistance in Mozambique: The Zambesi Valley, 1850–1921.* Berkeley, 1976.

Isaacman, Allen, and Barbara Isaacman. *Mozambique: From Colonialism to Revolution, 1900–1982.* Boulder, 1983.

Isaacman, Allen, and Richard Roberts, eds. *Cotton, Colonialism, and Social History in Sub–Saharan Africa,* Portsmouth, 1995.

Isaacman, Allen, and Anton Rosenthal. "Slaves, Soldiers and Police: Power and Dependency Among the Chikunda of Mozambique, ca. 1825–1920." In *The End of Slavery in Africa,* ed. Suzanne Miers and Richard Roberts. Madison, 1988.

Isaacman, Allen, et al. "'Cotton Is the Mother of Poverty': Peasant Resistance to Forced Cotton Production in Mozambique, 1938–1961." *International Journal of African Historical Studies* 13(1980), 581–615.

Jewswiecki, Bogumil. "African Peasants in the Totalitarian Colonial Society of the Belgian Congo." In *Peasants in Africa*, ed. Martin Klein. Beverly Hills, 1980.

Jones, William O. *Manioc in Africa*. Stanford, 1959.

Junod, Henri A. *The Life of a South African Tribe*. 2 vols. New York, 1962.

Junta de Exportação do Algodão. *Esboço do Reconhecimento Ecológico–Agrícola de Moçambique*. 2 vols. Lourenço Marques, 1955.

Kaplan, Temma. "Female Consciousness and Collective Action: The Case of Barcelona, 1910–1918." *Signs* 7(1982), 545–66.

Key, Geoffrey Kay. *Development and Underdevelopment: A Marxist Analysis*. New York, 1975.

Keys, P. W. "Report of the Inhambane and Limpopo District." *Official Report of the South East African Mission Conference of the Episcopal Methodist Mission Conference* 28(1938), 67–72.

Kitching, Gavin. *Class and Economic Change in Kenya*. New Haven, 1980.

Kolchin, Peter. *Unfree Labor American Slavery and Russian Serfdom*. Cambridge, 1987.

Laslett, Barbara, and Johanna Brenner. "Gender and Social Reproduction: Historical Perspectives." *Annual Review of Sociology* 15(1989), 381–404.

Lewin, L. "The Oligarchical Limitations of Social Banditry in Brazil: The Case of the 'Good' Thief, António Silvino." *Past and Present* 82(1979), 116–46.

Leys, Colin. *Underdevelopment in Kenya: The Political Economy of Neo–Colonialism*. Berkeley, 1974.

Likaka, Osumaka. "Forced Cotton Cultivation and the Colonial Work Ethic, 1936–1960." In *Canadian Journal of African Studies* (forthcoming).

_____ . "Forced Cotton Cultivation and Social Control." In *Cotton, Colonialism, and Social History in Sub–Saharan Africa*, ed. Allen Isaacman and Richard Roberts. Portsmouth, 1995.

Lynes, R. N. "The Agriculture of Moçambique." *Bulletin of the Imperial Institute* 9(1913), 102–10.

_____. *Mozambique, Its Agricultural Development*. London, 1913.

Machado, A. J. de Melo. *Entre os Macuas de Angoche*. Lisbon, 1970.

Magaia, Lina. *Dumba Nengue: Run For Your Life*. Trenton, 1988.

Mager, Anne. "'The People Get Fenced': Gender Rehabilitation and African Nationalism in the Ciskei and Border Region, 1945–1955." *Journal of Southern African Studies* 18(1992), 761–82.

Mandala, Elias. *Work and Control in a Peasant Economy: A History of the Lower Tchiri Valley, 1859–1960*. Madison, 1990.

Manghezi, Alpheus. "A Mulher e O Trabalho." *Estudos Moçambicanos* 3(1981), 45–56

Marcum, John. *The Angolan Revolution: The Anatomy of a Revolution*. Cambridge, 1969.

Marques, J. Montalvão. *Esboço Para Uma Monografia Agrícola do Posto–Sede dos Muchopes e dos Alguns Regulados do Chibuto*. Lisbon, 1958.

Martinez, Francisco Lerma. *O Povo Macua e a Sua Cultura*. Lisbon, 1989.

Martins, A. *O Soldado Africano de Moçambique*. Lisbon, 1936.

Marx, Karl. *Capital: A Critique of Political Economy*. 3 vols. Harmondsworth, 1976.

May, Jacques, and Donna L. McClellan. *The Ecology of Malnutrition in Seven Countries of Southern Africa and in Portuguese Guinea*. New York, 1971.

Miers, Suzanne, and Richard Roberts, eds. *The End of Slavery in Africa*. Madison, 1988.

Mitchell, Timothy. "Everyday Metaphors of Power." *Theory and Society* 19, 5(1990), 545–78.

Mondlane, Eduardo. "The Cotton Regime." *Mozambique Revolution* 46(1971), 18–23.

_____. *The Struggle for Mozambique*. Harmondsworth, 1969.

Monica, Maria Filomena. *Artesãos e Opérios: Industria, Capitalismo e Classe Operária em Portugal 1870–1934*, Lisbon, 1986.

Moore, Henrietta, and Megan Vaughan. *Cutting Down Trees: Gender, Nutrition, and Agricultural Change in the Northern Province of Zambia, 1890–1990*. Portsmouth, 1994.

Moore, M. P. "Cooperative Labour in Peasant Agriculture." *Journal of Peasant Studies* 2(1975), 270–91.

Moyana, João. "Produzir Algodão e Castanha de Cajú Não é Favor é Ordem do Estado." *Tempo* 836(19 October 1986), 12–15.

Mudenge, S. I. G. *A Political History of the Munhumutapa c.1400–1902.* Harare, 1988.

Myers, Gregory, and Harry West. "Land Tenure Security and State Farm Divestiture in Mozambique: Case Studies in Namatanda, Manica and Montepuez Districts." Research Paper, Land Tenure Center, University of Wisconsin–Madison, 1992.

Neil–Tomlinson, Barry. "The Growth of a Colonial Economy and the Development of African Labour: Manica and Sofala and the Mozambique Chartered Company, 1892–1934." In *Mozambique* (proceedings of a seminar at the Center of African Studies). University of Edinburgh, 1979.

_____. "The Nyasa Chartered Company, 1891–1929." *Journal of African History* 18(1977), 283–86.

Newitt, M. D. D. "Drought in Mozambique 1823–1831." *Journal of Southern African Studies* 15, 1(1988), 15–35.

_____. *Portugal in Africa: The Last Hundred Years.* New York, 1981.

_____. *Portuguese Settlement on the Zambezi: Exploration, Land Tenure and Colonial Rule in East Africa.* New York, 1973.

Official Journal of the South East African Mission Conference of the Methodist Episcopal Conference 11 (1927).

Official Report of the South East African Mission Conference at the Episcopal Methodist Conference 14 (1930).

Paul, John. *Memoirs of a Revolution.* London, 1975.

Pedro, J. Gomes. "A Fito Ecologia na Zonagem Algodoeira." *Trabalhos do Centro de Investigação Científica Algodoeira* 1(1948), 1–26.

Pélissier, René. *História de Moçambique.* 2 vols. Lisbon, 1987, 1988.

Penvenne, Jeanne. *African Workers and Colonial Racism: Mozambican Strategies for Survival in Lourenço Marques 1877–1962.* Portsmouth, 1994.

Pereira, Rui. "Antropologia Aplicada na Política Colonial Portuguesa do Estado Novo." *Revista Internacional de Estudos Africanos* 4/5(1986), 191–236.

Peridagão, José Henriques de Azevedo. "A Industria em Portugal: Para Um Inquerto." *Arquivo Universidade de Lisboa* 3(1916).

Peters, Pauline. "Gender, Developmental Cycles and Historical Process: A Critique of Recent Research on Women in Botswana." *Journal of Southern African Studies* 10, 1(1983), 100–122.

Pires, António J. *A Grande Guerra em Moçambique.* Porto, 1924.

Pitcher, M. Anne. "From Coercion to Incentive: The Portuguese Colonial Cotton Regime in Angola and Mozambique, 1946–1974." In *The Social History of Cotton in Colonial Africa,* ed. Allen Isaacman and Richard Roberts. Portsmouth, 1994.

_____. *Politics in the Portuguese Empire.* Oxford, 1993.

_____. "Sowing the Seeds of Failure: Early Portuguese Cotton Cultivation in Angola and Mozambique, 1820–1926." *Journal of Southern African Studies* 17, 1(1991), 43–70.

Polanah, Luis. *The Saga of a Cotton Capulana.* Translated by Tamara L. Bender. Edited by Allen Isaacman. Madison, 1981.

Popkins, Samuel. *The Rational Peasant.* Berkeley, 1979.

Popular Memory Group. "Popular Memory: Theory, Politics, Method." In *Making Histories: Studies in History Writing and Politics,* ed. Richard Johnson and others. Minneapolis, 1982.

Prentice, A. N. *Cotton, With Special Reference to Africa.* London, 1972.

Price, Richard. *Maroon Societies.* Baltimore, 1979.

Província de Moçambique. *Relatório da Administração da Circunscrição de Zavala—Sobre as Cooperativas da Sua Area*. Lourenço Marques, 1958.

Quintanilha, A. "The Problem of Cotton Production in Portuguese Africa." *South African Journal of Science* 44(1948), 44–49.

Reis, Carlos Manuel dos Santos. "Alimentação da Mãe Indígena e Aleitamento." *Anais do Instituto de Medicina Tropical* 10(1953), 1345–437.

_____. *A Nutrição no Ultramar Português*. 2 vols. Lisbon, 1973.

Reis, Diogo da Camara. "Os Macuas de Mogovolas." *Boletim da Sociedade de Moçambique* 31(1962), 5–40.

Reis, Morgado. "Main Food Areas and Nutritional Diseases in Mozambique." In *Comunicações Portuguesas Ao III Congresso da Associação Científica dos Países do Oceano Índico*. Lisbon, 1958.

Repartição Técnica de Estatística. *Estatística Agrícola*. Lourenço Marques, 1941–1960.

Repartição Técnica de Estatística. *Recenseamento Agrícola*. Lourenço Marques, 1940–1941.

Resende, Sebastião Soares de. *Ordem Anticomunista*. Lourenço Marques, 1950.

Ribeiro, E .K. de Queiroz. *O Algodão: Da Colheita à Industrialização*. Porto, 1947.

Richards, Paul. "Ecological Change and the Politics of African Land Use." *African Studies Review*, 26(1983), 1–72.

_____. *Indigenous Agricultural Revolution: Ecology and Food Production in West Africa*. London, 1985.

Rita–Ferreira, A. *O Movimento Migratório de Trabalhadores entre Moçambique e a África do Sul*. Lisbon, 1963.

Roberts, Richard. "The Coercion of Free Markets: Cotton, Peasants and Colonial State in the French Soudan, 1924–1932." In *Cotton, Colonialism and Social History in Sub–Sahara Africa*, ed. Allen Isaacman and Richard Roberts. Portsmouth, 1995.

_____. "Reversible Social Processes, Historical Memory, and the Production of History." *History in Africa* 17(1990), 341–49.

Rodney, Walter, Kapepwa Tambila, and Laurent Sago. *Migrant Labour in Tanzania During the Colonial Period*. Hamburg, 1983.

Roesch, Otto. "Migrant Labour and Forced Rice Production in Southern Mozambique: The Colonial Peasantry of the Lower Limpopo Valley." *Journal of Southern African Studies* 17, 2(1991), 239–70.

Rosas, Fernando. *Portugal Entre a Paz e a Guerra*. Lisbon, 1990.

Roseberry, William. "Beyond the Agrarian Question in Latin America." In *Confronting Historical Paradigms: Peasants, Labor and the Capitalist World System in Africa and Latin America*, ed. Fred Cooper et al. Madison, 1993.

Ross, Edward Alsworth. *Report on Employment of Native Labor in Portuguese Africa*. New York, 1925.

Salazar, A. de Oliveira., *Doctrine and Action: Internal and Foreign Policy of the New Portugal, 1928–1939*. London, 1939.

Salvador, A. R. Nunes. "Contribuição para o Estudo da Qualidade das Mandiocas em Ensaio no Posto Agrícola da Mahalamba." *Boletim da Sociedade de Estudos de Moçambique* 32(1963), 135–52.

Sarraut, Albert. *La Mise en Valeur des Colonies Français*. Paris, 1922.

Saul, John. "The Role of the Cooperative Movement." In *Socialism in Tanzania*, ed. Lionel Cliffe and John Saul. Dar es Salaam, 1973.

_____, ed. *A Difficult Road: The Transition to Socialism in Mozambique*. New York, 1985.

Schmidt, Elizabeth. *Peasants, Traders, and Wives: Shona Women in the History of Zimbabwe, 1870–1939*. Portsmouth, 1992.

Schofield, Sue. "Seasonal Factors Affecting Nutrition in Different Age Groups and Especially Preschool Children." *Journal of Development Studies* 11, 1(1974), 22–40.

Scott, James. *Domination and the Arts of Resistance: Hidden Transcripts*. New Haven, 1990.

_____. "State Simplifications: Nature, Space and People," University of Minnesota MacArthur Working Paper No. 3, Series 10, March 1994.

_____. *Weapons of the Weak: Everyday Forms of Peasant Resistance*. New Haven, 1985.

Sen, Amartya. *Poverty and Famines: An Essay on Entitlement*. Oxford, 1981.

Shlomowitz, Ralph. "Plantation and Smallholder: Comparative Perspectives from the World of Cotton and Sugar Cane Economies 1865–1939." *Agricultural History* 58(1984), 1–16.

Sikhondze, B. A. B. "The Development of Swazi Cotton Cultivation: Some Theoretical Problems." *Mohlomi: Journal of Southern African Studies* 6(1990)117–38.

Silva, M. A. de Andrade. "O Problema Alimentar de Moçambique." *Anais do Instituto de Medicina Tropical* 12(1955), 691–712.

Silva Cunha, J.M. da. *O Trabalho Indígena: Estudo do Direito Colonial*. Lisbon, 1949.

Soeiro, Álvaro Navarro, and Francisco Manuel Fernandes. "O Sisal de Moçambique." In *Assembleia Técnica da Associação dos Produtores de Sisal da Província de Moçambique*. Vol. 13. Braga, 1961.

Southern Rhodesia Census 1901–1936. Rhodesian Statistical Bureau, Salisbury.

Stoler, Ann. "Plantation Politics and Protest on Sumatra's Coast." *Journal of Peasant Studies* 13, 2(1986), 124–43.

Sunseri, Thaddeus. "Peasants and the Struggle for Labor in Cotton Regimes of the Rufiji Basin (Tanzania), 1885–1918." In *Cotton, Colonialism and Social History in Sub-Saharan Africa, ed.* Allen Isaacman and Richard Roberts. Portsmouth, 1995.

Taussig, Michael. "Culture of Terror—Space of Death: Roger Casement's Putumayo Report and the Explanation of Torture." *Comparative Studies in Society and History* 26, 3(1984), 467–97.

Tilly, Charles. "Routine Conflicts and Peasant Rebellions in Seventeenth–Century France." In *Power and Protest in the Countryside*, ed. Robert P. Weller and Scott E. Guggenheim. Durham, 1982.

Tosh, John. "Lango Agricultural Development during the Early Colonial Period: Land and Labor for a Cash Economy." *Journal of African History* 19, 3(1978), 415–40.

_____. "The Cash Crop Revolution in Tropical Africa: An Agricultural Reappraisal." *African Affairs* 79(1980), 415–39.

Torres, José. "A Agricultura no Distrito de Moçambique." *Boletim da Sociedade de Estudos da Colónia de Moçambique* (1932), 74.

Tracey, Hugh. *Chopi Musicians*. London, 1948.

Vail, David. *A History of Agricultural Innovation and Development in Teso District, Uganda*. Syracuse, 1972.

Vail, Leroy. "Mozambique's Chartered Companies: The Rule of the Feeble." *Journal of African History* 17(1976), 389–416.

Vail, Leroy, and Landeg White. *Capitalism and Colonialism in Mozambique: A Study of Quelimane District*. Minneapolis, 1980.

_____. "Forms of Resistance: Songs and Perceptions of Power in Colonial Mozambique." *American Historical Review* 88, 4(1983), 883–919.

_____. *Power and the Praise Poem*. Charlottesville, 1991.

_____. "Tawani Machambero!: Forced Rice and Cotton Cultivation on the Zambezi, 1938–1961." *Journal of African History* 19(1978), 239–63.

van Onselen, Charles. *Chibaro: African Mine Labour in Southern Rhodesia, 1900–1933*. London, 1976.

_____. *Studies in the Social and Economic History of the Witwatersrand. Vol. 2, New Nineveh*. London, 1982.

Van Zwanenberg, Roger. "The Development of Peasant Commodity Production in Kenya, 1920–1940." *Economic History Review* 27, 3(1974), 442–54.

Vaughan, Megan. *The Story of an African Famine: Gender and Famine in Twentieth–Century Malawi*. Cambridge, 1987.

von Rotenham, Dietrich. "Cotton Farming in Sukumaland." In *Smallholder Farming and Smallholder Development in Tanzania*, ed. Hans Ruthenberg. Munich, 1968.

"Voz de Mineiro, A." *Estudos Moçambicanos* 1(1980), 77–90.

Wallis, J. P. R., ed. *The Zambezi Expedition of David Livingstone*. 2 vols. London, 1956.

Walt, Gillian, and Angela Melamed. *Mozambique: Toward a People's Health Service*. London, 1983.

Warhurst, P. R. "The Tete Agreement." *Rhodesian History* 7(1970), 32–42.

Waterhouse, R. "Mozambique: Cotton Picks Up." *Africa Business* (March 1992), 22.

Watts, Michael. "On Political Diffidence: Non–Revolt, Resistance and Hidden Forms of Political Consciousness in Northern Nigeria, 1900–1945." In *Global Crises and Social Movements*, ed. Edmund Burke. Boulder, 1987.

_____. *Silent Violence: Food, Famine and the Peasantry in Northern Nigeria*. Berkeley, 1983.

Webster, David. "Migrant Labour, Social Formations and the Proletarianisation of the Chopi of Southern Mozambique." *African Perspectives* 1(1978), 157–74.

Wuyts, Marc. "Money, Planning and Rural Transformation in Mozambique." *Journal of Development Studies* 22(1991), 180–207.

Young, Sherilynn. "Fertility and Famine: Women's Agricultural History in Southern Mozambique." In *The Roots of Rural Poverty in Central and Southern Africa*, ed. R. Palmer and Q. N. Parsons. London, 1977.

Unpublished Theses and Papers

Adam, Yussuf. "Cooperativização Agrícola e Modificação das Relações de Produção no Período Colonial em Moçambique." Tesé de Licenciatura, Universidade Eduardo Mondlane, 1986.

Feliciano, José Fialho. "Antropologia Económica dos Thonga do Sul de Moçambique." Ph.D dissertation, Universidade Técnica de Lisboa, 1989.

Fortuna, Carlos. "Threading Through: Cotton Production, Colonial Mozambique, and Semi–Peripheral Portugal in the World Economy." Ph.D. dissertation, State University of New York at Binghamton, 1988.

Fuller, C. E. "An Ethnohistoric Study of Continuity and Change in Gwambe Culture." Ph.D. dissertation, Northwestern University, 1955.

Gillet, Ira. "Early Years in Africa." Manuscript. Milwaukee, Oregon, n.d.

Hafkin, Nancy. "Trade, Society and Politics in Northern Mozambique, 1753–1913." Ph.D. dissertation, Boston University, 1973.

Head, Judith. "State, Capital and Migrant Labour in Zambézia, Mozambique: A Study of the Labour Force of Sena Sugar Estates Limited." Ph.D. dissertation, University of Durham, 1980.

Likaka, Osumaka. "The Social Organization of Work." Research Paper. Minneapolis, 1991.

Lemos, Manuel Jorge Correia de. "Fontes Para O Estudo do Algodão em Moçambique: Documentos de Arquivo, 1938–1974." M.A. thesis, Arquivo Histórico de Moçambique, Universidade Eduardo Mondlane, 1984.

Ministério da Agricultura/Michigan State University, Department of Agriculture. "A Socio–Economic Survey in the Province of Nampula: Cotton in the Smallholder Economy." Working Paper no. 5E. January 1991.

O'Laughlin, Bridget. "Mbum–Beer parties: Structures of Production and Exchange in an African Social Formation." Ph.D. dissertation, Yale University, 1973.

Pachinuapa, Raimundo. "Dados Históricos dum Movimento Nacional Para Libertação Nacional." Maputo, 1988.

Pitcher, M. Anne. "Is State Intervention Worth the Price? Mozambique's Cotton Regime Under Salazar." Paper presented at Il Colóquio International em Ciências Socias Sabre a África de Língua Oficial Portuguesa.

Roesch, Otto. "Socialism and Rural Development in Mozambique: The Case of Aldeia Comunal 24 de Julho." Ph.D. dissertation, University of Toronto, 1986.

Young, Sherilynn. "Changes in Diet and Production in Southern Mozambique, 1855–1960." Paper delivered to British African Studies Association Conference, September 1976.

————, "Climate in Southern Mozambique: Identifying and Quantifying the Extent of and Periodicity of Twentieth–Century Drought." Paper presented at the African Studies Association Meeting, Toronto, November 4, 1994.

————. "Women in Transition: Southern Mozambique 1975–76: Reflections on Colonialism, Aspirations for Independence." Paper delivered at the Conference on the History of Women, College of St. Catherine, St. Paul, MN, 21 October 1977.

APPENDIX A

Concessionary Companies in Mozambique, 1950s

Name	Location	Activity	Enterprise	# Zones	Area (ha)
CAM	Moçambique, Cabo Delgado, Zambézia	cotton	corp.	23 (+1)	113,381
SAGAL	Cabo Delgado, Niassa	cotton	corp.	10 (+1)	45,049
João Ferreira dos Santos	Moçambique	other	family	6 (+1)	18,132
Sena Sugar Estates*	Zambézia, Manica e Sofala	other	corp.	2	5,886
CNA	Manica e Sofala	cotton	corp.	9	21,239
Zambézi Co.**	Tete	other	corp.	1	8,539
Lopes & Irmão	Zambézia	cotton	family	1	11,273
Monteiro & Giro	Zambézia	cotton	family	2 (+1)	12,695
SAN	Niassa, Moçambique	cotton	corp.	5 (+1)	32,946
Búzi Co.**	Manica e Sofala	other	corp.	2	8,866
Algodoeira do Sul do Save	Gaza, Inhambane	cotton	corp.	12 (+3)	39,501

*   foreign-owned
**   both Portuguese and foreign capital

Source: Fortuna, "Threading Through," 226.

APPENDIX B

Cotton Production, Select Southern Circumscriptions, 1940s

Year	Producers	Tons	Hectares [a] per producer	Kilograms[b] per producer	Escudos per producer
Guija					
1940	1,125	92	0.28	82	118
1941	816	20	0.50	24	34
1942	3,486	202	0.25	58	75
1943	8,931	202	0.25	23	29
1944	6,502	192	0.17	30	40
1945	3,456	234	0.25	68	92
1946	3,872	367	0.27	95	130
1947	6,633	446	0.31	67	105
1948	4,818	753	0.31	156	240
1949	6,307	1,166	0.37	185	346
Muchopes					
1940	230	17	0.32	73	100
1941	10,562	207	0.45	20	26
1942	10,386	223	0.25	21	20
1943	17,815	457	0.25	26	35
1944	18,754	847	0.19	45	60
1945	11,022	292	0.23	27	35
1946	11,148	673	0.20	60	82
1947	13,405	908	0.25	68	106
1948	8,190	579	0.26	71	110
1949	7,997	380	0.35	47	89
Zavala					
1940	437	95	0.83	218	298
1941	13,7114	207	0.13	22	30
1942	7,380	283	0.25	38	46
1943	10,300	469	0.25	46	54
1944	8,457	218	0.24	262	9
1945	14,022	446	0.26	32	38
1946	6,436	571	0.44	89	106
1947	8,386	1,354	0.51	161	252
1948	8,033	1,806	0.41	255	210
1949	1,310	657	1.69	501	926

Source: AIA, JEAC, "Areas Cultivadas, Produçao de Algodão-Caroço por Hectare e Número de Cultivadores Totais por Concelhos e Circunscriçoes."
[a] Rounded up to nearest hundredth of a hectare.
[b] Rounded up to the nearest kilogram.

APPENDIX C

Marketed Products,
Macomia Circumscription, 1946-1961 (metric tons)

Year	Peanuts	Manioc	Sorghum	Maize	Cotton
1946	277	947	242	76	21
1947	237	617	349	63	17
1948	144	1,133	127	15	29
1949	87	1,665	148	71	57
1950	24	333	14	63	37
1951	99	995	56	188	91
1952	33	373	26	29	288
1953	43	1,096	91	121	118
1954	55	221	190	68	188
1955	84	550	413	194	204
1956	32	686	107	31	57
1957	14	500	214	198	263
1958	84	1,041	224	98	274
1959	66	748	72	107	527

Source: RTE, *Recenseamento Agrícola* (1940–1941); RTE, *Estatística Agrícola* (1941–1960); Direcção Provinçal dos Serviços de Estatística Geral, *Estatística Agrícola* (1960–1964).

APPENDIX D

Marketed Products,
Nampula Circumscription, 1943–1959 (metric tons)

Year	Peanuts	Manioc	Sorghum	Maize	Cotton
1943	2258	818	190	1	1,510
1944	402	489	361	2	2,038
1945	1,220	635	321	3	1,325
1946	2,040	1,954	990	8	925
1947	1,232	989	191	2	1,108
1948	885	754	169	0	818
1949	138	183	248	0	1,169
1950	256	304	196	1	733
1951	702	1,044	242	3	1,198
1952	1,277	414	108	1	1,551
1953	692	927	91	0	1,156
1954	572	86	71	0	1,445
1955	1,174	233	91	0	799
1956	906	880	79	1	321
1957	851	867	79	9	1,668
1958	606	100	11	0	816
1959	172	94	70	0	1,407

Source: RTE, Recenseamento Agrícola (1940–1941); RTE, Estatística Agrícola (1941–1960); Direcção Provinçal dos Serviços de Estatística Geral, Estatística Agrícola (1960–1964).

APPENDIX E

Marketed Products,
Morrumbala Circumscription, 1946–1960 (metric tons)

Year	Peanuts	Manioc	Sorghum	Maize	Cotton
1946	22	63	591	1,896	1,055
1947	20	1	125	1,749	2,954
1948	32	74	236	1,078	3,278
1949	27	9	29	97	2,997
1950	10	12	161	2,416	2,653
1951	0	112	2	1,087	4,560
1952	1	26	9	1,855	3,594
1953	35	35	74	1,367	7,033
1954	72	2	0	0	7,276
1955	10	6	62	1,587	4,080
1956	43	44	32	1,996	4,007
1957	7	7	33	1,402	6,525
1958	2	0	59	866	5,405
1959	0	11	11	591	11,424

Source: RTE, *Recenseamento Agrícola* (1940–1941); RTE, *Estatística Agrícola* (1941–1960); Direcção Provinçal dos Serviços de Estatística Geral, *Estatística Agrícola* (1960–1964).

APPENDIX F

Marketed Products,
Mogovolas Circumscription, 1943–1960 (metric tons)

Year	Peanuts	Manioc	Sorghum	Maize	Cotton
1943	698	320	14	1	4,524
1944	2,893	726	5	0	5,446
1945	4,796	585	19	1	4,807
1946	3,237	1,028	143	2	4,956
1947	3,811	138	8	0	4,378
1948	2,707	382	1	1	3,591
1949	926	722	2	0	4,108
1950	1,399	185	1	0	3,400
1951	1,059	24	6	0	3,259
1952	3,626	146	8	2	2,409
1953	3,393	1,944	4	0	2,819
1954	2,546	3,150	1	0	3,190
1955	2,850	220	5	0	3,020
1956	4,442	531	5	1	1,182
1957	3,703	1,026	1	0	2,524
1958	3,194	97	0	0	1,753
1959	1,635	2	0	0	3,363

Source: RTE, *Recenseamento Agrícola* (1940–1941); RTE, *Estatística Agrícola* (1941–1960); Direcção Provinçal dos Serviços de Estatística Geral, *Estatística Agrícola* (1960–1964).

INDEX